Mathematics Explained for
primary teachers

With
online
materials

Education at SAGE

SAGE is a leading international publisher of journals, books, and electronic media for academic, educational, and professional markets.

Our education publishing includes:

- accessible and comprehensive texts for aspiring education professionals and practitioners looking to further their careers through continuing professional development

- inspirational advice and guidance for the classroom

- authoritative state of the art reference from the leading authors in the field

Find out more at: **www.sagepub.co.uk/education**

Mathematics Explained for primary teachers

4th edition

Derek Haylock

With online materials

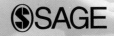

SAGE

Los Angeles | London | New Delhi
Singapore | Washington DC

© Derek Haylock 2010

First edition published 1995
Second edition published 2001
Third edition published 2005, reprinted 2006, 2007, 2008, 2009
This fourth edition published 2010

SAGE Publications Ltd
1 Oliver's Yard
55 City Road
London EC1Y 1SP

SAGE Publications Inc.
2455 Teller Road
Thousand Oaks, California 91320

SAGE Publications India Pvt Ltd
B 1/I 1 Mohan Cooperative Industrial Area
Mathura Road
New Delhi 110 044

SAGE Publications Asia-Pacific Pte Ltd
33 Pekin Street #02-01
Far East Square
Singapore 048763

Library of Congress Control Number: 2010922538

British Library Cataloguing in Publication data

A catalogue record for this book is available from the British Library

ISBN 978-1-84860-196-3
ISBN 978-1-84860-197-0 (pbk)

Typeset by C&M Digitals (P) Ltd, Chennai, India
Printed and bound in Great Britain by Ashford Colour Press Ltd
Printed on paper from sustainable resources

Contents

About the Author

Derek Haylock is an education consultant and author. He worked for over 30 years in teacher education, both initial and in-service, and was Co-Director of Primary Initial Teacher Training and responsible for the mathematics components of the primary programmes at the University of East Anglia (UEA), Norwich. He has considerable practical experience of teaching and researching in primary classrooms. His work in mathematics education has taken him to Germany, Belgium, Lesotho, Kenya, Brunei and India. He now works as an education consultant for a number of organizations, including the Training and Development Agency for Schools. As well as his extensive publications in the field of education, he has written seven books of Christian drama for young people and a Christmas musical (published by Church House/National Society).

Other books in education

Haylock, D. (1991) *Teaching Mathematics to Low Attainers 8–12*. London: Sage Publications.

Haylock, D. (2001) *Numeracy for Teaching*. London: Sage Publications.

Haylock, D. and McDougall, D. (1999) *Mathematics Every Elementary Teacher Should Know*. Toronto: Trifolium Books.

Haylock, D. and D'Eon, M. (1999) *Helping Low Achievers Succeed at Mathematics*. Toronto: Trifolium Books.

Browne, A. and Haylock, D. (eds) (2004) *Professional Issues for Primary Teachers*. London: Sage Publications.

Haylock, D. with Thangata, F. (2007) *Key Concepts in Teaching Primary Mathematics*. London: Sage Publications.

Haylock, D. and Cockburn, A. (2008) *Understanding Mathematics for Young Children: A Guide for Foundation Stage and Lower Primary Teachers, Fully Revised and Expanded Edition*. London: Sage Publications.

Haylock, D. with Manning, R. (2010) *Student Workbook for Mathematics Explained for Primary Teachers*. London: Sage Publications.

Acknowledgements

My thanks and genuine appreciation are due to the many trainee teachers and primary school teachers with whom I have been privileged to work on initial training and in-service courses in teaching mathematics: for their willingness to get to grips with understanding mathematics, for their patience with me as I have tried to find the best ways of explaining mathematical ideas to them, for their honesty in sharing their own insecurities and uncertainties about the subject – and for thereby providing me with the material on which this book is based. I also acknowledge my indebtedness to Marianne Lagrange, Matthew Waters, Jeanette Graham and their colleagues at Sage Publications for their unflagging encouragement and professionalism. And, finally, my thanks are due to my wife, Christina, without whose support I could not have even contemplated writing a fourth edition of this book.

The Student Workbook and the Website

To accompany this book there are two sources of supporting material. The first is the *Student Workbook for Mathematics Explained for Primary Teachers* (Haylock with Manning, 2010). This book, written with my colleague at UEA, Ralph Manning, has been produced specifically to accompany this fourth edition. For each of Chapters 6–29 of *Mathematics Explained* the workbook provides a set of tasks related to the mathematical content of that chapter, together with answers and further explanation. The tasks are of three kinds: checking understanding; using and applying; and learning and teaching.

The second is the *Mathematics Explained for Primary Teachers* website (www. sagepub.co.uk/haylock). Included on this website are 45 of the 62 check-ups from my book, *Numeracy for Teaching* (Haylock, 2001). This material relates directly to the demands of the Numeracy Test that must be passed by trainee teachers in England as a prerequisite for Qualified Teacher Status. Where relevant I indicate towards the end of various chapters the Check-Ups available on the website that can be used by readers looking for further practice – but with a focus on the application of the mathematical knowledge and skills to the job of being a teacher. In addition, the website contains a comprehensive glossary of the key terms used in this fourth edition of *Mathematics Explained for Primary Teachers*. This combines all the glossaries at the ends of chapters into a single list in alphabetical order.

Along with other relevant information, web links and assorted material, the website will also provide details of how the content of this book, chapter by chapter, links to primary school national curricula for England, Wales and Scotland and the level descriptions within each attainment target.

Introduction

Since the third edition of this book there have been a number of significant events in primary education in this country relevant to the learning and teaching mathematics. For example, there was the influential Williams Review of Mathematics Teaching in Early Years Settings and Primary Schools (Williams, 2008). This has reinforced again the key message of *Mathematics Explained*: the need for priority to be given in initial teacher training and professional development to primary school teachers developing secure subject knowledge in mathematics. One of the key recommendations in this review was the recruitment and training of mathematics consultants for every primary school in England, with 'deep mathematical subject knowledge and pedagogical knowledge' (Williams, 2008: 23). My intention in writing this fourth edition is to continue to provide material that will promote these qualities and in doing this to ensure that the book's coverage of mathematical subject and pedagogical knowledge is as comprehensive as possible. In terms of pedagogical knowledge I have, for example, increased substantially the number of Learning and Teaching Points in the new edition.

Then there was the Rose Review of the Primary Curriculum (Rose, 2009), the subsequent detailed proposals for a new primary school curriculum for England (DCSF/QCDA, 2010), including the curriculum for Mathematical Understanding (pp 44–51), and the revised level descriptions for Mathematics (QCDA, 2010: 28–33). These proposals indicated some of the ways in which children's experience of mathematics in primary schools are changing in the twenty-first century. In preparing this fourth edition I have added new material to reflect such changes. This includes increasing the emphasis on, for example: key skills and processes in mathematics; how mathematical understanding is used, applied and developed in other subject areas in the curriculum; budget problems and spreadsheets; the use of data-handling software in processing statistical data and representing it in graphical form; a greater range of graphical representations, including Venn diagrams, Carroll diagrams and scatter graphs; and an increased awareness of probability and risk.

Although the book is written from the perspective of teaching primary mathematics in England – the country in which I have worked for most of my career – it has been encouraging to note that teachers and mathematics educators in many other countries have found the previous editions to be helpful and relevant to their work. I am confident that this will continue to be the case.

Even well-qualified graduates feel insecure and uncertain about much of the mathematics they have to teach, as is demonstrated in Chapter 1 of the book, and appreciate a systematic explanation of even the most elementary mathematical concepts and procedures of the primary curriculum. In my long career in teacher education I have often reflected on what qualities make a good teacher. I have a little list. Top of the list is the following conviction. *The best teachers have a secure personal understanding of the structure and principles of what they are teaching.* This book is written to help primary teachers, present and future, to achieve this in mathematics. It sets out to explain the subject to primary school teachers, so that they in turn will have the confidence to provide appropriate, systematic and careful explanation of mathematical ideas and procedures to their pupils, with an emphasis on the development of understanding, rather than mere learning by rote. This is done always from the perspective of how children learn and develop understanding of this subject. Implications for learning and teaching are embedded in the text and highlighted as 'Learning and teaching points' distributed throughout each chapter.

Section A (Chapters 1–3) of this book is about Mathematical Understanding. Chapter 1, drawing on my research with trainee teachers, provides evidence for the need to develop understanding of mathematics in those who are to teach the subject in primary schools. Then there are two new chapters. Chapter 2 considers the distinctive contribution that mathematics makes to the primary curriculum and Chapter 3 is about pupils learning to learn mathematics with understanding. Sections B, C, D and E each focus on the content and principles of one of the four attainment targets for mathematics in England. These cover the content in the mathematics level descriptions (QCDA, 2010: 28–33) up to about level 6 – given that this is the level at which a not insignificant proportion of primary school children will be working at the age of 11 years. Section B covers Using and Applying Mathematics, giving this area of the mathematics curriculum more prominence than in previous editions. Section C covers Number and Algebra; Section D, Shape, Space and Measures; and Section E, Statistics.

SECTION A
MATHEMATICAL
UNDERSTANDING

1
Primary Teachers' Insecurity about Mathematics

In this chapter there are explanations of

- the importance of primary school teachers really understanding the mathematics they teach and being able to explain it clearly to the children they teach;
- attitudes of adults in general toward mathematics;
- mathematics anxiety in primary school teachers; and
- the insecurity about mathematics of many primary trainee teachers.

Understanding and explaining mathematics

Being a successful learner in mathematics involves constructing *understanding* through exploration, problem solving, discussion and practical experience – and through interaction with a teacher who has a clear grasp of the underlying structure of the mathematics being learnt. For children to enjoy learning mathematics it is essential that they should understand it; that they should make sense of what they are doing in the subject, and not just learn to reproduce learnt procedures and recipes that are low in meaningfulness and purposefulness.

One of the best ways for children to learn and understand much of the mathematics in the primary school curriculum is for a teacher who understands it to explain it to them. In the 1990s – when I wrote the first and much slimmer edition of this book – much of the criticism of primary school teaching of mathematics (Ofsted, 1993a; 1993b) suggested that there had been too great a reliance on approaches to the organization of children's activities that allowed insufficient opportunities for teachers to provide this explanation. One encouraging aspect of the National Numeracy Strategy (DfEE, 1999) in England was the increased emphasis on interactive whole-class teaching. This encouraged primary teachers to engage more with children in explanation, question and answer, and discussion, aimed at promoting understanding and confidence in mathematics.

Of course, there is more to learning mathematics than just a teacher explaining something and then following this up with exercises. The key processes of using and applying mathematics must always be at the heart of learning the subject – and these figure prominently in this book, particularly in Section B (Chapters 4 and 5). But children do need 'explanation' and there is now in England a greater awareness that primary teachers must organize their lessons and the children's activities in ways that give opportunities for them to provide careful, systematic and appropriate explanation of mathematical concepts, procedures and principles to groups of children. That many primary teachers have in the past neglected this aspect of teaching may possibly be associated with the prevailing primary ethos, which emphasized active learning and the needs of the individual child. But it seems to me to be more likely a consequence of their own insecurity about mathematics, which is a characteristic of too many primary school teachers. This insecurity has made it more likely that teachers will lean heavily on the commercial scheme to make their decisions about teaching for them.

This book is written to equip teachers with the knowledge and confidence they require to explain mathematical ideas to the children they teach. I have set out to provide explanations of all the key ideas that are taught in mathematics in primary schools in England, with the aim of improving primary teachers' own understanding and increasing their personal confidence in talking about these ideas to the children they teach. In order to ensure that the teacher understands the mathematical significance of some of the material they teach to children up to the age of 11 years, the mathematical content of some of the chapters goes further than the actual content of the primary curriculum. Confident teachers of mathematics know and understand more than they teach! They also need to be thoroughly competent in a range of numeracy skills, such as handling and interpreting data, in order to meet the day-to-day demands of their profession.

Attitudes to mathematics in adults

There are widespread confusions amongst the adult population in Britain about many of the basic mathematical processes of everyday life. This lack of confidence in basic mathematics appears to be related to the anxiety about mathematics and feelings of inadequacy in this subject that are common amongst the adult population. These phenomena are clearly demonstrated by surveys of adults' attitudes to mathematics (Cockcroft, 1982; Coben, 2003). Findings indicate that many adults, in relation to mathematical tasks, admit to feelings of anxiety, helplessness, fear, dislike and even guilt. The feeling of guilt is particularly marked amongst those with high academic qualifications, who feel that they ought to be more confident in their understanding of this subject. There is a perception that there are proper ways of doing mathematics and that the subject is characterized by questions to which your answers are either right or wrong. Feelings of failure, frustration and anxiety are identified by many adults as having their roots in unsympathetic attitudes of teachers and the expectations of parents. A project at King's College, London, looking at the attitudes of adults attending numeracy classes, found that the majority of such adults viewed themselves as failures and carried various types of emotional baggage from their schooldays. They spoke of their poor experience of schooling and of feeling that they had been written off by their mathematics teachers, usually at an early stage. Their return to the mathematics classroom as adults was accompanied by feelings of anxiety, even fear (Swain, 2004). Significantly, in a survey of over 500 adults in the UK, Lim (2002) identified three widely claimed myths about mathematics: it is a difficult subject; it is only for clever people; and it is a male domain.

Mathematics anxiety in primary teachers

Research into primary school teachers' attitudes to mathematics reveals that many of them continue to carry around with them these same kinds of 'baggage' (Briggs and Crook, 1991). There is evidence that many primary teachers experience feelings of panic and anxiety when faced with unfamiliar mathematical tasks (Briggs, 1993), that they are muddled in their thinking about many of the basic mathematical concepts which underpin the material they teach to children, and that they are all too aware of their personal inadequacies in mathematics (Haylock and Cockburn, 2008). The widespread view that mathematics is a difficult subject, and therefore only for clever people, increases these feelings of inadequacy – and the common perception that mathematics is a male domain exacerbates the problem within a subset of the teaching profession that continues to be largely populated by women. The importance of tackling these attitudes to the subject is underlined by the findings of Burnett and Wichman (1997) that primary teachers' (and parents') own anxieties about mathematics can often be passed on to the children they teach. It is really important not to generate mathematics anxiety in the children we teach, because anxiety affects our ability to perform to our potential. The research of Ashcraft and Moore (2009), for example, confirms that raising anxiety about mathematics produces a drop in performance in the subject, particularly in terms of the individual's access to their 'working memory'.

Trainee teachers' anxieties

The background for this book is mainly my experience of working with graduates enrolled on a primary one-year initial teacher-training programme. The trainee teachers I have worked with have been highly motivated, good-honours graduates, with the subjects of their degree studies ranging across the curriculum. The ages of these trainee teachers have usually ranged from about 21 to 40 years, with the mean age about 27. Over a number of years of working with such trainees, it has become clear to me that many of them start their course with a high degree of anxiety about having to teach mathematics. So an invitation was given for any trainees who felt particularly worried about mathematics to join a group who would meet for an hour a week throughout their course, to discuss their anxieties and to identify which aspects of the National Curriculum for mathematics appropriate to the age range they would be teaching gave them most concern. A surprisingly large number of trainees turned up for these sessions. Discussions with them revealed both those aspects of mathematics anxiety which they still carry around with them, derived clearly from their own experiences of learning mathematics at school, and the specific areas of mathematics they will have to teach for which they have doubts about their own understanding.

Below I recount many of the statements made by the primary trainee teachers in my group about their attitudes towards and experiences of learning mathematics. In reading these comments it is important to remember that these are students who have come through the system with relative success in mathematics: all must have GCSE grade C, or the equivalent, and can therefore be judged to be in something like the top 30% for mathematics attainment. Yet this is clearly not how they feel about themselves in relation to this subject. The trainees' comments on their feelings about mathematics can be categorized under five headings: (1) feelings of anxiety and fear; (2) expectations; (3) teaching and learning styles; (4) the image of mathematics; and (5) language. These categories reflect closely the findings of other studies of the responses towards mathematics of adults in general and primary teachers in particular.

Feelings of anxiety and fear

When these trainee teachers talk freely about their memories of mathematics at school, their comments are sprinkled liberally with such words as frightened, terror and horrific, and several recalled having nightmares! These memories were very vivid and still lingered in their attitudes to the subject today as academically successful adults:

I was very good at geometry, but really frightened of all the rest.

Maths struck terror in my heart: a real fear that has stayed with me from over 20 years ago.

I had nightmares about maths. They only went away when I passed my A level!

I had nightmares about maths as well: I really did, I'm not joking. Numbers and figures would go flashing through my head. Times tables, for example. I especially had nightmares about maths tests.

It worried me a great deal. Maths lessons were horrific.

Others recalled feelings of stupidity or frustration at being faced with mathematical tasks:

> I remember that I would always feel stupid. I felt sure that everyone else understood.

> Things used to get hazy and frustrating when I was stuck on a question.

Those of us who teach mathematics must pause and wonder what it is that we do to children that produces successful, intelligent adults who continue to feel like this about the subject.

Expectations

It seems as though the sources of anxiety for some trainee teachers were the expectations of others:

> It was made worse because Dad's best subject was maths.

> My teacher gave me the impression that she thought I was bad at maths. So that's how I was labelled in my mind. When I got my GCE result she said, 'I never thought you'd get an A!' So I thought it must just be a fluke. I still thought I was no good at maths.

But the most common experience cited by these trainees was the teacher's expectation that they *should* be able to deal successfully with all the mathematical tasks they were given. They recalled clearly the negative effect on them of the teacher's response to their failure to understand:

> There were few maths teachers who could grasp the idea of people not being mathematical.

> The teacher just didn't understand why I had problems.

> Teachers expect you to be good at maths if you're good at other things. They look at your other subjects and just can't understand why you can't do maths. They say to you, 'You should be able to do this … '.

> I remember when I was 7 I had to do 100 long divisions. The headmaster came in to check on our progress. He picked me up and banged me up and down on my chair, saying, 'Why can't you do it?' After that I wouldn't ask if I couldn't understand something.

Teaching and learning styles

The trainee teachers spoke with considerable vigour about their memories of the way mathematics was taught to them, recognizing now, from their adult perspective, that part of the problem was a significant limitation in the teaching style to which they were subjected:

> Surely not everyone can be bad at maths. Is it just that it's really badly taught?

> I remember one teacher who was good because she actually tried to explain things to me.

It was clear that most of the trainees in this group felt that they had been encouraged to learn by rote, to learn rules and recipes without understanding. This rote-learning style was then reinforced by apparent success:

> I was quite good at maths at school but I'm frightened of going back to teach it because I think I've probably forgotten most of what we learnt. I have a feeling that all I learnt was just memorized by rote and now it's all gone.

> I could rote learn things, but not understand them.

> I got through the exams by simply learning the rules. I would just look for clues in the question and find the appropriate process.

> I don't think I understood any of it. I got my O level, but that just tested rote learning.

The limitations of this rote-learning syndrome were sometimes apparent to the trainees:

> I found you could do simple problems using the recipes, but then they'd throw in a question that was more complex. Then when the recipe I'd learnt didn't work I became angry.

> We would be given a real-life situation but I would find it difficult to separate the maths concepts out of it.

But it seems that some teachers positively discouraged a more appropriate learning style:

> I was made to feel like I was a nuisance for trying to understand.

> Lots of questions were going round in my head but I was too scared to ask them.

I always tried to avoid asking questions in maths lessons because you were made to feel so stupid if you got it wrong. There must be ways of convincing a child it doesn't matter if they get a question wrong.

The following remark by one trainee in this context highlights how the role as a trainee teacher serves to focus the feeling of anxiety and inadequacy arising from the rote-learning strategy adopted in the past:

I have a real fear of teaching young children how to do things in maths as I just learnt rules and recipes. I have this dread of having to explain why we do something.

Image of mathematics

For some trainees, mathematics had an image of being a difficult subject, so much so that it was socially acceptable not to be any good at it:

Maths has an image of being hard. You pick this idea up from friends, parents and even teachers.

My Mum would tell me not to worry, saying, 'It's alright, we're all hopeless at maths!' It was as if it was socially acceptable to be bad at maths.

Among my friends and family it was OK to be bad at maths, but it's not acceptable in society or employment.

For some, the problem seemed to lie with the feeling that mathematics was different from other subjects in school because the tasks given in mathematics are seen as essentially convergent and uncreative:

Maths is not to do with the creativity of the individual, so you feel more restricted. All the time you think you've just got to get the right answer. And there is only one right answer.

There's more scope for failure with maths. It's very obvious when you've failed, because things are either right or wrong, so you feel a fool, or look a fool in front of the others.

Language

A major problem for all the trainee teachers was that mathematical language seemed to be too technical, too specific to the subject and not reinforced through their language use in everyday life:

> I find the language of maths difficult, but the handling of numbers is fine.

> Most of the words you use in maths you never use in everyday conversation.

> Some words seem to have different meanings in maths, so you get confused.

> I was always worried about saying the wrong things in maths lessons, because maths language seems to be so precise. I worry now that I'll say things wrong to children in school and get them confused. You know, like, 'Which is the bigger half?'

When we discussed the actual content of the National Curriculum programmes of study for mathematics, it became clear that the majority of the trainees' anxieties were related to language. Often they would not recognize mathematical ideas that they actually understood quite well, because they appeared in the National Curriculum in formal mathematical language, which they had either never known or forgotten through neglect. This seemed to be partly because most of this technical mathematical language is not used in normal everyday adult conversation, even amongst intelligent graduates:

> I can't remember what prime numbers are. Why are they called prime numbers anyway?

> Is a product when you multiply two numbers together?

> What's the difference between mass and weight?

> What is congruence? A mapping? Discrete data? A measure of spread? A quadrant? An inverse? Reflective symmetry? A translation? A transformation?

Even as a 'mathematician', I must confess that it is very rare for this kind of technical language to come into my everyday conversation, apart from when I am actually 'doing mathematics'. When this technical language was explained to the students, typical reactions would be:

> Oh, is that what they mean? Why don't they say so, then?

> Why do they have to dress it up in such complicated language?

Mathematics explained

Recognizing that amongst primary trainee teachers and, indeed, amongst many primary school teachers in general, there is this background of anxiety and confusion, it is clear to me that a major task for initial and in-service training is the promotion of positive attitudes towards teaching mathematics in this age range. The evidence from my conversations with trainee teachers suggests that to achieve this we need to shift perceptions of teaching mathematics away from the notion of teaching recipes and more towards the development of understanding. And we need to give time to explaining mathematical ideas, to the ironing out of confusions over the content and, particularly, the language of the mathematics National Curriculum. Some trainees' comments later in the year highlighted the significance to them of having mathematics explained. The emphasis on explaining and understanding paid off in shifts of attitudes towards the subject:

> It's the first time anyone has actually explained things in maths to me. I feel a lot happier about going into the classroom now.

> The course seems to have reawakened an interest in mathematics for me and exploded the myth that maths was something I had to learn by rote for exams, rather than understand.

> I was really fearful about having to teach maths. That fear has now declined. I feel more confident and more informed about teaching maths now.

These kinds of reactions have prompted me to write this book. It is my hope that by focusing specifically on explaining the language and content of the mathematics that we teach in the primary age range, this book will help other trainee teachers – and primary school teachers in general – to develop this kind of confidence in approaching their teaching of this key subject in the curriculum to children who are at such an important stage in their educational development.

Research focus

In the context of increasing government concern about the subject knowledge in mathematics of trainee teachers, a group of mathematics educators at the London Institute of Education audited primary trainee teachers' performance in a number of basic mathematical topics. Those topics in which the trainees had the lowest facility were making algebraic generalizations, Pythagoras's theorem, calculation of area, mathematical reasoning, scale factors and percentage increase. Significantly, trainees with poor subject knowledge in mathematics were found to perform poorly in their teaching of mathematics in the classroom when assessed at the end of their training (Rowland et al., 2000).

2
Mathematics in the Primary Curriculum

In this chapter there are explanations of

- the different kinds of reason for teaching mathematics in the primary school;
- the contribution of mathematics to everyday life and society;
- the contribution of mathematics to other areas of the curriculum;
- the contribution of mathematics to the learner's intellectual development;
- the importance of mathematics in promoting enjoyment of learning;
- how mathematics is important as a distinctive form of knowledge;
- how the essential content of the primary curriculum in England is not just about knowledge and skills but also about using and applying mathematics;
- the various components of using and applying mathematics in the primary curriculum in England; and
- the relationship of numeracy to mathematical understanding.

Why teach mathematics in the primary school?

What is distinctive about mathematics in the primary curriculum? Why is it always considered such a key subject? What are the most important things we are trying to achieve when we teach mathematics to children? To answer questions such as these we need to identify our aims in teaching mathematics to primary school children. Teachers are normally very good at specifying their short-term objectives – the particular knowledge or skills they want pupils to acquire in a lesson. But reflective teachers will also recognize the value of having a framework for longer-term planning, to ensure that the children receive an appropriate breadth of experience year by year as they progress through their primary education. I find it helpful, therefore, to identify at least five different kinds of **aims of**

teaching mathematics in primary schools. They relate to the contribution of mathematics to: (1) everyday life and society; (2) other areas of the curriculum; (3) the child's intellectual development; (4) the child's enjoyment of learning; and (5) the body of human knowledge. These are not completely discrete strands, nor are they the only way for structuring our thinking about why we teach this subject.

How does mathematics contribute to everyday life and society?

This strand relates to what are often referred to as **utilitarian** aims. We teach mathematics because it is useful for everyone in meeting the demands of everyday living. One of our aims is to introduce children to 'concepts, skills and thinking strategies that are useful in everyday life' (DCSF/QCDA, 2010: 44). Many everyday transactions and real-life problems, and most forms of employment, require confidence and competence in a range of basic mathematical skills and knowledge – such as measurement, manipulating shapes, organizing space, handling money, recording and interpreting numerical and graphical data, and using information and communications technology (ICT).

Teachers themselves, for example, need a large range of such skills in their everyday professional life – for example, in handling school finances and budgets, in organizing their timetables, in planning the spatial arrangement of the classroom, in processing assessment data, in interpreting inspection reports and in using ICT in their teaching. If in teaching mathematics we are to equip young people for the demands of everyday life then our approach to the subject must reflect the availability of ICT applications such as calculators and spreadsheets.

The relationship of mathematical processes to real-life contexts is demonstrated in this book particularly in the process of *modelling* which is introduced in Chapter 5 and which forms the basis of the discussion of addition, subtraction, multiplication and division structures in Chapters 6 and 9.

> **LEARNING and TEACHING POINT**
>
> In shaping, monitoring and evaluating their medium-term planning, teachers should ensure that sufficient prominence is given to each of the five reasons for teaching mathematics:
>
> 1. its importance in everyday life and society;
> 2. its importance in other curriculum areas;
> 3. its importance in relation to the learner's intellectual development;
> 4. its importance in developing the child's enjoyment of learning; and
> 5. its distinctive place in human knowledge and culture.

> **LEARNING and TEACHING POINT**
>
> Learning experiences for children that reflect the contribution of mathematics to everyday life and society could include, for example: (a) realistic and relevant financial and budgeting problems; (b) meeting people from various forms of employment and exploring how they use mathematics in their work; and (c) helping teachers with some of the administrative tasks they have to do that draw on mathematical skills.

How does mathematics contribute to other areas of the curriculum?

Learning experiences for children that reflect the application of mathematics to other curriculum areas could include, for example: (a) collecting, organizing, representing and interpreting data arising in science experiments or in enquiries related to historical, geographical and social understanding; (b) drawing up plans and meeting the demands for accurate measurement in technology and in design; (c) using mathematical concepts to stimulate and support the exploration of pattern in art, dance and music; and (d) using mathematical skills in cross-curricular studies such as 'transport' or 'a visit to France'.

This strand relates to the **application** of mathematics. We teach mathematics because it has applications in a range of contexts, including other areas of the curriculum. Much of mathematics as we know it today has developed in response to practical challenges in science and technology, in the social sciences and in economics. So, as well as being a subject in its own right, with its own patterns, principles and procedures, mathematics is a subject that can be applied and mathematical skills can support learning across the curriculum. The primary school teacher who is responsible for teaching nearly all the areas of the curriculum is uniquely placed to take advantage of opportunities that arise, for example, in the context of science and technology, in the arts, in history, geography and society, to apply mathematical skills and concepts purposefully in meaningful contexts – and to make explicit to the children what mathematics is being applied.

This is a two-way process: these various curriculum areas can also provide meaningful and purposeful contexts for introducing and reinforcing mathematical concepts, skills and principles. Following the Rose Review in 2009, cross-curricular studies are once again becoming a feature of primary education. Many teachers have welcomed the opportunity for 'enhancing children's mathematical understanding through making links to other areas of learning and wider issues of interest and importance' (DCSF/QCDA, 2010: 45). Cross-curricular studies will inevitably draw on and develop mathematical skills, for example, in organizing, representing and interpreting data – and can be planned with particular mathematical content in mind.

How does mathematics contribute to the child's intellectual development?

This strand includes what are sometimes referred to as *thinking skills*, but I am including here a broader range of aspects of the learner's **intellectual development**. We teach mathematics because it provides opportunities for developing important intellectual skills in problem solving, deductive and inductive reasoning, creative thinking and communication. Mathematics is important for primary school children because it introduces them to some key thinking strategies for solving problems and gives them opportunities to 'use logical reasoning, suggest solutions and try out different approaches to problems' (DCSF/QCDA, 2010: 45). These are distinctive characteristics of a person who thinks in a mathematical way.

Sometimes to solve a mathematical problem we have to reason logically and systematically, using what is called deductive reasoning. Other times, an insight that leads to a solution may require thinking creatively, divergently and imaginatively. So, not only does mathematics develop logical, deductive reasoning but – perhaps surprisingly – engagement with this subject can also foster creativity. So mathematics is an important context for developing effective problem-solving strategies that potentially have significance in all areas of human activity. But also in learning mathematics, children have many opportu-

> **LEARNING and TEACHING POINT**
>
> Learning experiences for children in mathematics should include a focus on the child's intellectual development, by providing opportunities to foster: (a) problem-solving strategies; (b) deductive reasoning, which includes reasoning logically and systematically; (c) creative thinking, which is characterized by divergent and imaginative thinking; (d) inductive reasoning that leads to the articulation of patterns and generalizations; and (e) communication of mathematical ideas orally and in writing, using both formal and informal language, and in diagrams and symbols.

nities to look for patterns. This involves inductive reasoning leading to the articulation of generalizations, statements of what is always the case. The process of using a number of specific instances to formulate a general rule or principle, which can then be applied in other instances, is at the heart of mathematical thinking.

Then finally, in this section, in terms of intellectual development we should note that in learning mathematics children are developing a powerful way of communicating. Mathematics is effectively a language, containing technical terminology, distinctive patterns of spoken and written language, a range of diagrammatic devices and a distinctive way of using symbols to represent and manipulate concepts. Children use this language to articulate their observations and to explain and later to justify or prove their conclusions in mathematics. Mathematical language is a key theme throughout this book.

How does mathematics contribute to the child's enjoyment of learning?

This strand relates to what is sometimes referred to as the **aesthetic** aim in teaching mathematics. We teach mathematics because it has an inherent beauty that can provide the learner with delight and enjoyment. I suspect that there may be some readers whose experience of learning mathematics in school may not resonate with this statement! But there really is potential for genuine enjoyment and pleasure for children in primary schools in exploring and learning mathematics. It is emotionally satisfying for children to be able to make coherent sense of the numbers, patterns and shapes they encounter in the world around them, for example, through the processes of classification and conceptualization. 'Children delight in using mathematics to solve a problem' (DCSF/QCDA, 2010: 4). Indeed they will often be seen to smile

Learning experiences for children in mathematics should ensure that children enjoy learning mathematics, by providing opportunities to: (a) experience the sense of pleasure that comes from solving a problem or a mathematical puzzle; (b) have their curiosity stimulated by formulating their own questions and investigating mathematical situations; (c) play small-group games that draw on mathematical skills and concepts; (d) experiment with pattern in numbers and shapes and discover relationships for themselves; and (e) have some beautiful moments in mathematics where they are surprised, delighted or intrigued.

with pleasure when they get an insight that leads to a solution; when they spot a pattern, discover something for themselves or make connections; when they find a mathematical rule that always works – or even identify an exception that challenges a rule. The extensive patterns that underlie mathematics can be fascinating, and recognizing and exploiting these can be genuinely satisfying. Mathematics can be appreciated as a creative experience, in which flexibility and imaginative thinking can lead to interesting outcomes or fresh avenues to explore for the curious mind. Throughout this book I aim to increase the reader's own sense of delight and enjoyment in mathematics, with the hope that this will be communicated to those they teach.

Why is mathematics important as a distinctive form of knowledge?

This strand is what the more pretentious of us would call the **epistemological** aim. Epistemology is the theory of knowledge. The argument here is that we teach mathematics because it is a significant and distinctive form of human knowledge with its own concepts and principles and its own ways of making assertions, formulating arguments and justifying conclusions. This kind of purpose in teaching mathematics is based on the notion that an educated person has the right to be initiated into all the various forms of human knowledge and to appreciate their distinctive ways of reasoning and arguing. For example, an explanation of a historical event, a theory in science, a doctrine in theology and a mathematical generalization are four very different kinds of statements, supported by different kinds of evidence and arguments.

   In mathematics, as we have indicated above, some of the characteristic ways of reasoning would be to look for patterns, to make and test conjectures, to investigate a hypothesis, to formulate a generalization and then to justify the generalization by means of a deductive argument (a proof). The most distinctive quality of mathematical knowledge is the notion of a mathematical statement being incontestably true because it can be deduced by logical argument either from the axioms (self-evident truths) of mathematics or from previously proven truths. Of course, children in primary schools will not be able to justify their mathematical conclusions by means of a formal proof, but they can experience many of the other distinctive kinds of mathematical processes and even at this age begin to demonstrate and explain why various things are always true.

Mathematics is also a significant part of our cultural heritage. Not to know anything about mathematics would be as much a cultural shortcoming as being ignorant of our musical and artistic heritage. Historically, the study of mathematics has been at the heart of most major civilizations. Certainly much of what we might regard as European mathematics was well known in ancient Chinese civilizations. Our number system has its roots in ancient Egypt, Mesopotamia and Hindu cultures. Classical civilization was dominated by great mathematicians such as Pythagoras, Zeno, Euclid and Archimedes. To appreciate mathematics as a subject should also include knowing something of how mathematics as a subject has developed over time and how different cultures have contributed to this body of knowledge. The Williams Review underlines the significance of this aspect of mathematics in the curriculum, suggesting that 'opportunities for children to engage with the cultural and historical story of both science and mathematics could have potential for building their interest and positive attitudes to mathematics' (Williams, 2008: 62).

> **LEARNING and TEACHING POINT**
>
> Primary school teachers should include as one of their aims for teaching mathematics: to promote awareness of some of the contributions of various cultures to the body of mathematical knowledge. This can be a fascinating component of history-based cross-curricular projects, such as the study of ancient civilizations.

What mathematics do we teach in the primary school?

The level descriptions for mathematics in the National Curriculum for England (QCDA, 2010), which cover both primary and secondary schools, are organized under four attainment targets. These provide a simple framework for describing the mathematics we teach in primary schools: (1) Using and Applying Mathematics; (2) Number and Algebra; (3) Shape, Space and Measures; and (4) Statistics.

At the head of the list of attainment targets, given appropriate prominence, is '**using and applying mathematics**'. This does not represent a discrete section of the mathematics curriculum. It is intended to be an integral component of all the mathematics that children do in school. The mathematics curriculum – and therefore this book – contains a huge amount of knowledge to be learnt, and a great number of skills to be mastered and concepts and principles to be understood. But it is a lifeless and purposeless subject if we do not also learn to use and apply all this knowledge and all these skills, concepts and principles. Williams (2008: 62) stresses the need 'to strengthen teaching that challenges and enables children to use and apply mathematics more often, and more effectively, than is presently the case in many schools.'

Williams argues that it is in experiences of using and applying mathematics that we have the best chance of fostering positive attitudes to mathematics: 'if children's interests are not kindled through using and applying mathematics in interesting and engaging

Using and applying mathematics is not just something for children to do after they have learnt some mathematical content, but should be integrated into all learning and teaching of the subject. Sometimes an appropriate approach to planning a sequence of mathematics lessons might be: introduce some new concept or skill; practise it; apply it in various problems. But not always! Sometimes a real-life problem that draws on a wide range of mathematical ideas can be used as a meaningful context in which to introduce some new mathematical concept or to provide a purposeful stimulus for children to extend their mathematical skills.

ways, and through learning across the full mathematics curriculum, they are unlikely to develop good attitudes to the subject' (Williams, 2008: 62). So teachers have to ensure that children get opportunities to learn not just mathematical content but also how to use and apply their mathematics. Sometimes this will consist of using the mathematical knowledge, skills, concepts and principles they have learnt to solve problems or pursue enquiries within mathematics itself. Other times it will involve applying mathematics to solve practical problems in the world around them or to support projects within other areas of the school curriculum.

The Number and Algebra attainment target includes learning about counting, place value and our number system, different kinds of numbers, the structures of the four basic number operations, mental strategies and written methods for calculations, remainders and rounding, various properties of numbers, fractions and ratios, calculations with decimals, proportion and percentages. It introduces children to algebraic thinking, through expressing generalizations in words and simple formula, coordinates and linear relationships. This mathematics is essentially the content of Section C of this book, Chapters 6–21.

Within the Shape, Space and Measures attainment target children learn to identify and classify 2-dimensional and 3-dimensional shapes, to use appropriate language to describe the properties of various shapes, and to recognize various families of shapes. They learn how to transform shapes in various ways, including reflections and rotations, and learn about different kinds of symmetry. They learn how to measure and how to estimate length, mass, capacity, time and angle, using non-standard and standard units. They learn about different metric units and how they are related. They are introduced to the area and perimeter of some simple two-dimensional shapes, and the volume of solid shapes. This mathematics is the subject of Section D of this book, Chapters 22–26.

The attainment target for Statistics in the primary school is about learning how to collect, organize, display and interpret various kinds of data, particularly using data-handling software. Children learn about frequency tables and how to use and interpret different ways of representing data pictorially, including Venn diagrams, Carroll diagrams, pictograms, block graphs, bar charts, line graphs, scatter graphs and pie charts. They learn how to calculate and use different kinds of averages. They begin to learn about probability and risk and how probability can be measured. This mathematics is covered in Section E of this book, Chapters 27–29.

What do children learn in using and applying mathematics in the primary school?

Much of this attainment target is about using and applying mathematics in real-life and cross-curricular contexts: 'children use mathematics as an integral part of class-room activities'. This leads on to the development of problem-solving strategies. These are used and developed not just in realistic problems set in real-life contexts, but also through what we might regard as essentially problems within mathematics itself: 'children develop their own strategies for solving problems and use these strategies both in working within mathematics and in applying mathematics to practical contexts'.

In practice, it makes little sense to categorize problems as either 'within mathematics' or in 'practical contexts'. There is really a continuum of contexts for using and applying mathematics. At one end are problems that are purely mathematical, just about numbers and shapes, in which the outcome is of no particular practical significance. An example is shown in Figure 2.1, where the challenge would be: how many different shapes can you make by joining five identical squares together edge to edge? At the other end of the continuum would be problems that are genuine, real-life situations that need to be solved. An example might be: how much orange squash should we buy to be able to provide three drinks for each player in the inter-school football tournament? But many other problems or investigations are set in real-life contexts, but are perhaps less genuine. An example might be: find out as many interesting things as you can about the way the page numbers are arranged on the sheets of a newspaper.

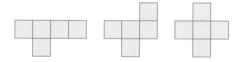

Figure 2.1 *How many different shapes can you make with five squares joined together like these?*

The using and applying mathematics attainment target also includes the development of mathematical reasoning: 'children show that they understand a general statement by finding particular examples that match it … they look for patterns and

LEARNING and TEACHING POINT

To develop the key processes involved in using and applying mathematics children should have opportunities to use mathematics in a range of tasks, including:

(a) activities within their everyday experience in the classroom, such as planning their timetable for the day, or grouping children for various activities;

(b) identifying and proposing solutions to genuine problems, such as where in the playground staff should park their cars;

(c) tackling artificial but realistic problems, such as estimating the cost for a family of four to go on a two-week holiday on the Norfolk Broads;

(d) applying mathematics in practical tasks, such as making a box to hold a set of calculators;

(e) solving mathematical problems, such as finding two-digit numbers that have an odd number of factors; and

(f) pursuing mathematical investigations, such as 'find out as much as you can about the relationships between different paper sizes (A5, A4, A3, and so on)'.

relationships.' The key processes in mathematical reasoning include those associated with recognizing patterns and relationships, making conjectures, formulating hypotheses, articulating and using generalizations.

Then, another clear strand is about the development of skills in communicating with mathematics: 'they explain why an answer is correct … presenting information and results in a clear and organised way … draw simple conclusions of their own and explain their reasoning.' It is in using and applying mathematics that children get the most powerful experience of communicating with mathematical language, symbols and diagrams. This will involve explaining insights, describing the outcomes of an investigation, providing convincing reasons for a conclusion they have drawn, or offering evidence to support a point of view.

Key processes in using and applying mathematics, such as modelling, problem solving, generalizing and creative thinking, are introduced and explained in detail in Section B (Chapters 4 and 5) and then developed as an integral component of subsequent chapters.

How does numeracy relate to mathematical understanding?

There was a time when 'numeracy' was understood to refer to no more than competence with numbers and calculations within the demands of everyday life – a small subset of the mathematics curriculum. The word was often preceded by the word 'basic'. So, it would amount to not much more than knowing your multiplication tables and being able to work out simple everyday calculations with money – most of which in reality would be done with calculators anyway. Then – apparently without any justification – in the early twenty-first century the National Numeracy Strategy in England chose to use the word synonymously with 'mathematics'. So everything in the primary mathematics curriculum suddenly became numeracy, and mathematics lessons in primary schools became 'the numeracy hour'. The 2010 proposal for the primary curriculum in England (DCSF/QCDA, 2010) sensibly brought back 'mathematics', in the section of the curriculum entitled 'Mathematical Understanding' – and gave a new lease of life to the word 'numeracy'.

Significantly, numeracy appears as one of the Essential for Learning and Life, which are aspects of learning to be embedded and developed across the curriculum. In this new understanding of the term, numeracy is clearly and specifically about the using and applying aspects of mathematics: 'Children use and apply mathematics confidently and competently in their learning and in everyday contexts. They recognise where mathematics can be used to solve problems and are able to interpret a wide range of mathematical data' (DCSF/QCDA, 2010:14). So, numeracy takes on a much more substantial meaning, including aspects like problem solving, using mathematical models of real-life situations (see Chapter 5) and communicating with mathematics. Encouragingly, the proposal to develop numeracy, understood in this way, across the curriculum has the potential to make the using and applying aspect of mathematics appropriately prominent in primary learning and teaching – and not just in mathematics lessons.

> **LEARNING and TEACHING POINT**
>
> In developing numeracy, children in primary schools should learn across the curriculum to:
>
> (a) represent and model situations using mathematics, using a range of tools and applying logic and reasoning in order to predict, plan and try out options;
>
> (b) use numbers and measurements for accurate calculation and an understanding of scale, in order to make reasonable estimations;
>
> (c) interpret and interrogate mathematical data in graphs, spreadsheets and diagrams, in order to draw inferences, recognise patterns and trends, and assess likelihood and risk; and
>
> (d) use mathematics to justify and support decisions and proposals, communicating accurately using mathematical language and conventions, symbols and diagrams.
>
> (DCSF/QCDA, 2010:14).

Research focus

In recent years there has been increased recognition of the important part that ICT should play in the mathematics curriculum. One of the most useful and accessible ICT devices is, of course, the simple hand-held calculator. But what should be the place of calculators in the primary mathematics curriculum? On the one hand, many mathematics educators would point to the many ways in which calculators can be used right across the primary age range, not just to do calculations, but to promote understanding of mathematical concepts and to explore patterns and relationships between numbers. On the other hand there are those – including some influential politicians and journalists who have strong views but little insight into the learning and teaching of mathematics – who would argue that calculators have no place at all, because they clearly must undermine children's calculation skills. This particular argument is not supported by the research evidence. For example, an Australian research project (Groves, 1993; 1994) explored the results achieved by using a calculator-aware number curriculum with young children from the reception class onwards. When these children reached the age of 8–9 years they were found to perform better in a number of key mathematical tasks than children two years older than them. These included: estimating the result of a calculation; solving real-life problems; understanding of place value, decimals and negative numbers; and interpreting calculator answers involving decimals.

Suggestions for further reading

1. Read the entries on 'Aims of mathematics teaching', 'Deductive and inductive reasoning' and 'Using and applying mathematics' in Haylock with Thangata (2007). Each entry in this book contains a definition of the 'concept', explanation and discussion, practical examples and related reading.
2. The contributors to White and Bramall (2000) explore the varied aims of learning and teaching mathematics, and consider to what extent the subject deserves the privileged status it has traditionally enjoyed in the school curriculum. Recommended for those with a philosophical bent.
3. In a chapter entitled 'Calculators for all?', in Thompson (2003), Williams and Thompson suggest that the National Numeracy Strategy in England failed to take the opportunity to articulate effective calculator practice in mathematics teaching in both Key Stages of primary schooling. Examples are given of exciting ways of using calculators with young children exploring the pattern and application of number.
4. Read an intelligent discussion of numeracy in the twenty-first century in Chapter 1 of Anghileri (2007).

Glossary of key terms introduced in Chapter 2

Aims of teaching mathematics: in describing the importance of mathematics in the primary curriculum a number of different kinds of aims in teaching mathematics can be identified; these can be classified as utilitarian, application, intellectual development, aesthetic and epistemological.

Utilitarian aim in teaching mathematics: mathematics is useful in everyday life and necessary in most forms of employment.

Application aim in teaching mathematics: mathematics has many important applications in other curriculum areas.

Intellectual development aim in teaching mathematics: mathematics provides opportunities for developing important intellectual skills in problem solving, deductive and inductive reasoning, creative thinking and communication.

Aesthetic aim in teaching mathematics: mathematical experiences in the primary school can provide delight, wonder, beauty and enjoyment.

Epistemological aim in teaching mathematics: mathematics should be learnt because it is a distinctive and important form of knowledge and part of our cultural heritage.

Using and applying mathematics: using the skills, knowledge, concepts and principles learnt in mathematics to solve problems, across a continuum from genuine problems in a real-life context to purely mathematical challenges; engaging in investigations and enquiries that develop key processes in mathematical reasoning; and communicating insights, reasoning, results and conclusions with mathematical language, diagrams and symbols.

3
Learning How To Learn Mathematics

In this chapter there are explanations of

- the fundamental importance of children in primary schools learning how to learn mathematics;
- the connections model for understanding number and number operations;
- the processes of recognizing equivalences and identifying transformations; and
- the process of classification.

What is meant by 'learning how to learn mathematics'?

When the National Curriculum for primary schools in England was being reviewed in 2008, I was invited to take part in a mathematics advisory group. To start the discussion we were asked to say what we considered was the most important thing for children to learn in mathematics at primary school. Reflecting on this question on the train down to London, I came up with my answer. The most important thing for children to learn in mathematics in the primary years is how to learn mathematics!

This conclusion is based on my experience of teaching mathematics to children of all ages and to adults, particularly those training to teach in primary schools. The biggest problem that I come across is that in learning this subject individuals can develop a rote-learning mind set. In essence, this means that they have stopped trying to make sense of what they are taught or asked to do in mathematics; they just sit there waiting for the teacher to tell them what to do with a particular type of question. They no longer want to understand. They see learning mathematics as a matter of learning a whole collection of routines and recipes for different kinds of questions. Sadly, they may even have learnt that to get the teacher's approval and the marks in mathematics tests you do not actually have to understand what is going on, you just have to remember the right procedures.

If children learn this in primary schools, then they have not learnt how to learn mathematics. The beauty of the subject is that it does all make sense. It can be understood. It can be learnt meaningfully. Our biggest challenge in teaching mathematics to primary school children, I am convinced, is to ensure that they move on to secondary education with a meaningful-learning mind set. This means that they are committed to learning with understanding. They have learnt how to learn with understanding, they expect to understand and will not be content until they do. They have had teachers who have valued children showing understanding more highly than just the accurate reproduction of learnt procedures.

The best teachers in primary schools want children to understand what they learn. But for a child to understand, they have to learn how to learn with understanding – and this requires teachers who understand what learning with understanding in mathematics is like and how it is demonstrated in children's responses to mathematical situations.

How is mathematics understood?

A simple way of talking about understanding is to say that to understand means to build up (cognitive) connections. When I have some new experience in mathematics, if I just try to learn it as an isolated bit of knowledge or a discrete skill, then this is what is called rote learning. All I can do is to try to remember it and to recall it when appropriate. If, however, I can connect it in various ways with other experiences and things I have learnt, then it makes sense. For example, if I am trying to learn the 8-times multiplication table and the teacher helps me to connect it with the 4-times table – which I already know – then I feel I am beginning to make some sense of what otherwise would seem to be a whole collection of arbitrary results. So, 7 eights, well, that is just double 7 fours: double 28, which makes 56. And, of course, when I struggle momentarily to recall 7 fours, well, that is just double 7 twos. And so on. So, in learning the multiplication tables, I am not just trying to recall a hundred different results, but I am constructing a network of connections, which helps me to make sense of all these numbers, to see patterns and to use relationships. As teachers, we want to encourage children all the time to make these and other kinds of connections, so this becomes the default setting for how they learn mathematics.

To understand many mathematical ideas – like number, subtraction, place value, fractions – we have to gradually build up these networks of connections, where each new experience is being connected with our existing understanding, and related in some way to other experiences. This is achieved through practical engagement with mathematical materials, through investigation and exploration, through talking about mathematics with the teacher and other learners, and through the teacher's explanation and asking the right kinds of questions – but, above all, through the learner's own cognitive response, which has been shaped by prior successful learning to look for connections and relationships in order to learn in a meaningful way.

In the rest of this chapter I shall explain four key processes that are at the heart of understanding in primary school mathematics: (1) a connections model of understanding number and number operations; (2) equivalence; (3) transformation; and (4) classification.

What is the connections model of understanding?

Figure 3.1 illustrates a simple connections model that I find helpful for promoting understanding in number and number operations. This model identifies the four kinds of things that children process and manipulate when doing number work in primary schools: language, pictures, symbols and practical/real-life experience. This diagram represents many of the most important connections to be established in understanding number and number operations. Making any one of these kinds of connections – connecting language with symbols, connecting pictures with language, connecting real-life experience with symbols, and so on – contributes to the learner's understanding.

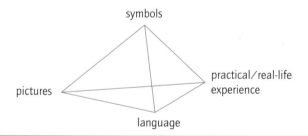

Figure 3.1   *A model for understanding number work: making connections*

Language in this model includes formal mathematical language: subtract, multiply, divide, equals, and so on. It also includes more informal language appropriate to various contexts: taking away, so many lots of so many, sharing, is the same as, makes, and so on. In particular, it includes key patterns of language, such as in these examples: 8 is 3 more than 5 and 5 is 3 less than 8; 12 shared equally between 4 is 3 each. By *pictures*, I have in mind all kinds of charts, graphs, pictograms and sorting diagrams and, especially, the picture of number as provided in number strips and number lines. *Symbols* are those we use to represent numbers and number operations, equality and inequality: 3, ¾, 0.78, +, −, ×, ÷, =,

<, >, and so on. *Practical/real-life experiences* includes any kind of engagement with physical objects, such as counters, coins, blocks, fingers, containers, groups of children, board games, toys. This also includes any real-life situations, such as shopping, measuring, travelling, cooking, playing in the playground, whether actual or imagined.

So, developing understanding of a concept in number work can be thought of as building up cognitive connections between these four components. Throughout this book number concepts are explained in this way, with an emphasis on connecting the relevant language, pictures and concrete experiences with the mathematical symbols. For example, in Chapter 6 the concept of place value is explained in terms of: key language, such as 'exchanging one of these for ten of these'; pictures, such as the number line; concrete materials such as coins and blocks; and then making the connections between all these and the symbols used in our place-value number system. If we as teachers aim to promote understanding in mathematics, rather than just learning by rote, then the key to this is to teach it in a way that encourages children to make connections.

> **LEARNING and TEACHING POINT**
>
> Use question-and-answer sessions with the class and with groups of children specifically to ensure that they are making connections from their experience of doing mathematical tasks. For example in promoting understanding of subtraction, start with a real-life situation such as: when playing a board game, Tom is on square 13 and wants to land on square 22, what score does he need? Connect it with language, such as what do we add to 13 to make 22? What is 22 subtract 13? Connect it with a picture: what do we do on a number line to work this out? Connect it with symbols: what would we enter on a calculator to work this out? (22 – 13 =).

What are equivalences and transformations?

Recognizing similarities and differences are fundamental cognitive processes by means of which we organize and make sense of all of our experiences. They have particular significance in the development of understanding in mathematics. In this context we refer to forming equivalences (by asking the question, what is the same?) and identifying transformations (by asking the question, what is different? Or, how has it changed?). So, an equivalence is formed when we identify some mathematical way in which two or more numbers or shapes or sets (or any other kind of mathematical entities) are the same. And a transformation is identified when we specify what is different between two entities and what has to be done to one to change it into the other.

Can you give some examples of equivalences?

The process of forming equivalences is widespread in the experience of children learning mathematics with understanding. It is part of the process of developing mathematical concepts and is a powerful tool for manipulating mathematical ideas. In the early stages of learning number, for example, children learn to recognize that there is something the same about, say, a set of five beakers and a set of five children. These two collections are different from each other (beakers are different from children), but there is something significantly the same about them, which can be recognized by matching one beaker to each child. Both sets are described by the adjective 'five', which indicates a property they share. Forming equivalences like this contributes to the child's understanding of the number five and numbers in general. Understanding number is explored further in Chapter 6.

This example illustrates how many abstract mathematical concepts are formed by identifying equivalences, recognizing things that are the same or properties that are shared. Geometry provides many such examples. In learning the concept of 'square', for example, children may sort a set of two-dimensional shapes into various subsets. When they put all the squares together in a subset, because they are 'all the same shape', they are recognizing an equivalence. The shapes may not all be the same in every respect – they may differ in size or colour, for example – but they are all the same in some sense; they share the properties that make them squares; there is an equivalence. Any one of them could be used if we wanted to show someone what a square is like, or to do some kind of investigation with squares.

> **LEARNING and TEACHING POINT**
>
> To promote the formation of equivalences and the recognition of transformations, frequently ask children the questions: In what ways are these the same? How are they different? How could this change into that? For example, look at the numbers in a set (for example, 3, 6, 9, 12, 15, 18, 21, 24, 27, 30) and ask, what is the same about them? (They are all multiples of 3.) Select two numbers from the set (for example, 15 and 30) and ask, how are these two different from each other? (15 is smaller than 30, 30 is larger than 15, and so on.) How can one number be changed into the other number? (Double the 15, halve the 30, and so on.) Follow the same approach with sets of shapes.

This kind of thinking is powerful and is fundamental to learning and doing mathematics. It enables the learner to hold in their mind one conceptual idea (such as 'five' or 'square') which is an abstraction of their experiences of many specific examples of the concept, all of which are in some sense the same, all of which are equivalent in this respect. In doing this, the learner combines a number of individual experiences of specific exemplars, which have been recognized as being the same in some sense, into one abstraction.

And examples of transformations?

Making sense of the relationship between two mathematical entities (numbers, shapes, sets, and so on) often comes down to recognizing that they are the same but different. Whenever we form equivalences by seeing something that is the same about some mathematical objects, we have to ignore the ways in which they are different. When we take into account what is different, we focus on the complementary process of transformation. We identify a transformation when we specify what we have to do to one thing to change it into another, different thing. Sometimes we focus on the equivalence and sometimes on the transformation. For example, children have to learn that $\frac{2}{3}$ and $\frac{4}{6}$ are equivalent fractions. They are not identical – two slices of a pizza divided into three equal slices is not in every respect the same as four slices of a pizza divided into six equal slices. But there is something very significantly the same about these two fractions: we do get the same amount of pizza! In making this observation we focus on the equivalence. But when we observe that you change $\frac{2}{3}$ into $\frac{4}{6}$ by multiplying both top number and bottom number by 2 then we focus on the transformation. We explore equivalent fractions further in Chapter 17.

In Figure 3.2, the two shapes can be considered equivalent because we can see a number of ways in which they are the same: for example, they are both rectangles with a diagonal drawn, and they are the same length and height. However one is a transformation of the other, because they are mirror images. So we may identify some differences: for example, if you go from A to B to C to D and back to A, in one shape you go in a clockwise direction and in the other in an anticlockwise direction. So understanding mirror images and reflections in geometry comes down to recognizing how shapes change when you reflect them (the transformation) and in what ways they stay the same (equivalence). Equivalence and transformation are the major themes of Chapter 24 where we see that a key aspect of mathematical reasoning involves looking at sets of shapes and asking: What is the same about all these shapes? What do they have in common? Or – when we transform a shape in some way – what has changed and what has stayed the same?'

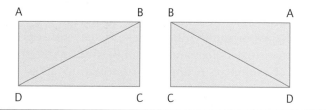

Figure 3.2   *What is the same? What is different?*

This interaction of equivalence and transformation is also central to understanding the principle of conservation in number and measurement. In the context of measurement conservation is explained in Chapter 22. In terms of **conservation of number**, the principle is illustrated in Figure 3.3. Young children match two rows of counters, blue and grey, say, and recognize that they are the same number. There is an equivalence, established by the one to one matching. If one of the rows (B) is then spread out, they have to learn to recognize that, even though the row of counters has been transformed, there is still the same number of counters. This transformation preserves the equivalence. This is a crucial aspect of young children's understanding of number. Children who are in the early stages of understanding number may not yet see number as something that is conserved when the set of objects is transformed – and may perceive that B is now a greater number than A.

Figure 3.3   *Understanding conservation of number*

What is classification in mathematics?

The identification of equivalences is at the heart of the key process of **classification**. Children have to learn to classify numbers and shapes according to a range of criteria and to assign them to various sets. For example, they classify numbers as odd or even, as one-digit or two-digit, as less than 100, as multiples of 3, as factors of 30, as positive or negative, and so on. They classify two-dimensional shapes as triangles or quadrilaterals, as squares, as oblongs, as regular or irregular, as symmetric, and so on; and three-dimensional shapes as cubes or cuboids, as prisms, as pyramids, as spheres, and so on.

Figure 3.4 illustrates the process of classification. In each case here a rule has been used to sort (a) a set of shapes and (b) a set of numbers into exemplars and non-exemplars. Children can be challenged to articulate the rule and to use it to sort some more shapes or numbers. In these cases, the sets of exemplars are: (a) triangles with two sides equal; and (b) single-digit numbers. Sometimes when we do this the set of exemplars is important enough for us to give it a name. For instance, in example (a) we call the triangles that satisfy the rule of having two equal sides 'isosceles triangles' (see Chapter 25). In this way classification in mathematics enables us to develop and understand new concepts – and then to use these as building blocks for forming higher-order concepts. For example, the concept of 'isosceles triangle' uses as building blocks earlier concepts such as triangle and lines of equal lengths. We explore some important classifications of numbers in Chapter 14, and classification of shapes particularly in Chapter 25. Classification is also a key process in the early stages of handling data and pictorial representation, as explained in Chapter 27.

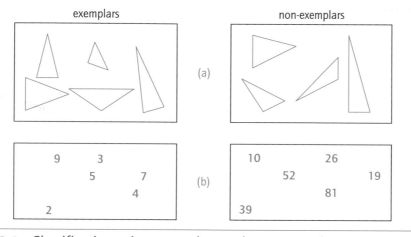

Figure 3.4 *Classification using exemplars and non-exemplars*

Research focus

One of the most famous and influential early researchers into how children learn and understand was the Swiss psychologist and philosopher, Jean Piaget (1896–1980). His work provides a number of intriguing insights into the learning of key mathematical concepts (see, for example, Piaget, 1952), even though many of his findings have subsequently been challenged. What I have talked about as 'networks of connections', Piaget called 'schemas' (Piaget, 1953). He investigated how schemas were developed through the learner relating new experiences to their existing cognitive structures. In many cases, the new experience can be adopted into the existing schema by a process that Piaget called 'assimilation': this is when the new experience can be related to the existing schema just as it is. But sometimes, in order to take on board some new experience, the existing schema has to be modified, reorganized. This process Piaget called 'accommodation'. For example, a child may be developing a schema for multiplication, using multiplication by numbers up to 10. When they encounter multiplication by numbers greater than 10, this new experience can usually be assimilated fairly smoothly into the existing multiplication schema. Part of this schema might be the notion that multiplying makes things bigger. When the learner encounters multiplication by a fraction (such as $20 \times \frac{1}{4} = 5$) this does not fit with this aspect of the existing schema. How can you multiply 20 by something and get an answer smaller than 20? To understand this will require a significant accommodation: a reorganization of the existing schema. If this cannot be achieved, the new experience cannot be understood, it can only be learnt by rote. A key role for teachers of mathematics is helping the learner to accommodate new experiences when they provide significant challenges to the learner's existing understanding.

Suggestions for further reading

1. Chapter 1 of Haylock and Cockburn (2008) is on understanding mathematics. In this chapter we outline and illustrate in more detail the connections model for understanding, as well as the ideas of transformation and equivalence, with a particular focus on younger children learning mathematics.
2. The entries on 'Making connections', 'Rote learning', 'Meaningful learning', 'Equivalence' and 'Transformations', in Haylock with Thangata (2007) expand some of the central ideas introduced in this chapter.
3. Turner and McCullough (2004) emphasize teaching methods in primary mathematics that seek to establish relationships between language, symbols and pictorial representation.
4. Rowland et al. (2009) is a book that will help primary teachers to understand how they can develop their own mathematical subject knowledge in ways that will make their own teaching more effective. Look particularly at chapter 5 on making connections in teaching.

Self-assessment questions

3.1: In developing understanding of addition, what connections might young children make between the symbols, $5 + 3 = 8$, and (a) formal mathematical language; (b) practical experience with fingers and informal mathematical language; and (c) the picture of counting numbers shown in Figure 3.5?

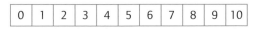

Figure 3.5   *A number strip*

3.2: Refer to Figure 3.2 and the associated commentary. Suggest two further ways in which the two shapes are the same as each other and two further ways in which they are different.

Further practice

From the Student Workbook

Each section of the workbook contains three or four tasks that focus on the teaching and learning of the mathematical content of the related chapter of this book, with an emphasis throughout on promoting understanding.

Glossary of key terms introduced in Chapter 3

Rote-learning mind set: a tendency in a learner to learn new material as isolated pieces of knowledge or skills, without making cognitive connections with existing networks of connections; a preference for relying on memorization and recall, rather than seeking to understand.

Meaningful learning mind set: a commitment in the learner to making sense of new material, to understanding it, by making cognitive connections with existing understanding; a preference for understanding rather than just learning by rote.

Connections model: a model for understanding number and number operations, expressed in terms of the learner making cognitive connections between language, symbols, pictures and practical/real-life experiences.

Equivalence: the mathematical term for any relationship in which one mathematical entity (number, shape, set, and so on) in some sense is the same as another; in identifying an equivalence we focus on what is the same, regardless of how the entities are different.

Transformation: the mathematical term for any process which changes a mathematical entity (number, shape, set, and so on) into another; in identifying a transformation we focus on what is different, what has changed, even though some things may still be the same.

Conservation of number: the principle that a number remains the same under certain transformations; for example, the number of items in a set does not change when the items are rearranged or spread out.

Classification: a key process in understanding mathematics, in which some numbers or some shapes (exemplars) are recognized as sharing a specified property or satisfying some criterion, which distinguishes them from other number or shapes (non-exemplars); for example, positive whole numbers may be classified as even or odd.

SECTION B
USING AND APPLYING MATHEMATICS

4
Key Processes in Mathematical Reasoning

In this chapter there are explanations of

- generalization;
- conjecturing and checking;
- the language of generalization;
- counter-examples and special cases;
- hypothesis and inductive reasoning;
- explaining, convincing, proving and deductive reasoning; and
- thinking creatively in mathematics.

What is generalization in mathematics?

In Chapter 2, in considering the epistemological reasons for teaching mathematics, I argued that to understand mathematics we need to have a good grasp of not just the terms, concepts and principles that are used in the subject but also the distinctive ways in which we reason and make and justify our assertions in this subject. These key processes of mathematical reasoning are the focus of this chapter. In order to illustrate these processes I have to use mathematical concepts and results that are explained in later chapters in this book. So do not worry too much at this stage if you struggle a bit with some of the details of the examples used; try to focus on the key processes involved and note the chapters you will need to give special attention to later.

Generalization is one of these significant ways of reasoning in mathematics. To make a generalization is to make an observation about something that is always true or always the case for all the members of a set of numbers, or a set of shapes, or even a set of people. To say that the diagonals of a square always bisect each other at right angles is to make a generalization that is true for all squares. To recognize that every other number when you count is an even number is to make a true generalization about the set of counting numbers. To say that any Member of Parliament is paid more than every primary school teacher in the UK is to make a generalization – which may or may not be justified. It is possible to make generalizations that prove to be invalid, of course. In Chapter 20, where I explain the basic ideas of algebra, we will see how the process of making generalized statements is the fundamental process of algebraic thinking. We will see there the central role played by algebraic symbols in representing variables and enabling us to articulate generalizations. To introduce here some of the key components of the process of making generalizations, we will look at the mathematical investigation illustrated in Figure 4.1. In this investigation we construct a series of square picture frames, using small square tiles, and tabulate systematically the number of tiles needed for different sizes of frame to identify the underlying numerical pattern.

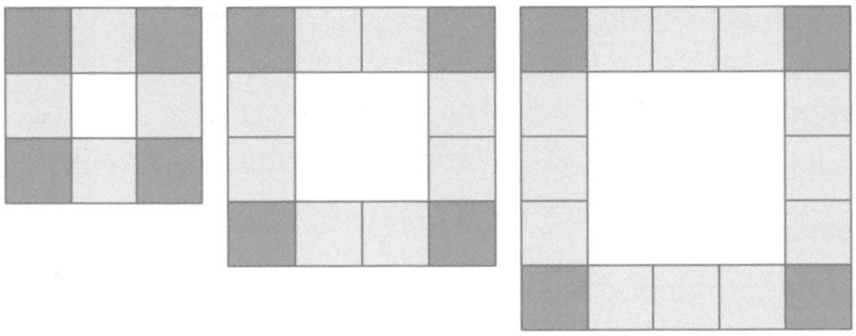

Number of tiles along the edge n	Number of tiles in the frame f
3	8
4	12
5	16
6	...
7	...
100	?

Figure 4.1   *How many tiles are needed to make a square picture frame?*

Having got to this stage, we might **conjecture** that for a frame of side 6 we would need 20 tiles respectively. We would check to see whether our conjecture is true, by actually building the frame. Then we might spot and articulate something that appears to be always true here, a *generalization*: 'the rule is that to get the next number of tiles you always add 4' – and perhaps build a few more frames to check this.

We may even reason our way to articulating a more sophisticated generalization: 'to find the number of tiles in the frame you multiply the number along the edge by 4 and subtract 4'. This rule would enable us to determine how many tiles are needed for a frame of side 100, for example: multiply 100 by 4 and subtract 4, giving a total of 396 tiles required. We would check this rule against all the examples we have. When we are confident in using algebraic notation (see Chapter 20), we might express this generalization as $f = 4n - 4$ (where n is a whole number greater than 2).

On the way, we might have attempted one or two generalizations that proved to be false. For example, we might have looked at the frames and thought intuitively that the number of tiles must be just 4 times the number along the edge. However, any frame that we use to check this generalization provides a **counter-example**, showing that it is false.

Then we might ask ourselves, what about a frame of side 2? Does that fit the rule? Or is it a **special case**? Well, the rule works, but we could not use the resulting construction as a picture frame! And what about a frame of side 1? The rule tells us that we need 0 tiles, which is a very strange result. These cases will lead us to refine our generalization, perhaps to apply only to frames where the number of tiles along the edge is greater than 2.

After all this, our sophisticated generalization that $f = 4n - 4$ is still only a **hypothesis**. We have not actually provided an *explanation* or a *convincing argument* or what mathematicians would call a **proof** that it must be true in every case. (This is your challenge in self-assessment question 4.4 at the end of this chapter.)

So, from this example of a mathematical investigation, we can identify the following as some of the key processes of reasoning mathematically: making conjectures, using the language of generalization, using counter-examples and recognizing special cases, hypothesizing, explaining, convincing and proving. These are explained further in the rest of this chapter.

What is a conjecture in mathematics?

The word *conjecture* is often used in the context of mathematical problem solving and investigating. It refers to an assertion that something might be true, at the stage when there has not yet been produced the evidence necessary to decide whether or not it is true. A conjecture is usually followed, therefore, by some appropriate mathematical process of checking. This experience of conjecturing and checking is fundamental to reasoning mathematically.

For example, a child might make a conjecture that 91 is a prime number (see Chapter 14). To say this is a conjecture means that they do not know for sure at this stage that 91 is a prime number, but they have a hunch that it might be. After a little bit of exploration, dividing 91 in turn by 2, 3, 5 and then 7, they find that

7 divides into 91, 13 times, so 91 is not prime. So the conjecture was wrong, but we have done some useful mathematics by considering it as a possibility and checking it out. Another child might be given a collection of containers and by examining them make a conjecture that the flower vase has the greatest capacity (see Chapter 22). To check this conjecture the

child might carefully fill each of the other containers in turn with water and pour this into the empty flower vase. This might lead to the conclusion that the conjecture was correct.

What is the language of generalization?

Another child notices that there are exactly three multiples of 3 (3, 6 and 9) in the set of whole numbers from 1 to 10 inclusive. The child then makes the conjecture that there will be another three in the set of whole numbers from 11 to 20 inclusive. Checking leads to the confirmation of this conjecture, since 12, 15 and 18 are the only multiples of 3 in the range. Excited by this discovery, the child then goes on to wonder if there are three multiples of 3 in every decade. (By *decade*, we mean 1–10, 11–20, 21–30, 31–40, and so on.) The child's thinking has moved from specific cases to the general. This is now a *generalization*. This is good mathematical thinking, whether or not it turns out to be a valid generalization. (The reader is invited to check the validity of this generalization in self-assessment question 4.1 at the end of this chapter.)

So, a generalization is an assertion that something is true in a number of cases, or even in every case. To make a generalization in words we will often use one or other of the following bits of language: always; every; each; any; all; if ... then ... . It is also possible in English to imply 'always' without actually stating it and to do some nifty things with negatives. Here, for example, is a (true) generalization about multiples (see Chapter 14) stated in nine different ways:

- Multiples of 6 are always multiples of 2.
- Every multiple of 6 is a multiple of 2.
- Each multiple of 6 is a multiple of 2.
- Any multiple of 6 is a multiple of 2.
- All multiples of 6 are multiples of 2.
- If a number is a multiple of 6 then it is a multiple of 2.
- A multiple of 6 must be a multiple of 2.
- There is no multiple of 6 that is not a multiple of 2.
- If a number is not a multiple of 2 then it is not a multiple of 6.

Note that the reverse statement of a true generalization is not necessarily true. For example, it is *not* true to say: if a number is a multiple of 2 then it is a multiple of 6. This statement is still a generalization, but it happens to be a false one.

What are counter-examples and special cases?

A *counter-example* is a specific case that demonstrates that a generalization is not valid. For example, to show the falsity of the generalization made at the end of the previous paragraph, we could use the number 14 as a counter-example. This would involve pointing out that 14 is a multiple of 2 (so it satisfies the 'if' bit of the statement), but it is not a multiple of 6 (so it fails the 'then' bit).

Here is an example of a generalization in the context of shape: all rectangles have exactly two lines of symmetry. At first sight this looks like a sound generalization, but then we may recall that squares are rectangles and they have four lines of symmetry. So a square is a counter-example showing the generalization to be false. Sometimes a counter-example will lead us to modify our generalization rather than discarding it altogether. The generalization above, for example, could be modified to refer to 'all rectangles except squares' or 'all oblong rectangles' (see Chapter 25).

Here's another example: someone might make the generalization that all prime numbers are odd. Someone else then points out that 2 is a counter-example, being a prime number that is even (see Chapter 14). However, this can be recognized as a *special case*. The generalization can therefore be modified, by excluding the special case, changing the set of numbers to which the generalization applies, as follows: all prime numbers greater than 2 are odd.

Often 0 or 1 will turn out to be special cases that need checking. For example, when investigating fractions we might notice that $\frac{1}{3}$ is less than $\frac{1}{2}$, $\frac{1}{4}$ is less than $\frac{1}{3}$, $\frac{1}{5}$ is less than $\frac{1}{4}$, $\frac{1}{6}$ is less than $\frac{1}{5}$, and so on, and generalize this by observing that every time you increase the bottom number by 1 the fraction gets smaller. Being very sophisticated we might come up with the statement that for any positive whole number n, $\frac{1}{n}$ is less than $\frac{1}{(n-1)}$. However, we would have to exclude 1 from this generalization, because that would give us $\frac{1}{1}$ is less than $\frac{1}{0}$, which is nonsense because $\frac{1}{0}$ is not a real number (division by zero is not possible). In this example, 1 is a special case. (Fractions are explained in Chapter 17.)

In another investigation, a child discovers that all square numbers have an odd number of factors. (See Chapter 15 for a discussion of square numbers.) This is a correct generalization, apart from the special case of zero. The teachers asks, 'What about zero? Is that a square number? If so, how many factors does it have?' Well, 0 is technically a square number, since $0^2 = 0$. However, every positive whole number is a factor of zero! (Note that $0 \times 1 = 0$, $0 \times 2 = 0$, $0 \times 3 = 0$ and so on.) So, it is necessary to exclude zero as a special case by making the generalization as follows: all square numbers greater than 0 have an odd number of factors.

What is a hypothesis?

The word *hypothesis* is usually used to refer to a generalization that is still a conjecture and which still has to be either proved to be true, or shown to be false by means of a counter-example. Often a hypothesis will emerge by a process of **inductive reasoning**, by looking at a number of specific instances that are seen to have something in common and then speculating that this will always be the case. For example, some children might investigate what happens when you add together odd and even numbers. They might spot that in all the examples they try an odd number added to an even number gives an odd number as the answer. So they conjecture that this is always the case. This is a hypothesis, obtained by inductive reasoning. It always seems to be the case, and every example we check seems to work. But, however many cases we check, it is still only a hypothesis – until such time as we produce some kind of a *proof* that it must work in every case.

This is an important point, because sometimes a hypothesis may appear to be correct to begin with but then let you down later. For example, someone might assert that all numbers that are 1 less or 1 more than a multiple of 6 are prime numbers. To start with this looks like a pretty good hypothesis: 5, 7, 11, 13, 17, 19, 23 are all prime. You might think that if something works for the first seven numbers you try it will always work. But the next number, 25, lets us down.

Hypotheses also turn up frequently in the context of probability and statistical data (see Section E). For example, the assertion made by one child that a boy is more likely than a girl to have a digital watch would be a hypothesis that primary children might investigate, testing it by the collection and analysis of data from a sample of boys and girls. The evidence in this case would only lend support to the hypothesis, not prove it conclusively, of course.

What is the difference between an explanation and a proof?

Proof is a peculiarly mathematical way of reasoning. If a generalization is written in the form of a statement using the 'if … then … ' language, a mathematical proof is a series of logical deductions that starts from the 'if … ' bit and leads to the 'then … ' bit. Proof therefore involves **deductive reasoning**.

I thought you should at least see what a formal mathematical proof might look like, even though in primary school teaching you will not need to able to reproduce something like this. So here is a typical example: a proof that all multiples of 6 are multiples of 2. First we write what we have to prove in the 'if … then … ' version: if a natural number is a multiple of 6 then it is a multiple of 2. We then introduce some algebraic symbols to enable us to manipulate the mathematical concepts involved here. So, what we have to do is to construct a logical argument which starts with 'If a natural number n is a multiple of 6' and concludes with 'n is a multiple of 2'. Often the steps in the argument are connected by the symbol $\Rightarrow$, meaning 'which implies'. So, here's the proof by deduction:

> If a natural number n is a multiple of 6,
> then $n = 6 \times k$, for some positive whole number k
> $\Rightarrow n = (2 \times 3) \times k$
> $\Rightarrow n = 2 \times (3 \times k)$ (using the associative law of multiplication, see Chapter 11)
> $\Rightarrow n = 2 \times m$, where m is the positive whole number equal to $3 \times k$
> $\Rightarrow n$ is a multiple of 2.

Clearly, primary children (and their teachers) should not be expected to produce proofs of their hypotheses like this. They can, however, be encouraged to try to formulate *explanations* as to why their generalizations are valid. In some cases they may even formulate a *convincing argument* that the generalization must be valid.

For example, consider the generalization made above that an odd number added to an even number always gives an odd number as the answer. A child may be able to provide or at least follow an explanation along these lines. The odd number is made by adding some 2s and a 1 and the even number is made just by adding some 2s. If you add them together you get lots of 2s, plus the extra 1 – which must therefore be an odd number. Or, having made the generalization above that all square numbers greater than zero have an odd number of factors, some primary children could offer or at least follow an explanation as to why this must be so. Here's the basis of the argument:

> For all numbers other than squares, like 28, the factors can be linked in pairs: 1×28, 2×14, 4×7. Because they come in pairs, the total number of factors must be even. But with a square number, like 36, as well as the pairs of factors (1×36, 2×18, 3×12, 4×9) there is an extra factor, in this case 6, because this is the number that is multiplied by itself to give 36. So the total number of factors must be odd.

This is not a formal mathematical proof, but it is perhaps a convincing explanation.

Some hypotheses can be proved to be true by a method called **proof by exhaustion**. This is a method of proof that can be employed for a generalization that relates to only a finite number of cases. It might then be possible to check every single case – in other words, to exhaust all the possibilities. This is a method of proof that can be accessible to primary school children in appropriate examples, but it requires a high level of systematic thinking. For example, Figure 4.2 shows four shapes with perimeters of 12 units drawn using the

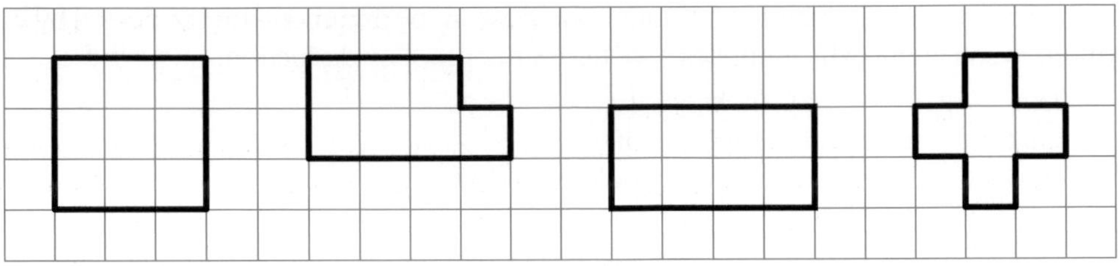

Figure 4.2   *Four shapes with perimeters of 12 units*

lines on a square grid. Of these four shapes, the square has the largest area – just count the number of square units inside each shape. (Area and perimeter are explained in Chapter 26.)

Can we prove that whatever shape we draw with a perimeter of 12 units on the grid it will have an area smaller than that of the square? This could be rephrased as a generalization, using the 'if … then …' format, as follows: if any shape, other than a square, with a perimeter of 12 units is constructed using the lines on a square grid then the area of the shape will be less than that of the square. Now we can actually *prove* this to be true fairly easily, because the number of different shapes that can be made is finite. So we can exhaust all the possibilities by drawing all the possible shapes and checking that in every case the area is less than that of the square.

What are axioms?

Some of the generalizations we use in mathematics are called **axioms**. An axiom is a statement that is taken to be true, usually because it is self-evidently true, but which cannot be proved as such. An axiom is one of the building blocks of mathematical reasoning. It is a statement that we have to accept as true, otherwise we would just not be able to get on and do any mathematics. Two examples of axioms that we will discuss in this book are the commutative law of addition and the commutative law of multiplication (see Chapters 7 and 10). These axioms, respectively, tell us, for example, that $3 + 5 = 5 + 3$ and $3 \times 5 = 5 \times 3$, and that these would work whatever two numbers we used. Another example would be the transitive property of the inequality 'greater than', which we will explain in Chapter 22. This axiom allows us to conclude that, if a number A is greater than some number B, which in turn is greater than some number C, then A must be greater than C. We can explain these laws, we can give examples of what they mean and we can seen how they are used – but we never question their truth or feel the need to prove them. These kinds of generalizations are not hypotheses up for discussion and investigation. They are axioms of mathematics.

Is generalizing only for the older, more able primary children?

Our discussion of key processes in using and applying mathematics has led us into some challenging mathematics, so it is timely to remind ourselves that the process of forming generalizations occurs at a range of different levels and at all ages in primary school learning and teaching. At the simplest level, young children are making and using generalizations when they identify a pattern of beads on a string and continue a pattern: blue, red, yellow, yellow, blue, red, yellow, yellow, and so on. When children learn to count beyond 20, they do this by recognizing a pattern for each group of 10 numbers and make a generalization that every time you get to 9 you move on to the next multiple of 10. Once this is established they generalize the pattern further in order to go beyond 100. When a 9-year-old observes that all the numbers in the 5-times table end in 5 or 0, they are making a generalization.

Children of differing abilities in mathematics will make different levels of generalization. For example, looking at a sequence such as 6, 11, 16, 21, 26 …, some 10-year-olds will be able to generalize this only at the level of seeing the pattern in the digits (6, 1, 6, 1, 6 …). Others will formulate a rule for continuing the sequence: you always add 5. More able children will observe that all the numbers in the sequence are the numbers in the 5-times table plus 1.

The most able children will sometimes show an even higher level of generalization when they identify a mathematical principle that can be generalized and applied in other situations. Here's an actual example from my classroom-based research with a small group of mathematically able 11-year-olds. They were working with me on average speeds (see Chapter 28). I gave them the following problem:

> **LEARNING and TEACHING POINT**
>
> The facility with which children formulate generalizations is one of the key ways of recognizing genuine mathematical ability – more significant than performance in routine calculations. The ability to generalize principles, to remember them and to apply them in other situations is a particular characteristic of children who are gifted in mathematics.

> On a journey from A to B I average 30 mph. On the return journey I average 60 mph. What is my overall average speed?

Intuitively, the immediate response was 45 mph. We checked the conjecture, by assuming that the distance from A to B was 60 miles. This meant 2 hours there and 1 hour back; that is a total of 120 miles in 3 hours, average speed 40 mph! Less than the average of the two speeds. We tried other distances and always got the same answer. I then posed this problem:

> If I cycle from home to the university when a strong north wind is blowing, it adds 5 mph to my average speed on the way there and reduces by 5 mph my average speed

on the return journey. When is the journey quicker? When there is a wind? When there is no wind? Or does it make no difference?

Intuition might lead us to think it makes no difference. But it was interesting to note how adeptly the more able children were able to use the experience of the previous problem not to fall into this trap, by reasoning in terms of general principles, as follows. Say you usually cycle at 10 mph (note: they are assuming the principles will be the same whatever speed is used). In the wind, that would be 15 mph there and 5 mph back. The average of these two speeds is still 10 mph, but the average speed will be less than the average of the two speeds (generalizing the principle from the previous problem), so it will take you longer. The distance does not matter (again generalizing what they had learnt in the previous problem), so assume it is 15 miles. Then without a wind it takes you 3 hours there and back. With a wind it takes you 1 hour there and 3 hours back, 4 hours in total.

Reasoning like this is exciting to observe and is what makes mathematics such a powerful subject. The ability to extract from the result of one problem a principle that can be generalized and applied in other problems is one of the most significant characteristics of children who are mathematically gifted. The reader might now try self-assessment question 4.7, which actually uses the same mathematical principle.

How would I recognize creative thinking in mathematics?

Creative thinking involves being able to break away from routines and stereotype methods, to think flexibly and to generate original ideas and approaches to problems. The opposite of creativity is rigidity and fixation. For example, some 10-year-olds were given the following questions:

(a) Find two numbers that have a sum of 10 and a difference of 4.
(b) Find two numbers that have a sum of 20 and a difference of 10.
(c) Find two numbers that have a sum of 15 and a difference of 3.
(d) Find two numbers that have a sum of 19 and a difference of 5.
(e) Find two numbers that have a sum of 10 and a difference of 3.

The majority quickly concluded that (e) was impossible. In the previous questions they had established a procedure that worked. This was essentially to run through all the possible pairs of whole numbers that add to the given sum, until they came to a pair with the required difference. This procedure does not work in (e). Most of the children were unable to break from this mental set, even though they all had sufficient competence with simple fractions and decimals to get the solution (3.5 and 6.5). Some children did, however, get this solution and these were the children who generally showed more inclination to think creatively in mathematics.

Most of the questions we give children in mathematics have one correct answer and therefore require what is called **convergent thinking**. Creativity is usually associated with **divergent thinking**. To give opportunities for flexible and original responses, therefore, we should sometimes give children more open-ended tasks, such as these:

- Find lots of different ways of calculating 98 × 32.
- Which numbers could go in the boxes: ($\square + \square$) × $\square$ = 12? Give as many different answers as you can.
- To answer a mathematics question Jo arranged 24 cubes as shown in Figure 4.3. What might the question have been?
- How many different two-dimensional shapes can you make by fitting together six square tiles (not counting rotations and reflections)?
- If I tell you that 33 × 74 = 2442, write down lots of other results you can work out from this without doing any hard calculations.
- Three friends went for a meal. Ali's bill was £12, Ben's was £15 and Cassie's was £19. Make up as many questions as you can that could be answered from this information.
- What's the same about 16 and 36? Write down as many answers as you can think of.

Creative thinking will be shown by: fluency, coming up with many responses; flexibility, using many different ideas and; originality, using ideas that few other children in the group use. For example, the responses of one creative 11-year-old to the question 'What is the same about 16 and 36?' included mathematical ideas such as even, whole numbers, multiples, digits, square numbers, less than, greater than, between, divisibility and factors, Some of the responses were highly original, such as 'they are both greater than 15.9999' and 'they are both factors of 144'.

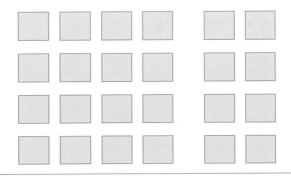

Figure 4.3 *What was the question?*

In problem solving, it is usually the teacher who poses the problem. However the teacher can encourage creative thinking by giving children the opportunity to pose their own problems. This is possible in more open mathematical investigations or enquiries. Examples might be: find out as many interesting mathematical things as you can about the windows in the school building; look at this educational supplies catalogue and pose some interesting mathematical problems you might like to enquire into; think of something you do not like about the school timetable and come up with a way of making it better.

Research focus

In a study of **creativity in mathematics** (Haylock, 1997), 11–12-year-olds were assessed on their ability to overcome fixations and to produce appropriate but divergent responses in a range of mathematical tasks. It emerged that children with equal levels of mathematics attainment in conventional terms can show significantly different levels of mathematical creativity. It was found that the higher the level of attainment the more possible it is to discriminate between children in terms of the indicators of mathematical creativity. The high-attaining children with high levels of mathematical creativity were distinguished from the high-attaining children with low creativity by a number of characteristics: they had significantly lower levels of anxiety and higher self-concepts; they tended to be broad coders in the way they processed information; and they were more willing to take reasonable risks in mathematical tasks. One implication is that children may be more likely to think more creatively if they learn mathematics in a context in which they are encouraged to take risks and to back their hunches even if sometimes this results in their getting things wrong.

Suggestions for further reading

1. The entries on 'Creativity in mathematics' and 'Generalization', in Haylock with Thangata (2007) offer further insights into some of the key processes introduced in this chapter.
2. Recommended for those who teach younger children is Threlfall's chapter entitled 'Repeating patterns in the early primary years', in Orton (2004). This shows how the recognition of pattern in the activities of younger children forms the basis for developing the process of generalization.
3. Read the chapter by Jones entitled 'The problem with problem-solving', in Thompson (2003). Jones suggests some ways of interpreting the idea of problem solving in mathematics that will enable the primary teacher to put problem-solving experiences and children's reasoning skills at the heart of their teaching of the subject.

4. Pound (2006) shows how young children can be enabled to enjoy thinking mathematically. The book outlines a curriculum for promoting mathematical thinking in the early years and provides guidance on observing, planning and supporting mathematical thinking.

Self-assessment questions

4.1: (a) Show that the child's suggestion that there are exactly three multiples of 3 in every decade is not a correct generalization. (b) Then consider this generalization: there are exactly four multiples of 3 in every third decade (i.e. 21–40, 51–60, 81–90, and so on). True or false?

4.2: Which of these generalizations are true and which are false? If false, give a counter-example.

   (a) Any number greater than 5 is greater than 10.
   (b) If a number is not a multiple of 3 then it is not a multiple of 6.
   (c) Any quadrilateral (four-sided figure) with all sides equal is a square.

4.3: Prove by exhaustion the following: if a shape other than a square is constructed on a square grid from 4 square units, then the perimeter of the shape is greater than that of the square.

4.4: In the picture frame investigation (see Figure 4.1 and the accompanying commentary) the hypothesis was formulated that the number of tiles needed is 4 times the number along the edge, minus 4. Give a convincing explanation as to why this must be true.

4.5: A child makes a chain of equilateral triangles, using matchsticks (see Figure 4.4). The child finds that 3 matchsticks are needed to make one triangle, 5 to make 2 triangles, 7 to make 3 triangles, and so on. Formulate a generalization that will enable you to find how many matchsticks are needed to make a chain of 100 triangles. Can you provide a convincing explanation for your generalization? What about zero triangles? Does this fit your generalization or is it a special case?

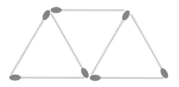

Figure 4.4   *A chain of 3 triangles needs 7 matchsticks*

4.6: Write down three digits and write them down again, hence making a six-digit number (for example, 346 346). Use a calculator to check the hypothesis that all such numbers must be divisible by 7, 11 and 13. Why is this? (Hint, calculate $7 \times 11 \times 13$.)

4.7: One week Jo spent all her pocket money on toys costing 50p each. Next week she spent the same amount on toys costing £1 each. Jack got the same pocket money for these two weeks and spent it all on toys costing 75p each. Who got the most toys? Or did they get the same number?

4.8: In a science laboratory there are two flasks of water, a small one and a large one. The temperature of the water in the small flask is held steady at 50 °C. When the temperature of the water in the large flask reaches 60 °C the temperature difference between the two flasks is 10 °C. When it reaches 70 °C the temperature difference is 20 °C. What is the temperature of the large flask when the difference in the temperatures is (a) 30 °C? (b) 50 °C? (c) 70 °C?

Further practice

From the Student Workbook

Each section of the workbook contains three or four tasks that focus on key processes in using and applying the mathematical content of the related chapter of this book. Many of them focus on the key processes outlined in this chapter.

Glossary of key terms introduced in Chapter 4

Generalization: in mathematics an assertion that something is true for all the members of a set of numbers or shapes or people. A generalization may be true (for example, 'all multiples of 12 are multiples of 3') or false (for example, 'no women can read maps').

Conjecture: an assertion the truth of which has not yet been established or checked by the individual making it.

Counter-example: a specific instance that shows a generalization to be false.

Special case: a specific instance that does not fit an otherwise true generalization and may have to be removed from the set to which the generalization is applied.

Hypothesis: a generalization that someone might make, which they have yet to prove to be true in every case.

Proof: a complete and convincing argument to support the truth of an assertion in mathematics, which proceeds logically from the assumptions to the conclusion.

Inductive reasoning: in mathematics, the process of looking at a number of specific instances that are seen to have something in common and then speculating that this will always be the case.

Deductive reasoning: reasoning based on logical deductions.

Proof by exhaustion: a method for proving a generalization by checking every single case to which it applies.

Axiom: in mathematics, a statement that is taken to be true, usually because it is self-evident, but which cannot be proved. For example, $a + b = b + a$ for all numbers a and b.

Convergent thinking: the kind of thinking involved in seeking the one and only correct answer to a mathematical question.

Divergent thinking: the opposite of convergent thinking; thinking characterized by flexibility, generating many different kinds of response in an open-ended task.

Creativity in mathematics: identified by overcoming fixations and rigidity in thinking; by divergent thinking, fluency, flexibility and originality in the generation of responses to mathematical situations.

5
Modelling and Problem Solving

In this chapter there are explanations of

- three approaches to calculations: algorithms, adhocorithms and calculators;
- the key process of mathematical modelling;
- the contribution of electronic calculators to this process;
- interpreting answers obtained on calculators; and
- problem solving.

How should children do calculations?

This chapter has a focus on two further processes of using and applying mathematics: mathematical modelling and problem solving. First, though, I want to say something about calculations. When we engage in mathematical modelling of real-life situations and solving problems there will often be calculations to do on the way, but we should regard these calculations as mere tools needed to do the real mathematics. So, in starting this chapter with talking about calculation, my intention is not to give the impression that this is what doing mathematics is all about, but to put it firmly in its place, so that we can then focus on more important stuff!

Now, there are essentially three ways in which we can do a calculation, such as an addition, a subtraction, a multiplication or a division. For example, consider the problem of finding the cost of 16 items at 25p each. To solve this we may decide to work out 16×25.

One approach to this would be to use an **algorithm**. The word 'algorithm' (derived from the name of the ninth-century Arabian mathematician, Al-Khowarizmi) refers to a step-by-step process for obtaining the solution to a mathematical problem or, in this case, the result of a calculation. In number work we use the word to refer to the formal, paper-and-pencil methods that we might use for doing calculations, which, if the procedures are followed correctly, will always lead to the required result. These would include, for example, subtraction by decomposition and long division. So, solving the problem above using an algorithm might involve, for example, performing the calculation for 16×25 as shown in Figure 5.1, using the method known as long multiplication.

$$
\begin{array}{r}
16 \\
\times\ \ 25 \\
\hline
320 \\
80 \\
\hline
400 \\
\hline
\end{array}
$$

Figure 5.1   *Using an algorithm for 16×25*

A second approach would be to use one of the many informal methods for doing calculations, which are actually the methods that most numerate adults employ for the calculations they encounter in everyday life. For example, to solve the problem above, we might:

- make use of the fact that four 25-pences make £1, so 16 of them must be £4; or
- work out ten 25s (250), four 25s (100) and two 25s (50) and add these up, to get 400; or
- use repeated doubling and reason, 'two 25s is 50, so four 25s is 100, so eight 25s is 200, so sixteen 25s is 400'.

This kind of approach, in which we make ad hoc use of the particular numbers and relationships in the problem in question, I like to call an **adhocorithm** – my own invented word, not yet in the dictionaries! These informal, ad hoc approaches to calculations should be recognized as being equally as valid as the formal, algorithmic approaches. They have the advantage that they are based on our own personal level of confidence with numbers and number operations. They are based on and encourage understanding of the relationships between numbers – because, unlike algorithms, they are not applied mechanically and cannot rely on rote learning. In Chapters 8, 9, 11 and 12, I discuss various algorithms and adhocorithms for each of the four operations.

Then, a third way of doing this calculation is just use to use a *calculator*, entering 16, ×, 25, = and reading off the result (400). Many people are not convinced that there is any mathematics involved in using a calculator; I have even heard people suggest they should be banned from the classroom! The argument is that all you have to do is to press the buttons and the machine does all the thinking for you. This is a common misconception about calculators. Even in the simple example above we have to decide what calculation to put into the calculator and interpret the result as £4. In fact, using a calculator to solve a practical problem involves us in a fundamental mathematical process called **mathematical modelling**.

What is mathematical modelling?

We are not talking here about making models out of card or other materials. Mathematical modelling is the process whereby we use the abstractions of mathematics to solve problems in the real world. For example, how would you work out how many boxes you need to hold 150 calculators if each box holds just 18 calculators? You might use one of the calculators to work out 150 divided by 18. This would give you the result 8.3333333. That's a bit more than 8 boxes. So you would actually need 9 boxes. If you only had 8 boxes there would be some calculators which could not be fitted in, although the calculator answer does not tell you directly how many. The four steps involved in the reasoning here provide essentially an example of the process called mathematical modelling. This process is summarized in Figure 5.2.

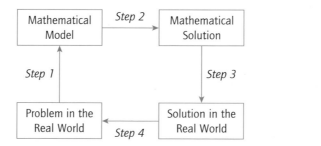

Figure 5.2   *The process of mathematical modelling*

In step 1 of this process a problem in the real world is translated into a problem expressed in mathematical symbols. (Strictly, the term 'modelling' is usually used for problems expressed in algebraic symbols, but since the four steps involved are essentially the same, we can adapt the idea and language of modelling and apply them to word problems being translated into number statements.) So, in this example, we shall say that the real-world problem about buying boxes to hold calculators is *modelled* by the mathematical expression 150 ÷ 18. Then in step 2 the mathematical symbols are manipulated in some way – this could be by means of a mental or written calculation or, as on this occasion, by pressing keys on a calculator – in order to obtain a mathematical solution, 8.3333333. Step 3 is to interpret this mathematical solution back in the real world – for example, by saying that this means '8 boxes and a bit of a box'. The final step is to check the result against the constraints of the original situation. In this case, by considering the real situation and recognizing that 8 boxes would leave some calculators not in a box, the appropriate conclusion is that you actually need 9 boxes.

So in this process there are basically four steps:

1. Set up the mathematical model.
2. Obtain the mathematical solution.
3. Interpret the mathematical solution back in the real world.
4. Check the solution with the reality of the original situation.

There is potentially a fifth step: if the solution does not make sense when checked against the reality of the original problem, then you may have to go round the cycle again, checking each stage of the process to determine what has gone wrong.

It is important to note that the calculator does only the second of the steps in the process of mathematical modelling. You will have done all the others. Your contribution is significant mathematics. In a technological age, in which most calculations are done by machines, it surely cannot be disputed that knowing which calculation to do is more important than being able to do the calculation. As will be seen in Chapters 7 and 10, recognizing which operations correspond to various real-world situations (step 1 above) is not always straightforward. These chapters indicate the range of categories or structures of problems that children should learn to model with each of the operations of addition, subtraction, multiplication and division.

Is there much to learn about the interpretation of a calculator result?

The interpretation of the calculator result (step 3) is also far from being an insignificant aspect of the process. For example, in the problem above, the interpretation of the result 8.3333333 required a decision about what to do with all the figures after the decimal point.

When we carry out a calculation on a calculator to solve a practical problem, particularly those modelled by division, we can get three kinds of answer:

- An exact, appropriate answer.
- An exact but inappropriate answer.
- An answer that is a **truncation**.

In the last two cases, we normally have to round the answer in some way to make it appropriate to the real-world situation (**rounding** is considered in more detail in Chapter 13).

For example, consider these three problems, all with the same mathematical structure:

> **LEARNING and TEACHING POINT**
>
> Discuss with children real-life problems, particularly in the context of money, that produce calculator answers that require different kinds of interpretation, including those with: (a) an exact, appropriate answer; (b) an exact but inappropriate answer; and (c) an answer that has been truncated.

1. How many apples at 15 p each can I buy with 90p?
2. How many apples at 24 p each can I buy with 90p?
3. How many apples at 21 p each can I buy with 90p?

For problem (1) the mathematical model is $90 \div 15$, so we might enter '$90 \div 15 =$' on to a calculator and obtain the result 6. In this case there is no difficulty in interpreting this result back in the real world. The answer to the problem is indeed exactly 6 apples. The calculator result is both exact and appropriate.

For problem (2) we might enter '$90 \div 24 =$' and obtain the result 3.75. This is the exact answer to the calculation that was entered on the calculator. In other words, it is the solution to the mathematical problem that we used to model the real-world problem. It is correctly interpreted as 3.75 apples. But, since greengrocers sell only whole apples, clearly the answer is not appropriate. In the final step of the modelling process – checking the solution against the constraints of reality – the 3.75 apples must be rounded to a whole number of apples. We would conclude that the solution to problem (2) is that we can actually afford only 3 apples.

For problem (3) we might enter '$90 \div 21 =$' on to the calculator and find that we get the result 4.2857142. This is not an exact answer. Dividing 90 by 21 actually produces a **recurring decimal**, namely, 4.285714285714 … , with the 285714 repeating over and over again without ever coming to an end. Since a simple calculator can display only eight digits, it *truncates* the result, by throwing away all the extra digits. Of course, in this case, the bits that are thrown away are relatively tiny and the error involved in this truncation process is fairly insignificant. We can interpret the result displayed on the calculator as 'about 4.2857142 apples'. But again, when we compare this with the real-world situation, we must recognize the constraints of purchasing fruit and round the answer in some way to give a whole number of apples. The obvious conclusion is that we can afford only 4 apples.

Another problem in interpretation arises when the calculator result in a money problem gives only one figure after the decimal point. For example, here is a problem in the real world: how much for 24 marker pens at £1.15 each? We might model this with the mathematical expression, 24×1.15 (step 1). Handing over the donkey work (step 2) to a calculator gives the result 27.6. Primary children have to be taught how to interpret this (step 3) as £27.60 (not 27 pounds, 6 pence), to draw the conclusion (step 4) that the total cost of the 24 marker pens is £27.60.

What is problem solving all about?

The skills, concept and principles of mathematics that children master should be used and applied to solve problems. It is the nature of the subject that applying what we learn in solving problems must always be a central component of mathematical reasoning.

A **problem**, as opposed to something that is merely an exercise for practising a mathematical skill, is a situation in which we have some givens and we have a goal, but the route from the givens to the goal is not immediately apparent. This means, of course, that what is a problem for one person may not be a problem for another. If you tackled some mathematical questions with me you might think that I am a good problem-solver. However, it might just be that I

Figure 5.3   *The three Gs of problem solving*

have seen them all before so that for me they are not actually problems! For a task to be a problem, there must be for the person concerned a (cognitive) gap between the givens and the goals, without an immediately obvious way for the gap to be bridged. I call these the three Gs of problem solving: the given, the goal and the gap, as shown in Figure 5.3.

There are many strategies that can be used to help people solve problems, but the most important of these are the most obvious: make sure you understand what you are given; make sure you understand what the goal is. Clarify the givens and clarify the goal. The arrow in Figure 5.3 goes both ways; this is an indication of another problem-solving strategy, which is that, as well as working from the givens to the goal, you can work backwards

from the goal towards the givens. You can also identify sub-goals, which involves recognizing intermediate steps between the givens and the goal. For example, if the problem is to find out how much it would cost to redecorate the classroom an intermediate goal might be to find the total area of the walls and ceiling.

What kind of problems should primary school children tackle in mathematics?

Problem solving in primary school mathematics can take many forms. Some children will be particularly motivated by purely mathematical problems, either numerical or spatial, such as those shown in Figure 5.4.

Problem 1:   Place three numbers in the boxes so that the top two boxes total 20, the bottom two total 43 and the top and bottom boxes total 37.

Problem 2:   Complete the drawing so that the arrowed line is a line of symmetry.

I am fairly confident that most readers will have all the mathematical knowledge and skills that are required to solve these two problems. The first problem requires no more

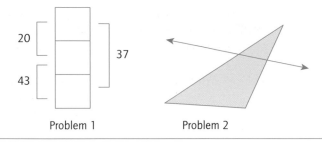

Problem 1   Problem 2

Figure 5.4   *Two purely mathematical problems*

than addition and subtraction, and the second just understanding about reflections and using a ruler. But I am equally confident that for most readers it will not be immediately apparent what has to be done to achieve the goal in each case. This is what makes these tasks problems, rather than merely exercises. I shall leave these two problems for the reader to complete (in self-assessment question 5.5) and to reflect on the strategies they use, particularly in terms of clarifying the givens and the goal.

Other children will be more motivated by genuine real-life problems, particularly if they have immediate purpose and practical relevance. Examples of such problems that I have used with children include:

Problem 3: How should we rearrange the classroom chairs and tables for practical work in groups of four?

Problem 4: Plan our class trip to Norwich Castle Museum and ensure that it all goes smoothly.

Problems such as these require the application of a wide range of numerical and spatial skills. Problem 3, for example, required considerable practical measurement, knowledge of units of length and use of decimal notation, making a simple scale drawing, division by 4 and dealing with remainders, as well as a degree of spatial imagination. Problem 4 involved calculations with money, drawing up a budget, calculator skills, timetabling, estimating, average speed (of the coach), as well as a range of communication skills. Both problems involved children in clarifying what they were given, what they needed to know, and what was the goal and identifying a number of sub-goals.

Genuine problems like these are clearly more engaging for children than artificial problems; but we have to recognize that in practice many of the problems that we pose for children, although set in real-life and practical contexts, will inevitably be rather artificial in nature. But children in primary schools can still be intrigued by problems like these, where they put themselves in an imaginary quasi-realistic situation:

Problem 5: You are a zookeeper with £1000 budget to buy some snakes, costing £40 each, and some baby alligators, costing £100 each. If you spend all your money, how many snakes and baby alligators might you buy?

Problem 6: You are a teacher planning to take up to 80 children on a camp. What's the best number of children to take if you plan to put them in groups of 3, 4, 5 and 6 for various activities and you do not want any children to be left out of a group for any activity?

These problems are left for the reader to solve, as self-assessment question 5.6 below.

Research focus

The assumption in this chapter has been that there are real benefits for children across the primary school age range in providing them with explicit experiences of the process of mathematical modelling. This has been demonstrated in research by English (2004) and English and Watters (2005). English observed upper primary school children working collaboratively on authentic problems that could be modelled by mathematics. She identified a number of significant aspects of learning taking place, both mathematical and social. These included: interpreting and reinterpreting given information; making appropriate decisions; justifying reasoning; posing hypotheses; and presenting arguments and counter-arguments. English and Watters (2005: 59) outline similar findings with younger learners and conclude from the evidence of research in this field that 'the primary school is the educational environment where all children should begin a meaningful development of mathematical modelling'.

Suggestions for further reading

1. Read chapter 10 of Anghileri (2007) for an interesting analysis of problem solving in primary mathematics, illustrated by some illuminative examples.
2. Fairclough's chapter entitled 'Developing problem-solving skills in mathematics', in Koshy and Murray (2002), provides some lively examples of problems used in the primary classroom to illustrate her analysis of different types of mathematical problems and how to teach primary children to be problem solvers.
3. Chapter 10 of Haylock and Cockburn (2008) is on using and applying mathematics. In this chapter we illustrate how mathematical modelling is one of the distinctive ways of thinking mathematically, which can be fostered even in younger children.
4. The entries on 'Modelling process', 'Problem solving' and 'Using and applying mathematics', in Haylock with Thangata (2007), offer further insights into some of the key processes discussed in this chapter.

Self-assessment questions

5.1: How much altogether for three books costing £4.95, £5.90 and £9.95? Use a calculator to answer this question, then identify the steps in the process of mathematical modelling in what you have done.

5.2: What does each person pay if three people share equally a restaurant bill for £27.90? Use a calculator to answer this question. Is the calculator result: (a) an exact, appropriate answer; (b) an exact but inappropriate answer; or (c) an answer that has been truncated? Identify the steps in the process of mathematical modelling in what you have done.

5.3: Repeat question 5.2 with a bill for £39.70.

5.4: How many months will it take me to save £500 if I save £35 a month? Use a calculator to answer this question. Is the calculator result: (a) an exact, appropriate answer; (b) an exact but inappropriate answer; or (c) an answer that has been truncated? Identify the steps in the process of mathematical modelling in what you have done.

5.5: Solve problems 1 and 2 given earlier in this chapter (see Figure 5.4).

5.6: Solve problems 5 and 6 given earlier in this chapter.

Further practice

From the Student Workbook

Using and applying questions are provided in each section of the workbook, including many opportunities to model situations with mathematics and to develop problem-solving skills.

On the website (www.sagepub.co.uk/haylock)

Check-Up 4: Using a four-function calculator for money calculations

Glossary of key terms introduced in Chapter 5

Algorithm: in number work, a standard, written procedure for doing a calculation, which, if followed correctly, step by step, will always lead to the required result; examples of algorithms are subtraction by decomposition, long multiplication and long division.

Adhocorithm: my term for any informal, non-standard way of doing a calculation, where the method used is dependent on the particular numbers in the problem and the relationships between them.

Mathematical modelling: the process of moving from a problem in the real world, to a mathematical model of the problem, then obtaining the mathematical solution, interpreting it back in the real world, and finally checking the result against the constraints of the original problem.

Truncation: this is what a calculator does when it has to cut short an answer to a calculation by throwing away some of the digits after the decimal point, because it does not have room to display them all. For example, a calculator with space for only 8 digits in the display might truncate the result 987.654321 to 987.65432.

Rounding: in this chapter, transforming an answer that is not an exact whole number into a whole number, either the whole number above (rounding up) or the one below (rounding down). (See also Chapter 13.)

Recurring decimal: a decimal, which might be the result of a division calculation, where one or more digits after the decimal point repeat over and over again, for ever. For example, 48 ÷ 11 is equal to 'four point three six recurring' (4.36363636 ... with the '36' being repeated over and over again, for ever).

Problem: in mathematics, a situation consisting of some givens and a goal, with a cognitive gap between them; this constitutes a problem for an individual if the way to fill the gap between the givens and the goal is not immediately obvious.

SECTION C
NUMBER AND ALGEBRA

6
Number and Place Value

In this chapter there are explanations of

- the difference between numerals and numbers;
- the cardinal and ordinal aspects of number;
- natural numbers and integers;
- rational, irrational and real numbers;
- the Hindu-Arabic system of numeration and the principles of place value;
- some contrasts with numeration systems from other cultures;
- digits and powers of ten;
- two ways of demonstrating place value with materials;
- how the number line supports understanding of place value;
- the role of zero as a place holder;
- the extension of the place-value principle to tenths, hundredths, thousandths;
- the decimal point as a separator in the contexts of money and measurement; and
- locating numbers written in decimal notation on a number line.

What is the difference between a 'numeral' and a 'number'?

A **numeral** is the symbol, or collection of symbols, that we use to represent a number. The number is the concept represented by the numeral, and therefore consists of a whole network of connections between symbols, pictures, language and real-life situations. The same number (for example, the one we call 'three hundred and sixty-six') can be represented by different numerals – such as 366 in our Hindu-Arabic, place-value system, and

CCCLXVI using Roman numerals (see Figure 6.5 later in this chapter and the accompanying commentary). Because the Hindu-Arabic system of numeration is now more or less universal, the distinction between the numeral and the number is easily lost.

What are the cardinal and ordinal aspects of number?

A numeral, such as 3, together with the associated word 'three', has a wide range of situations and contexts to which it can be connected. The two most significant for young children are the cardinal and ordinal aspect of number.

The learner's first experience of number is likely to be as an adjective describing a small set of objects: two brothers, three sweets, five fingers, three blocks, and so on. This idea of a number being a description of a set of things is called the **cardinal aspect of number**. By the process of one-to-one matching between sets containing the same number, as shown in Figure 6.1, the learner is able to recognize that there is

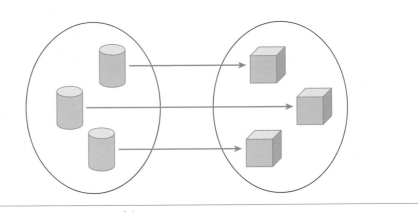

Figure 6.1   *One-to-one matching*

something the same about the sets; in other words, they identify an equivalence. The property that is shared by all sets of three things, for example, is then abstracted to form the concept of 'three' as a cardinal number, existing in its own right, independent of any specific context.

But this is not by any means the only aspect of number that the young learner encounters. Numbers are much more than just a way of describing sets of things.

Young children also encounter numbers used as labels to put things in order. For example, they turn to page 3 in a book. They play games on the number strip in the playground and find themselves standing on the space labelled 3. They learn that they are 3 years old and that next birthday they are going to be 4. One of the tricycles in the playground is labelled 3 and this has to be parked in the space labelled 3, which is once again between 2 and 4. The numerals and words being used here do not represent cardinal numbers, because they are not referring to sets of three things. In these examples 'three' is one thing, which is labelled three because of the position in which it lies in some ordering process. This is called the **ordinal aspect of number**. Numbers in this sense tell you what order things come in: which thing is first, which is second, which is third, and so on.

The most important experience of the ordinal aspect of number is when we represent numbers as locations on a number strip (see Figure 3.5 in Chapter 3) or as points on a number line, as shown in Figure 6.2. We shall make considerable use of this image of number as we explore understanding of number operations in subsequent chapters.

There is a further way in which numerals are used, sometimes called the *nominal* aspect. This is where the numeral is used as a label or a name, without any ordering implied. The usual example to give here would be a number 7 bus. Calling it number 7 is not much different from calling it the East Acton bus. It just identifies the bus and distinguishes it from buses on other routes. When we see a number 7 bus, we do not expect it to be followed by a number 8 and then a number 9 – in fact, we may well expect it to be followed by two more number 7s, as is the habit of buses. Having said that, I should make clear that when various bus services are listed in numerical order in a timetable their numbers are then being used in an ordinal way.

Figure 6.2   *Numbers as points on a line*

What are natural numbers and integers?

How many numbers are there between 10 and 20? This is a question I like to ask primary trainee teachers when we start to think about understanding number. The most common response is nine: namely, the numbers 11, 12, 13, 14, 15, 16, 17, 18 and 19. Some trainees answer a different question and give the answer ten, which is the difference between 10 and 20. Others give the answer eleven, choosing to include the 10 and the 20, in an unorthodox use of the word 'between'. All of these answers assume that when I say 'number' I mean the numbers we use for counting: {1, 2, 3, 4, 5, 6, ... }, going on for ever. These are what mathematicians choose to call the set of **natural numbers**. As we have seen above natural numbers can have both cardinal and ordinal interpretations.

How many numbers are there that are less than 10? That's another interesting question! Some say nine, just counting the natural numbers from 1 to 9. Most include 0 (zero) and give the answer ten. But others have the insight to include negative numbers in their understanding of 'numbers', and give responses such as 'there is an infinite number' or 'they go on for ever'. So, we can extend our understanding of what constitutes a number to what mathematicians call the set of **integers**: { ... , −5, −4, −3, −2, −1, 0, 1, 2, 3, 4, 5, ...} now going on for ever in both directions. Integers build on the ordinal aspect of number, by extending the number line in the other direction, as shown in Figure 6.3, labelling the points to the left of zero as negative numbers.

The mathematical word 'integer' is related to words such as 'integral' (forming a whole) and 'integrity' (wholeness). So the set of integers is simply the set of all whole numbers. But this includes both **positive integers** (whole numbers greater than zero) and **negative integers** (whole numbers less than zero), and zero itself. The integer −4 is properly named 'negative four', rather than 'minus four' as is the habit of weather forecasters; **minus** is an alternative word for subtraction. Likewise, the integer +4 is named 'positive four', not 'plus four'; **plus** is an alternative word for addition. Of course, the integer +4 is another way of referring to the natural number 4, so we would not normally write +4, or say 'positive four', but would simply write 4 and say 'four' – unless in the context it were particularly

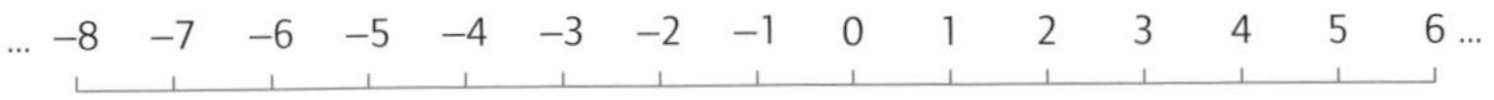

... −8 −7 −6 −5 −4 −3 −2 −1 0 1 2 3 4 5 6 ...

Figure 6.3 *Extending the number line*

helpful to signal the distinction between the negative and the positive integers. So we note that the set of integers includes the set of natural numbers. Integers are explained in greater detail in Chapter 16.

What are rational and real numbers?

When you read the question above that asked how many numbers are there between 10 and 20, you may have been bursting to say, 'It's an infinite number!' Yes, of course, there is no limit to how many numbers there are between 10 and 20. There's $14\frac{1}{2}$ for a start; and 16.07 and 19.9999999; and endless other numbers using fractions and decimals. So 'number' can also include numbers like these, as well as all the integers. When we extend our concept of what is a number to include fractions and decimals (which are a particular kind of fraction) we get the set of **rational numbers**.

The term 'rational' derives from the idea that a fraction represents a *ratio*. The technical definition of a rational number is any number that is the ratio of two integers. Decimal fractions are explained later in this chapter, fractions and other fractions and ratios in Chapter 17. But a few examples here may help to illustrate the concept of a rational number.

$\frac{3}{8}$ is a rational number, because it is the ratio of 3 to 8 (3 divided by 8).
0.8 is a rational number, because it is the ratio of 8 to 10 (8 divided by 10).
$14\frac{1}{2}$ is a rational number, because it is the ratio of 29 to 2 (29 divided by 2).
16.07 is a rational number, because it is the ratio of 1607 to 100 (1607 divided by 100).
23 is a rational number, because it is the ratio of 23 to 1 (23 divided by 1).
−7 is a rational number, because it is the ratio of −7 to 1 (−7 divided by 1).

In simple terms, the set of rational numbers includes all fractions, including decimal fractions (which are just tenths, hundredths, thousandths and so on), as well as all the integers themselves. Rational numbers enable us to subdivide the sections of the number line between the integers and to label the points in between, as shown in Figure 6.4.

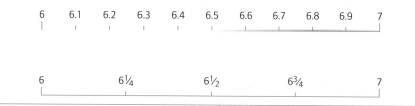

Figure 6.4   *Some rational numbers between 6 and 7*

Now, the reader may be thinking that the set of rational numbers must include all the numbers there are. But, in fact, there are other **real numbers** that cannot be written down as exact fractions or decimals – and are therefore not rational. Believe it or not, there is a limitless number of points on the number line that cannot be represented by rational numbers. These are numbers like square roots or cube roots (see Chapter 15) that do not work out exactly.

For example, there is no fraction or decimal that is exactly equal to the square root of 50 (written as $\sqrt{50}$). This means there is no rational number that when multiplied by itself gives exactly the answer 50. We can get close. In fact, we can get as close as we want. But we cannot get exactly 50. Using a calculator, I could discover that $\sqrt{50}$ is somewhere between 7.07 and 7.08. I find that 7.07×7.07 (= 49.9849) is just less than 50 and 7.08×7.08 (= 50.1264) is just greater than 50. If we went to further decimal places, we could decide that it lies somewhere between 7.0710678 and 7.0710679. But neither of these rational numbers is the square root of 50. Neither of them when multiplied by itself would give 50 exactly. And however many decimal places we went to – you will just have to believe me about this – we could never get a number that gave us 50 exactly when we squared it. But $\sqrt{50}$ is a real number – in the sense that it represents a real point on a continuous number line, somewhere between 7 and 8. It represents a real length. For example, using Pythagoras's theorem (which is explained in Chapter 15), we could work out that the length of the diagonal of a square of side 5 units is $\sqrt{50}$ units. So this is a real length, a real number, but it is not a rational number. It is called an **irrational number**.

There is no end of irrational numbers, all of them representing real lengths and real points on the number line. Some examples would be: $\sqrt{8}$, $\sqrt{17.3}$, $\sqrt[3]{50}$ (the cube root of 50), and that favourite number of mathematicians, π (pi: see Chapter 26). So, what mathematicians call the set of real numbers includes all rational numbers – which include integers, which in turn include natural numbers – and all irrational numbers. We think of it as the set of all numbers that can be represented by real lengths or by points on a continuous number line.

I can imagine that some readers are now wondering if there are numbers other than real numbers. If your appetite for number theory is really that insatiable, you will have to look elsewhere to find out how mathematicians use the idea of an *imaginary number* (like the square root of –1) to construct things called *complex numbers*.

What is meant by 'place value'?

The system of numeration we use today is derived from an ancient Hindu system. It was picked up and developed by Arab traders in the ninth and tenth centuries and quickly spread through Europe. Of course, there have been many other systems developed by various cultures through the centuries, each with their particular features. Comparing some of these with the way we write numbers today enables us to appreciate the power and elegance of the Hindu-Arabic legacy. There is not space here to go into much detail, but the history of different numeration systems is a fascinating topic, with considerable potential for cross-curriculum work in schools, which will repay further study by the reader.

The Egyptian hieroglyphic system, used as long ago as 3000 BC, for example, had separate symbols for ten, a hundred, a thousand, ten thousand, a hundred thousand and a million. The Romans, some 3000 years later, in spite of all their other achievements, were using a numeration system which was still based on the same principle as the Egyptians, but simply had symbols for a few extra numbers, including 5, 50 and 500. Figure 6.5 illustrates how various numerals are written in these systems and, in particular, how the numeral 366 would be constructed. Looking at these three different ways of writing 366 demonstrates clearly that the Hindu-Arabic system we use today is far more economic in its use of symbols. The reason for this is that it is based on the highly sophisticated concept of **place value**.

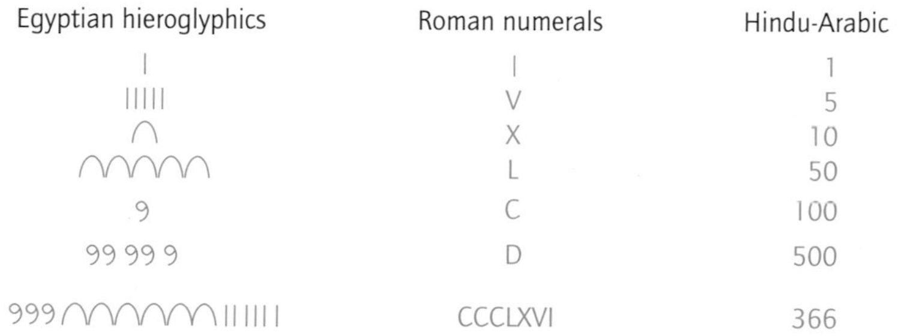

Egyptian hieroglyphics	Roman numerals	Hindu-Arabic
I	I	1
IIIII	V	5
∩	X	10
∩∩∩	L	50
9	C	100
99 99 9	D	500
999 ∩∩∩ IIIIII	CCCLXVI	366

Figure 6.5 *Some numbers written in different numeration systems*

In the Roman system, for example, to represent three hundreds, three Cs are needed, and each of these symbols represents the same quantity, namely, a hundred. Likewise, in the Egyptian system, three 'scrolls' are needed, each representing a hundred. But, in the Hindu-Arabic system we do not use a symbol representing a hundred to construct three hundreds: we use a symbol representing three! Just this one symbol is needed to represent three hundreds, and we know that it represents three hundreds, rather than three tens or three ones, because of the *place* in which it is written. The two sixes in 366, for example, do not stand for the same number: reading from left to right, the first stands for six tens and the second for six ones, because of the places in which they are written.

So, in our Hindu-Arabic place-value system, all numbers can be represented using a finite set of **digits**, namely, 0, 1, 2, 3, 4, 5, 6, 7, 8, 9. Like most numeration systems, no doubt because of the availability of our ten fingers for counting purposes, the system uses ten as a **base**. Larger whole numbers than 9 are constructed using **powers** of the base: ten, a hundred, a thousand, and so on. Of course, these powers of ten are not limited and can continue indefinitely with higher powers. This is how some of these powers are named, written as numerals, constructed from tens, and expressed as powers of ten in symbols and in words:

A million $\qquad$ $1000000 = 10 \times 10 \times 10 \times 10 \times 10 \times 10 = 10^6$ (ten to the power six)

A hundred thousand $\quad 100000 = 10 \times 10 \times 10 \times 10 \times 10 \qquad = 10^5$ (ten to the power five)

Ten thousand $\qquad 10000 = 10 \times 10 \times 10 \times 10 \qquad = 10^4$ (ten to the power four)

A thousand $\qquad 1000 = 10 \times 10 \times 10 \qquad = 10^3$ (ten to the power three)

A hundred $\qquad 100 = 10 \times 10 \qquad = 10^2$ (ten to the power two)

Ten $\qquad 10 = 10 \qquad = 10^1$ (ten to the power one)

The place in which a digit is written then represents that number of one of these powers of ten. So, for example, working from right to left, in the numeral 2345 the 5 represents 5 ones, the 4 represents 4 tens, the 3 represents 3 hundreds and the 2 represents 2 thousands. Perversely, we work from right to left in determining the place values, with increasing powers of ten as we move in this direction. But, since we read from left to right, the numeral is read with the largest place value first: 'two thousands, three hundreds, four tens, and five'. Certain conventions of language then transform this into the customary form, 'two thousand, three hundred and forty-five'. So, the numeral 2345 is essentially a clever piece of shorthand, condensing a complicated mathematical expression into four symbols, as follows:

LEARNING and TEACHING POINT

In explaining place value to children use the language of 'exchanging one of these for ten of those' as you move right to left along the powers of ten, and 'exchanging ten of these for one of those' as you move left to right.

$$(2 \times 10^3) + (3 \times 10^2) + (4 \times 10^1) + 5 = 2345.$$

Notice that each of the powers of ten is equal to ten times the one below: a hundred equals 10 tens, a thousand equals 10 hundreds, and so on. This means that whenever you have accumulated ten in one place this can be **exchanged** for one in the next place to the left. This principle of being able to 'exchange one of these for ten of those' as you move right to left along the powers of ten, or to 'exchange ten of these for one of those' as you move left to right, is a very significant feature of the place-value system. It is essential for understanding the way in which we count. For example, the next number after 56, 57, 58, 59 … is 60, because we fill up the units position with ten ones and these are exchanged for an extra ten in the next column.

This principle of exchanging is also fundamental to the ways we do calculations with numbers. It is the principle of 'carrying one' in addition (see Chapter 9). It also means that when necessary we can exchange one in any place for ten in the next place on the right, for example, when doing subtraction by decomposition (see Chapter 9).

What are the best ways of explaining place value in concrete terms?

There are two sets of materials that provide particularly effective concrete embodiments of the place-value principle and therefore help us to explain the way our number system works. They are (1) base-ten blocks and (2) 1p, 10p and £1 coins.

Figure 6.6 shows how the basic place-value principle of exchanging one for ten is built into these materials, for ones, tens and hundreds. Note

that the ones in the base-ten blocks are sometimes referred to as units, the tens as longs and the hundreds as flats. With the blocks, of course, ten of one kind of block can actually be put together to make one of the next kind. With the coins it is simply that ten ones are *worth* the same as one ten, and so on.

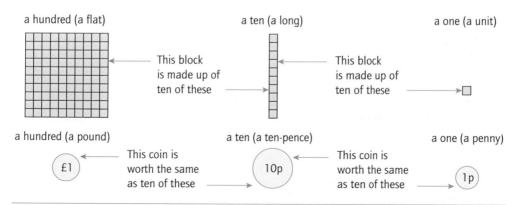

Figure 6.6 *Materials for explaining place value*

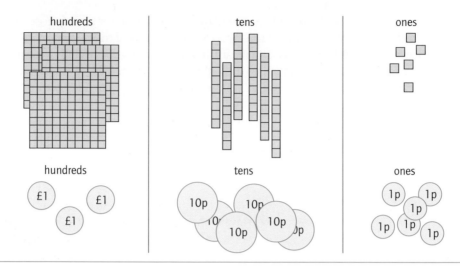

Figure 6.7 *The number 366 in base-ten blocks and in coins*

Figure 6.7 shows the number 366 represented with these materials. Notice that with both the blocks and the coins we have 3 hundreds, 6 tens and 6 ones; this collection of blocks is equivalent to 366 units; and the collection of coins is worth the same as 366 of the 1p coins. Representing numbers with these materials enables us to build up images which can help to make sense of the way we do calculations such as addition and subtraction by written methods, as will be seen in Chapter 9.

How does the number line support understanding of place value?

As we have seen already, the **number line** is an important image that is particularly helpful for appreciating where a number is positioned in relation to other numbers. This ordinal aspect of a number is much less overt in the representation of numbers using base-ten materials. Figure 6.8 shows how the number 366 is located on the number line. The number-line image shows clearly: that it comes between 300 and 400; that it comes between 360 and 370; and that it comes between 365 and 367. The significant mental processes involved in locating the position of the number on the number line are: counting in 100s; counting in 10s; and counting in 1s. First you

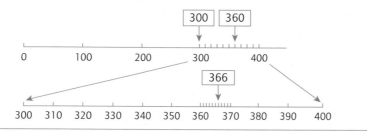

Figure 6.8   *The number 366 located on the number line*

count from zero in 100s until you get to 300: 100, 200, 300; then from here in 10s until you get to 360: 310, 320, 330, 340, 350, 360; and then in 1s from here until you get to 366: 361, 362, 363, 364, 365, 366. The number-line image is also particularly significant in supporting mental strategies for calculations, as will be seen in Chapter 8.

What is meant by saying that zero is a place holder?

The Hindu-Arabic system was not the only one to use a place-value concept. Remarkably, about the same time as the Egyptians, the Babylonians had developed a system that incorporated this principle, although it used sixty as a base as well as ten. But a problem with their system was that you could not easily distinguish between, say, three and three sixties. They did not have a symbol for zero. It is generally thought that the Mayan civilization of South America was the first to develop a numeration system that included both the concept of place value and the consistent use of a symbol for zero.

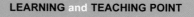

LEARNING and TEACHING POINT

Incorporate some study of numeration systems into history-focused topics such as Egyptian and Mayan civilizations, and use this to highlight the advantages and significance of the place-value system we use today.

Figure 6.9 shows 'three hundred and seven' represented in base-ten blocks. Translated into symbols, without the use of a zero, this would easily be confused with thirty-seven: 37. The zero is used therefore as a **place holder**; that is, to indicate the position of the tens' place, even though there are no tens there: 307. It is worth noting, therefore, that when we see a numeral such as 300, we should not think to ourselves that the 00 means 'hundred'. It is the *position* of the 3 that indicates that it stands for 'three hundred'; the function of the zeros is to

LEARNING and TEACHING POINT

Give particular attention to the function and meaning of zero when writing and explaining numbers to children. The zero in 307 does not say 'hundred'. The 3 says 'three hundred' because of the position it is in. The zero says 'no tens'.

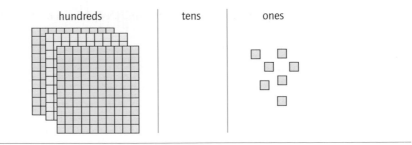

Figure 6.9   *Three hundred and seven in base-ten blocks*

make this position clear whilst indicating that there are no tens and no ones. This may seem a little pedantic, but it is the basis of the confusion that leads some children to write, for example, 30045 for 'three hundred and forty-five'.

How does the place-value system work for quantities less than one?

It works in exactly the same way. Once the principle of being able to 'exchange one of these for ten of those' is established, we can continue with it to the right of the units position, with tenths, hundredths, thousandths, and so on. These positions are usually referred to as *decimal places* and are separated from the units by the **decimal point**. Since a tenth and a hundredth are what you get if you divide a unit into ten and a hundred equal parts respectively, it follows that one unit can be exchanged for ten tenths, and one tenth can be exchanged for ten hundredths. In this way the principle of 'one of these being exchanged for ten of those' continues indefinitely to the right of the decimal point, with the values represented by the places getting progressively smaller by a factor of ten each time.

> **LEARNING and TEACHING POINT**
>
> Articulate the words 'tenths' and 'hundredths' very carefully when explaining decimal numbers; otherwise children may think you are saying 'tens' and 'hundreds'.

A useful way to picture decimals is to explore what happens if we decide that the 'flat' piece in the base-ten blocks represents 'one whole unit'. In this case the 'longs' represent tenths of this unit and the small cubes represent hundredths. Then the collection of blocks shown in Figure 6.7 above is now made up of 3 units, 6 tenths and 6 hundredths. This quantity is represented by the decimal number 3.66. Similarly the blocks in

> **LEARNING and TEACHING POINT**
>
> Explain decimal numbers by using the flat pieces in the base-ten materials to represent units; then the longs can represent tenths and the small cubes can represent hundredths.

Figure 6.9 would now represent the decimal number 3.07, that is, 3 units, no tenths and 7 hundredths.

Do you have to explain tenths, hundredths and decimal places when you introduce decimal notation in the contexts of money or measurement?

If we decide to call a pound coin the 'unit', then the collection of coins in Figure 6.7 now represents the number 3.66, since the ten-penny coins are tenths of a pound and the penny coins are hundredths of a pound. This makes sense, since this amount of money written in pounds, rather than in pence, is recorded conventionally as £3.66.

In terms of decimal numbers in general, the function of the decimal point is to indicate the transition from units to tenths. Because of this a decimal number such as 3.66 is read as 'three point six six', with the first figure after the point indicating the number of tenths and the next the number of hundredths. It would be confusing to read it as 'three point sixty-six', since this might be taken to mean three units and sixty-six tenths.

There is a different convention, however, when using the decimal point in recording money: the amount £3.66 is read as 'three pounds sixty-six'. In this case there is no confusion about what the 'sixty-six' refers to: the context makes clear that it is 'sixty-six pence'. In practice, it is in money notation like this that children first encounter the decimal point. In this form we use the decimal point quite simply as something that separates the pounds from the pennies – so that £3.66 represents simply 3 whole pounds and 66 pence – without any awareness necessarily that the first 6 represents 6 tenths of a pound and the next 6 represents 6 hundredths. It is because the decimal point here is effectively no more than a **separator** of the pounds from the pennies that we have the convention of always writing two figures after the point when recording amounts of money in pounds. So, for example, we would write £3.20 rather than £3.2, and read it as 'three pounds twenty (meaning twenty pence)'. By contrast, if we were working with pure decimal numbers then we would simply write 3.2, meaning '3 units and 2 tenths'.

Since there are a hundred centimetres (cm) in a metre (m), just like a hundred pence in a pound, the measurement of length in centimetres and metres offers a close parallel to recording money. So, for example, a length of 366 cm can also be written in metres, as 3.66 m. Once again the decimal point is seen simply as something that separates the 3 whole metres from the 66 centimetres. In this context it is helpful to exploit children's familiarity with money notation and press the parallel quite strongly, following the same convention of writing two figures after the point when expressing lengths in metres, for example, writing 3.20 m rather than 3.2 m. We can then interpret this simply as three metres and twenty centimetres. I shall explain in Chapter 18 how this convention is very useful when dealing with additions and subtractions involving decimals.

This principle then extends to the measurement of mass (or, colloquially, weight: see Chapter 22) where, because there are a thousand grams (g) in a kilogram (kg), it is best, at least to begin with, to write a mass measured in kilograms with three figures after the point. For example, 3450 g written in kg is 3.450 kg. The decimal point can then simply be seen as something that separates the 3 whole kilograms from the 450 grams. Similarly, in recording liquid volume and capacity, where there are a thousand millilitres (ml) in a litre, a volume of 2500 ml is also written as 2.500 litres, with the decimal point separating the 2 whole litres from the 500 millilitres.

So, when working with primary school children, it is not necessary initially to explain about tenths and hundredths when using the decimal point in the context of money, length and other measurement contexts. To begin with we can use it simply as a separator and build up the children's confidence in handling the decimal notation in these familiar and meaningful contexts. Later, of course, money and measurement in general will provide fertile contexts for explaining the ideas of tenths, hundredths and thousandths. For example, a decimal number such as 1.35 can be explained in the context of length by laying out in a line 1 metre stick, 3 decimetre rods (tenths of a metre) and 5 centimetre pieces (hundredths of a metre), as shown in Figure 6.10.

Figure 6.10 *The decimal number 1.35 shown as a length*

This can then be connected with the number-line image of numbers, where 1.35 is now represented by a point on a line: the point you get to if you start at zero, count along 1 unit, 3 tenths and then 5 hundredths, as shown in Figure 6.11. Note again how this image

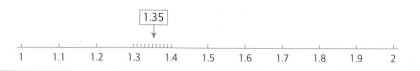

Figure 6.11 *The decimal number 1.35 as a point on a number line*

of the number line enables us to appreciate the position of the number 1.35 in relation to other numbers, the ordinal aspect: for example, it lies between 1 and 2; it lies between 1.3 and 1.4; it lies between 1.34 and 1.36.

Research focus

Since the essence of our number system is the principle of place value, it seems natural to assume that a thorough grasp of place value is essential for young children before they can successfully move on to calculations with two- or three-digit numbers. Thompson has undertaken a critical appraisal of this traditional view (Thompson, 2000). Considering the place-value principle from a variety of perspectives, Thompson concludes that the principle is too sophisticated for many young children to grasp. He argues that many of the mental calculation strategies used by children for two-digit addition and subtraction are based not on a proper understanding of place value but on what he calls *quantity value*. This is being able to think of, say, 47 as a combination of 40 and 7, rather than 4 tens and 7 units. A subsequent research study with 144 children aged 7 to 9 years (Thompson and Bramald, 2002) demonstrated that only 19 of the 91 children who had successful strategies for adding two-digit numbers had a good understanding of the place-value principle. Approaches to teaching calculations with younger children that are consistent with these findings would include: delaying the introduction of column-based written calculation methods; emphasis on the position of numbers in relation to other numbers through spatial images such as hundred squares and number lines; practice of counting backwards and forwards in 1s, 10s, 100s; and mental calculation strategies based on the ideas of quantity value.

Suggestions for further reading

1. Chapter 2 of Haylock and Cockburn (2008) is about understanding number and counting. We outline the mathematical development of number, through natural numbers, integers and rational numbers to real numbers. Although the aim is to enhance the primary teacher's own awareness of the nature of number from a mathematical perspective, the implications for teaching are also considered.

2. Chapter 6 of Hughes (1986) is on written number systems of other cultures. This draws some fascinating parallels between the written numeration systems of various cultures and the representations of number used by young children.
3. Chapter 3 of Nunes and Bryant (1996) is on understanding numeration systems. The authors provide an insightful and scholarly study of young children's understanding of numeration systems.
4. Chapter 4 of Ryan and Williams (2007) discusses the development of number concepts. The authors provide practical examples to show how teachers can reduce the likelihood of mathematical misconceptions developing in the children they teach.
5. Chapter 6, 'Highlighting the learning process', written by Littler and Jirotková, in Cockburn and Littler (2008), explores some of the difficulties children encounter with place value.
6. Chapters 3–5 of Wright et al. (2006) provide an excellent exploration of how children come to understand number and counting, with good suggestions for learning activities.

Self-assessment questions

6.1: What is the next number after 199?

6.2: A teacher says, 'There are 32 children in class 6 and none of them has reached level 4 in mathematics.' Which of the numbers in this statement use the cardinal aspect of number and which the ordinal aspect?

6.3: (a) How many numbers are there between 0 and 20? (b) How many integers are there between 0 and 20?

6.4: Is 1.4142 a rational number? Is it a real number? Is it an integer?

6.5: Is $\sqrt{2}$ a rational number? Is it a real number?

6.6: Arrange these numbers in order from the smallest to the largest, without converting them to Hindu-Arabic numbers: DCXIII, CCLXVlI, CLXXXVIII, DCC, CCC. Then convert them to Hindu-Arabic, repeat the exercise and note any significant differences in the process.

6.7: Add one to four thousand and ninety-nine.

6.8: Write these numbers in Hindu-Arabic numerals, and then write them out in full using powers of ten: (a) five hundred and sixteen; (b) three thousand and sixty; and (c) two million, three hundred and five thousand and four.

6.9: I have 34 one-penny coins, 29 ten-penny coins and 3 one-pound coins. Apply the principle of 'exchanging ten of these for one of those' to reduce this collection of coins to the smallest number of 1p, 10p and £1 coins.

6.10: Interpret these decimal numbers as collections of base-ten blocks (using a 'flat' to represent a unit) and then arrange them in order from the smallest to the largest: 3.2, 3.05, 3.15, 3.10.

6.11: There are a thousand millimetres (mm) in a metre. How would you write lengths of 3405 mm and 2500 mm in metres?

6.12: How should you write: (a) 25p in pounds; (b) 25 cm in metres; (c) 7p in pounds; (d) 45 g in kilograms; (e) 50 ml in litres; and (f) 5 mm in metres?

6.13: Fill in the boxes with single digits: on a number line, 3.608 lies between □ and □; it lies between □.□ and □.□; it lies between □.□□ and □.□□; it lies between □.□□□ and □.□□□.

Further practice

From the Student Workbook

Tasks 1–4: Checking understanding of number and place value
Tasks 5–7: Using and applying number and place value
Tasks 8–11: Learning and teaching of number and place value

Glossary of key terms introduced in Chapter 6

Numeral: the symbol used to represent a number; for example, the number of children in a class might be represented by the numeral 30.

Cardinal aspect of number: the idea of a number as representing a set of things. This idea of number has meaning only in terms of non-negative integers.

Ordinal aspect of number: the idea of a number as representing a point on a number line. This idea of number as a label for putting things in order has meaning for negative as well as positive numbers.

Natural numbers: the set of numbers that we use for counting, 1, 2, 3, 4, 5, and so on, going on for ever.

Integer: a whole number, positive, negative or zero.

Positive integer: an integer greater than zero. The integer +4 is correctly referred to as 'positive four'. Usually the + sign is understood and the integer is just written as 4 and referred to as 'four'.

Negative integer: a number less than zero. The integer −4 is correctly referred to as 'negative four'.

Minus and **Plus.** synonyms for 'subtract' and 'add' respectively. Strictly speaking, it is incorrect to refer to negative integers and positive integers as 'minus numbers' and 'plus numbers', as is often done by weather forecasters.

Rational number: a number that can be expressed as the ratio of two integers (whole numbers). All whole numbers and fractions are rational numbers, as are all numbers that can be written as exact decimals.

Real number: any number that can be represented by a length or by a point on a continuous number line. The set of real numbers consists of all rational and all irrational numbers.

Irrational number: a number that is not rational; for example $\sqrt{2}$ is irrational because it cannot be written exactly as one whole number divided by another.

Place value: the principle underpinning the Hindu-Arabic system of numeration in which the position of a digit in a numeral determines its value; for example, '6' can represent six, sixty, six hundred, six tenths, six hundredths, and so on, depending on where it is written in the numeral.

Digits: the individual symbols used to build up numerals in a numeration system; in our Hindu-Arabic system the digits are 0, 1, 2, 3, 4, 5, 6, 7, 8 and 9.

Base: the number whose powers are used for the values of the various places in the place-value system of numeration; in our system the base is ten, so the places represent powers of ten, namely, units, tens, hundreds, thousands, and so on.

Power: a way of referring to a number repeatedly multiplied by itself; for example, $10 \times 10 \times 10 \times 10$ is referred to as '10 to the power 4', abbreviated to 10^4.

Exchange: the principle at the heart of our place-value system of numeration, in which ten in one place can be exchanged for one in the next place to the left, and vice versa; for example, 10 hundreds can be exchanged for 1 thousand, and 1 thousand can be exchanged for 10 hundreds.

Number line: a straight line in which points on the line are used to represent numbers, emphasizing particularly the order of numbers and their positions in relation to each other.

Place holder: the role of zero in the place-value system of numeration; for example, in the numeral 507 the 0 holds the tens place to indicate that there are no tens here. Without the use of zero as a place holder there would just be a gap between the 5 and the 7.

Decimal point: a punctuation mark (.) required when the numeration system is extended to include tenths, hundredths and so on; it is placed between the digits representing units and tenths.

Separator: the function of the decimal point in the contexts of money and other units of measurements, where it serves to separate, for example, pounds from pence, or metres from centimetres..

7
Addition and Subtraction Structures

In this chapter there are explanations of

- two different structures of real-life problems modelled by addition;
- the contexts in which children will meet these structures;
- the commutative law of addition;
- four different structures of real-life problems modelled by subtraction; and
- the contexts in which children will meet these structures.

What are the different kinds of situation that primary children might encounter to which the operation of addition applies?

This chapter is not about doing addition and subtraction calculations, but focuses first on understanding the mathematical structures of these operations. Essentially it is concerned with step 1 of the modelling process (see Figure 5.2) introduced in Chapter 5: setting up the mathematical model corresponding to a given situation. The approach taken for each of addition and subtraction in this chapter is to identify the range of situations that children have to learn to connect with the operation. The following two chapters then consider step 2 of the modelling process, the mental and written methods for doing the actual calculations.

There are two basic categories of real-life problems that are modelled by the mathematical operation we call addition. The problems in each of these categories may vary in terms of their content and context, but essentially they all have the same structure. I have coined the following two terms to refer to the structures in these two categories of problems:

- the aggregation structure; and
- the augmentation structure.

Distinguishing between these two addition structures is not always easy, nor is it necessarily helpful to try to do so. But I find it is useful in teaching to have them in mind to ensure that children have opportunities to experience the full range of situations and, most importantly, the associated language that they have to learn to connect with addition.

What is the aggregation structure of addition?

I use the term **aggregation** to refer to a situation in which two (or more) quantities are combined into a single quantity and the operation of addition is used to determine the total. For example, there are 15 marbles in one circle and 17 in another: how many marbles altogether? This idea of 'how many (or how much) altogether' is the central notion in the aggregation structure (see Figure 7.1). In this example notice that the two sets do not overlap. They are called **discrete sets**. When two sets are combined into one set they form what is called the **union of sets**. So another way of describing this addition structure is 'the union of two discrete sets'. This notion of addition mainly builds on the cardinal aspect of number, the idea of number as a set of things (see Chapter 6).

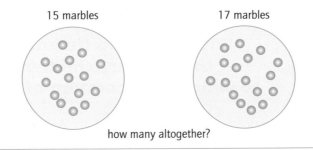

15 marbles   17 marbles

how many altogether?

Figure 7.1 *Addition as aggregation*

What is the augmentation structure of addition?

I use the term **augmentation** to refer to a situation where a quantity is increased by some amount and the operation of addition is required in order to find the augmented or increased value. For example, the price of a bicycle costing £149 is

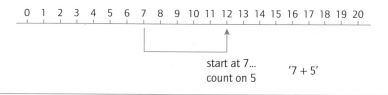

Figure 7.2   *Addition as augmentation*

increased by £25: what is the new price? This is the addition structure which lies behind the idea of counting on along a number line and which we might use with young children for experiencing simple additions such as, say, 7 + 5: 'start at 7 and count on 5' (see Figure 7.2). Because it is connected so strongly with the image of moving along a number line, this notion of addition mainly builds on the ordinal aspect of number (see Chapter 6).

It should just be mentioned at this stage that if the number added were a negative number, then the addition would not result in an increase, but in a *decrease*. This extension of the augmentation structure to negative numbers is discussed in Chapter 16, which deals with positive and negative integers.

What are some of the contexts in which children will meet addition in the aggregation structure?

First and most simply, children will encounter this structure whenever they are putting together two sets of objects into a single set, to find the total number. For example, combining two discrete sets of children (25 boys and 29 girls, how many altogether?); combining two separate piles of counters (46 red counters, 28 blue counters, how many altogether?). Second, and, in terms of relevance, most importantly, children will encounter the aggregation structure in the context of money. This might be, for example, finding the total cost of two or more purchases, or the total bill for a number of services. The question will be, 'How much altogether?'

> **LEARNING and TEACHING POINT**
>
> Ensure that children experience the two addition structures in a range of relevant contexts, including money (shopping, bills, wages and salaries) and various aspects of measurement. Then they also have to recognize addition in situations of aggregation in the contexts of measurements, such as length and distance, mass, capacity and liquid volume, and time. For example, addition would be the operation required to find the total distance for a journey if I have already travelled 63 miles and then do a further 45 miles; or to find the total time for the journey if the first stage has taken me 85 minutes and the second stage takes 65 minutes.

What are some of the contexts in which children will meet addition in the augmentation structure?

The most important and relevant context for this structure is again that of money, particularly the idea of increases in price or cost, wage or salary. Another context that has relevance for children is temperature, where addition would model an increase in temperature from a given starting temperature. A significant context for use with younger children is their age: 'You are 6 years old now, how old will you be in 4 years' time?' This is a good way for younger children to experience 'start at six and count on 4'. The key language that signals the operation of addition is that of 'increasing' or 'counting on'. This idea may also be encountered occasionally, but not often, in other measurement contexts, such as length (for example, stretching a length of elastic by so much), mass (for example, putting on so many kilograms over Christmas) and time (for example, increasing the length of the lunch break by so many minutes).

What is the commutative law of addition?

It is clear from Figure 7.1 that the problem there could be represented by either 15 + 17 or by 17 + 15. Which set is on the left and which on the right makes no difference to the total number of marbles. The fact that these two additions come to the same result is an example of what is called the **commutative law of addition**. To help remember this technical term, we could note that commuters go both ways on a journey. So the commutative law of addition is simply the principle that an addition can go both ways: for example, 17 + 15 = 15 + 17. The principle is an axiom (see Chapter 4) – a self-evident fact – one of the fundamental building blocks of arithmetic. We can state this commutative law formally by the following generalization, which is true whatever the numbers a and b:

> **LEARNING and TEACHING POINT**
>
> Make explicit to children the principle of the commutative law of addition. Show them how to use it in addition calculations, particularly by starting with the bigger number when counting on. Explain that subtraction does not have this property.

$a + b = b + a.$

The significance of this property is twofold. First, it is important to realize that subtraction does *not* have this commutative property. For example, 10 − 5 is not equal to 5 − 10. Second, it is important to make use of commutativity in addition calculations. Particularly when using the idea of counting on, it is nearly always best to start with the bigger number. For example, it would not be sensible to calculate 3 + 59 by starting at 3 and counting on 59! The obvious thing to do is to use the commutative law mentally to change the addition to 59 + 3, then start at 59 and count on 3.

What are the different kinds of situation that primary children might encounter to which the operation of subtraction applies?

There is a daunting range of situations in which we have to learn to recognize that the appropriate operation is subtraction. I find it helpful to categorize these into at least the following four categories:

- the partitioning structure;
- the reduction structure;
- the comparison structure; and
- the inverse-of-addition structure.

It is important for teachers to be aware of this range of structures, to ensure that children get the opportunity to learn to apply their number skills to all of them. Being able to connect subtraction with the whole range of these situations and to switch freely from one to the other is also the basis for being successful and efficient at mental and informal strategies for doing subtraction calculations. For example, to find out how much taller a girl of 167 cm is than a boy of 159 cm (which is the comparison structure), a child may recognize that this requires the subtraction '167 − 159', but then do the actual calculation by interpreting it as 'what must be added to 159 to get 167?' (which is inverse of addition).

> **LEARNING and TEACHING POINT**
>
> Familiarity with the range of subtraction structures will enable children to interpret a subtraction calculation in a number of ways and hence increase their ability to handle these calculations by a range of methods.

It helps us to connect these mathematical structures with the operation of subtraction if we ask ourselves the question: what is the calculation I would enter on a calculator in order to solve this problem? In each case the answer will involve using the subtraction key. It is one of the baffling aspects of mathematics that the same symbol, as we shall see particularly with the example of the subtraction symbol, can have so many different meanings.

What is the partitioning structure of subtraction?

The **partitioning** structure refers to a situation in which a quantity is partitioned off in some way or other and subtraction is required to calculate how many or how much remains. For example, there are 17 marbles in the box, 5 are removed, how many are left? (See Figure 7.3.) The calculation to be entered on a calculator to correspond to this situation is '17 − 5'. Partitioning is the structure that teachers (and consequently their children) most frequently connect with the subtraction symbol. Because it is linked in the early stages so strongly with the idea of a set of objects, it builds mainly on the cardinal aspect of number.

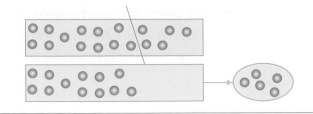

Figure 7.3   *Subtraction as partitioning*

It cannot be stressed too strongly that subtraction is not just 'take away'. As we shall see, partitioning is only one of a number of subtraction structures. So teachers should not overemphasize the language of 'take away, how many left' at the expense of all the other important language identified below that has to be associated with subtraction.

What is the reduction structure of subtraction?

The **reduction** structure is similar to 'take away' but it is associated with different language. It is simply the reverse process of the augmentation structure of addition. It refers to a situation in which a quantity is reduced by some amount and the operation of subtraction is required to find the reduced value. For example: if the price of a bicycle costing £149 is reduced by £25, what is the new price? The calculation that must be entered on a calculator to solve this problem is '149 − 25'. The essential components of this structure are a starting point and a reduction or an amount to go down by. It is this subtraction structure that lies behind the idea of counting back along a number line, as shown in Figure 7.4. Because of this connection, the idea of subtraction as reduction builds on the ordinal aspect of number.

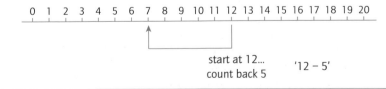

Figure 7.4   *Subtraction as reduction*

What is the comparison structure of subtraction?

The **comparison** structure refers to a completely different set of situations, namely, those where subtraction is required to make a comparison between two quantities, as for example in Figure 7.5. How many more blue cubes are there than red cubes? The calculation to be entered on a calculator to correspond to this situation is '12 − 7'. Subtraction of the smaller number from the greater enables us to determine the *difference*, or to find out *how much greater* or *how much smaller* one quantity is than the other.

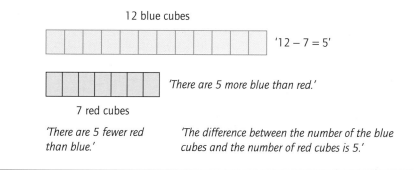

12 blue cubes

'12 − 7 = 5'

'There are 5 more blue than red.'

7 red cubes

'There are 5 fewer red than blue.'

'The difference between the number of the blue cubes and the number of red cubes is 5.'

Figure 7.5 *Subtraction as comparison*

Because making comparisons is such a fundamental process, with so many practical and social applications, the ability to recognize this subtraction structure and the confidence to handle the associated language patterns are particularly important. Comparison can build on both the cardinal aspect of number (comparing the numbers of objects in two sets) and the ordinal aspect (finding the gap between two numbers on a number line).

What is the inverse-of-addition structure of subtraction?

The **inverse-of-addition** structure refers to situations where we have to determine what must be added to a given quantity in order to reach some target. The phrase 'inverse of addition' underlines the idea that subtraction and addition are **inverse processes**. The concept of inverse turns up in many situations in mathematics, whenever one operation or transformation undoes the effect of another one. For example, moving 5 units to the left on a number line is the inverse of moving 5 units to the right: do one and then the other and you finish up back where you were. When we think of subtraction as the inverse of addition we mean, for example, that since 28 + 52 comes to 80, then 80 − 52 must be 28. The subtraction of 52 undoes the effect of adding 52. Hence to solve a problem of the form 'what must be added to X to give Y?' we subtract X from Y.

LEARNING and TEACHING POINT

Asking the question 'what is the calculation to be entered on a calculator to solve this problem?' helps to focus the children's thinking on the underlying mathematical structure of the situation.

An example of an everyday situation with this structure would be: the entrance fee is 80p, but I have only 52p, how much more do I need? Even though the question is about adding something to the 52p, the calculation that must be entered on a calculator to solve this problem is a subtraction, 80 − 52. Figure 7.6 shows how this subtraction structure might be interpreted as an action on the number line: starting at 52 we have to determine what must be added to get to 80. This is a particularly important structure to draw on when doing subtraction calculations by mental and informal strategies.

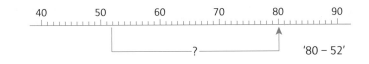

Figure 7.6   *Subtraction as inverse of addition*

What are some of the contexts in which children will meet the partitioning subtraction structure?

LEARNING and TEACHING POINT

Children should experience problems with all the different subtraction structures in a range of practical and relevant contexts, including money (shopping, bills, wages and salaries) and various aspects of measurement.

First, this structure is encountered whenever we start with a given number of things in a set and a subset is taken away (removed, destroyed, eaten, killed, blown up, lost or whatever). In each case the question being asked is, 'how many are left?' It also includes situations where a subset is identified as possessing some particular attribute and the question asked is, 'how many are not?' or 'how many do not?' For instance, there might be 58 children from a year group of 92 going on a field trip. The question, 'how many are not going?' has to be associated with the subtraction, 92 − 58. (See the discussion of complement of a set in Chapter 27.)

Then the structure has a number of significant occurrences in the context of money and shopping. For example, we might plan to spend £72 from our savings of £240 and need to work out how much would be left (that is, carry out the subtraction, 240 − 72).

Finally, there are various practical situations in the context of measurement where we encounter the partitioning subtraction structure: for example, when we have a given length of some material, plan to cut off a length of it and wish to calculate how much will be left; or where we have some cooking ingredients measured by mass or volume, plan to use a certain amount in a recipe and wish to calculate how much will be left.

What are some of the contexts in which children will meet subtraction in the reduction structure?

Realistic examples of the reduction structure mainly occur in the context of money. The key idea which signals the operation of subtraction is that of 'reducing', for example, reducing prices and costs, cutting wages and salaries. For example, if a person's council tax of £625 is cut by £59, the reduced tax is determined by the subtraction, 625 − 59. The structure may also be encountered occasionally in other measurement contexts, such as reduction in mass or temperatures falling.

What are some of the contexts in which children will meet subtraction in the comparison structure?

Wherever two numbers occur we will often find ourselves wanting to compare them, to determine the difference, or to find out how much greater or smaller one is than the other.

In particular, the process of comparison is a central idea in all measurement contexts, as we shall see in Chapter 22. The table below provides examples of the extensive language

LEARNING and TEACHING POINT

Take every opportunity to promote the language of comparison and ordering throughout the primary age range, not just in mathematics lessons.

that children might use in various contexts in primary mathematics to compare and order quantities. These are arranged in two columns, so that alongside a comparison with the greater quantity as the subject of the sentence ($A > B$) is the equivalent statement with the lesser quantity as the subject ($B < A$). For example, when children compare two objects by balancing them on some weighing scales, their observations would be both 'the bottle is heavier than the book' and 'the book is lighter than the bottle'.

A > B	B < A
A set of 21 has more items than a set of 19.	A set of 19 has fewer items than a set of 21.
£3.50 is more than £2.95.	£2.95 is less than £3.50.
$\frac{1}{2}$ is larger than $\frac{1}{3}$.	$\frac{1}{3}$ is smaller than $\frac{1}{2}$.
Australia is bigger than Britain.	Britain is smaller than Australia.
Anna is taller than Ben.	Ben is shorter than Anna.
The pencil is longer than my finger.	My finger is shorter than the pencil.
The ceiling is higher than the light.	The light is lower than the ceiling.
London is further than Ipswich.	Ipswich is nearer than London.
The corridor is wider than the door.	The door is narrower than the corridor.
The teddy is fatter than the rabbit.	The rabbit is thinner than the teddy.
The bottle is heavier than the book.	The book is lighter than the bottle.
The jug holds more than the bottle.	The bottle holds less than the jug.
Oranges cost more than bananas.	Bananas cost less than oranges.
Fruit juice is dearer than milk.	Milk is cheaper than fruit juice.
A maths lesson takes longer than music.	Music takes less time than a maths lesson.
Music is later than literacy.	Literacy is (earlier) sooner than music.
Music happens after literacy.	Literacy happens before music.
Mrs Jones is older than Ben.	Ben is younger than Mrs Jones.
Ben is faster (quicker) than Mrs Jones.	Mrs Jones is slower than Ben.
Inside is hotter (warmer) than outside.	Outside is colder (cooler) than inside.

This table illustrates the huge significance of the language and experience of comparison in children's learning. Subtraction is involved when, having made a comparison to identify which is the greater or lesser quantity, we then go on to ask: how many more? How many fewer? How much greater? How much less? How much heavier? How much lighter? And so on.

The child might first compare the numbers of items in two sets (for example, the numbers of marbles in two bags, the numbers of cards in two packs, the numbers of children in two classes, the numbers of counters in two piles, the numbers of pages in two books, and so on). To do this they have to connect the situation and the associated language of 'difference', 'how many more?', 'how many fewer?' with the operation of subtraction.

Then in the context of money they would encounter this subtraction structure whenever they are comparing the prices of articles or the costs of services. If holiday package A costs £716 and package B costs £589, then we would ask questions such as: 'how much more expensive is A?' 'How much cheaper is B?' 'How much dearer is A?' 'How much more does A cost than B?' 'How much less does B cost

> **LEARNING and TEACHING POINT**
>
> When comparing two quantities, A and B, as well as asking about the difference, always use at least two other forms of the question, one making the greater quantity the subject, the other the lesser. For example: how many more in A? How many fewer in B? How much greater is A? How much less is B? How much longer is A? How much shorter is B? How much heavier is A? How much lighter is B? How much earlier is A? How much later is B?

than *A*?' Note the range of language patterns used here – and that in each case the question is answered by the same subtraction, 716 – 589. Also, subtraction might be used to compare salaries and wages: for example, how much more does the police officer earn than the teacher? Or, to put it another way, how much less does the teacher earn than the police officer?

If a child has measured the heights of Anna and Ben, there would be a subtraction involved in comparing their heights, to determine how much taller is Anna than Ben and how much shorter is Ben than Anna. The calculation enables us to say, for example, 'Anna is 2.5 cm taller than Ben' or 'Ben is 2.5 cm shorter than Anna'. If the child had measured the masses of the bottle and the book, they could compare them by asking 'how much heavier is the bottle?' or 'how much lighter is the book?' – and again subtraction is required to be able to say, for example, 'the bottle is 65 g heavier than the book' or 'the book is 65 g lighter than the bottle'.

What are some of the contexts in which children will meet subtraction in the inverse-of-addition structure?

This subtraction structure is often the most difficult for primary children to recognize, because the language associated with it, such as 'how much more is needed?' and 'what must be added?', signals the idea of addition rather than subtraction.

There are many commonplace situations where we encounter this structure: for example, any situation where we have a number of objects or a number of individuals and we require some more in order to reach a target. The most convincing examples for many will be in the context of sport. For example, if I have scored 180 in darts how many more do I need to reach 401? This corresponds to the subtraction, 401 – 80. If we are chasing a score of 235 in cricket and we have scored 186 with eight overs remaining, how many more runs do we need? The calculation to be entered on a calculator to answer this is 235 – 186.

Other examples of the inverse-of-addition structure occur in the context of measurement, such as: how much further do you have to drive to complete a journey of 345 miles if you have so far driven 196 miles?

Perhaps the most relevant instances of the inverse-of-addition subtraction structure occur in the context of money. For example, if we have saved £485 towards a holiday costing £716, we will need to do the subtraction, 716 – 485, in order to calculate how much more we need to save. Again, if the reader is uncertain about the assertion that this situation is an example of subtraction, it will help to ask: what is the calculation you would enter on a calculator to work this out?

Of course, when calculating a subtraction like 716 – 485 without a calculator, we might very well use a number-line image and the idea of adding on from 485 to get to 716. For example, we could add 15 to get from 485 to 500, another 200 to get to 700, and another 16 to get to 716, as shown in Figure 7.7. This is a powerful mental strategy, as we shall see in the next chapter. It reinforces the importance of children associating subtraction with the full range of structures discussed above. This is not just so that they will know when a situation requires a subtraction calculation, but also that when a subtraction calculation is required they can interpret it in a number of different ways in order to deal with it.

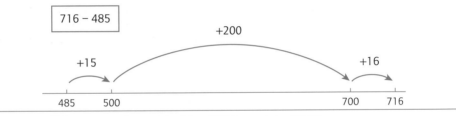

Figure 7.7   *What must be added to 485 to get to 716?*

Research focus

A significant study of children's responses to word problems involving addition and subtraction was undertaken in Israel by Nesher and Teubal (1975). They analysed the responses of about 85 children aged 7 years to four word problems: a problem using 'more' requiring addition (87% successful), one using 'less' requiring addition (64% successful), one using 'less' requiring subtraction (81% successful), and one using 'more' requiring subtraction (43% successful). These results suggested that there were particular difficulties for children in recognizing the correct operation in problems where the verbal cues 'more' (suggesting addition) and 'less' (suggesting subtraction) appeared to lead the children to select the wrong operation. The lowest success rate was in the subtraction problem where the word 'more' was used: 'The milkman brought 11 bottles of milk on Sunday; that was 4 more than he brought on Monday; how many did he bring on Monday?' They concluded that children tended to look for key words and to respond to them, rather than try to understand and grasp the logical structure of the problem. Their findings suggest, for example, that there is a need for teachers to focus particularly on children's grasp of the logical structure of situations incorporating subtraction as the inverse of addition.

Suggestions for further reading

1. In Chapter 7 of Haylock (1991) I explain why being able to recognize the operations of addition, subtraction, multiplication and division in a range of structures and contexts is a primary objective for numeracy. The chapter draws on experience of working with low attainers on this objective. Classroom activities for promoting children's grasp of these ideas are included.
2. Chapter 3 of Haylock and Cockburn (2008) is on understanding addition and subtraction, This chapter will provide the opportunity to visit again some of the ideas about addition and subtraction structures explained above, from the perspective of teaching younger children. It includes examples of small-group and class activities for children, designed to promote understanding through making connections.
3. Chapter 6 of Nunes and Bryant (1996), on giving meaning to addition and subtraction, is recommended for readers who want to dig more deeply into children's understanding of the ideas of addition and subtraction. The focus is on children's development from pre-school to age 7 years.

Self-assessment questions

7.1: Make up a problem that corresponds to the addition, 5.95 + 6.99, using the aggregation structure in the context of shopping.

7.2: Make up a problem that corresponds to the addition, 1750 + 145, using the augmentation structure in the context of salaries.

7.3: Make up a problem that corresponds to the addition, 15 + 25 + 55 + 20 + 65, using the aggregation structure in the context of time.

7.4: There are 256 pages in my book. I have so far read 178 of them. How many more pages do I have to read? What is the calculation to be entered on a calculator to answer this? Of what subtraction structure is this an example?

7.5: I am 62 and my daughter is 35. How many years younger than me is she? What is the calculation to be entered on a calculator to answer this? Of what subtraction structure is this an example?

7.6: Make up a problem that corresponds to the subtraction, 4.95 − 3.99, using the comparison structure in the context of shopping.

7.7: Make up a problem that corresponds to the subtraction, 250 − 159, using the partitioning structure and the phrase 'how many do not ... '.

7.8: Make up a problem corresponding to 989 − 650 that uses the inverse-of-addition structure in the context of shopping.

Further practice

> **From the Student Workbook**
>> Tasks 12–14: Checking understanding of addition and subtraction structures
>> Tasks 15–16: Using and applying addition and subtraction structures
>> Tasks 17–19: Learning and teaching of addition and subtraction structures

Glossary of key terms introduced in Chapter 7

Aggregation: the process modelled by addition in which two quantities are combined into a single quantity and addition is used to determine the total. The key language is 'how many altogether?'

Discrete sets: two (or more) sets that do not overlap, having no members in common; for example, the set of boys and the set of girls in a class are discrete sets.

Union of sets: the set formed when two (or more) sets are combined to form a single set. The union of two discrete sets is an example of the aggregation structure of addition.

Augmentation: the process modelled by addition in which a given quantity is increased by a certain amount and addition is used to determine the result of the increase. This structure includes 'start at … count on by …'.

Commutative law of addition: the principle that the order of two numbers in an addition calculation makes no difference to their sum. In symbols, the commutative law of addition states that, whatever the numbers a and b, $a + b = b + a$.

Partitioning (subtraction structure): the process modelled by subtraction in which a quantity is partitioned off or taken away from a given quantity and subtraction is used to determine how many are left (or how much is left). The key idea is 'take away … how many (much) left?'

Reduction: the process modelled by subtraction in which a given quantity is reduced by some amount and subtraction is used to determine the result of the reduction. This structure includes 'start at … count back by … '.

Comparison: the process modelled by subtraction in which two quantities are compared and subtraction is used to find the difference, or how much greater or less one is than the other.

Inverse of addition: the process modelled by subtraction in which the question asked is 'what must be added?' in order to reach some target.

Inverse processes: two processes, one of which has the effect of undoing the effect of the other. For example: add 7 and subtract 7; double and halve; turn clockwise through a right angle and turn anticlockwise through a right angle.

8
Mental Strategies for Addition and Subtraction

What is the associative law of addition?

Like the commutative law ($a+b=b+a$) discussed in the previous chapter, the **associative law** is a fundamental property of addition and an axiom of arithmetic. Written formally, as a generalization, it is the assertion that for any numbers a, b and c:

$$a + (b + c) = (a + b) + c.$$

Using a particular example, this might be: $7 + (13 + 18) = (7 + 13) + 18$. The brackets indicate which addition should be done first. In simple terms, the associative law says that if you have three numbers to add together you get the same answer whether you start by adding the second and third or start by adding the first and second. In the example above, it's probably easier to start by adding the 7 and 13, but you get the same answer if you start with 13 + 18. I like to remember the associative law by thinking of it as a picture of three political parties: sometimes the party in the centre associates with the right and sometimes it associates with the left, but it does not make any difference!

This law allows us to write down 7 + 13 + 18, without using any brackets to indicate which two numbers should be added first. We can choose whichever we prefer. The commutative and associative laws combined give us the freedom to add a string of numbers together in any order we like. For example, 7 + (13 + 18) could be changed as follows:

$$
\begin{aligned}
& 7 + (13 + 18) \\
=\ & 7 + (18 + 13) && \text{(using the commutative law)} \\
=\ & (7 + 18) + 13 && \text{(using the associative law)} \\
=\ & (18 + 7) + 13 && \text{(using the commutative law)} \\
=\ & 18 + (7 + 13) && \text{(using the associative law)} \\
=\ & 18 + (13 + 7) && \text{(using the commutative law)} \\
=\ & (18 + 13) + 7 && \text{(using the associative law)} \\
=\ & (13 + 18) + 7 && \text{(using the commutative law).}
\end{aligned}
$$

We shall see below that deciding on the most efficient way of adding up various bits of numbers is an important strategy for informal calculations, so the associative and commutative laws of addition are important – even though most people use them without realizing it or without referring to them explicitly.

An important point to make about associativity is that subtraction does *not* have this property. For example, 25 − (12 − 8) is not equal to (25 − 12) − 8. This means that we cannot write 25 − 12 − 8 to mean both of these! The convention is that 25 − 12 − 8 means (25 − 12) − 8, that is, that the subtractions are done in order from left to right, unless brackets are used to indicate otherwise.

How important is mental calculation?

The ability to calculate mentally using a range of strategies is recognized as being an important component of numeracy. It is a reasonable expectation that most children in primary schools should be able to learn to add and subtract using informal, mental strategies with three-digit numbers. This does not mean, of course, that they do not write anything down. They may need to write the question down for a start, so they do not forget it – and it may be helpful to support their mental calculation with a few jottings along the way or with a picture such as a number line.

It is now generally realized that most of the problems that children encounter in calculations in primary schools are associated with them being introduced too early to formal algorithms, written in a vertical format. Vertical layouts for additions and subtractions especially lead children to treat the digits in the numbers as though they are individual numbers and then to combine them in all kinds of bizarre and meaningless ways. Mental strategies by their very ad hoc nature lead you to build on what you understand and to use methods that make sense to you.

LEARNING and TEACHING POINT

Make it clear to children and parents (and grandparents) that there is no 'proper' way of doing a calculation and that an effective mental or informal method is as valid as a formal written method.

The decision as to which strategy to employ is guided by the actual numbers in the problem. For example, very few of us would use the same strategy for calculating 201 – 20 and 201 – 197. The first I would do essentially by counting back in tens from 201, and the second by counting on from 197. Both of these are very simple subtractions, of course, when written down horizontally and done by mental methods. But the potential for error when these are written down as vertical calculations and tackled by the conventional algorithm is considerable, as illustrated in Figure 8.1 (see self-assessment question 8.2 at the end of this chapter). A good suggestion is that children should be thoroughly confident in additions and subtractions written in horizontal format, using mental and informal strategies, before they are introduced to the vertical layout algorithms. Greater sharing of such methods, through open discussion and specific teaching of some of the key mental strategies, will undoubtedly lead to greater confidence with number.

LEARNING and TEACHING POINT

When formal written methods have been taught, encourage children still to look for an easier way to do additions and subtractions by mental and informal methods first, before resorting to formal written algorithms.

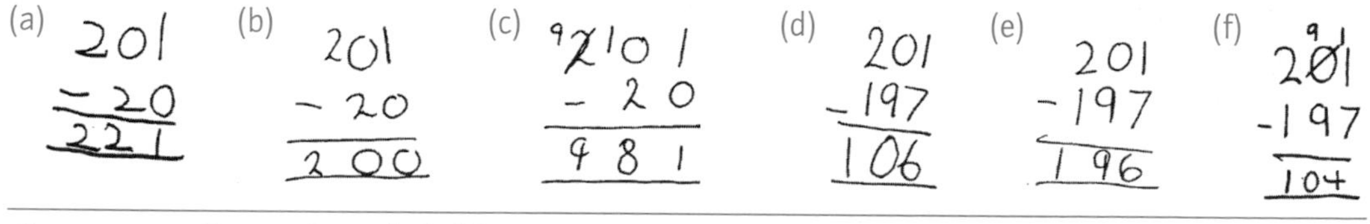

Figure 8.1 *Examples of children's errors in vertical layout of subtractions*

How does counting forwards and backwards help in mental calculations?

In Chapter 7 we saw how addition could be understood as counting on and subtraction as counting back, and that these ideas were strongly linked with movements

LEARNING and TEACHING POINT

Confidence in counting backwards and forwards in ones, tens and hundreds is an essential prerequisite for effective mental calculation, so these skills should be taught specifically and reinforced frequently.

along a number line. These ideas are also central to much mental and informal calculation. Doing additions and subtractions on a hundred square (see Figure 8.2) provides children with a strong image that supports the process of counting on and back in ones and tens. So 57 + 3 done by counting on in ones is associated with a movement to the right along a row: 57 … 58, 59, 60. And 57 − 3 done by counting back in ones is associated with a movement to the left along a row: 57 … 56, 55, 54. Then 57 + 30 done by counting on in tens is seen as a movement down a column: 57 … 67, 77, 87. And 57 − 30 done by counting back in tens is seen as a movement up a column: 57 … 47, 37, 27.

These are important strategies that can be extended to counting in hundreds and which we combine with other strategies when we become more proficient mental calculators. A good target is that children should be able to count on or back in ones, tens and hundreds from any given number (up to three digits) by about the age of 9 years.

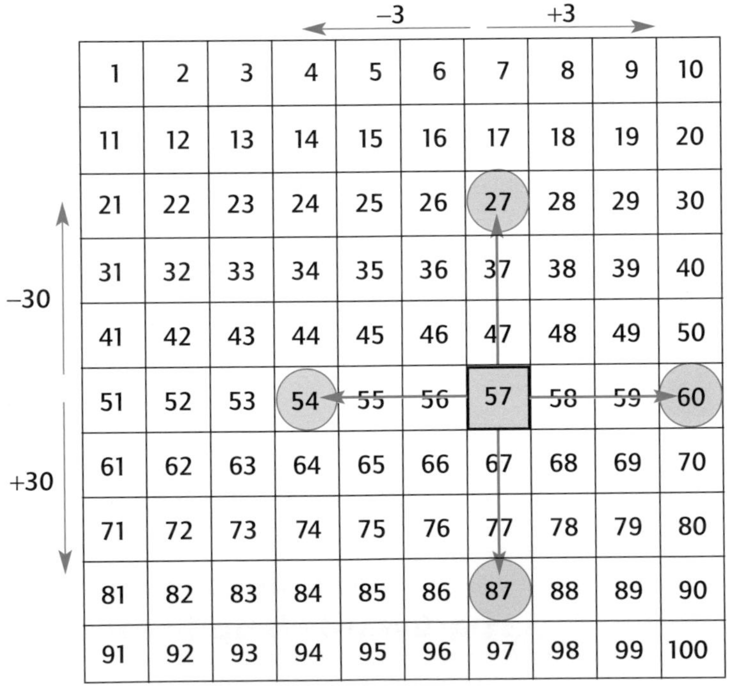

Figure 8.2 *Using a hundred square*

How do we use multiples of 10 and 100 as stepping stones?

Notice what happens when we add 5 to 57 on a hundred square. We have to break the 5 down into two bits, 3 and 2. The 3 gets us to the next **multiple of 10** (60) and then we have 2 more to count on. This process of using a multiple of ten (60) as a **stepping stone** is an important mental strategy for addition and subtraction. (*Note*: multiples of 10 are 10, 20, 30, 40, 50, 60, … and so on. Multiples are discussed more fully in Chapter 14.)

Here is how we might use this idea of a stepping stone for calculating, say, 57 + 28. First, we could count on in 10s, to deal with adding the 20: 57 … 67, 77. Then break the 8 up into 3 and 5, to enable us to use 80 as a stepping stone: 77 + 8 = 77 + 3 + 5 = 80 + 5 = 85.

A number-line diagram is a very useful image for supporting this kind of reasoning. Children can be taught to use an **empty number line**, which is simply a line on which they can put whatever numbers they like, not worrying about the scale, just ensuring that numbers are in the right order relative to each other. Figure 8.3 shows an empty number-line representation of the calculation of 57 + 28, using 80 as a stepping stone.

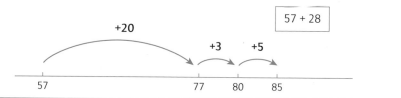

Figure 8.3 *Using a multiple of 10 as a stepping stone on an empty number line*

Figure 8.4 shows how we might use multiples of 100 as stepping stones for calculating 542 – 275, using an empty number line. Using the inverse-of-addition structure, the subtraction can be interpreted as, 'What do you add to 275 to get 542?' This is done in three steps (25 + 200 + 42), with 300 and 500 as convenient stepping stones lying between the 275 and the 542.

What is front-end addition and subtraction?

Most formal written algorithms for addition and subtraction work from right to left, starting with the units. In mental calculations it is much more common to work from left to

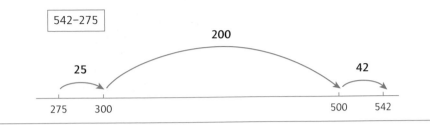

Figure 8.4 *Using multiples of 100 as stepping stones in a subtraction*

right. This makes more sense, because you deal with the biggest and most significant bits of the numbers first. One strategy is mentally to break the numbers up into hundreds, tens and ones, and then to combine them bit by bit, starting at the front end – that is, starting by adding (or subtracting) the hundreds. So, for example, given 459 + 347, we would think of the 459 as (400 + 50 + 9) and the 347 as (300 + 40 + 7). This process is sometimes called **partitioning into hundreds, tens and ones**. We would then use the freedom granted to us by the associative and commutative laws to add these bits in any order we like. The **front-end approach** would deal with the hundreds first (400 + 300 = 700), then the tens (50 + 40 = 90, making 790 so far), then the ones (for example, 790 + 9 = 799; 799 + 7 = 799 + 1 + 6 = 806). Notice that I have used 800 as a stepping stone for the last step here.

Writing this out in full, in a way which might explain my thinking to someone else:

$$459 + 347 = (400 + 50 + 9) + (300 + 40 + 7)$$
$$= (400 + 300) + (50 + 40) + (9 + 7)$$
$$= 700 + 90 + 9 + 7$$
$$= 799 + 7 = 799 + 1 + 6 = 800 + 6 = 806.$$

We will quite often use the front-end approach to get us started in a subtraction done mentally. For example, for 645 – 239, we would immediately deal with the hundreds (600 – 200 = 400) leaving us simply to think about 45 – 39. This gives us 6, so the answer is 400 + 6 = 406.

What is compensation in addition and subtraction?

You can often convert an addition or subtraction question into an easier question by temporarily adding or subtracting an appropriate small number. For example, many people would evaluate 673 + 99 by adding 1 temporarily to the 99, so the question becomes 673 + 100. This gives 773. Now take off the extra 1, to get the answer 772. This strategy is sometimes called **compensation**. Figure 8.5(a) shows how this way of finding 673 + 99 looks when carried out on an empty number line.

The trick in the strategy is always to be on the lookout for an easier calculation than the one you have to do. This will often involve temporarily replacing a number ending

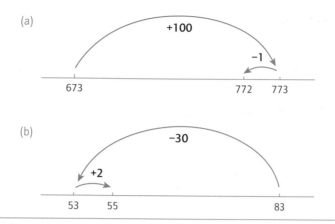

Figure 8.5 *Using compensation to calculate (a) 673 + 99 and (b) 83 – 28*

in a 9 or an 8 with the next multiple of 10. For example, the subtraction, 83 – 28, can temporarily be changed into the much easier calculation, 83 – 30, which gives 53, with 2 to be added to this to compensate for the fact that we've actually taken away 2 more than required. This is illustrated on an empty number line in Figure 8.5(b).

The strategy can be used to change any subtraction into an easier one. For example, 453 – 178 looks a bit daunting. I would rather do 453 – 180. (But remember: I will have taken away 2 more than I should and this will have to be added on again later.) If I'm still struggling with 453 – 180, I could instead choose to do 453 – 200, which is 253. (Now I have to remember there's an extra 20 to add on.) So the answer is 253 + 20 + 2, which is a relatively easy addition, giving 275.

This approach is particularly effective with precisely those subtractions that cause most problems using the decomposition algorithm (see Chapter 9): those with zeros in the first number. For example, Figure 8.6(a) shows a typical error made by a 9-year-old boy attempting to calculate 101 – 97 set out in vertical format. He was then given the question in horizontal format and encouraged to work it out mentally. This he did successfully by first dealing with 100 – 97 by counting back and then compensating. Figure 8.6(b) is his response to the invitation to 'write down how you did it in a way that shows your thinking to someone else'.

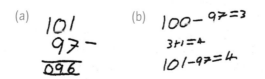

Figure 8.6 *(a) A 9-year-old's unsuccessful attempt to calculate 101 – 97; and (b) his successful use of compensation*

Here is a more challenging example, written out in a way that might explain the thinking to someone else:

To calculate:	$4003 - 3196$
Add 4 to the second number:	$4003 - 3200$
Add 800 to the second number:	$4003 - 4000 = 3$
Now compensate:	$3 + 4 + 800 = 807.$

Obviously to use this strategy you have to be very good at recognizing what you need to make a number up to the next multiple of 10, the next multiple of 100, and so on. There are other ways of using the strategy of compensation, all of which amount to changing one or more of the numbers in order to produce an easier calculation. We can use this approach to exploit our confidence in handling multiples of five, to relate additions and subtractions to doubles, or simply to replace one of the numbers by a more 'friendly' number. These are explained below.

How should the symbol for 'equals' be used in recording calculations?

As children begin to make more detailed written records of their calculations they can be encouraged to use the equals sign (=) to link only those things that are actually equal, as has been done in all the examples in this chapter. There is a tendency for children (and some teachers) to abuse the equals sign by employing it rather casually just to link the steps in a calculation, without it having any real meaning. For example, it is not uncommon to see this kind of thing written down: $103 - 87 = 103 - 90 = 13 + 3 = 16$. Only the final equals sign here connects two expressions that are actually equal. Although this kind of recording is acceptable behaviour in the privacy of your own scribbling-pad, you should be warned that it is likely seriously to upset pedantic mathematicians if done in public.

While I am being pedantic, I might just mention the word 'sum'. Mathematically, a **sum** is the result of the *addition* of two or more numbers. Colloquially the word 'sum' is often used to refer to any *calculation*. Strictly, it should apply only to additions. So, for example, '$103 - 87$' and '$(256 + 14) \div 30$' are not sums.

How do multiples of 5 help in mental additions and subtractions?

Multiples of 5 (5, 10, 15, 20, 25, 30, …) are particularly easy to work with. Young children quickly learn to relate simple additions and subtractions to fives. For example, a 5-year-old might think of $6 + 7$ as '5 and 1 and 5 and 2', and proceed by first combining the fives. This tendency to relate numbers to multiples of 5 is no doubt related to the way our early experience of counting on our fingers leads us to perceive 6, 7, 8 and 9 as '5 and some more'. It is then reinforced by our experience of handling coins. We can exploit this confidence with multiples of 5 in many additions and subtractions done mentally. For example, 37 + 26 could be related to 35 + 25, which we would probably find much easier. This can be taught as a specific strategy. Here are some examples, written out in full to show what would, of course, be a mental process:

$$37 + 26 \;=\; (35 + 25) + 2 + 1 \;=\; 60 + 2 + 1 \;=\; 63$$
$$77 + 24 \;=\; (75 + 25) + 2 - 1 \;=\; 100 + 2 - 1 \;=\; 101$$
$$174 - 46 \;=\; (175 - 45) - 1 - 1 \;=\; 130 - 1 - 1 \;=\; 128.$$

How do you relate additions and subtractions to doubles?

Sometimes in additions and subtractions we can exploit the fact that most people are fairly confident with the processes of doubling and halving. Even quite young primary school children will quickly show confidence with doubles, no doubt because they have two sets of fingers on which to learn to calculate. So it is found that young children will often exploit their facility with doubles to calculate '**near-doubles**'. For example, many 5-year-olds would think of 6 + 7 as 'double 6 and 1 more'. This is

another example of compensation, of course, turning the calculation into what most of us would find to be an easier one.

Using our facility for doubling larger numbers could lead us to look at, for example, 36 + 37 and think 'double 36 and 1 more'. Here are some more examples of how we might use our confidence with doubling and halving to get us started on some additions and subtractions:

48 + 46 could be related to double 46: 46 + 46 = 92, so 48 + 46 = 92 + 2 = 94.
62 + 59 could be related to double 60: 60 + 60 = 120, so 62 + 59 = 120 + 2 − 1 = 121.
54 − 28 could be related to half 54 (27): 54 − 27 = 27, so 54 − 28 = 27 − 1 = 26.
54 − 28 could be related to half 56 (28): 56 − 28 = 28, so 54 − 28 = 28 − 2 = 26.

How do you use 'friendly' numbers?

Most of us would much prefer to deal with 742 − 142 than 742 − 146, because the 142 and 742 are much more **friendly** than the 146 and the 742. We always have as an option in addition and subtraction to use the compensation approach and temporarily replace one

LEARNING and TEACHING POINT

Teach children specifically the strategies outlined in this chapter and give them opportunities to discuss different ways of tackling additions and subtractions by mental methods supported by jottings and empty number line diagrams.

of the numbers in a calculation with one that is more friendly. This is especially useful in subtraction:

To calculate $742 - 146$
Change the 146 to 142: $742 - 142 = 600$
Now compensate: $742 - 146 = 600 - 4 = 596$.
Or,
Change the 742 to 746: $746 - 146 = 600$
Now compensate: $742 - 146 = 600 - 4 = 596$.

Research focus

In a research project with children aged 6–9 years in Queensland, Australia, Heirdsfield and Cooper (1997) found that introducing children too early to formal written algorithms for addition and subtraction limits their willingness and ability to develop a range of mental strategies and a good number sense. When presented with a calculation written in horizontal format and invited to find the answer mentally, the majority of such children tended to use a mental strategy based on the formal written method. Interestingly, the children showed a greater range of mental strategies when the calculation was presented as a word problem. Clearly, the range of addition and subtraction structures embedded in real-life situations suggests different ways of doing the calculations, some of which they had not specifically been taught in school. The researchers also found that children who were most successful in mental addition and subtraction had two key skills: very secure knowledge of number facts and a good sense of computational estimation.

Suggestions for further reading

1. Harries and Spooner (2006) is an accessible exploration of the range of mental processes in number work and the various images that can support them. The book manages to combine a theoretical perspective with sound practical advice for the primary classroom.
2. Part 3 of the guidance on teaching mental strategies produced to support the Numeracy Strategy in England (QCA, 1999a) deals with addition and subtraction strategies.
3. Read the chapter by Rousham entitled 'The empty number line: a model in search of a learning trajectory?' in Thompson (2003). The author draws on the experience of primary teachers in Holland who have used the empty number line as an aid for promoting mental strategies in addition and subtraction with marked success.
4. Chapters 6–9 of Wright et al. (2006) is an insightful analysis of how younger children come to understand addition and subtraction and to develop skills in handling these operations mentally.

Self-assessment questions

8.1: (a) What sign should go in the box to make this true: $67 - (20 - 8) = (67 - 20) \, \square \, 8$? Try this with some other numbers and state a general rule. (b) What sign should go in the box to make this true: $67 - (20 + 8) = (67 - 20) \, \square \, 8$? Try this with some other numbers and state a general rule.

8.2: Identify the errors made by the children in the examples in Figure 8.1.

8.3: Find the answer to $538 + 294$ by the front-end approach, partitioning the numbers into hundreds, tens and ones, then starting with the hundreds and working from left to right.

8.4: Calculate $423 + 98$ mentally, using compensation.

8.5: Calculate $297 + 304$ mentally, by relating it to a double.

8.6: Calculate $494 + 307$ mentally, using 500 as a stepping stone.

8.7: Calculate $26 + 77$ mentally, by relating the numbers to multiples of 5.

8.8: Calculate $1000 - 458$ mentally, using compensation.

8.9: Calculate $819 - 523$ mentally, by making one of the numbers more friendly.

8.10: Calculate $732 - 389$ mentally, by adding-on from 389, using 400 and 700 as stepping stones.

8.11: Do these using any mental strategies that seem appropriate: (a) $974 - 539$; (b) $400 - 237$; (c) $597 + 209$; (d) $7000 - 6$; (e) $7000 - 6998$.

Further practice

From the Student Workbook

Tasks 20–22: Checking understanding of mental strategies for addition and subtraction

Tasks 23–26: Using and applying mental strategies for addition and subtraction

Tasks 27–29: Learning and teaching of mental strategies for addition and subtraction

On the website (www.sagepub.co.uk/haylock)

Check-Up 10: The commutative laws

Check-Up 11: The associative laws

Check-Up 23: Mental calculations, adding lists

Glossary of key terms introduced in Chapter 8

Associative law of addition: the principle that if there are three numbers to be added it makes no difference whether you start by adding the first and second, or by adding the second and third. In symbols, this law states that, for any three numbers a, b and c, $(a + b) + c = a + (b + c)$.

Multiple of 10:   a number that can be divided exactly by 10. So the multiples of 10 are 10, 20, 30, 40, 50, 60, 70, 80, 90, 100, 110, 120, and so on. Similarly, multiples of 100 are 100, 200, 300, and so on.

Stepping stone: usually a multiple of 10 or 100 used to break down an addition or subtraction into easier steps. For example, to find what has to be added to 37 to get to 75, the numbers 40 and 70 might be used as stepping stones.

Empty number line: a number line without a scale, used to support mental and informal additions and subtractions; numbers involved in the calculation can be placed anywhere on the line provided they are in the right order relative to each other.

Partitioning into hundreds, tens and ones: breaking a number up into hundreds, tens and ones as an aid to using it in a calculation. For example, 476 when partitioned is $400 + 70 + 6$.

Front-end approach: a method for doing a calculation that focuses first on the digits at the front of the number. For example, to add 543 and 476, a front-end approach would start by adding the 500 and 400.

Compensation: a strategy that involves replacing a number in a calculation with an easier number close to it and then compensating for this later. For example, to subtract 38 you could subtract 40 instead and compensate by adding on the additional 2 at the end.

Sum: the result of doing an addition; for example, 25 is the sum of 17 and 8. The word 'sum' should not be used as a synonym for 'calculation'.

Near-double: when two numbers involved in an addition are nearly the same, such as $46 + 48$; or when one number involved in a subtraction is nearly double or half of the other, such as $87 - 43$. Such calculations can be done by treating them as exact doubles and then compensating.

'Friendly' numbers: two numbers that are related to each other in a way that makes a calculation particularly easy; for example, $457 - 257$. Often a calculation can be made easier by replacing one of the numbers with a more friendly number close to it and then compensating later.

9
Written Methods for Addition and Subtraction

In this chapter there are explanations of

- a variety of ways of introducing column addition and subtraction;
- the idea of 'carrying' in the formal addition algorithm;
- the decomposition method for doing subtraction calculations;
- the equal additions method for subtraction;
- how the two methods differ and why decomposition is preferred;
- the problem with zeros in the top number in a subtraction calculation; and
- the constant difference method for subtraction.

How can you introduce children to column addition?

When children begin to work with three-digit numbers they can be introduced to **column addition**: various ways of laying out their calculations that line up the hundreds, tens and ones in columns. These should build on some of the mental strategies outlined in the previous chapter, particularly the idea of partitioning the numbers into hundreds, tens and ones. Figure 9.1(a) shows how a 9-year-old might record the calculation, 372 + 247, using this strategy and lining up the hundreds, tens and ones in columns. Figure 9.1(b) shows an alternative layout for recording the same thinking, which can then be abbreviated to the version in Figure 9.1(c). These ways of recording are a useful, informal introduction to what we might call 'the formal addition algorithm', which is shown in Figure 9.1(d). The major source of error in using this format is that it encourages children to think of the digits as separate numbers, losing any sense that they represent hundreds, tens or ones. The layouts in Figures 9.1(a), (b) and (c) have the advantage that they do not obscure the meaning of the digits and children should

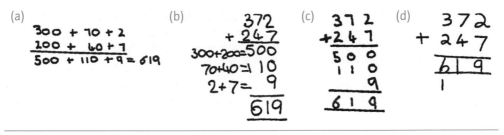

Figure 9.1   *Four ways of recording 372 + 247 as a column addition*

still be consciously aware that they are handling hundreds, tens and ones. Note that these layouts allow you to use the more natural procedure of working from left to right, dealing with the largest bits of the numbers first, as in the 'front-end' approach discussed in Chapter 8. Discussion of various ways of setting out calculations such as these also reinforces the important message that there is no 'proper' way of doing a calculation.

How do you explain what's going on when you 'carry one' in addition?

The conventional, formal written algorithm (shown in Figure 9.1(d)) is a very condensed and abstract record of a calculation. Teachers might therefore help children to understand what is going on here by making clear links between the written record and the manipulation of some form of base-ten materials that incorporate place-value principles (see Chapter 6). These could be, for example, base-ten blocks (units, longs and flats) or coins (pennies, ten-pences and pounds), representing the ones, tens and hundreds.

To explain addition, then, I will use £1, 10p and 1p coins, which will be referred to as 'hundreds', 'tens' and 'ones'. Some teachers prefer to refer to the 'ones' as 'units'. I have no strong views about this and tend to switch freely between the two words. Clearly the principle that 'ten of these can be exchanged for one of those' applies to the ones and the tens, and to the tens and the hundreds. The process could equally well be experienced with base-ten blocks.

So, to take an example: 356 + 267. This calculation is set out with coins as shown in Figure 9.2, with 356 interpreted as 3 hundreds, 5 tens and 6 ones, and 267 interpreted as 2 hundreds, 6 tens and 7 ones. The two numbers now have to be combined to find the total. So where do you start? The standard algorithm usually involves working from right to left, that is, starting with the ones. To some extent this procedure of working from right to left conflicts with the natural mental strategy of starting with the digits with the greatest value and so working from left to right. When it comes to using the standard addition algorithm, all I can say is that with experience you find that it's easier to be systematic and to avoid getting in a muddle if you work from right to left. But, in fact, it really does not matter as long as you remember and apply correctly the principle that 'ten of these can be exchanged for one of those'.

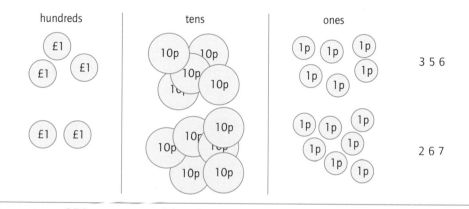

Figure 9.2 *356 + set out with coins*

So, in Figure 9.2, we first put together all the ones, making thirteen in all. Ten of these can then be exchanged at the bank for a ten. Since this ten is literally 'carried' from the bank and placed in the tens column, the language of **'carrying one'** is very appropriate – provided it is clear that we are carrying 'one of these' (that is a ten) and not carrying 'a one'.

The coins at this stage are arranged as shown in Figure 9.3. This also shows the recording so far, in which there is a direct relationship between what is done with the symbols and what has been done with coins. The 3 written in the ones column corresponds to the three remaining one-penny coins. The 1 written below the line in the tens column corresponds to the one ten which has been carried from the bank in exchange for ten ones.

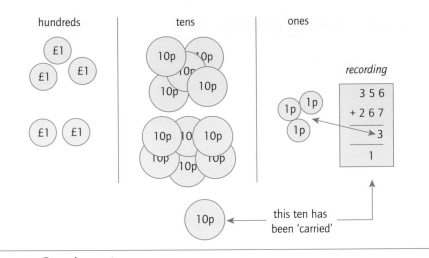

Figure 9.3 *Carrying a ten*

Next all the tens are combined: that's the 5 tens in the top row, plus the 6 tens in the next row, plus the 1 ten that has been carried. This gives a total of 12 tens. Ten of these are then exchanged for a hundred. So once again we are 'carrying one', but this time, of course, it is 'one hundred'. Figure 9.4 shows the situation at this stage and, once again, the direct correspondence between the recording in symbols and the manipulation of the coins.

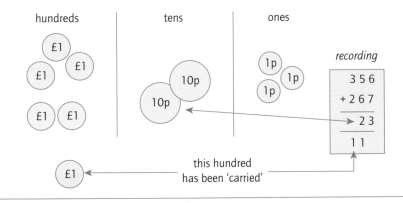

Figure 9.4 *Carrying a hundred*

The final stage in this calculation is to combine the hundreds: that's the 3 hundreds in the top row, plus the 2 hundreds in the next row, plus the 1 hundred that has been carried, giving a total of 6 hundreds. Figure 9.5 shows the final arrangement of the coins, with the 6 hundreds, 2 tens and 3 ones corresponding to the answer to the addition, namely 623.

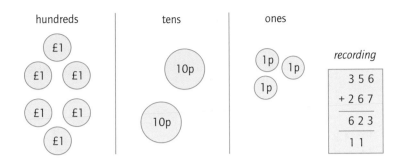

Figure 9.5 *The result of adding 356 and 267*

What about introducing column subtraction?

Subtractions are straightforward when each digit in the first number is greater than the corresponding digit in the second. For example, in calculating 576 – 324 we just take the 3 hundreds away from the 5 hundreds, the 2 tens away from the 7 tens, and the 4 units away from the 6 units, to get the answer 252. The problem comes when one (or more) of the digits in the first number is smaller than the corresponding digit in the second number, for example, 448 – 267. Of course, this is not a difficult calculation when tackled by some of the mental strategies outlined in the previous chapter. But, as the numbers get bigger, children will need to develop some kind of standard written procedure for **column subtraction**, lining up the hundreds, tens and ones in columns.

Historically, in Britain, there have been essentially two formal written algorithms for subtraction. Nowadays, nearly all primary schools, if they teach children a subtraction algorithm, use the method known as subtraction by **decomposition**. This has more or less completely ousted the method that most people of my age were taught at school, namely, the method of **equal additions**. These methods are explained later in this chapter. There is no real need to try to master the method of equal additions. However, you will find it informative to try to understand it and, as we shall see later, it can be the basis for a novel approach to subtraction calculations. The reason for the widespread adoption of the method of decomposition is that it is much easier to *understand*, in the sense of making connections between the manipulation of concrete materials, the manipulations of the symbols and the corresponding language. Subtraction by equal additions can only really be taught to children by rote, as a procedure to be followed blindly with little real understanding of

> **LEARNING and TEACHING POINT**
>
> When children need a formal algorithm for subtraction, teach the method of decomposition. But explain the method in a way that encourages understanding of the process, not just as a recipe without meaning.

what is going on. The shift towards decomposition therefore coincided with a greater emphasis in teaching on learning mathematics with understanding.

Children can be introduced to the idea of lining up the hundreds, tens and ones in columns for subtraction using the same format as is suggested in Figure 9.1(a) for introducing addition. Figure 9.6 shows some ways in which some children recorded their informal calculation of 448 – 267, all of which start by partitioning the numbers into hundreds, tens and ones.

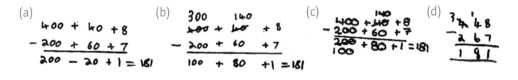

Figure 9.6   *Four ways of calculating 448 – 267 using column subtraction*

In the approach shown in Figure 9.6(a) the child has worked from left to right, subtracting the hundreds, then the tens, then the ones. The recording of –20 in the tens column does not require a sophisticated understanding of negative numbers. It can be understood simply as meaning that we have taken away 40 of the 60 in the second number, so we still have 20 to be taken away. The final step of calculating 200 – 20 + 1 is done mentally.

In Figure 9.6(b), the child is introduced to the idea of decomposition and encouraged to work from right to left. The thought process is as follows: starting with the ones, 8 – 7 = 1; then on to the tens; 40 take away 60 is a problem; so take 100 from the next column and add this to the 40, making 140; then 140 – 60 = 80; then deal with the hundreds; 300 – 200 = 100. The final calculation 100 + 80 + 1 is again done mentally.

Figure 9.6(c) shows a novel application of the idea of decomposition. The child uses a front-end approach, working from left to right. Having dealt with 400 – 200 = 200, the child then encounters the problem of 40 – 60. To deal with this, 100 is taken from the 200 in the answer in the hundreds column and added on to the 40. This gives 140 – 60 = 80.

The layout of Figure 9.6(b) especially is a helpful introductory procedure prior to the development of the formal decomposition algorithm shown in Figure 9.6(d). As with addition, the formal algorithm for subtraction is a highly condensed and abstract form of recording and can become a meaningless routine in which digits are manipulated without any thought as to what they represent. Again, to promote understanding of what is going on here, teachers might discuss with children the corresponding manipulation of some base-ten materials to represent hundreds, tens and ones. This would involve putting out a pile of hundreds, tens and ones to represent the first number, then taking away the second number, exchanging a hundred for ten tens, or a ten for ten ones when necessary. As with addition, children should be helped to connect the manipulation of the materials with the written record, step by step.

So how does subtraction by decomposition work?

As with addition calculations, the key to explaining the method is a sound grasp of place value and the use of some appropriate concrete embodiments of number, such as coins or base-ten blocks.

I will explain the method of decomposition with base-ten blocks, using the example of 443 – 267. First, the 443 is set out with base-ten blocks, as shown in Figure 9.7: 4 hundreds, 4 tens and 3 units. The task is to take 267 away from this collection of blocks, that is, to remove 2 hundreds, 6 tens and 7 units.

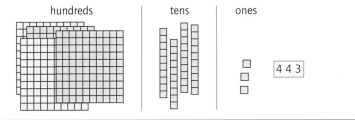

Figure 9.7   *The number 443 set out with base-ten blocks*

As with addition, the natural place to start might be to take away the biggest blocks first, that is, working from left to right, and this is how most of us would deal with a calculation of this kind if doing it mentally or by informal written methods. But again the standard written algorithm actually works from right to left. This is certainly not essential, but it is usually tidier to do it this way. So we start by trying to remove 7 units from the collection of blocks in Figure 9.7. Since there are only 3 units there we cannot do this – yet. So we pick up one of the tens, take it to the box of blocks and exchange it for ten units.

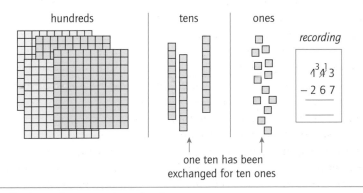

one ten has been exchanged for ten ones

Figure 9.8   *Exchanging one ten for ten ones*

Figure 9.8 shows the situation at this stage and the corresponding recording. Notice how the recording in symbols corresponds precisely to the manipulation of the materials. We have crossed out the 4 tens in the top number and replaced it by 3, because one of these tens has been exchanged for units and we do indeed now have 3 tens in our collection. The little 1 placed beside the 3 units in the top number is to indicate that we now have 13 units. We are now in a position to take away the 7 units as required, leaving 6 units. This is recorded as in Figure 9.9.

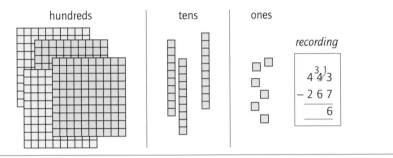

Figure 9.9   *After 7 units have been taken away*

The next step is to deal with the problem of removing 6 tens when we have only 3 of them. So we take one of the hundreds and exchange it for 10 tens, producing the situation shown in Figure 9.10. The recording indicates that after the exchanging process we now have 3 hundreds and 13 tens. We can now complete the subtraction, taking away first the 6 tens and then the 2 hundreds.

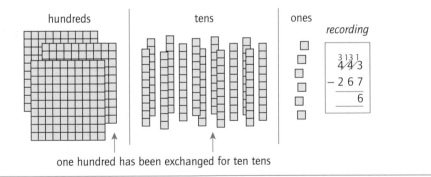

one hundred has been exchanged for ten tens

Figure 9.10   *Exchanging one hundred for 10 tens*

Figure 9.11 shows the final arrangement of the blocks, with the remaining 1 hundred, 7 tens and 6 units corresponding to the result of the subtraction, namely 176.

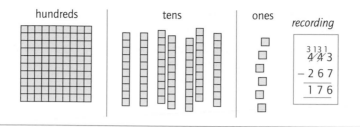

Figure 9.11 *The result of subtracting 267 from 443*

There are three important points to note about this method. First, there is the quite natural idea of exchanging a block in one column for ten in the next column to the right when necessary. Second, there is the strong connection between the manipulation of the materials and the recording in symbols, supported by appropriate language. Third, notice that all the action in the recording takes place in the top line, that is, in the number you are working on, not the number you are subtracting.

LEARNING and TEACHING POINT

Encourage children to set out subtraction calculations in vertical format generously, to give themselves plenty of room for their working.

How does the method of equal additions differ from this?

The method of equal additions differs in all three of these respects. It does not use the principle of exchange, it is not naturally rooted in the manipulation of materials and the method involves working on both numbers simultaneously. Although the method is not normally taught these days, it will actually prove to be quite useful to explain it. My explanation will be merely in terms of numbers, without the support of coins or blocks, simply because the method is not easily understood in these terms.

The method is based on the comparison structure of subtraction (see Chapter 7) and uses the principle that the difference between two numbers remains the same if you add the same number to each one. For example, the difference between your height and my height is still the same if we stand together on a table rather than on the floor! Faced with the subtraction, 443 – 267, the person using equal additions would manipulate the symbols as shown in Figure 9.12.

Unable to deal with '3 take away 7', we add 10 to both numbers, as shown in Figure 9.12(b). But we do this in a subtle way. In the top number this 10 is added to the units digit, increasing the 3 to 13. This is shown by writing a little 1 in front of the 3. In the bottom number the 10 is added to the tens column, increasing the 6 to 7. I show this by striking through the 6 and writing 7, whereas some people indicate this by writing a little one

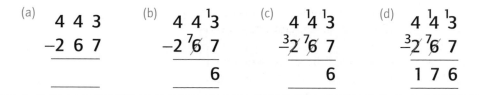

Figure 9.12   *The method of equal additions*

somewhere in the tens column: various systems of recording are used for this step, but the principle of adding ten to both numbers is the same.

In Figure 9.12(b) we can now deal with the units, writing in 6 in the answer, but are faced with the problem of '4 subtract 7' in the tens column. We apply the same principle of adding the same thing to both numbers, but this time we actually add 100, as shown in Figure 9.12(c). This appears as 10 tens in the top number, increasing the number of tens from 4 to 14. Simultaneously, in the bottom number we add one to the hundreds digit, increasing it from 2 to 3. We are then able to complete the subtraction as shown in Figure 9.12(d). The reader may be encouraged to note that both methods produce the same answer.

What is 'borrowing' in subtraction?

I really do not know. Back in the last century when we did equal additions we were taught to say, 'Borrow one and pay it back'. I have never understood this phrase, since it is not at all clear from whom we were borrowing or even whether we were paying it back to the same source. I have therefore come to the conclusion that it was merely something to say to yourself, with no meaning, simply as a reminder that there were two things to do. We could equally well have said, 'Pick one up and put one down'. The intriguing thing is, though, that this language of 'borrowing' has actually survived the demise of the method for which it was invented! It is still commonplace to hear teachers talking about 'borrowing one' when explaining the method of decomposition to children. I find this unhelpful. We are not 'borrowing one' in decomposition, we are '*exchanging* one of these for ten of those'.

Of course, in practice no one ever thought consciously that what they were doing, for example, was adding ten or a hundred to both numbers: they were simply 'borrowing one and paying it back'! Thus subtraction by equal additions was always taught by rote, with no real attempt to understand what was going on. This is the real advantage of decomposition: that there is the potential in the method for children to understand it in terms of concrete experiences of coins or blocks, connected to the meaningful language of exchange.

The reader may wonder therefore why everyone did not always teach the method of decomposition. The reason is that, unfortunately, there is sometimes a slight problem in using the decomposition method when there is a zero in the top number. A modification in the process of decomposition is required, whereas with equal additions zeros in the top number make no difference to the routine. However, the modification is a natural process, still easily understood if related strongly to concrete materials and the appropriate language of exchange.

> **LEARNING and TEACHING POINT**
>
> Do not talk about 'borrowing' when teaching subtraction by decomposition. This is meaningless and unhelpful. The language to use is 'exchanging'.

What is the problem in decomposition with a zero in the top number?

Figure 9.13 shows the steps involved in tackling 802 − 247 by decomposition. In Figure 9.13(a) the person doing the calculation is faced with the problem of '2 subtract 7'. The decomposition method requires a ten to be exchanged for ten units, but in the 802 the zero indicates that there are no tens. This is the problem! However, it is not difficult to see that the thing to do is to go across to the hundreds column and exchange one of these for 10 tens, as shown in Figure 9.13(b), then to take one of these tens and exchange it for ten units, as shown in Figure 9.13(c). The subtraction can then be completed, as in Figure 9.13(d). Of course, all this can be carried out and understood easily in terms of base-ten blocks or coins, representing hundreds, tens and ones (units).

However, let me remind you that these subtractions with zeros in the first number, which are most problematic when done by the formal decomposition algorithm, are often very straightforward when tackled using mental strategies such as compensation, as explained in Chapter 8. For example, 802 − 247 is a cinch if you start with 802 − 250 and then compensate for the additional 3 taken away. The method of constant differences explained below is an alternative approach that is also particularly effective when there are zeros in the first number.

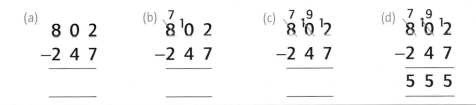

Figure 9.13   *The problem of a zero in the top number*

What is the constant difference method?

LEARNING and TEACHING POINT

Discuss with children how the principle of adding the same thing to both numbers (or subtracting the same thing from both) can convert a subtraction question into an easier calculation. This constant difference method is a genuine alternative for children who get confused by decomposition and is often easier for subtractions with a zero in the first number.

Surprisingly, in view of what I have said above, the principle of equal additions is not redundant, but is actually an important tool in the collection of strategies that we might use for mental or informal methods of doing subtraction calculations. But it does not have to be just 10 or 100 that you add. For instance, to work out 87 – 48 we could simply add 2 to both numbers and change it to 89 – 50, thus converting it into a much easier calculation. This adhocorithm can almost be developed into an algorithm that some children might find more to their liking than the formal method of decomposition. I call it the **constant difference method**, because as we change the subtraction into easier subtractions, we keep the difference between the numbers constant.

So, for example, returning to 802 – 247, we could proceed like this:

The problem is 802 – 247
Add 3 to both numbers: 805 – 250 (that makes it easier)
Add 50 to both numbers: 855 – 300 (that makes it really easy!)
So the answer is 555.

This approach can be combined where appropriate with subtracting the same thing from both numbers. For example, to calculate 918 – 436:

The problem is 918 – 436 (no problem with the units)
Subtract 6 from both: 912 – 430 (getting easier)
Add 70 to both numbers: 982 – 500 (really easy!)
So the answer is 482.

With a bit of practice, this method of converting the second number into a multiple of 10 or a multiple of 100 by adding the same thing to both numbers, or subtracting the same thing from both numbers, can become extremely efficient and just as quick as any other.

Research focus

A study of the errors made by 2500 children in the USA in the decomposition method for doing subtraction (Brown and Burton, 1978; Burton, 1981) identified the most common 'bugs'. These included: subtracting the smaller digit in a column from the larger, regardless of which one is on the top line; and writing zero in the answer in any column where the digit in the top line is smaller than the one in the second line (for example, '3 take away 5, cannot do it, so put down 0'). All the other most common bugs were in subtractions with a zero in the top number: crossing out the 0, replacing it with 9, but leaving the digit in the next column to the left unchanged; and using incorrect rules for subtracting from zero, for example, $0 - 4 = 4$ or $0 - 4 = 0$. If zero occurs in the tens column and exchange is needed to deal with the units, then common bugs were: skipping the zero and exchanging one hundred for ten ones; just inserting the required ten units without any exchanging at all; and exchanging from the tens column in the second number. All these can be observed in any primary classroom where the method of decomposition is taught as a meaningless procedure, a recipe to be learnt by rote, without the emphasis on understanding that has been promoted in this chapter. This research is usefully summarized by Resnick (1982).

Suggestions for further reading

1. Read the chapter by Brown entitled 'Influences on the teaching of number in England', in Anghileri (2001b). This historical survey of the ideological and social influences on the way number and calculations are taught in England sheds light on how the position and importance of standard written algorithms in the mathematics curriculum have varied over time, and how we have got to where we are today.
2. Section 3.7 of the research-based book by Dickson, Brown and Gibson (1984) deals with number operations and computational procedures. This section provides an informative summary of the problems associated with standard written algorithms (for all four operations) and the kinds of errors that children make most often. The reader should note the authors' tendency to use the term 'borrowing' inappropriately.
3. Part 3 of the guidance on teaching written calculations produced to support the Numeracy Strategy in England (QCA, 1999b) deals with addition and subtraction strategies.

Self-assessment questions

9.1: Using the same kind of explanation with coins as that given above, work through the addition of 208, 156 and 97.
9.2: Using the column addition layout in Figure 9.1(a), what would be the last line in the calculation of $357 + 587$?
9.3: Practise the explanation of the process of subtraction by decomposition using coins (1p, 10p and £1 to represent ones, tens and hundreds) and appropriate examples, such as $623 - 471$.
9.4: Using the column subtraction layout in Figure 9.6(b), what would be the last line in the calculation of $652 - 464$?
9.5: Practise the explanation of the process of decomposition using base-ten blocks to represent units, tens, hundreds and thousands, with examples with zero in the first number, such as $2006 - 438$.
9.6: Find the answer to $2006 - 438$ using the constant difference method.

Further practice

Glossary of key terms introduced in Chapter 9

Column addition and **column subtraction:** ways of setting out an addition or subtraction calculation in which the ones, tens, hundreds and thousands (and so on) in the numbers in the calculation are arranged in columns.

Carrying (one): in an addition calculation the process of replacing ten in one column by one in the column to the left; for example, 10 tens are replaced by 1 hundred, which is carried to the hundreds column.

Decomposition (subtraction): the column method of subtraction which uses the principle of exchange to overcome the difficulty caused when the digit to be subtracted in a particular column is less than the one it is being subtracted from; for example, if there are not sufficient tens in the top number to do the subtraction in that column, one of the hundreds is exchanged for 10 tens.

Equal additions: a formal procedure for doing subtraction calculations, based on the idea of adding 10 or 100 or 1000 (and so on) to both numbers, thus keeping the difference the same; the method is no longer taught in British primary schools because decomposition is easier to understand in terms of the manipulation of base-ten materials.

Constant difference method: an informal, ad hoc method for doing subtraction calculations, based on the idea that the difference between the two numbers does not change if you add the same number to both or subtract the same number from both.

10
Multiplication and Division Structures

In this chapter there are explanations of

- two different structures of real-life problems modelled by multiplication;
- the contexts in which children will meet these multiplication structures;
- the commutative law of multiplication;
- the idea of a rectangular array associated with multiplication;
- three different structures of real-life problems modelled by division; and
- the contexts in which children will meet these division structures.

What are the different kinds of situation to which the operation of multiplication applies?

This chapter is not about doing multiplication and division calculations, but focuses on understanding the mathematical structures of these operations. Chapters 10–12 follow the pattern used in Chapters 7–9 for addition and subtraction. First, in this chapter, we identify the range of situations that children have to learn to connect with the operations of multiplication and division. So here we are concerned essentially with step 1 of the modelling process introduced in Chapter 5: setting up the mathematical model corresponding to a given situation. Then in the following two chapters we will consider step 2 of the modelling process, the mental and written methods for doing multiplication and division calculations.

LEARNING and TEACHING POINT

Familiarity with the range of multiplication and division structures discussed in this chapter will enable children to interpret multiplication and division calculations in a variety of ways and hence increase their ability to handle these calculations by a range of mental and written methods.

We can identify at least two categories of situation that have a structure that corresponds to the mathematical operation represented by the symbol for multiplication. These two structures, which are essentially extensions of the two structures of addition discussed in Chapter 4, are

- the repeated aggregation structure; and
- the scaling structure.

As well as being the basis for their understanding of the operation itself, experience of these different structures associated with multiplication is essential for developing children's confidence in a range of mental and written calculation methods. For example, a key mental strategy for multiplication makes use of doubling, which is based on the scaling structure.

What is the repeated aggregation structure for multiplication?

Repeated aggregation (or repeated addition) is the elementary idea that multiplication means 'so many sets of' or 'so many lots of'. If I have '10 sets of 3 counters' then the question, 'how many counters altogether?', is associated with the multiplication, 3×10 (see Figure 10.1). This structure is simply an extension of the aggregation structure of addition, with, for example, the

repeated addition, $3 + 3 + 3 + 3 + 3 + 3 + 3 + 3 + 3 + 3$, becoming the multiplication, 3×10.

Figure 10.1 *Multiplication as repeated aggregation, 3×10*

What is the scaling structure for multiplication?

The **scaling** structure is a rather more difficult idea. It is an extension of the augmentation structure of addition. In that structure addition means increasing a quantity by a certain amount. With multiplication we also increase a quantity, but we increase it by a *scale factor*. So multiplication by 10 would be interpreted in this structure as scaling a quantity by a factor of 10, as illustrated in Figure 10.2.

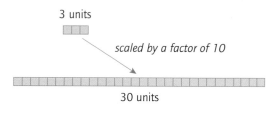

3 units

scaled by a factor of 10

30 units

Figure 10.2 *Multiplication as scaling, 3 × 10*

It should be mentioned here that multiplication by a number less than 1 would correspond to a scaling that *reduces* the size of the quantity, not increases it. For example, scaling 3 by a factor of 0.5 would reduce it to 1.5, corresponding to the multiplication, $3 \times 0.5 = 1.5$.

I'm not sure whether 3 × 5 means '3 lots of 5' or '5 lots of 3'

Which of the pictures in Figure 10.3 would we connect with 3 × 5? If I were to be really pedantic, I suppose I would have to say that, strictly speaking, 3 × 5 means '5 lots of 3'. You start with 3, and multiply it by 5. That is, you reproduce the three, five times in all, as illustrated in Figure 10.3(a). But I would prefer to let the meaning of the symbol be determined by how it is used. It seems to me that, in practice, people use the symbols 3 × 5 to mean both '3 lots of 5' and '5 lots of 3', in other words,

both the examples shown in Figures 7.3(a) and 7.3(b). I am happy therefore to let 3 × 5 refer to both (a) and (b). And the same goes for 5 × 3. One symbol having more than

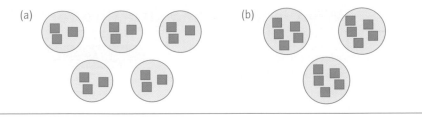

Figure 10.3   *(a) 5 sets of 3; (b) 3 sets of 5*

one meaning is something we have to learn to live with in mathematics – as well as being a feature that makes mathematical symbols so powerful in their application.

The underlying mathematical principle here is what is called the **commutative law of multiplication**. This refers to the fact that when you are multiplying two numbers together the order in which you write them down does not make any difference. We have already seen in Chapter 4 that addition also has this property. We recognize this commutative property formally by the following generalization, which is true whatever the numbers a and b: $b \times a = a \times b$.

LEARNING and TEACHING POINT

Teach children how to use the commutative principle to help in learning multiplications facts. For example, if they know seven 5s then they know five 7s.

There are two important points to note about the commutative property in relation to multiplication. First, it is important to realize that division does *not* have this property. For example, $10 \div 5$ is not equal to $5 \div 10$. Second, use of the commutative property enables us to simplify some calculations. For example, many of us would evaluate '5 lots of 14' by changing the question to the equivalent, '14 lots of 5' – because fives are much easier to handle than fourteens! Grasping the principle of commutativity also cuts down significantly the number of different results we have to memorize from the multiplication tables: for example, if I know the 9-times table, because it has such a strong pattern built into it, then I also know nine 7s (the same as seven 9s), nine 8s (the same as eight 9s), and so on.

Is there a picture that can usefully be connected with the multiplication symbol?

It is interesting to note first that the commutative property of multiplication is by no means obvious. Other than by counting the numbers in each picture, we would not immediately recognize that (a) and (b) in Figure 10.3 have the same number of counters. So this picture is not especially helpful. But there is one very significant picture of multiplication that does make this commutative property obvious. This is the association of multiplication with the image of a **rectangular array**. Figure 10.4 shows some examples of rectangular arrays that correspond to 3×5 (or 5×3). This is the image of

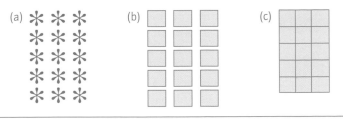

Figure 10.4 *Examples of rectangular arrays for 3 × 5*

multiplication that we should carry round in our heads, particularly when we want to talk to children about multiplication and to illustrate our discussions with diagrams. This picture really does make the commutative property transparently obvious. We can actually see that 3 sets of 5 and 5 sets of 3 come to the same thing, because the array can be thought of as 3 rows of 5, using vertical rows, or 5 rows of 3, using horizontal rows.

There are other good reasons for strongly associating this image of a rectangular array with multiplication. For example, this idea leads on naturally to the use of multiplication for determining the area of a rectangle. In example (c) in Figure 10.4, 3 × 5 gives the number of square units in the rectangle and therefore determines its area. We can extend this idea to develop an effective method for multiplying together larger numbers (scc Chapter 12).

Apart from 'so many sets of so many,' are there other contexts in which children meet multiplication in the repeated aggregation structure?

Any situation in which we aggregate a certain number of portions of a given quantity – such as mass, liquid volume, length and time – provides an application of this multiplication structure. For example: finding the total mileage for 42 journeys of 38 miles each (42 × 38); finding the total volume of drink required to fill 32 glasses if each holds 225 ml (32 × 225); finding the total time required for 12 events each lasting 25 minutes (12 × 25).

But, not surprisingly, the most important context will be shopping, particularly where we have to find the cost of a number of items given the *unit cost*. Two important words here are *each* and *per*. For example, we might need to find the cost of 25 cans of drink at 39p *each* (25 × 39). Or we might purchase 25 tickets at £3.50 *per* ticket (25 × 3.50). In both cases we have to associate the language and the structure of the example with

LEARNING and TEACHING POINT

Help children to use the word *per* with confidence and to associate the practical problems about *unit cost* and *cost per unit of measurement* with the corresponding multiplications.

the operation of multiplication. Then there are important situations where we encounter repeated aggregation in the context of *cost per unit of measurement*. For example, if we purchase 28 litres of petrol at £1.23 per litre, we should recognize that a multiplication (28 × 1.23) is required to determine the total cost, although in practice the petrol pump will do it for us. Likewise, we should connect multiplication with situations such as finding the cost of so many metres of material given the cost per metre, or someone's earnings for so many hours of work given the rate of pay per hour, and so on.

What are some of the contexts in which children will meet multiplication in the scaling structure?

Most obviously, this structure is associated with scale models and scale drawings. For example, if a scale model is built using a scale factor of 1 to 10, then each linear measurement in the actual object is 10 times the corresponding measurement in the model. Similarly, if we have made a plan of the classroom using a scale factor 1 to 100 and the width of the whiteboard in the drawing is 2 cm, then the width of the actual whiteboard will be 200 cm (2 × 100).

This is also the multiplication structure that lies behind the idea of a **pro rata increase**. For example, if we all get a 13% increase in our salary, then all our salaries get multiplied by the same scale factor, namely, 1.13 (see Chapter 19 for an explanation of percentage increases). The simplest experience of this structure is when we talk about *doubling* or *trebling* a given quantity: this is simply increasing the given quantity by applying the scale factors 2 or 3 respectively.

Then we also sometimes use this multiplication structure to express a comparison between two numbers or amounts, where we make statements using phrases such as 'so many times as much (or as many)' or 'so many times bigger (longer, heavier, and so on)'. For example, 125 × 3 would be the calculation corresponding to this situation: John earns £125 a week, but his brother earns three times as much; how much does his brother earn? The phrase *three times as much* is what should prompt the association with multiplication by 3.

What are the different kinds of situation to which the operation of division applies?

There is a wide range of situations in which we have to learn to recognize that the appropriate operation is division. These can be categorized into at least the following three structures:

- the equal-sharing structure;
- the inverse-of-multiplication structure; and
- the ratio structure.

As with the other operations of addition, subtraction and multiplication, it helps us to connect these mathematical structures with the operation of division if we ask ourselves the question: 'What is the calculation I would enter on a calculator in order to solve this problem?' In each case the answer will involve using the division key on the calculator. As we saw earlier, particularly with subtraction in Chapter 7, one of the difficulties in understanding the meanings of the symbols we use in mathematics is that one symbol can have a number of strikingly different meanings. This is certainly the case with the division symbol.

> **LEARNING and TEACHING POINT**
>
> Division is not just 'sharing'. Equal sharing is only one division structure. Teachers should not overemphasize the language and imagery of sharing at the expense of the other important language and imagery that is associated with division, particularly division as the inverse of multiplication.

What is the equal-sharing structure for division?

The **equal-sharing** structure refers to a situation in which a quantity is shared out equally into a given number of portions and we are asked to determine how many or how much there is in each portion. For example, 20 marbles might be *shared equally between* 4 children in a game, as shown in Figure 10.5. The calculation to be entered on a calculator to correspond to this situation is 20 ÷ 4. This is the structure that teachers most naturally connect with division and which is strongly associated with the language 'sharing' and 'how many (or how much) each?'

> **LEARNING and TEACHING POINT**
>
> The key phrases to use in problems with the equal-sharing structure of division are *sharing equally between* and *how many (much) each?*

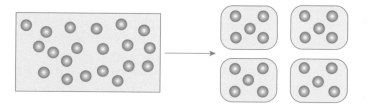

Figure 10.5 *Division as equal sharing, 20 ÷ 4*

What is the inverse-of-multiplication structure for division?

The **inverse-of-multiplication** structure interprets 20 ÷ 4 in a completely different way, as shown in Figure 10.6. Now the question being asked is: 'How many groups of 4 marbles are there in the set of 20 marbles?'

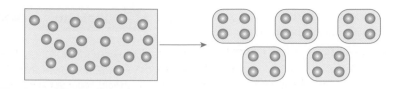

Figure 10.6   *Division as inverse of multiplication, 20 ÷ 4*

Figures 10.5 and 10.6 are equally valid interpretations of the division, 20 ÷ 4, even though they are answering two different questions:

Figure 10.5: share 20 equally into 4 groups. How many in each group? (equal sharing)
Figure 10.6: share 20 into groups of 4. How many groups? (inverse of multiplication)

The phrase 'inverse of multiplication' underlines the idea that division and multiplication are inverse processes – just as addition and subtraction were seen to be inverse processes in Chapter 7. This means, for example, that since 6 × 9 comes to 54, then 54 ÷ 9 must be 6. The division by 9 'undoes' the effect of multiplying by 9. Hence to solve a problem of the form 'what must *A* be multiplied by to give *B*?' we divide *B* by *A*. For example: how many tickets costing £1.50 each do I need to sell to raise £90? The calculation that must be entered on a calculator to solve this problem is the division, 90 ÷ 1.50.

The actual problems that occur in practice which have this inverse-of-multiplication structure can be further subdivided. First, there are problems that incorporate the notion of **repeated subtraction** from a given quantity, such as 'how many sets of 4 can I get from a set of 20?' So the process of sharing out the 20 marbles in the above example can be thought of as *repeatedly subtracting* sets of 4 marbles from the set of 20 until there are none left, counting the number of sets as you do this.

Second, there are those problems that incorporate the idea of **repeated addition** to reach a target, such as 'how many sets of 4 do you need to get a set of 20?'. For example, the question, 'how many groups of 4 marbles are there in a set of 20 marbles?' could mean, in practical terms, *repeatedly adding* sets of 4 marbles until the target of 20 is achieved, counting the number of sets required as you do this.

In Chapter 13 we shall see that this distinction between the repeated subtraction idea and the repeated addition idea in the inverse-of-multiplication structure is particularly significant when the answer to the division is not a whole number.

What is the ratio structure for division?

The **ratio** structure for division refers to situations where we use division to compare two quantities. In Chapter 7 we saw that in a situation where a comparison has to be made between two numbers, two sums of money or two measurements of some kind, one way to make the comparison is by subtraction, focusing on the *difference* between the quantities. For example, if A earns £300 a week and B earns £900 a week, one way of comparing them is to state that B earns £600 more than A, or A earns £600 less than B. The 600 is the result of the subtraction, 900 − 300. But we could also compare A's and B's earnings by looking at their *ratio*, stating, for example, that B earns *three times more* than A. The three here is now the result of the division, 900 ÷ 300. This process is simply the inverse of the scaling structure of multiplication described above, since what we are doing here is finding the scale factor by which one quantity must be increased in order to match the other. In the above example, the question would be, by what factor must 300 be multiplied to give 900?

What about remainders?

The reader may have noticed that all the examples of division used in this chapter so far have had whole-number answers and no **remainders**. In practice, most division questions do not work out nicely like this, of course. For example, a teacher may want to put the 32 children in her class into six equal groups for some activity. The mathematical model is '32 ÷ 6 − 5, remainder 2'. This means that sharing 32 equally into 6 groups gives 5 in each group, with 2 remaining not in a group. Alternatively, using the inverse-of-multiplication structure, the teacher's plan might be to put the 32 children into groups of 6. The mathematical model is again '32 ÷ 6 = 5, remainder 2', but now the interpretation is that there can be 5 groups of 6 children, with once again 2 children not in a group. Remainders do not occur where division is used to model situations with the ratio structure. For example, if we were calculating how many times greater than a journey of 6 km is a journey of 32 km, the division calculation is once again 32 ÷ 6, but the solution '5, remainder 2' would not make any sense in this context. The solution would have to be something like '5.33 times greater' (rounded to two decimal places). The interpretation and handling of remainders and rounding are covered in detail in Chapter 13.

What are some of the contexts in which children will meet division in the equal-sharing structure?

At first sight we might think that sharing is a very familiar experience for children: sharing sweets, sharing pencils, sharing books, sharing toys, and so on. But this idea of sharing a

LEARNING and TEACHING POINT

As far as possible, avoid talking about 'sharing' when explaining division. Instead, talk about 'sharing equally between'. Each word in this phrase is crucial to children's understanding of the equal-sharing structure.

set into subsets corresponds to division only under certain conditions. First, the set must be shared into *equal* subsets, which is certainly not always the case in children's experience of sharing. Second, it is important to note that the language is *sharing between* rather than *sharing with*. Children's normal experience is to share sets of things *with* a number of friends. Division requires sharing *between* a number of people. The division 12 ÷ 3 does not correspond to 'I have 12 marbles and I share them *with* my 3 friends'. The situation required is: 'Share 12 marbles equally *between* 3 people'. This is a somewhat artificial process and may not be encountered as often in the children's experience as we might imagine. So, sharing does not always correspond to division: it must be not just 'sharing', nor just 'sharing equally', but 'sharing equally between'.

In the context of measurement it is not difficult to come up with imaginary situations where we might share a given quantity into a number of equal portions. Cutting up a 750-cm length of wood into 6 equal lengths, or pouring out 750 ml of wine equally into 6 glasses, or sharing out 750 g of chocolate equally between 6 children, for example, all correspond to the division 750 ÷ 6. But these problems do feel like situations contrived for mathematics lessons rather than genuine problems.

The context of money does, however, provide some of the more natural examples in real life for this structure of the division operation. For example, a group of people might share a prize in a lottery, or share a bill in a restaurant: in both cases it is likely that we would *share equally between* the people in the group. An important class of everyday situations is where items are sold in multiple packs: a familiar requirement is to want to know the price per item. So, for example, if a shop is selling a pack of 9 blank CDs for £7.92, the cost per CD, in pence, is found by the division 792 ÷ 9. We can think to ourselves that a set of 792 pence is being shared equally between the 9 CDs.

LEARNING and TEACHING POINT

Children should experience all the division structures in a range of practical and relevant contexts, including especially shopping, rates of pay and the many kinds of problems associated with the word *per*, such as *price per unit*.

This then extends naturally to the idea of price per unit of measurement. For example, to find the cost per pint of a 6-pint bottle of milk costing 210p, we should recognize that the calculation to be entered on a calculator is the division, 210 ÷ 6. It is as though a set of 210 pence is being shared out equally between the 6 pints, giving 35p for each pint. Once again the word 'per', meaning 'for each', plays an important part in our understanding of this kind of situation.

This idea of 'per' turns up in numerous other situations in everyday life. For example, when calculating for a purchase how many or how much we get per penny or per pound, when finding miles per litre, determining how much someone earns per hour, an average speed in miles per hour, the number of words typed per minute, and so on: all these situations would correspond to the operation of division using the equal-sharing structure.

What are some of the contexts in which children will meet division in the inverse-of-multiplication structure?

There are many practical situations in which a set is to be sorted out into subsets of a given size and the question to be answered is, 'how many subsets are there?' For example, the head of a school with 240 children may wish to organize them into classes of 30 children. How many classes do we need? This is modelled by 240 ÷ 30, in other words, how many 30s make 240? Then the teacher with a class of 30 children may wish to organize them into groups of 5 children and asks: how many groups? This is modelled by 30 ÷ 5. In other words, how many 5s in 30?

Once again, the structure extends quite naturally into the context of money. A familiar question is: How many of these can I afford? This kind of question incorporates the idea of *repeated subtraction from a given quantity*. For example, how many items costing £6 each can I buy with £150? The question is basically 'how many 6s can I get out of 150?' We could imagine repeatedly spending (subtracting) £6 until all the £150 is used up. Similar situations occur in the context of measurement. For instance, the question, 'how many 150-ml servings of wine from a 750-ml bottle?' is an example of the inverse-of-multiplication structure of division, in the context of liquid volume and capacity, corresponding to the calculation, 750 ÷ 150. In other words, how many 150s make 750? Again the notion of repeated subtraction from a given quantity is evident here. We can imagine repeatedly pouring out (subtracting) 150-ml servings, until the 750 ml is used up.

Then there are problems in the context of money and measurement that ask the question: How many do we need? This kind of question incorporates the idea of *repeated addition to reach a target*. For example, how many items priced at £6 each must I sell to raise £150? We could imagine repeatedly adding £6 to our takings until we reach the target of £150. In spite of the language used, the problem is modelled by the division, 150 ÷ 6.

The word 'per' turns up again in this division structure. For example, if we know the price per kg of potatoes is £1.25 (125p), then we might find ourselves asking a question like, 'how many kilograms can I get for £10 (1000p)?' Similarly, if I save £1.25 (125p) per week, I might ask the question, 'how long will it take me to save £10?' Or, if the price of petrol is 125p per litre, the question might be, 'how many litres can I get for £10?' Each of these is, of course, an instance of 'how many 125s make 1000?', so they are again examples of the inverse-of-multiplication structure, corresponding in these cases to the division, 1000 ÷ 50.

Exactly the same mathematical structure occurs in finding the time for a journey given the average speed. For example, the question, 'how long will it take me to drive 1000 miles, if I average 50 miles per hour?', is equivalent to the question, 'how many 50s make 1000?', and hence, using the inverse-of-multiplication structure, to the division, 1000 ÷ 50.

What about situations using the ratio division structure?

LEARNING and TEACHING POINT

Primary children can be introduced to the idea of using division to find the ratio between two quantities in order to compare them, but the results are difficult to interpret if they are not whole numbers.

Many primary school children can learn to recognize the need to use division to compare two quantities by ratio. Situations where comparisons could be made between numbers in sets, between amounts of money or between measurements of various kinds are readily available. The problem is, however, that in practice, unless the questions are contrived carefully, the answers tend to be quite difficult to interpret. It's easy enough to deal with, say, comparing two children's journeys to school of 10 minutes and 30 minutes, and, using division (30 ÷ 10 = 3), making the statement that one child's journey is three times longer than the other. But it's a huge step from interpreting a statement like that with whole numbers to making sense of, say, comparing the heights of two children, 125 cm and 145 cm, using a calculator to do the division (145 ÷ 125 = 1.16), and concluding that one child is 1.16 times taller than the other.

Research focus

In a word problem like 'Spinach costs 65p a bag, how much for 3 bags?' the 65 is sometimes called the **multiplicand** (the number being multiplied) and the 3 the **multiplier**. The result of the multiplication is called the **product**. De Corte, Verschaffel and Van Coillie (1988) studied how well children aged 10 to 11 years could recognize multiplication structures in a series of word problems, involving whole numbers and decimals less than 1. They found that children were very successful (98%, 99%) in recognizing the operation required to be multiplication when the multiplier was a whole number, regardless of whether the multiplicand was a whole number or a decimal less than 1. But the facility dropped dramatically (to 32%) when the multiplicand was a whole number but the multiplier a decimal less than 1 (for example, 'Milk costs 90p a litre, how much for 0.8 litre?') The explanation for this is twofold. First, the idea of multiplication as repeated addition does not fit easily with a multiplier less than 1. Second, children seem to have the (mistaken) idea that multiplication always makes things bigger, whereas in this case the product is smaller than the multiplicand.

Suggestions for further reading

1. Chapter 4 of Haylock and Cockburn (2008) is about understanding multiplication and division. This chapter will provide the opportunity to visit again some of the ideas about multiplication and division structures explained above, from the perspective of teaching younger children.
2. Chapter 7 of Nunes and Bryant (1996) is entitled 'The progress to multiplication and division'. This is recommended for readers who want to dig more deeply into children's understanding of the ideas of multiplication and division. The authors show how multiplicative reasoning begins in children as young as 5 years and outline the development of children's understanding of multiplication and division through the primary age range, drawing on significant research in this field.
3. Wright et al. (2006) provide strategies for assessing younger children's understanding of early ideas of multiplication and division, and suggest ways of developing children's understanding of these operations.

Self-assessment questions

10.1: Give two problems associated with the multiplication 29 × 12, one using the idea of '29 lots of 12' and the other using '12 lots of 29'.
10.2: Make up a problem using the repeated aggregation structure and the word *per*, in the context of shopping, corresponding to the multiplication, 12 × 25.
10.3: A box of yoghurts consists of 4 rows of 6 cartons arranged in a rectangular array. How would you use this as an example to illustrate the commutative property of multiplication?
10.4: A model of an aeroplane is built on a scale of 1 to 25. Make up a question about the model and the actual aeroplane, using the scaling structure.
10.5: A headteacher earning £2827 a month gets a 12% pay rise. Model this situation with a multiplication by a scale factor and use a calculator to find her new monthly salary.
10.6: The real car is 300 cm long and the model car is 15 cm long: how many times longer is the real car? ('That is, what is the scale factor?') What is the calculation to be entered on a calculator to answer this? Of what division structure is this an example?
10.7: A sack of apples weighing 25 kilograms costs £12: what is the price per kilogram-weight of apples? What is the calculation to be entered on a calculator to answer this? Of what structure of division is this an example?

10.8:   How many CDs costing £12.50 each can I afford to buy with £100? What is the calculation to be entered on a calculator to answer this? Of what division structure is this an example?

10.9:   How many months do I need to save up £300 if I save £12 a month? What is the calculation to be entered on a calculator to answer this? Of what division structure is this an example?

10.10: Make up a problem that corresponds to the division, 60 ÷ 4, using the equal-sharing structure in the context of shopping.

10.11: Make up a problem that corresponds to the division, 60 ÷ 4, using the inverse-of-multiplication structure, incorporating the idea of repeated subtraction from a given quantity, in the context of shopping.

10.12: Make up a problem using the ratio structure in the context of salaries. Use a calculator to answer your own problem.

Further practice

From the Student Workbook

Tasks 39–41: Checking understanding of multiplication and division structures
Tasks 42–44: Using and applying multiplication and division structures
Tasks 45–47: Learning and teaching of multiplication and division structures

Glossary of key terms introduced in Chapter 10

Repeated aggregation: the process modelled by multiplication related to the idea of 'so many sets of so many'; also called repeated addition.

Scaling of quantity: the process modelled by multiplication in which a given quantity is increased by a scale factor; doubling and trebling are examples of scaling by factors of 2 and 3, respectively. Scaling by a factor less than 1 (for example, halving) reduces the size of the quantity.

Commutative law of multiplication: the principle that the order of two numbers in a multiplication calculation makes no difference. For example, $5 \times 7 = 7 \times 5$. In symbols, the commutative law of multiplication states that, whatever the numbers a and b, $a \times b = b \times a$.

Rectangular array: a set of objects or shapes arranged in rows and columns, in the shape of a rectangle; for example, 7 rows of 5 counters, or a 7 by 5 grid of squares. Rectangular arrays are important images to be associated with multiplication.

Per: an important word in multiplication and division situations, meaning 'for each'; used, for example, in problems about cost per unit of measurement.

Pro rata increase: an increase applied, for example, to salaries or prices, in which each amount is increased by the same scale factor.

Equal sharing: the process modelled by division in which a set of items or a given quantity is shared equally between a number of individuals; the key phrase in the equal-sharing structure of division is 'shared equally between'.

Inverse of multiplication: the process modelled by division in which the question is 'how many groups of a given number are there in a given set?' For example, 'how many 4s make 20?' corresponds to $20 \div 4$.

Repeated subtraction (division):   one of the ways of experiencing the inverse-of-multiplication structure of division by repeatedly subtracting a quantity from a given amount; for example, 'how many times can £6 be taken away from £24 until there is nothing left?' is connected with $24 \div 6$.

Repeated addition (division):   one of the ways of experiencing the inverse-of-multiplication structure of division by repeatedly adding a quantity to reach a given target; for example, 'how many payments of £6 are required to make a total of £24?' is connected with $24 \div 6$.

Ratio: the inverse of the scaling structure of multiplication, where division is used to compare two quantities; for example, the ratio of £36 to £12 is 3; this is represented by the division $36 \div 12 = 3$.

Remainder: in a division situation that does not work out exactly, the surplus number after an equal sharing or grouping has been completed. For example, $45 \div 7 = 6$, remainder 3. This could mean 45 shared equally between 7 gives 6 each, with 3 not shared out; or it could mean that 6 subsets of 7 can be made from a set of 42, with 3 not in a subset.

Multiplicand: the number or quantity that is to be multiplied – a word not often used nowadays.

Multiplier: the number by which a multiplicand is multiplied.

Product: the result of a multiplication; for example, the product of 37 and 27 is 999.

11
Mental Strategies for Multiplication and Division

In this chapter there are explanations of

- the commutative, associative, distributive laws of multiplication;
- the distributive laws of division;
- quotient, dividend and divisor;
- how these laws are used in multiplication and division calculation strategies;
- some prerequisite skills for being efficient in mental multiplication and division calculations;
- how factors can be used to simplify multiplications;
- how doubling can be used as an ad hoc approach to multiplication;
- the use of ad hoc additions and subtractions in multiplication and division; and
- the constant ratio method for a division calculation.

What are the commutative, associative and distributive laws of multiplication?

We have already met commutative laws, first in Chapter 7, where it was explained as a fundamental property of addition, and then in Chapter 10, where the corresponding commutative law of multiplication was explained in detail. In Chapter 8 the associative law of addition was explained. We now meet the **associative law of multiplication**. There are also two further important laws of multiplication, what are called the **distributive laws**.

For completeness, here are all four of the fundamental laws of multiplication, written formally as algebraic generalizations

Commutative law of multiplication:　$a \times b = b \times a$
Associative law of multiplication:　$(a \times b) \times c = a \times (b \times c)$
Distributive laws of multiplication:　$(a + b) \times c = (a \times c) + (b \times c)$
　　　　　　　　　　　　　　　　$(a - b) \times c = (a \times c) - (b \times c)$

whatever numbers are chosen for a, b and c.

Written down baldly, as they are above, the three fundamental laws of multiplication look a bit daunting and obscure. But, rather like Monsieur Jourdain in *Le Bourgeois Gentilhomme*, who discovered to his delight that he had been speaking prose for more than 40 years without knowing it, readers can be assured that they probably use one or another of these laws unconsciously every time they undertake a multiplication calculation!

How are these laws used in multiplication calculations?

The commutative law allows you to decide which of the two numbers in a multiplication question is the multiplicand and which the multiplier. Take as an example the calculation of 5×28. First, I might prefer to think of this as 28 fives, rather than five 28s, simply because I am better at my 5-times table than I am at my 28-times table. It is the commutative law that allows me to switch the order of two numbers in a multiplication freely like this:

$5 \times 28 = 28 \times 5$.

Now to work out 28×5, I could think of the 28 as 14×2, choose to do 2×5 first (to get 10) and then multiply this by 14 (that is, $14 \times 10 = 140$). What I am using here is the associative law. I am 'associating' the 2 with the 5, rather than with the 14, in order to make the calculation easier:

$(14 \times 2) \times 5 = 14 \times (2 \times 5)$.

An alternative approach to calculating 28×5 would be to split the 28 into $20 + 8$ and then to multiply the 20 and 8 separately by the 5, to get 100 and 40, which add up to 140. This is using the distributive law! The multiplication by 5 is being 'distributed' across the addition of 20 and 8. Written down formally the first step of this strategy might look like this:

$(20 + 8) \times 5 = (20 \times 5) + (8 \times 5)$.

Finally, we could choose to think of the 28 as $30 - 2$ and then 'distribute' the multiplication by 5 across this subtraction: 30×5 is 150, 2×5 is 10, so the answer is $150 - 10$, which is 140. This is using the second of the distributive laws of multiplication:

$(30 - 2) \times 5 = (30 \times 5) - (2 \times 5)$.

The commutative and associative laws together give us the freedom to rearrange two or more numbers in a product in any order we wish. For example,

$$
\begin{aligned}
(5 \times 3) \times 8 \quad &= 5 \times (3 \times 8) && \text{(using the associative law)} \\
&= 5 \times (8 \times 3) && \text{(using the commutative law)} \\
&= (5 \times 8) \times 3 && \text{(using the associative law)} \\
&= (8 \times 5) \times 3 && \text{(using the commutative law)} \\
&= 40 \times 3 = 120.
\end{aligned}
$$

This means that we can write down $5 \times 3 \times 8$ without any brackets, recognizing that we can multiply the numbers together in any order we like.

The distributive laws give us the option to deal with a complicated multiplication in easy stages, breaking up the numbers into easier components. We shall see below that these three laws are really all we need to become very efficient at multiplication with informal mental strategies.

What are quotients, dividends and divisors?

These are three technical words that are used in the context of division calculations. They correspond to the words used in multiplication, introduced at the end of the previous chapter: product, multiplicand and multiplier. **Quotient, dividend and divisor** are the terms used to identify the numbers in a division calculation. They are perhaps not often used in teaching, but it is useful to have them available here to help in explaining division strategies. The result of dividing one number by another is called the *quotient*. For example, if 56 is divided by 8 (that is, $56 \div 8 = 7$) the quotient is 7. The first number in the division, that which is to be divided (in this example, 56), is called the dividend. The number by which it is *divided* (in this example, 8) is called the *divisor*.

Are there any fundamental laws of division?

We have already noted in Chapter 10 that division (like subtraction) is not commutative. We should note here that division is also not associative (again like subtraction).

For example, $(24 \div 6) \div 2$ is not equal to $24 \div (6 \div 2)$. Dealing with the divisions in the brackets first, in the first of these we get the answer 2, whereas in the second we get the answer 8.

But, like multiplication, division can be *distributed* across addition and subtraction. There are the following two **distributive laws for division**:

Distributive laws of division:
$$(a + b) \div c = (a \div c) + (b \div c)$$
$$(a - b) \div c = (a \div c) - (b \div c)$$

whatever numbers are chosen for a, b and c (provided c does not equal 0).

The proviso about c not being equal to zero is because division by zero is not possible. Informally the first of these laws means that if the dividend can be thought of as the sum of two numbers $(a + b)$, then you can divide each of a and b separately by the divisor (c) and add up the results. And the second means that if the dividend can be thought of as the difference between two numbers $(a - b)$ then you can divide each of a and b separately by the divisor (c) and find the difference between the results.

Again, the reader should recognize these as the basis of some very familiar procedures in the way we handle division calculations. We often employ this principle to simplify division questions. For example, since $45 = 30 + 15$, you can split $45 \div 3$ into two easier divisions: $30 \div 3$ and $15 \div 3$, giving us 10 add 5, which is 15. Written formally, we see that it is the first of the distributive laws for division being used here:

$$(30 + 15) \div 3 = (30 \div 3) + (15 \div 3).$$

The trick here was to transform the 45 into $30 + 15$, being aware that with a divisor of 3, numbers like 30 and 15 are easily dealt with. In using the distributive law in an ad hoc approach we should always look for numbers that are easy to handle with the particular divisor. So, to take another example, when tackling $143 \div 11$, I might make use of the fact that 99 is a good number to have around when dividing by 11, and think of 143 as $99 + 44$ as follows:

$143 \div 11$	$= (99 + 44) \div 11$
$(99 + 44) \div 11$	$= (99 \div 11) + (44 \div 11)$ (using the distributive law)
	$= 9 + 4 = 13.$

Of course, there is no need to set out the working as formally as I have done here. It will probably be done mentally with a few numbers written down to keep track of where you are. Here is an example where we might use the same trick but with subtraction, for calculating $162 \div 9$. The trick here is to spot that 162 is not too far from 180, which is an easy number to divide by 9. So we think of 162 as $180 - 18$:

$$162 \div 9 \qquad = (180 - 18) \div 9$$
$$(180 - 18) \div 9 \qquad = (180 \div 9) - (18 \div 9) \text{ (using the distributive law)}$$
$$= 20 - 2 = 18.$$

Again, there is no need to set out the working in full like this, unless, like me, you are trying to explain your strategy to someone else.

What are the prerequisite skills for being efficient at mental strategies for multiplication and division?

The first prerequisite is that you know thoroughly and can recall instantly all the results in the multiplication tables up to 10×10. If you are still struggling with this basic knowledge then develop some strategies for working out what you do not know from what you do know.

For example, if you are not sure of the product of 6 and 8, start with $6 \times 2 = 12$, double it to get $6 \times 4 = 24$ and double it again to get $6 \times 8 = 48$. Then, if you cannot remember the product of 7 and 8, but you now know $6 \times 8 = 48$, you can get $7 \times 8 = 56$ by adding on another 8. Or you could use $5 \times 8 = 40$ and $2 \times 8 = 16$ to deduce that $7 \times 8 = 40 + 16$. As suggested in our discussion of learning to learn mathematics with understanding in Chapter 3, this is all about encouraging children to make connections.

> **LEARNING and TEACHING POINT**
>
> Make sure children are thoroughly confident with their multiplication tables up to 10×10 before they embark on multiplying bigger numbers and teach children some strategies for working out multiplication results they do not know from those they do know.

The second prerequisite is that you should be able to derive from any one of these results a whole series of results for multiplications involving multiples of 10 and 100. For example, knowing $7 \times 8 = 56$, we should be able to deduce the following:

$$
\begin{array}{rclcl}
70 & \times & 8 & = & 560 \\
7 & \times & 80 & = & 560 \\
70 & \times & 80 & = & 5600 \\
7 & \times & 800 & = & 5600 \\
700 & \times & 8 & = & 5600 \\
70 & \times & 800 & = & 56000 \\
700 & \times & 80 & = & 56000.
\end{array}
$$

It helps enormously just to notice that the total number of zeros written in the numbers on the left-hand side of each of these results is the same as the extra number of zeros written after the 56 on the right-hand side. To help understand this, using the example 700 × 80, we can think of the 700 as 7 × 100 and the 80 as 8 × 10. Then the whole calculation becomes: 7 × 100 × 8 × 10. Using the freedom granted to us by the commutative and associative laws of multiplication to rearrange this how we like, we can think of it as (7 × 8) × (100 × 10), which leads to 56 × 1000 = 56000.

The third prerequisite is that you should be able to recognize all the division results that are simply the inverses of any of the above results. For example:

$$56 \div 8 = 7$$
$$56 \div 7 = 8$$
$$560 \div 8 = 70$$
$$5600 \div 70 = 80$$
$$56000 \div 800 = 70$$

Once you have these skills in place you will be able to use a wide range of strategies, such as:

- the use of factors as an ad hoc approach to multiplication;
- the use of doubling as an ad hoc approach to multiplication;
- ad hoc additions and subtractions in multiplication;
- ad hoc additions and subtractions in division; and
- the constant ratio method for division.

How can factors be used as an ad hoc approach to multiplication?

When we think of a number such as 6 as 3 × 2 we are splitting it up into what are called **factors**. A factor of any natural number is a natural number by which it can be divided exactly without any remainder; factors are discussed in more detail in Chapter 14. As we have already seen above, we can use the associative law to enable us to multiply by each factor in turn, in order to simplify a product.

For example, one way to tackle 37×6 would be to think of the 6 as 3×2:

$$37 \times 6 = 37 \times (3 \times 2)$$
$$= (37 \times 3) \times 2 \quad \text{(using the associative law)}$$
$$= 111 \times 2 = 222.$$

This strategy is particularly effective when there are numbers ending in 5 around, since they are especially easy to multiply by 2 or 4. For example, to calculate 26×15, I would jump at the opportunity to make use of the fact that $2 \times 15 = 30$. To achieve this, we split the 26 into factors as 13×2:

$$26 \times 15 = (13 \times 2) \times 15$$
$$= 13 \times (2 \times 15) \quad \text{(using the associative law)}$$
$$= 13 \times 30 = 390.$$

Similarly, when I see 25 in a multiplication, such as 25×32, I immediately look to see if I can use the fact that $25 \times 4 = 100$. In this example, we can get the 4 we are looking for by splitting the 32 into factors as 4×8:

$$25 \times 32 = 25 \times (4 \times 8)$$
$$= (25 \times 4) \times 8 \quad \text{(using the associative law)}$$
$$= 100 \times 8 = 800.$$

Again, it should be stressed that I am writing these out in detail only to explain the mathematical basis of what will be essentially a mental process. Figure 11.1 shows some examples of an 11-year-old using factors to assist with some multiplications, writing down her method in a way that shows her thinking to someone else.

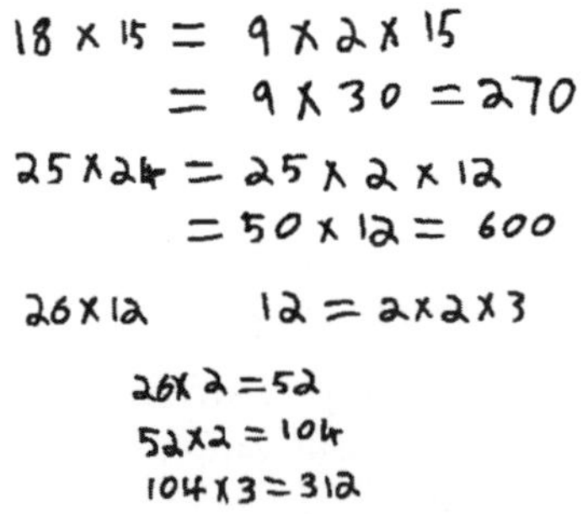

$$18 \times 15 = 9 \times 2 \times 15$$
$$= 9 \times 30 = 270$$
$$25 \times 24 = 25 \times 2 \times 12$$
$$= 50 \times 12 = 600$$
$$26 \times 12 \qquad 12 = 2 \times 2 \times 3$$
$$26 \times 2 = 52$$
$$52 \times 2 = 104$$
$$104 \times 3 = 312$$

Figure 11.1   *An 11-year-old using factors in multiplication*

How can doubling be used as an ad hoc approach to multiplication?

We have previously noted (in Chapter 8) that we can make use of our confidence in doubling numbers in informal approaches to additions and subtractions. We can also deal with *any* multiplication with whole numbers simply by a process of doubling! Approaches to multiplication based on doubling have in fact been around much longer than has what people regard as the 'traditional' method for long multiplication. The trick here is

to note that any number can be obtained by adding together some of the following numbers (called the powers of 2): 1, 2, 4, 8, 16, 32, 64 … and so on. For example, 23 = 16 + 4 + 2 + 1. This means that we can multiply a number by 23 (using the distributive law) in bits, multiplying by 16, 4, 2 and 1, and adding up the results. For example, to calculate 26 × 23 the working might look like this:

First, by repeatedly doubling the 26 and then selecting the results for the multipliers that add to 23 (16, 4, 2 and 1):

$$26 \times 1 = 26$$
$$26 \times 2 = 52$$
$$26 \times 4 = 104$$
$$26 \times 8 = 208$$
$$26 \times 16 = 416$$
$$\text{So, } 26 \times 23 = 416 + 104 + 52 + 26 = 598.$$

Again, I have provided more detail than would be necessary for an informal calculation, as illustrated in Figure 11.2 in which an 11-year-old uses this method in a shopping context.

Figure 11.2 *Using doubling to find the cost of 13 items at £17 each*

How can you use ad hoc additions and subtractions in multiplication

As with all calculations we can always make use of those number facts and relationships with which we are confident to find our own individual approaches that make sense to us. Again there is great value in encouraging children, even in primary schools, to build on their growing confidence with number to develop their own approaches and to share different approaches to the same calculation. The distributive law gives us the freedom to break up a number in a multiplication calculation in any way we like, using an ad hoc combination of additions and subtractions of whatever numbers are easiest to handle.

For instance, here are two ad hoc ways of evaluating 26 × 34. First, by breaking up the 26 into 10 + 10 + 2 + 2 + 2, on the basis that I am confident in multiplying by 10 and by 2, we can transform 26 × 34 into (10 × 34) + (10 × 34) + (2 × 34) + (2 × 34) + (2 × 34), as follows:

$$
\begin{aligned}
10 \times 34 &= 340 \\
10 \times 34 &= 340 \\
2 \times 34 &= 68 \\
2 \times 34 &= 68 \\
2 \times 34 &= 68 \\
\text{So, } 26 \times 34 &= 884
\end{aligned}
$$

Visually, this method is represented by the diagram in Figure 11.3. The trick in this kind of approach is to make sure you only ever multiply by easy numbers, like 1, 2, 5 and 10.

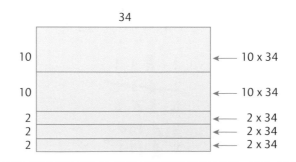

Figure 11.3   *An ad hoc approach to 26 × 34 (diagram not to scale)*

A second ad hoc approach to this calculation would be to think of the 34 as 10 + 10 + 10 + 5 – 1, so that 26 × 34 becomes (26 × 10) + (26 × 10) + (26 × 10) + (26 × 5) – (26 × 1), as follows:

$$
\begin{aligned}
26 \times 10 &= 260 \\
26 \times 10 &= 260 \\
26 \times 10 &= 260 \\
\underline{26 \times 5} &= \underline{130} \\
\text{So, } 26 \times 35 &= 910 \quad \text{(adding, to get thirty-five 26s)} \\
\underline{26 \times 1} &= \underline{26} \quad \text{(one 26 to be subtracted)} \\
\text{So, } 26 \times 34 &= 884
\end{aligned}
$$

LEARNING and TEACHING POINT

Provide children with plenty of practice in mental multiplication by 1, 2, 5, 10, 20 and 50: this is all that is required by way of multiplication to be efficient in doing multiplications and divisions using ad hoc addition and subtraction.

And how can you use ad hoc additions and subtractions in division?

You can sometimes make a division much simpler by writing it as the sum or difference of numbers that are easier to divide by the given divisor. For example, if you have your wits about you, given 608 ÷ 32 you might spot that it would have been much nicer if the question had been 640 ÷ 32 (answer 20). So, we could deal with this division as follows:

$$
\begin{aligned}
608 \div 32 &= (640 - 32) \div 32 \\
&= (640 \div 32) - (32 \div 32) \\
&= 20 - 1 = 19.
\end{aligned}
$$

In practice, the context of the problem that gave rise to the calculation will often suggest an appropriate ad hoc approach. For example, in Figure 11.4 a child is calculating how many classes of 32 children would be needed for a school of 608. The child's approach is to build up to the given total of 608, by an ad hoc process of addition, using

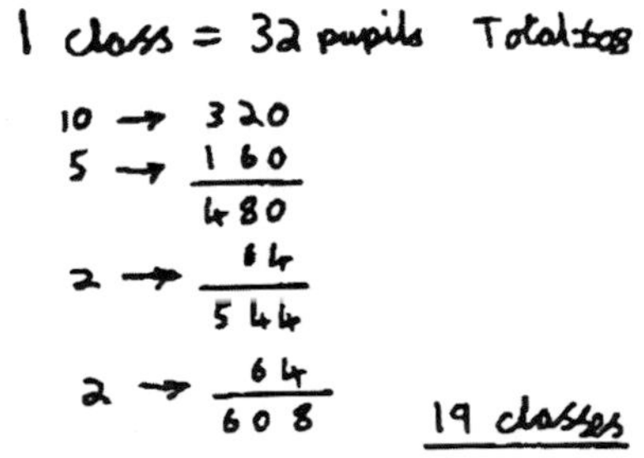

Figure 11.4 *Ad hoc addition used to solve a division problem*

first 10 classes, then another 5, then a further 2 and another 2. Formally, the child is breaking the 608 up into $320 + 160 + 64 + 64$ and distributing the division by 32 across this addition as follows:

$$608 \div 32 = (320 + 160 + 64 + 64) \div 32$$
$$= (320 \div 32) + (160 \div 32) + (64 \div 32) + (64 \div 32)$$
$$= 10 + 5 + 2 + 2 = 19.$$

The child's own way of writing down the thinking involved is clear and is, of course, perfectly acceptable. Many children are very successful in dealing with division calculations by this kind of ad hoc addition, building up to the given target. In the next chapter I will explain how an approach based on ad hoc subtraction can be used to develop an efficient written method for division calculations.

What is the constant ratio method for division?

We have here a parallel with the constant difference method for subtraction explained in Chapter 9. We make use of this important principle: that we do not change the answer to a division calculation if we multiply both the numbers by the same thing. To understand the **constant ratio method of division** think of the division in terms of the ratio structure: if both quantities are scaled by the same factor, then their ratio does not change – just as when you add the same thing to two numbers their difference does not change. For instance, all these divisions give the same result as $6 \div 2$ ($= 3$), because in each case the two numbers 6 and 2 have been multiplied by the same scale factor:

$60 \div 20$	(multiply both numbers by 10)
$12 \div 4$	(multiply both numbers by 2)
$30 \div 10$	(multiply both numbers by 5)
$6000 \div 2000$	(multiply both numbers by 1000).

This principle can be illustrated in the context of money. For example, imagine that we are comparing two prices, £3.75 and £1.25, by dividing one by the other to find the ratio. If we change the prices into pence (multiplying both numbers by 100) the ratio stays the same: $3.75 \div 1.25 = 375 \div 125$.

The division $75 \div 5$ can be used to demonstrate the application of this principle. Multiply both numbers by 2 and the question becomes: $150 \div 10$. So the answer is clearly 15. This approach is particularly useful when it comes to divisions involving decimals, as we shall see in Chapter 18. For example, to handle 6 ÷ 1.5, which looks tricky, we could multiply both numbers by 2, to give 12 ÷ 3, which is easy!

We can also use the reverse principle: that we do not change the answer to a division calculation if we *divide* both the numbers by the same thing. I might use this principle if I was dealing with, for example, 648 ÷ 24, as follows:

648 ÷ 24 is the same as 324 ÷ 12   (dividing both numbers by 2)
324 ÷ 12 is the same as 108 ÷ 4   (dividing both numbers by 3)
108 ÷ 4 is the same as 54 ÷ 2   (dividing both numbers by 2), which is 27.

These two principles can be combined, as in the following example, where I might spot that multiplying both numbers by 2 would turn 225 ÷ 15 into an easier question:

225 ÷ 15 = 450 ÷ 30 (multiplying both numbers by 2)
        = 45 ÷ 3   (dividing both numbers by 10)
        = 15.

Although this constant ratio method is mathematically sound, the reader should be warned that it could lead you astray if you are dealing with a division that does not work out exactly and you wish to give the answer *with a remainder*. For example, if the question was 48 ÷ 5 and you doubled both numbers you would produce the equivalent ratio 96 ÷ 10. The exact value of this quotient (9.6) is indeed the correct answer to 48 ÷ 5. However, 96 ÷ 10 expressed as '9, remainder 6' is not the correct result for 48 ÷ 5, because the remainder has been doubled as well.

In Chapter 17, we shall use this principle (that you do not change the ratio if you multiply or divide both numbers by the same thing) in explaining the idea of equivalent fractions.

Research focus

Squire, Davies and Bryant (2004) studied the ability of children aged 9 and 10 years to use the commutative and distributive laws in multiplication questions. The children showed a much better than expected understanding of commutativity, but a very poor grasp of the distributive law. A question would be preceded by a cue, designed to prompt the application of the distributive law. For example, for the question, 'How many squares in a bar of chocolate 27 squares long and 21 squares wide?' the following cue would be given: 'In a bar of chocolate that is 26 squares long and 21 squares wide there are altogether 546 squares.' The most common response was to select the answer 547 from the available options. The children tended therefore to think that adding one to one of the numbers in the multiplication added one to the answer. This is a major possible misunderstanding on which to focus explicitly in teaching mental strategies for multiplication.

Suggestions for further reading

1. Chapter 4 of Fraser and Honeyford (2000), written in a clear and straightforward style that can be understood by non-professionals, provides an outline of the more informal approaches to written calculations (for all four operations) that are now being embraced by many primary schools.
2. Part 4 of the guidance on teaching mental calculation strategies produced to support the Numeracy Strategy in England (QCA, 1999a) deals with multiplication and division. Skills and strategies discussed include knowledge of multiplication and division facts, multiplying and dividing by multiples of 10 and by single-digit numbers, multiplying by 2-digit numbers, doubling and halving.
3. Robinson's chapter on 'Teaching mental calculations', in Koshy and Murray (2002) provides practical guidance on teaching mental strategies for all four operations. It encourages teachers to encourage children to think flexibly about and structure numbers.

Self-assessment questions

11.1:   What is the product of 1, 2, 3, 4 and 5?
11.2:   A carton holds 6 bottles of squash. I have 288 bottles to put in cartons. How many cartons will I need? In the division calculation arising from this problem, which number is the dividend, which the divisor and which the quotient?
11.3:   How would the commutative law help in calculating the number of children in 25 groups of 16?
11.4:   Shozna calculated 25×24 by writing it as $25 \times (4 \times 6)$ and then using the associative law. Complete Shozna's calculation.
11.5:   Sam calculated 25×24 by writing it as $25 \times (20 + 4)$ and then using the distributive law. Complete Sam's calculation.
11.6:   Bev calculated 22×38 by writing it as $22 \times (40 - 2)$ and then using the distributive law. Complete Bev's calculation.
11.7:   Deduce eight other multiplication results, involving 4, 40, 400, 9, 90 and 900, from the result $4 \times 9 = 36$.
11.8:   Use an ad hoc method, based on factors, to find 48×25.
11.9:   Use the fact that $26 = 2 + 8 + 16$ and the doubling strategy to find 103×26.
11.10: Use the fact that $26 = 10 + 10 + 2 + 2 + 2$ to find 103×26.

11.11: Use the distributive law and the fact that $154 = 88 + 66$ to find the answer to $154 \div 22$; now do this again using the fact that $154 = 220 - 66$.

11.12: Find $483 \div 21$ by ad hoc addition of groups of 21, building up to the total of 483.

11.13: Find $385 \div 55$ by using the constant ratio method.

Further practice

From the Student Workbook

Tasks 48–50: Checking understanding of mental strategies for multiplication and division

Tasks 51–53: Using and applying mental strategies for multiplication and division

Tasks 54–56: Learning and teaching of mental strategies for multiplication and division

On the website (www.sagepub.co.uk/haylock)

Check-Up 12: The distributive laws

Check-Up 18: Mental calculations, multiplication strategies

Check-Up 19: Mental calculations, division strategies

Glossary of key terms introduced in Chapter 11

Associative law of multiplication: the principle that if there are three numbers to be multiplied together it makes no difference whether you start by multiplying the first and second, or by multiplying the second and third. In symbols, this law states that, for any three numbers a, b and c, $(a \times b) \times c = a \times (b \times c)$.

Distributive laws of multiplication: the laws that allow you to distribute a multiplication across an addition or across a subtraction. For example, 28×4 can be split up into 25×4 add 3×4, or 30×4 subtract 2×4. Formally, the laws state that for any numbers, a, b and c, then $(a + b) \times c = (a \times c) + (b \times c)$ and $(a - b) \times c = (a \times c) - (b \times c)$.

Quotient, divisor and dividend: technical names for the three numbers involved in a division calculation; for example, in $999 \div 37 = 27$, the 999 is the dividend, 37 is the divisor and 27 is the quotient.

Distributive laws of division: the laws that allow you to distribute a division across an addition or across a subtraction. For example, $92 \div 4$ can be split up into $80 \div 4$ add $12 \div 4$, or $100 \div 4$ subtract $8 \div 4$. Formally, the laws state that for any numbers, a, b and c (provided c is not zero), then $(a + b) \div c = (a \div c) + (b \div c)$ and $(a - b) \div c = (a \div c) - (b \div c)$.

Factor: a natural number by which a given natural number can be divided exactly, without a remainder; for example, 7 is a factor of 28.

Constant ratio method for division: a method for simplifying a division calculation by multiplying the dividend and the divisor by the same thing, or by dividing them by the same thing, thus keeping the ratio the same. For example, $180 \div 15$ can be simplified to $360 \div 30$, by doubling both numbers; and $360 \div 30$ can then be simplified to $36 \div 3$, by dividing both numbers by 10.

12
Written Methods for Multiplication and Division

 In this chapter there are explanations of

- the long multiplication algorithm;
- a simpler method for multiplication using areas of rectangles;
- the grid method for multiplication;
- the difficulty of understanding long division;
- the ad hoc subtraction method of doing division calculations; and
- the algorithm known as short division.

How do you make sense of long multiplication?

The standard algorithm for multiplying together two numbers with two or more digits is usually called **long multiplication**. Figure 12.1 shows how the method might be set out for calculating 26×34.

$$
\begin{array}{r}
2\,6 \\
\times\,3\,4 \\
\hline
7\,8\,0 \\
1\,0\,4 \\
\hline
8\,8\,4 \\
\hline
\end{array}
$$

7 8 0 ◄——— this is 26×30
1 0 4 ◄——— this is 26×4
8 8 4 ◄——— this is 26×34

Figure 12.1 *Long multiplication, 26×34*

The method is based on the distributive law for multiplication distributed over addition, explained in the previous chapter. Effectively what happens is that one of the numbers is broken up into the sum of its tens and units, and the multiplication by the other number is distributed across these. Applying this principle to 26 × 34, we can think of it as 26 × (30 + 4) and get the answer by multiplying the 26 first by the 30 and then by the 4, and then adding up the results. This is precisely what goes on in long multiplication, as shown in Figure 12.1. But the problem with the method is that multiplications like 26 × 30 and 26 × 4 are themselves quite difficult calculations and there is consequently some potential for errors and confusion.

So is there a simpler method for multiplication of two-digit numbers that is easier to understand?

Yes, of course there is a simpler method! It is based on the idea of splitting up *both* the numbers being multiplied into tens and units. So the 26 becomes 20 + 6 and the 34 becomes 30 + 4. Then we have to multiply the 20 by the 30, the 20 by the 4, the 6 by the 30 and the 6 by the 4. To make sense of this we can visualize the multiplication as a question of finding the number of counters in a rectangular array of 26 by 34 (see Chapter 10), as shown in Figure 12.2. Thinking of the 26 and the 34 as 20 + 6 and 30 + 4

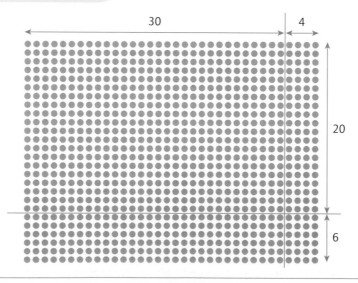

Figure 12.2 *A simpler approach for 26 × 34*

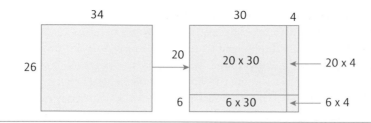

Figure 12.3 *Using area to interpret 26 × 34*

respectively suggests that we can split the array up into four separate rectangular arrays of counters, representing 20 × 30, 20 × 4, 6 × 30 and 6 × 4.

Drawing pictures with hundreds of counters in them, like Figure 12.2, helps to explain the method, but it is clearly very tedious. A more efficient picture, therefore, uses the idea, suggested in Chapter 10, that we can extend the notion of a rectangular array into that of the area of a rectangle. We can then explain 26 × 34 very simply using the diagram shown in Figure 12.3. The answer to the multiplication is then obtained by working out the areas of the four separate rectangles and adding them up. This can be called the **areas method** for multiplication. The actual calculation can be written out as follows:

$$
\begin{aligned}
20 \times 30 &= 600 \\
6 \times 30 &= 180 \\
20 \times 4 &= 80 \\
6 \times 4 &= 24 \\
\hline
&\; 884
\end{aligned}
$$

Once you have grasped this approach, it becomes unnecessary to draw the rectangles every time. The steps in the calculation can be set out in a grid, as shown below. Because of this, many teachers call this the **grid method**:

	30	4
20	600	80
6	180	24

780 + 104 = 884

Can this method be used with three-digit numbers?

The method extends quite easily to multiplications involving three-digit numbers. Figure 12.4 shows a rough sketch that might be used to visualize 348 × 25. (The rectangles in the

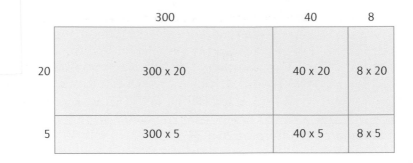

Figure 12.4   *The area approach applied to 348 × 25*

diagram are not drawn to scale.) Clearly, in this example, there are now six bits to deal with separately, and then to be added. This leads to the calculation being set out, for example, as follows, with the six products in the right hand column being summed to give 348 × 25 = 8700.

$$
\begin{aligned}
300 \times 20 &= 6000 \\
40 \times 20 &= 800 \\
8 \times 20 &= 160 \\
300 \times 5 &= 1500 \\
40 \times 5 &= 200 \\
8 \times 5 &= 40 \\
\hline
&\,8700
\end{aligned}
$$

> **LEARNING and TEACHING POINT**
>
> Note again the importance of children being thoroughly confident in multiplication with multiples of 10 and 100 (for example, 300 × 20) as a prerequisite for going on to multiply two- and three-digit numbers. Keep reinforcing these basic skills.

Using the grid format, the steps in this calculation could be set out as follows:

	300	40	8	
20	6000	800	160	
5	1500	200	40	
	7500 +	1000 +	200	= 8700

Multiplications of this level of difficulty are about as far as most primary school children would need to go.

What about long division?

The conventional algorithm for division, usually known as **long division**, can involve some tricky multiplications and is, to say the least, not easy to make sense of. Figure 12.5 illustrates the method for 648 ÷ 28. I'll talk you through this. The first step is to ask how many 24s are there in 64? The answer to this question is 2, which is written above the 4 in

648. You then write the product of 2 and 24 (48) under the 64 and subtract, giving 16. The 8 in the 648 is then dragged down and written next to the 16, making 168 in this row. You then ask how many 24s are there in 168? The answer to this is 7, which is written above the 8 in 648. You then write the product of 7 and 24 (168) under the 168 and subtract it, giving zero. So 648 ÷ 24 = 27, with no remainder. That's what you do, but does it make much sense? It really is quite difficult to explain what is going on here. What are you actually doing when you divide the 24 into 64? What does the 48 mean?

$$
\begin{array}{r}
27 \\
24\overline{)648} \\
48 \\
\overline{168} \\
168 \\
\overline{0}
\end{array}
$$

Figure 12.5　*Long division, 648 ÷ 24*

Why do you have to write various numbers where you write them? If you can successfully get children to master this method you will probably have to rely on rote learning rather than learning with understanding, which as we have seen in Chapter 3 undermines the priority we would give to children learning how to learn mathematics.

Is there a simpler alternative that makes more sense?

In my view, long division is a method that could well be laid to rest in the twenty-first century. With the ready availability of calculators we do not need to be able to do complicated divisions by paper-and-pencil algorithms. I would encourage therefore the use of a more ad hoc method, described below, which builds on the mental and informal approaches to division discussed in Chapter 11. It works very well with problems up to the level of difficulty with which most people should be able to cope – dividing a three-digit number by a two-digit number. The **ad hoc subtraction** approach (sometimes called 'chunking') builds on the individual's personal confidence with multiplication and the process is easily understood.

So, we will look again at the division, 648 ÷ 24. The method uses the inverse-of-multiplication structure and the idea of repeated subtraction, explained in Chapter 10. Hence the question is interpreted as: how many 24s make 648? (Not 'share 648 between 24'.) We approach this step by step, using whatever multiplications we are confident with, repeatedly subtracting from the dividend various multiples of the divisor, in an ad hoc manner.

For example, we should know easily that ten 24s make 240. We subtract this 240 from the 648. That leaves us with 408 to find. At this stage our working might be as shown in

	(a)		648 ÷ 24		(b)		648 ÷ 24		(c)		648 ÷ 24		(d)		648 ÷ 24

(a)
10	648 ÷ 24
	240
	408

(b)
10	648 ÷ 24
	240
	408
10	240
	168

(c)
10	648 ÷ 24
	240
	408
10	240
	168
2	48
	120

(d)
10	648 ÷ 24
	240
	408
10	240
	168
2	48
	120
2	48
	72
2	48
	24
1	24
27	0

Figure 12.6   *Ad hoc subtraction approach to 648 ÷ 24*

Figure 12.6(a). Try another ten 24s. That's a further 240, leaving us with 168, as shown in Figure 12.6(b). We do not have enough for a further ten 24s, so we might try two 24s (or one 24, if we prefer it, or whatever we are confident to do mentally). This gives us the situation shown in Figure 12.6(c). And so we proceed, until we have used up all the 648, as shown in Figure 12.6(d). Totting up the numbers of 24s we've used down the left-hand side gives us the answer to the calculation: $10 + 10 + 2 + 2 + 2 + 1 = 27$.

Someone with greater confidence with multiplication might get to the result more quickly, as shown in Figure 12.7. Here I have gone straight in with twenty 24s (that is, $20 \times 24 = 480$), followed this up with five 24s (that is, $5 \times 24 = 120$) and finished off with two 24s (that is, $2 \times 24 = 48$). The beauty of this method is that each individual can approach the calculation in a way that suits them and draws on their personal level of confidence with number relationships. We should note, however, that you would not get far with this method for division by a two-digit number if you were

> **LEARNING and TEACHING POINT**
>
> Provide children with plenty of practice in mental multiplication by 1, 2, 5, 10, 20 and 50: this is all that is required by way of multiplication to be efficient in doing divisions by the ad hoc repeated subtraction method. Children who are not fluent in subtraction are not yet ready to go on to written methods for division calculations.

20	648 ÷ 24
	480
	168
5	120
	48
2	48
27	0

Figure 12.7   *648 ÷ 24 with fewer steps*

not fluent in subtraction. And it also helps to be really at ease with multiplying by at least 1, 2, 5, 10, 20 and 50. The reader should compare this method with the reverse process of ad hoc addition of multiples of the divisor building up to the given dividend, explained in the previous chapter.

Does this method work when there's a remainder?

Yes. Take as an example 437 ÷ 18 (Figure 12.8). This time I have started with twenty 18s, because I can do that in my head easily (20 × 18 = 360), then followed it up with two 18s and a further two 18s. At this stage I am left with 5. Since this is less than the divisor, 18, I can go no further. The answer to the question is therefore '24 remainder 5'. The meaning of this answer will, of course, depend on the actual practical situation that gave rise to the calculation. Remainders in various division situations are discussed in Chapter 13.

$$
\begin{array}{r|l}
 & 437 \div 18 \\
\hline
20 & 360 \\
\hline
 & 77 \\
2 & 36 \\
\hline
 & 41 \\
2 & 36 \\
\hline
24 & \text{rem } 5
\end{array}
$$

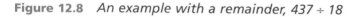

Figure 12.8 *An example with a remainder, 437 ÷ 18*

What about short division?

Short division is the standard algorithm often used for dividing by a single-digit number. It can be demonstrated clearly using the equal-sharing structure for division and either coins (1p, 10p and £1) or base-ten blocks to represent the numbers. For example, Figure 12.9 shows the division, 75 ÷ 5, interpreted with 10p and 1p coins. The 7 tens and 5 ones in the dividend are to be shared equally between five recipients.

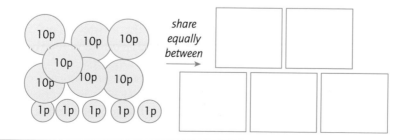

Figure 12.9 *Interpreting 75 ÷ 5*

In Figure 12.10, 1 ten has been given to each of the five recipients and the remaining 2 tens have been exchanged for 20 ones. There is therefore a total of 25 ones still to be shared out. When this is done each recipient gets 1 ten and 5 ones. Hence the answer is clearly 15.

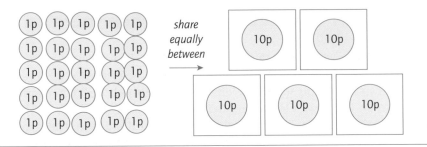

Figure 12.10 *Dealing with the tens for 75 ÷ 5*

One of the standard ways of recording this process is shown in Figure 12.11. The little 2 represents the 2 tens that have been exchanged for 20 ones; written in front of the 5, it indicates that at that stage there are 25 ones to be shared out. The 15 written above the line represents the 1 ten and 5 ones that each of the recipients gets when 75 is shared between five.

$$\begin{array}{r} 1\;5 \\ 5\overline{)7\;{}^{2}5} \end{array}$$

Figure 12.11 *Short division, 75 ÷ 5*

LEARNING and TEACHING POINT

You might wish to teach short division as a method for dividing by a single-digit number, explaining the procedure with coins or base-ten blocks. Or you might decide to teach only the ad hoc subtraction method, using this for both single-digit and two-digit divisors.

The problem with this explanation is that, in practice, when using the short division algorithm, particularly with bigger numbers, you probably do not use the equal-sharing structure consistently, but switch between this and the inverse-of-multiplication structure. So, for example, in Figure 12.12(a), tackling 438 ÷ 6, the first question I find myself asking might be: can I share 4 (hundreds) between 6? Since the answer is 'no' (at least, not without breaking down the hundreds into tens), I exchange these 4 hundreds for 40 tens, giving a total of 43 tens, and so I am now looking at '43 tens to be shared between 6'. I now find myself saying: How many 6s in 43? I have switched from sharing to inverse of multiplication. The answer is 7 with 1 (ten) remaining, which is exchanged for 10 ones, giving a total of 18 ones still to be shared out between the 6. Again, I will probably switch to inverse

Figure 12.12 *Short division, 438 ÷ 6*

of multiplication and think: How many 6s in 18? The calculation is completed as shown in Figure 12.12(b). But the explanation gets unwieldy and very wordy.

Many primary teachers opt to teach older children the short division algorithm for dividing by single-digit numbers but teach the ad hoc subtraction method I have outlined above for divisions by two-digit numbers. On balance, I prefer when teaching division by a single-digit number to use this as an opportunity to introduce the ad hoc subtraction approach, rather than plump for the standard short division algorithm. Figure 12.13 shows this repeated subtraction method applied to the two examples just considered, namely, 75 ÷ 5 and 438 ÷ 6. Clearly, the method gets easier the more fluent we are with mental multiplication. One of the reasons I prefer to use it for single-digit divisors is that it encourages children to handle calculations like 50 × 6 and 20 × 6 mentally, thus building up the confidence they need for the more challenging divisions using two-digit divisors.

Figure 12.13 *The ad hoc subtraction alternative to short division*

Research focus

A study of over 500 children in England and the Netherlands (Anghileri, 2001a) revealed the impact on children's performances of the different standard methods for division that had been taught in primary schools in the two countries. The Dutch approach had been to progress from repeated subtraction of the divisor to more and more efficient subtraction of multiples of the divisor, using essentially the written procedure proposed in this chapter (see Figures 12.6, 12.7, 12.8 and 12.13). The traditional short-division algorithm (see Figure 12.11 and 12.12) was taught much more in English schools and took precedence over informal methods. This had the clear disadvantages of being inflexible and disguising the number relationships involved. It was clear that the Dutch approach proved to be more successful because it had the flexibility for individuals to use the knowledge of multiplication facts with which they were confident. It also gave children access to division by two-digit numbers much earlier.

Suggestions for further reading

1. Chapter 6 of Anghileri (2001b) is entitled 'Intuitive approaches, mental strategies and standard algorithms'. Drawing on data from both British and Dutch schools, Anghileri explores the progression from intuitive approaches to division calculations and key mental strategies to different versions of standard algorithms.
2. The National Council of Teachers of Mathematics (NCTM), an influential US organization for promoting mathematics education, has produced a whole book all about teaching and learning algorithms (NCTM, 1998).
3. Part 4 of the guidance for teaching written calculations produced for the National Numeracy Strategy (QCA, 1999b) deals with multiplication and division. There are some good examples of children's recording and generally the approaches advocated show a commitment to processes built on understanding rather than rote learning.
4. Chapter 2 of Thompson (2003) is entitled 'Deconstructing the National Numeracy Strategy's approach to calculation'. In this interesting chapter Thompson questions some of the assumptions in the National Numeracy Strategy in England (DfEE, 1999) about the way in which primary children's mental strategies prepare the way for standard written methods.

Self-assessment questions

12.1: Use the method of Figure 12.3 to find 42×37.
12.2: Use the method of Figure 12.4 to find 345×17.
12.3: Write down the values of: 7×3, 7×5, 7×10. Now find $126 \div 7$, using the method of ad hoc subtraction.
12.4: Write down the values of: 23×2, 23×5, 23×10, 23×20. Now find $851 \div 23$, using the method of ad hoc subtraction.
12.5: Write down the values of: 8×5, 8×10, 8×50. Now find $529 \div 8$, using the method of ad hoc subtraction.

Further practice

From the Student Workbook

Tasks 57–59: Checking understanding of written methods for multiplication and division

Tasks 60–62: Using and applying written methods for multiplication and division

Tasks 63–65: Learning and teaching of written methods for multiplication and division

On the website (www.sagepub.co.uk/haylock)

Check-Up 24: More multiplication strategies

Check-Up 25: More division strategies

Glossary of key terms introduced in Chapter 12

Long multiplication: a condensed and formal written algorithm for multiplying two numbers, based on the distributive law for multiplication. In this procedure, for example, 426×37 is calculated in two steps, 426×30 and 426×7.

Areas method for multiplication: a more expanded approach to multiplication of two numbers, in which the two numbers are interpreted as the sides of a rectangle and their product is the area. In this procedure, 426×37 is calculated as the sum of six areas: 400×30, 400×7, 20×30, 20×7, 6×30 and 6×7.

Grid method for multiplication: an alternative way of recording the steps in the areas method, without actually drawing the rectangle.

Long division: a condensed and formal written method for division by two-digits numbers (and larger). The procedure is difficult to understand and involves some tricky multiplications; learners have to be able to recall accurately a complicated sequence of steps.

Ad hoc subtraction: an acceptable written method for doing division calculations, in which ad hoc multiples of the divisor are subtracted from the dividend until no more can be subtracted. The method is easier to understand than long division and learners can operate at their own level of confidence with number relationships.

Short division: a compact standard algorithm for a division calculation involving a single-digit divisor. The divisor is divided into each digit in turn, working from left to right, with any remainders being transferred to the next column.

13
Remainders and Rounding

 In this chapter there are explanations of

- the different interpretations required for the results of division calculations done on a calculator and those done by methods which produce a remainder;
- the relationship between the answer with a remainder and the calculator answer;
- the way in which the context determines whether to round a result up or down;
- the idea of rounding to the nearest something; and
- how to give answers to so many decimal places or significant figures.

How do the figures after the decimal point in a calculator answer to a division calculation relate to the remainder?

Consider the problem of seating 250 children in coaches that hold 60 children each. Using the process of mathematical modelling (see Chapter 5), we could model this problem with the division, 250 ÷ 60. It is instructive to contrast the kind of reasoning involved in interpreting the answer to this division calculation when we do it with a calculator or without a calculator. If we divide 250 by 60, using whatever mental or written procedure we are confident with, we would get to the result '4 remainder 10'. To interpret this result we should note that the 'remainder 10' does not stand for 10 coaches; it represents the 10 children who would have no seats if you ordered only 4 coaches.

When we do the calculation on a calculator, however, and get the result '4.1666666', the '.1666666' represents a bit of a coach, not a bit of a child. So, in this example, the figures after the decimal point represent a bit of a coach, whereas the remainder represents a number of children. They are certainly not the same thing. This is a very significant observation, requiring careful explanation to children, through discussion of a variety of examples.

The way we interpret back in the real world the mathematical solution to a calculation involving a division actually depends on:

- whether the way we have done the calculation led to an answer with a remainder or an answer with figures after the decimal point; and
- whether the problem giving rise to the division is an *equal-sharing* structure or an *inverse-of-multiplication* structure (see Chapter 10).

How does the interpretation of the results differ for the different division structures?

Consider the division, 150 ÷ 18. If I do this by mental or written methods I may get to the result '8 remainder 6'. But if I do it on a calculator I get '8.3333333'.

First, we will analyse how these results are interpreted if the problem that gave rise to the calculation is an *equal-sharing* structure, of the form '150 things shared equally between 18'. For example: if I share 150 pencils equally between 18 people, how many do they each get? In interpreting the answer '8 remainder 6', the remainder represents the 6 pencils left over after you have done the sharing, giving 8 pencils to each person. But the figures after the decimal point in the calculator answer (the .3333333 part of 8.3333333) represent the portion of a pencil that each person would get if you *were* able to share out the remainder equally. This would, of course, involve cutting up the pencils into bits. So both the remainder and the figures after the decimal point in this example refer to pencils, although the first refers to pencils left over and the second to portions of pencils received if the left-overs are shared out.

Whether or not you can actually share out the remainder in practice will, of course, depend on what you are dealing with. For example, people and pencils are not usually cut up into smaller bits, so the answer with the remainder is actually more useful. But lengths, areas, weights and volumes can be usually further subdivided into smaller units, so the calculator answer might make more sense in examples in measurement contexts.

Now consider the interpretation of the two results if the problem that gave rise to 150 ÷ 18 is an *inverse-of-multiplication* structure. This might be a question of the form: 'How many sets of 18 can you get from 150 things?' For example: how many boxes that hold 18 pencils each do you need to store 150 pencils? Now we notice that the remainder 6 represents the surplus of pencils after you have filled up 8 boxes of 18. The figures after the decimal point in the calculator answer (the .3333333 part of 8.3333333) then represent what fraction this surplus is of a full set of 18. In our example, the .3333333 means the fraction of a box that would be taken up by the 6 remaining pencils. So the *remainder* in this division problem represents surplus pencils, but the *figures after the decimal point* represent 'a bit of a box'. In simple language, we might say either 'we need eight boxes and there will be six pencils left over', referring to the answer with the remainder, or 'we need eight boxes and a bit of a box', referring to the answer with figures after the decimal point.

How can you get from the calculator answer to the remainder, and vice versa?

We will compare the calculator answer for a division calculation (100 ÷ 7) with the answer with a remainder obtained by some written or mental method:

- Calculator: 100 ÷ 7 = 14.285714.
- Written or mental method: 100 ÷ 7 = 14 remainder 2.

Note that the calculator answer is truncated (see Chapter 5). If the calculator were able to display more than eight digits the result would actually continue as 14.285714285714285714 …, with the sequence of digits '285714' repeated over and over again, for ever. This is what is called a *recurring decimal*.

Now, the 14 is common to both answers. The question is, how does the .285714 in the first answer relate to the remainder 2 in the second? The easiest way to see this is to imagine that the division is modelling a problem with an equal-sharing structure in a measuring context; for example, sharing 100 cl (that is, a litre) of wine equally between 7 glasses (for reference, a centilitre is one-hundredth of a litre). The 14 represents 14 whole centilitres of wine in each portion, and the remainder 2 represents 2 centilitres of wine left over. If this 2 cl is also shared out between the 7 glasses, then each glass will get a further portion of wine corresponding to the answer to the division, 2 ÷ 7. Doing this on the calculator gives the result 0.2857142, which is clearly the same as the bit after the decimal point in the calculator answer to the original question, allowing for the calculator's truncation of the result. So the figures after the decimal point are the result of *dividing the remainder by the divisor*.

   This means, of course, that, since multiplication and division are inverse processes, the remainder should be the result of multiplying the bit after the decimal point by the divisor. Checking this with the above example, we would multiply 0.2857142 by 7 and expect to get the remainder, 2. What I actually get on my calculator is 1.9999994, which is *nearly* equal to 2, but not quite. The discrepancy is due to the tiny bit of the answer to 2 ÷ 7 that the calculator discarded when it truncated the result.

   Another way of getting from the calculator answer (14.285714) to the remainder (2) is simply to multiply the whole number part of the calculator answer (14) by the divisor (7) and subtract the result (98) from the dividend (100). The reasoning here is that the 14 represents the 14 whole centilitres in each glass. Since there are 7 glasses, this amounts to 98 cl (since $14 \times 7 = 98$). Taking this 98 cl away from the original 100 cl leaves the remainder of 2 cl.

   So, in summary, allowing for small errors resulting from truncation:

- The figures after the decimal point are the result of dividing the remainder by the divisor.
- The remainder is the result of multiplying the figures after the decimal point by the divisor.
- The remainder is also obtained by multiplying the whole number part of the calculator answer by the divisor and subtracting the result from the dividend.

What about rounding?

Numbers obtained from measurements or as the results of calculations in practical situations often require **rounding** in some way for us to be able to make sense of them and to use them. Sometimes we round up and sometimes we round down. The first consideration must always be the *context* that gives rise to the numbers.

   For example, when buying wallpaper most people find it helpful to round *up* in their calculation of how many rolls to purchase, to be on the safe side and to avoid an extra trip to the DIY store. On the other hand if we were planning to catch the 8.48 train we might well decide to round this time *down* to 'about a quarter to nine', since rounding this time *up* to 'about ten to nine' might result in our missing the train. So sometimes the context requires us to round *down* in our calculations and sometimes to round *up*. This consideration of the context is much more important than any rule we might remember from school about digits being greater or smaller than five.

What about rounding the result of a division calculation?

Consider these two examples, both of which are problems modelled by 44 ÷ 6, with the inverse-of-multiplication structure. Both are of the form 'how many sixes make 44?'

> Example 1: You can fit six children on a bench. How many benches do you need if you have 44 children to be seated?
>
> Example 2: A pencil costs 6p. How many pencils can you buy with 44p?

For each example I might enter '44 ÷ 6 =' on my calculator and get the result 7.3333333 displayed. The answer is a recurring decimal (7.333333 … with the 3s continuing for ever), which has been truncated by the calculator to show just eight figures. It is interpreted as 'about 7.3333333 benches'. Clearly, in example 1, you cannot in practice bring in 7.3333333 benches. Since seven benches would not be enough for everyone to get a seat, you conclude that eight benches are needed. In this case the context determines that you round the 7.3333333 *up* to 8. Then, in example 2, obviously in practice you can only purchase whole pencils, so the answer 'about 7.3333333 pencils' must again be rounded. In this case, however, the context determines that you round the answer *down*. You can clearly afford only 7 pencils.

In explaining what is going on to children, we could talk about the '.3333333' in example 1 as representing 'a bit of a bench'. We need 7 benches and a bit of a bench: so we must get 8 benches, otherwise some people will be left standing. Similarly, the '.3333333' in example 2 represents 'a bit of a pencil': we can afford 7 pencils and a bit of a pencil, but we will only be able to buy 7 pencils.

These two examples illustrate the point noted in Chapter 10 that a division problem with the inverse-of-multiplication structure often takes one of two forms. First, there are those that incorporate the idea of *repeated addition to reach a target*, such as problems that use the question, 'how many do we need?' Problems of this kind, such as example 1 above, require a calculator answer with superfluous figures to be rounded *up*. Then there are those that incorporate the idea of *repeated subtraction from a given quantity*, such as problems that use the question, 'how many can we afford?'. Problems of this kind, such as example 2 above, require a calculator answer with superfluous figures to be rounded *down*.

This analysis will be useful for teachers in generating division problems for children, to ensure that the children are given examples of both kinds and therefore experience a range of situations where the contexts require both rounding up and rounding down.

> **LEARNING and TEACHING POINT**
>
> When considering practical division problems with the inverse-of-multiplication structure that do not work out exactly when done on a calculator, discuss from the context whether to round up or to round down.

What about the rule of rounding up when the next digit is 5 or more?

In practice it is the context that most often deter-mines that we should round up or that we should round down. In some situations, however, there is a convention that we should round an answer to the nearest something. In fact, such situations are fairly rare in practice, since there is more often than not a contextual reason for rounding up or down, particularly when dealing with money. One situation where 'rounding to the nearest something' is often employed is in recording measurements.

Think of examples from everyday life where measurements are recorded in some form. It is nearly always the case that the measurement is actually recorded to the nearest something. For example, when the petrol pump says that I have put 15.8 litres in my tank this presumably means that the amount of petrol I have taken is really 15.8 litres to the nearest tenth of a litre. So it could actually be slightly more than that or slightly less. When I stand on the bathroom scales and record my weight as 11 stone 3 pounds, I am actually record-ing my weight to the nearest pound: sometimes I have to decide whether the pointer on the scales is nearer to, say, 3 pounds or 4 pounds. When I read that someone has run 100 metres in 9.84 seconds, I would deduce from the two deci-mal places in the answer that the time is rounded to the nearest one-hundredth of a second. In all these examples the measurement is recorded to the nearest some-thing. The reasons for this are sometimes the limitations of the measuring device and sometimes simply that no practical purpose would be served by having a more accurate measurement.

It is in the handling of statistical data that the convention of rounding to the near-est something is employed most frequently. For example, you may well need to round your answer in this way when calculating averages (means). If my scores one cricket season are 50, 34, 0, 12, 0 and 43, I would calculate my average score by adding these up and dividing by 6 (see Chapter 28 for a discussion of averages). Doing this on a calculator I get the result 23.166666.

Normally I would not wish to record all these figures, so I might round my average score to the nearest whole number, which would be 23, or possibly to the nearest tenth, which would be 23.2.

How does the process of rounding to the nearest something work?

It is helpful to note that the concept of 'nearest' is essentially a spatial one. It helps in this process, therefore, to imagine the position of the number concerned on a number line, as shown in Figure 13.1. Clearly the decision to round down or up is determined by whether the number is less or more than halfway along the line between two marks on the scale. The crucial questions in this process are always:

- what number would be halfway between the two marks on the scale?
- is my number less than or greater than this?

To express 23.166666 to the nearest whole number, we have to decide between 23 and 24. The number halfway between 23 and 24 is 23.5, so we round *down* to 23, because our number is *less* than 23.5. But to express 23.166666 to the nearest tenth we have to decide between 23.1 and 23.2. The number halfway between 23.1 and 23.2 is 23.15, so we round *up* to 23.2, because our number is greater than 23.15.

This is just the same principle as when you are rounding to the nearest ten, the nearest hundred, the nearest thousand, and so on. For example, imagine I had worked out the estimated cost for renovating a classroom to be £8357. In discussions with the governors I might find it appropriate to round this figure to the nearest hundred, or even the nearest thousand. To the nearest hundred I have to choose between £8300 and £8400. Halfway between these two figures is £8350. My figure of £8357 is more than this, so I would round *up* and say that we estimate the cost to be about £8400. But if it is sufficient

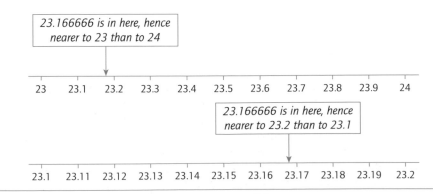

Figure 13.1 *Rounding to the nearest something*

to discuss the cost to the nearest thousand, then I now have to choose between £8000 and £9000. Once again I ask what is halfway between these two figures. The answer is clearly £8500 and, since my estimated cost of £8357 is less than this, we would round *down* and say that the cost is going to be about £8000, to the nearest thousand.

But what do you do if the number you are dealing with is exactly halfway between your two marks on the scale?

Someone always asks this question. My answer is normally not to do anything. There really is not much point, for example, in pretending to round a figure like £8500 to the nearest thousand, because there is not a 'nearest' thousand! Just give it as £8500 and leave it at that. If I normally work my batting average out to the nearest whole number and one year it happens to come out exactly as 23.5, well, I think I will just leave it like that: at least I will be able to deduce from my records that I did a bit better than last year when my average to the nearest whole number was 23.

What about rounding to so many decimal places and significant figures?

When we are rounding a number like 23.166666, it is unnecessarily complex to talk about rounding it to the nearest tenth, hundredth, thousandth, ten thousandth, and so on. Apart from anything else, most of us find it difficult to articulate a word like 'thousandth' in a way that distinguishes it from 'thousand'. It is much easier therefore to talk about rounding *to so many decimal places*.

For example, 23.166666 is:

23, when rounded to the nearest whole number
23.2, when rounded to one decimal place
23.17, when rounded to two decimal places
23.167, when rounded to three decimal places
23.1667, when rounded to four decimal places.

A bit trickier, but often more appropriate, is the idea of rounding to so many **significant figures**. A full consideration of this is properly beyond the scope of this book, but for the sake of completeness I will try to clarify the main idea. The point is that in many practical situations we are really only interested in the approximate size of an answer to a calculation, and just the first two or three figures are normally enough.

If you are applying for a new job, you are not going to get terribly concerned about whether the salary offered is £27 437 or £27 431. In either case, the salary is about £27 400. When you are talking about thousands of pounds the choice between an additional

£37 or £31 is not likely to be particularly significant. If, however, I am buying a pair of trousers then the difference between £37 and £31 becomes quite significant. It is this kind of reasoning that is the basis of the practice of rounding to a certain number of significant figures.

Giving the two salaries above as 'about £27 400' is the result of rounding them *to three significant figures*. The first significant figure – indeed the most significant figure – is the 2, since this represents the largest part of the salary, namely, ten thousand pounds. Then the 7 and the 4 are the second and third significant figures respectively. This might be all we want to know, since we would reckon that the figures in the tens and units columns are relatively insignificant. In most practical situations like these, when approximate answers are required it is rarely useful to use more than three significant figures. Below are some simple examples of rounding to significant figures.

> On my monthly trip to the supermarket I spend £270.96. When I get home my wife asks me how big the bill was.

- Exact statement: *The bill came to £270.96.*
- Using just one significant figure: *The bill came to about £300.* (This is to the nearest hundred pounds.)
- Using two significant figures: *The bill came to about £270.* (This is to the nearest ten pounds.)
- Using three significant figures: *The bill came to about £271.* (This is to the nearest pound.)

> A father left £270 550 to be shared equally between four children.

- *Mathematical model: 270 550 ÷ 4 = 67 637.5*
- Exact solution: *They each inherit £67 637.50.*
- To two significant figures we say: *They each inherit about £68 000.* (This is giving the amount of money to the nearest thousand pounds.)
- To three significant figures we say: *They each inherit about £67 600.* (This is giving the amount of money to the nearest hundred pounds.)
- To four significant figures we say: *They each inherit about £67 640.* (This is giving the amount of money to the nearest ten pounds.)

Research focus

A reasonable expectation is that a primary school teacher should be able spontaneously to generate a range of division problems with remainders in real-life contexts that shows an awareness of the different structures of division and the various ways of interpreting the remainder depending on the context that are discussed in this chapter. An interesting and relevant piece of research conducted with elementary school trainee teachers in the USA by Silver and Burkett (1994) focused on their ability to relate division problems with remainders to real-life situations. The trainees were asked to generate a range of problems in real-life contexts that corresponded to the following division: $540 \div 40 = 13$, remainder 20. The responses were categorized into those having a 'partitive division structure' (what I have called the equal-sharing structure) and those with a 'quotitive division structure' (what I have called the inverse-of-multiplication structure). Within these they identified those problems in which the correct approach is:

(a) 'to increment the quotient if a remainder occurs' (that is, to round up); for example, '40 ants can fit on a leaf – if there are 540 ants trying to cross the river how many leaves must the ants gather?'
(b) 'to ignore the remainder' (that is, effectively, to round down); for example, 'There are 540 balls – how many bags can you fill with 40 balls?'
(c) 'to give the remainder as the solution'; for example, 'If you have 540 cans of food and each of 40 needy families must get the same number of cans, how many cans are left over?'

Only two-thirds of the trainees were able to generate a problem that showed a proper understanding of the relationship between the division and at least one structure. A common error in posing problems in the equal-sharing structure was the failure to specify sharing equally. Additionally, about 25% of the problems posed had some unreasonable aspect to them, such as a highly implausible condition (like each student in a school having 13 lockers) or solutions that required breaking up objects like eggs, children or dogs into fractional parts. The authors suggest that this is indicative of a tendency to dissociate formal school mathematics from the real-world and express their concern that elementary school teachers without a better understanding of the relationship between mathematical computation and real-world contexts might perpetuate this dissociation in their own children's learning of the subject.

Suggestions for further reading

1. Have a look particularly at the helpful section on rounding to so many significant figures in the context of measurement, in chapter 7 of Graham (2008).
2. Some straightforward material for further practice of rounding to so many decimal places and to so many significant figures can be found in section 1, chapter 4, of Haighton et al. (2004).

Self-assessment questions

13.1: A teacher wants to order 124 copies of a mathematics book costing £5.95. She must report the total cost of the order to the year-group meeting. What is the mathematical model of this problem? Obtain the mathematical solution, using a calculator. Interpret the mathematical solution as an exact statement back in the real world. What would the teacher say if she reports the total cost to the nearest ten pounds? What would the teacher say if she reports the total cost to three significant figures?

13.2: Would you round your calculator answers up or down in the following situations?

(a) There are 327 children on a school trip and a coach can hold 40. How many coaches are needed? (327 ÷ 40 = …)

(b) How many cakes costing 65p each can I buy with £5? (500 ÷ 65 = …)

13.3: Here is a division calculation: 320 ÷ 50 = 6, remainder 20. Make up two realistic problems that correspond to this division, one of which has the answer 7 and the other of which has the answer 6.

13.4: What is the average (mean) height, to *the nearest centimetre*, of 9 children with heights, 114 cm, 121 cm, 122 cm, 130 cm, 131 cm, 136 cm, 139 cm, 146 cm, 148 cm? (Add the heights; divide by 9; round to the nearest centimetre.)

13.5: There were 1459 goals in 462 matches in a football league one season. How many goals is this per match, on average? (1459 ÷ 462 = …) Do this on a calculator and give the answer: (a) rounded to the nearest whole number; (b) rounded to one decimal place; and (c) rounded to two decimal places.

13.6: A batch of 3500 books is to be shared equally between 17 shops. Using a calculator, I get 3500 ÷ 17 = 205.88235. How many books are there for each shop? What is the remainder?

Further practice

From the Student Workbook

> Tasks 66–68: Checking understanding of remainders and rounding
> Tasks 69–71: Using and applying remainders and rounding
> Tasks 72–74: Learning and teaching of remainders and rounding

On the website (www.sagepub.co.uk/haylock)

> Check-Up 16: Rounding answers

Glossary of key terms introduced in Chapter 13

Rounding: the process of approximating an answer to a calculation to an appropriate degree of accuracy; this can be done by rounding up or rounding down or rounding to the nearest something. For example, £25.37 rounded up to the next ten pence is £25.40 and rounded down to the next ten pence is £ 25.30; rounded to the nearest ten pence it is £25.40, because it is nearer to this than to £25.30.

Significant figures: the digits in a number as you read from left to right; for example, in 25.37 the first significant figure is the 2, then the 5, then the 3 and then the 7. This number rounded to two significant figures is 25 and rounded to three significant figures is 25.4.

14
Multiples, Factors and Primes

 In this chapter there are explanations of

- multiples, including lowest common multiple;
- some ways of spotting multiples of various numbers;
- digital sums and digital roots;
- factors, including highest common factor;
- the transitive property of multiples and factors; and
- prime numbers and composite (rectangular) numbers.

What are multiples?

First it should be made clear that the concepts in this chapter relate only to natural numbers (see Chapter 6). These are the numbers we use for counting: 1, 2, 3, 4, 5, 6, and so on, continuing ad infinitum. So when you read the word 'number' in this chapter it refers to one of these. We are therefore excluding zero, negative numbers and anything other than positive whole numbers.

The **multiples** of any given (natural) number are obtained by multiplying the number in turn by each of the natural numbers. For example:

- multiples of 3 are: 3, 6, 9, 12, 15, 18, 21, 24, 27, 30, 33, 36, 39, 42, 45, and so on;
- multiples of 7 are: 7, 14, 21, 28, 35, 42, 49, 56, 63, 70, 77, 84, 91, and so on; and
- multiples of 37 are: 37, 74, 111, 148, 185, 222, 259, 296, 333, 370, and so on.

It is instructive to generate the multiples of a given number using the kind of simple, four-function calculator that you would get in a primary school, with a constant facility (most have this). Enter the number, for example, 37, on to the calculator, press, then repeatedly press the equals button. The calculator responds by repeatedly adding 37 to itself and thus produces the multiples of 37. Be warned that various calculators have different logics. This process works on the calculator I have on my desk and the one I have on my computer, but not my scientific calculator.

The mathematical relationship 'is a multiple of' applied to numbers possesses what is called the **transitive property**. Formally, this means that if A is a multiple of B and B is a multiple of C then it follows that A is a multiple of C. This is illustrated in general terms in Figure 14.1(a). Figure 14.1(b) gives an example: any number that is a multiple of 6, such as 24, must also be a multiple of 3, because 6 itself is a multiple of 3. Applying this principle, we can deduce that all multiples of 6 are multiples of 3 (but not vice versa). Similarly, all multiples of 28 must be multiples of 7, because 28 is itself a multiple of 7.

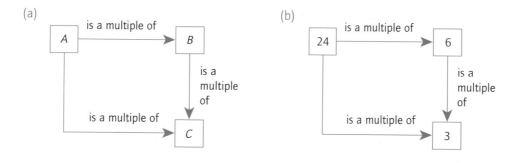

Figure 14.1   *The transitive property of multiples*

Is there anything else to know about multiples?

Being able to recognize multiples and having an awareness of some of the patterns and relationships within them help to develop a high level of confidence and pleasure in working with numbers. For example, this pattern in the multiples of 37 may appeal to some readers:

$3 \times 37 = 111$
$6 \times 37 = 222$
$9 \times 37 = 333$

$$12 \times 37 = 444$$
$$15 \times 37 = 555$$
$$18 \times 37 = 666$$

The pattern in the multiples of 9, with the tens digit increasing by one and the units digit decreasing by one each time, is a useful aid for learning the 9-times table:

$$1 \times 9 = 09$$
$$2 \times 9 = 18$$
$$3 \times 9 = 27$$
$$4 \times 9 = 36$$
$$5 \times 9 = 45$$
$$6 \times 9 = 54$$
$$7 \times 9 = 63$$
$$8 \times 9 = 72$$
$$9 \times 9 = 81$$
$$10 \times 9 = 90$$

There are a number of ways of spotting certain multiples. For example, you will surely be able to tell at a glance that all these numbers are multiples of ten: 20, 450, 980, 7620. That is using a very obvious pattern, namely, that all multiples of 10 end with the digit zero and all numbers ending in zero are multiples of 10. Similarly, you probably know that all multiples of two (even numbers) have 0, 2, 4, 6 or 8 as their final digit; and that all multiples of five end in 0 or 5.

There is a simple way to spot whether a number greater than 100 is a multiple of 4. Since 100 is a multiple of 4, then any multiple of 100 is a multiple of 4. So, given, for example, 4528, we can think of it as 4500 + 28. We know that the 4500 is a multiple of 4, because it's a multiple of 100. So all we need to decide is whether the 28 is a multiple of 4, which it is. So if you have a number with three or more digits you need only look at the last two digits to determine whether or not you are dealing with a multiple of 4.

Would you spot immediately that all these are multiples of nine: 18; 72; 315; 567; and 4986? If so, you may be making use of the **digital sum** for each number. This is the number you get if you add up the digits in the given number. If you then add up the digits in the digital sum, and keep going with this process of adding the digits until a single-digit answer is obtained, the number you get is called the **digital root**. For example, 4986 has a digital sum of 27. This is itself a multiple of nine! This is true for any multiple of 9: the digital sum is itself a multiple of 9. If you then add up the digits of this digital sum (2+7) you get the single-digit number, 9, which is therefore the digital root. Fascinatingly, the digital root of a multiple of 9 is always 9.

Here is a summary of some useful tricks for spotting various multiples:

- Every natural number is a multiple of 1.
- All even numbers (numbers ending in 0, 2, 4, 6 or 8) are multiples of 2.
- A number that has a digital sum that is a multiple of 3 is itself a multiple of 3.
- The digital root of a multiple of 3 is always 3, 6 or 9.
- If the last two digits of a number give a multiple of 4 then it is a multiple of 4.
- Any number ending in 0 or 5 is a multiple of 5.
- Multiples of 6 are multiples of both 3 and 2. So, any even number with a digital root of 3, 6 or 9 must be a multiple of 6.
- If the last three digits of a number give a multiple of 8 then the number is a multiple of 8.
- A number that has a digital sum that is a multiple of 9 is itself a multiple of 9.
- The digital root of a multiple of 9 is always 9.
- Any number ending in 0 is a multiple of 10.

What is a 'lowest common multiple'?

If we list all the multiples of each of two numbers, then inevitably there will be some multiples common to the two sets. For example, with 6 and 10, we obtain the following sets of multiples:

- Multiples of 6: 6, 12, 18, 24, 30, 36, 42, 48, 54, 60, 66, …
- Multiples of 10: 10, 20, 30, 40, 50, 60, 70, …

The numbers common to the two sets are: 30, 60, 90, 120, and so on. The smallest of these (30) is known as the **lowest common multiple**. The lowest common multiple of 6 and 10 is therefore the smallest number that can be split up into groups of 6 and into groups of 10. This concept occurs in a number of practical situations. For example, a class of 30 children is the smallest class-size that can be organized into groups of 6 children for mathematics and teams of 10 for games. Or, if I have to feed one plant every six days and another plant every ten days, then the lowest common multiple indicates the first day on which both plants have to be fed, namely, the thirtieth day. Or, if I can only buy a certain kind of biscuit in packets of 10 and I want to share the biscuits equally between 6 people, the number of biscuits I buy must be a multiple of both 6 and 10; so the smallest number I can purchase is the lowest common multiple, which is 30 biscuits. In Chapter 17 we shall see that the lowest common multiple of the bottom numbers can be useful when comparing two fractions or when doing additions and subtractions with fractions.

What is a factor?

The concept of *factor* (see glossary for Chapter 11) is simply the reverse of multiple. If *A* is a multiple of *B* then *B* is a factor of *A*. For example, 24 is a multiple of 6, so 6 is a factor of 24, as illustrated in Figure 14.2. Colloquially, we say '6 goes into 24'.

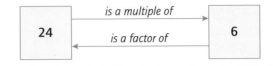

Figure 14.2 *If A is a multiple of B then B is a factor of A*

LEARNING and TEACHING POINT

Let children use calculators to find all the factors of various numbers. Use interesting numbers, like your age, the year, the number of children in the school, the school telephone number, perfect squares, prime numbers.

So the factors of 24 are all those natural numbers by which 24 can be divided exactly: 1, 2, 3, 4, 6, 8, 12 and 24. Notice that 1 and 24 are included as factors of 24. Of course, 1 is a factor of all numbers and every number is a factor of itself. The ability to recognize quickly all the factors of a given number is very useful and is another indication of an individual's confidence and familiarity with numbers. For example, with a set of 24 people we should know instantly that they can be put into groups of 2, 3, 4, 6, 8 or 12. This makes a number like 24, with lots of factors, much more useful for many practical purposes than a number like 23, which has no factors other than 1 and itself.

The idea of a *rectangular array*, introduced in Chapter 10, provides a good illustration of the concept of a factor. Figure 14.3 shows all the different rectangular arrays possible with a set of 24 crosses. The dimensions of these arrays are all the possible pairs of factors of 24: 1 and 24, 2 and 12, 3 and 8, 4 and 6.

```
X X X X X X X X X X X X X X X X X X X X X X X X        X X X X
                    1 by 24                             X X X X
                                                        X X X X
                                     X X X X X X X X     X X X X
X X X X X X X X X X X X               X X X X X X X X     X X X X
X X X X X X X X X X X X               X X X X X X X X     X X X X
           2 by 12                       3 by 8           4 by 6
```

Figure 14.3 *Factors of 24 shown in rectangular arrays*

A calculator can be used to determine whether or not a number is a factor of a given number. Divide the given number by the possible factor: if the answer is a whole number it is a factor, otherwise it is not. For example, is 23 a factor of 1955? Using a calculator, I get $1955 \div 23 = 85$, so 23 *is* a factor of 1955. Is 15 a factor of 1955? Using a calculator, I get $1955 \div 15 = 130.33333$, so 15 is *not* a factor of 1955.

The mathematical relationship, 'is a factor of', also possesses the transitive property as illustrated in Figure 14.4. So, for example, any factor of 12 must be a factor of 24, because 12 is a factor of 24.

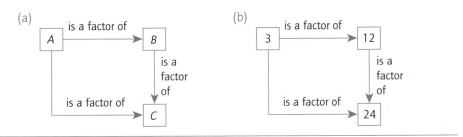

Figure 14.4 *The transitive property of factors*

What about the 'highest common factor'?

This is a similar idea to the lowest common multiple. If we list all the factors of two numbers, the two sets of factors may have some numbers in common. (Since 1 is a factor of all numbers they must at least have this number in common!) The largest of these common factors is called the **highest common factor**. For example, with 24 and 30 we have the following two sets of factors:

- Factors of 24: 1, 2, 3, 4, 6, 8, 12, 24.
- Factors of 30: 1, 2, 3, 5, 6, 10, 15, 30.

The factors in common are 1, 2, 3 and 6. So the highest common factor is 6. This concept occurs in a number of practical situations. For example, imagine that two classes in a year group have 24 and 30 children respectively, and that we wish to divide them up into a number of groups, with each class of children shared equally between the groups. The number of groups must clearly be a factor of both 24 and 30. The largest possible number of groups is therefore 6, since this is the highest common factor. Or, imagine that some teachers in a primary school require 40 exercise books a term and others require 32. It would be convenient to store the exercise books in packs of 8, so that some teachers can pick up 5 packs and others 4 packs. Why 8? Because 8 is the highest common factor of 40 and 32.

What is a prime number?

Any number that has precisely two factors, and no more than two, is called a **prime number**. This is the strict mathematical definition. In practice we think of a prime number as a number that cannot be divided exactly by any number apart from 1 and itself. So, for example, 7 is a prime number because it has precisely two factors, namely 1 and 7. But 10 is not a prime number because it has four factors, namely 1, 2, 5 and 10. A number, such as 10, with more than two factors is sometimes called a **composite number**, or, because it can be arranged as a rectangular array with more than one row (see Figure 14.5), a *rectangular number*. Prime numbers cannot be arranged as rectangular arrays, other than with a single row. The first twenty prime numbers are: 2, 3, 5, 7, 11, 13, 17, 19, 23, 29, 31, 37, 41, 43, 47, 53, 59, 61, 67 and 71.

LEARNING and TEACHING POINT

Use rectangular arrays to illustrate the concepts of factor, prime number and composite (rectangular) number.

(a) X X X X X   (b)

X X X X X   X X X X X X X

10   7

Figure 14.5   *(a) 10 is a composite number; (b) 7 is a prime number*

Notice that according to the strict mathematical definition, the number 1 is *not* a prime number since, uniquely, it has only one factor (itself). So 1 is the only number that is neither prime nor composite. The exclusion of 1 from the set of prime numbers often puzzles students of mathematics. The reason is related to the most important property of prime numbers: given any composite number whatsoever, there is only one combination of prime numbers that multiplied together give the number.

I will illustrate this with the number 24. This number can be obtained by multiplying together various combinations of numbers, such as: 2×12, $2 \times 2 \times 6$, $1 \times 2 \times 3 \times 4$, and so on. If, however, we stipulate that only *prime* numbers can be used, there is only one combination that will produce 24: namely, $2 \times 2 \times 2 \times 3$. This is called the **prime factorization** of 24. This is such a powerful property of prime numbers that it would be a pity to mess it up by allowing 1 to be a prime number! If we did, then the prime factorization of 24, for example, would not be unique, because we could also get to 24 with $1 \times 2 \times 2 \times 2 \times 3$, or $1 \times 1 \times 2 \times 2 \times 2 \times 3$, and so on. The theorem that states that there is only one prime factorization of any composite number is considered to be so important in number theory that it is actually called the fundamental theorem of arithmetic. So you had better not undermine it by calling 1 a prime number!

The study of primes is a fascinating branch of number theory. Nowadays computers are employed to search for very large numbers that are prime. At the time of writing, to my knowledge, the largest known prime number is '$2^{43112609} - 1$'. (This means 43 112 609 twos multiplied together, minus 1: this produces a number with nearly 13 million digits!) This prime number was discovered on 15 September 2008 by volunteers in a computer-based research project called the Great Internet Mersenne Prime Search. This prime number won for them a $100 000 prize that had been offered for finding the first prime number with more than 10 million digits. By the time you read this there may well be a new 'largest known prime number', since searching for larger and larger primes continues to be encouraged by the offer of a prize of $150 000 for finding the first prime number with more than 100 million digits! However, when they find one this big, it will definitely not be the largest prime number, because, as the Greek mathematician, Euclid, proved, as long ago as 300 BC, there is no largest prime number. The really annoying facet of prime numbers is that there is no pattern or formula that will generate the complete set of prime numbers.

What is the point of learning about multiples, factors and primes?

I recall once, in response to this question, asking a student whether she felt differently about the numbers 47 and 48. I was surprised to be told that she did not! To me, 48 seems such a friendly number, flexible and amenable. If I have 48 in a group there are so many ways I can reorganize them: 6 sets of 8, 3 sets of 16, 4 sets of 12, and so on. By contrast, 47 is such an awkward number! The difference, of course, is that 47 is prime, but 48 has lots of factors. This is all part of what is sometimes called 'having a feel for number'. Our confidence in responding to numbers in the everyday situations where they occur will be improved enormously by having this kind of feel for numbers; by being aware of the significant relationships between them; and by recognizing at a glance which properties they possess and which they do not. And the more we are aware of properties like multiples, factors and primes, the more we learn to delight in the pattern and fascination of number. Being able to spot at a glance which car registration numbers are multiples of eleven, or how many of the hymn numbers in church on Sunday morning are prime, might be diverting but is of no immediate practical use.

> **LEARNING and TEACHING POINT**
>
> Encourage children to be fascinated by number and patterns in number. By exploring the properties of multiples, factors and prime numbers build up children's feel for number and therefore their confidence in responding to numerical situations.

However it all leads to yet greater confidence when we have to respond to numerical situations that do matter. Whether the reader is convinced or not by this argument will, no doubt, be evident in the level of enthusiasm with which they tackle the self-assessment questions that follow.

Research focus

Two researchers in Canada (Zazkis and Liljedahl, 2004) investigated how teachers in elementary schools understood prime numbers. They found that many of them had some knowledge of what prime numbers were, often in terms of their being numbers that cannot be factorized, but were unable to implement this knowledge in a number of problem-solving tasks. The teachers' difficulties seemed to stem from the fact that their concept of primes was based on what they are not, rather than on what they are. Drawing on their evidence from the ways in which these teachers had constructed their understanding and some of their apparent misunderstandings (like 'prime numbers are small'), the researchers concluded that the major difficulty with prime numbers is that there is not a symbol or icon to connect with the concept.

Suggestions for further reading

1. Take a break from maths and read a novel! Doxiadis (2000) features Goldbach's Conjecture (the conjecture that every even number after 2 is the sum of two primes). It is the delightful story of Uncle Petros, an ageing recluse who was once a brilliant mathematician and who staked everything on being able to solve a problem that has defied all attempts at proof for over three centuries.
2. Section 2.3 ('Numbers and number sequences') of Hopkins, Pope and Pepperell (2004) provides an opportunity to reinforce the material in this chapter on multiples, factors and primes. The reader can learn also about the Sieve of Eratosthenes and factor trees.

Self-assessment questions

14.1: Continue the pattern shown earlier in this chapter for certain multiples of 37, until the pattern breaks down.

14.2: Multiply each of these numbers by 9 (use a calculator if necessary) and check that the digital root of the result in each case is 9: (a) 47; (b) 172; and (c) 9876543.

14.3: Use some of the methods for spotting multiples to decide whether the following numbers are multiples of 2, 3, 4, 5, 6, 8, or 9: (a) 2652; (b) 6570; and (c) 2401.

14.4: These car registration numbers are all multiples of 11: (a) 561; (b) 594; (c) 418; (d) 979; and (e) 330. Add up the two outside digits and subtract the middle one. Do this with a few more three-digit multiples of 11. Can you state a rule?

14.5: What is the smallest number of people that can be split up equally into groups of 8 and groups of 12? What mathematical concept is used in solving this problem?

14.6: Find all the factors of (a) 95; (b) 96; and (c) 97. Which of these two numbers would be most flexible as a year-group size for breaking up into smaller-sized groups for various activities?

14.7: List all the factors of 48 and 80. What are the common factors? If there are 48 blue chairs and 80 red chairs to be arranged in rows, with the same combination of reds and blues in each row, how can this be done?

14.8: List all the prime numbers between 70 and 100.

14.9: By trying each prime number in turn, using a calculator to help you, find the prime numbers that multiply together to give 4403.

14.10: Starting with 1, add 4, add 2, add 4, add 2, and continue this sequence until you pass 60. How many of the answers are prime?

Further practice

From the Student Workbook

Tasks 75 – 77: Checking understanding of multiples, factors and primes

Tasks 78 – 82: Using and applying multiples, factors and primes

Tasks 83 – 85: Learning and teaching of multiples, factors and primes

Glossary of key terms introduced in Chapter 14

Multiples of a number: the set of numbers obtained by multiplying a given natural number by each of the natural numbers in turn; for example, the multiples of 4 are 4, 8, 12, 16, 20, and so on; a multiple of 4 is therefore any number that can be divided exactly by 4.

Transitive property: a property that any given mathematical relationship may or may not possess; the property is that if A is related to B and B is related to C then it always follows that A is related to C. Each of the relationships 'is a factor of' and 'is a multiple of' is transitive.

Digital sum: the sum of all the digits in a given natural number; for example, the digital sum of 8937 is 27 ($8 + 9 + 3 + 7$).

Digital root: the result of finding the digital sum of the digital sum of a natural number repeatedly until a single digit answer is obtained; for example 8937 has a digital sum of 27 (because $8 + 9 + 3 + 7 = 27$) and therefore a digital root of 9 (because $2 + 7 = 9$).

Lowest common multiple: for two (or more) natural numbers the smallest number that is a multiple of both (or all) of them.

Highest common factor: for two (or more) natural numbers the highest number that is a factor of both (or all) of them; for example, the highest common factor of 24 and 36 is 12. For 'factor' see Glossary for Chapter 11.

Prime number: a natural number that has precisely two factors (namely, 1 and itself). The first ten prime numbers are 2, 3, 5, 7, 11, 13, 17, 19, 23 and 29.

Composite (rectangular) number: a natural number that has more than 2 factors. A composite number can be illustrated as a rectangular array with more than one row; for example, 21 is a composite number (with factors 1, 3, 7 and 21) and can be arranged as 3 rows of 7. All non-prime numbers except 1 are composite.

Prime factorization: writing a given natural number as the product of prime numbers; for example, the prime factorization of 63 is $3 \times 3 \times 7$. Each composite number has a unique prime factorization.

15
Squares, Cubes and Number Shapes

In this chapter there are explanations of

- square numbers;
- cube numbers;
- square roots and cube roots;
- the trial and improvement method for finding square roots and cube roots using a calculator;
- use of the inequality signs (>, <) for recording 'greater than', 'less than' and 'lies between';
- the relationship between sequences of geometric patterns and sets of numbers;
- triangle numbers; and
- the theorem of Pythagoras.

Why are some numbers called squares? A square is a shape, isn't it?

Connecting pictures with number concepts helps to build up our understanding and confidence, as was seen in the previous chapter with concepts like 'factor' and 'multiple'. In particular we saw that a prime number, like 7, could be represented as a rectangle of dots only with one row, whereas a composite (rectangular) number, like 10, could be shown as a rectangular array with more than one row (see Figure 14.5). Now, some rectangles have equal sides: these are the rectangles that are called **squares** (see Chapter 25). So numbers, such as 1, 4, 9, 16, 25, and so on, which can be represented by square arrays, as shown in Figure 15.1, are called **square numbers**. If we use an array of small squares, called **square units**, as in Figure 15.1(b), rather than just dots, as in Figure 15.1(a), then the number of squares in the array also corresponds to the total area. For example, the

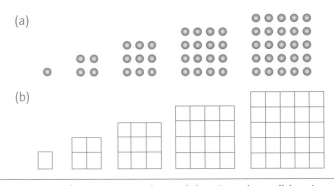

(a)

(b)

Figure 15.1   *Pictures of square numbers: (a) using dots; (b) using square grids*

area of the 5 by 5 square grid is 25 square units. Square numbers are also composite (rectangular) numbers, just as squares are rectangles. (Strictly speaking, there is one exception: the number 1 is considered a square number but, as we saw in the previous chapter, it is neither prime nor composite.)

This explains the geometric idea of square numbers. The arithmetic idea that corresponds to this is that a square number is any number that is obtained by multiplying a (whole) number by itself. The number 16 is represented in Figure 15.1 by 4 rows of 4 dots, or 4 rows of 4 squares, which, of course, corresponds to the multiplication 4×4. Likewise, the representation of 25 as a square corresponds to 5×5. There is a special mathematical notation that can be used as shorthand for writing 5×5. This is 5^2, which means simply that there are two fives to be multiplied together. This is read as 'five **squared**' or 'five to the power two' (see the discussion about powers of 10 in Chapter 6).

The square numbers can be obtained easily using a basic, non-scientific calculator. For example, to find 6 squared, just enter: 6, ×, =. This sequence of keys multiplies 6 by itself. (This works on most basic calculators, but may be different on some. A scientific calculator would have a specific squaring function.) This is the numerical pattern for the set of square numbers:

$$1 \times 1 = 1^2 = 1$$
$$2 \times 2 = 2^2 = 4$$

$3 \times 3 = 3^2 = 9$
$4 \times 4 = 4^2 = 16$
$5 \times 5 = 5^2 = 25$
$6 \times 6 = 6^2 = 36$, and so on.

What about cube numbers?

Just as some numbers can be represented by square arrays, there are those, such as 1, 8 and 27, that can be represented by arrangements in the shape of a **cube**. These **cube numbers** are not specifically in the primary curriculum, although they will turn up in exploring the volumes of cubes with older children. Figure 15.2 shows how the first three cube numbers are constructed from small cubes, called **cubic units**. The first three cube numbers are made from 1 cubic unit, from 8 cubic units and from 27 cubic units, respectively. The 27, for example, is produced by 3 layers of cubes, with 3 rows of 3 cubes in each layer, and is therefore equal to $3 \times 3 \times 3$. The number of cubic units in the whole construction corresponds to the total volume of the cube. For example, the volume of the 3 by 3 by 3 cube is 27 cubic units. It is difficult, of course, to represent these cubic constructions in a two-dimensional picture, so readers are encouraged to build various-sized cubes from cubic units and to generate these cube numbers for themselves.

The same kind of notation is used for cube numbers as for square numbers: $3 \times 3 \times 3$ is abbreviated to 3^3 and read as 'three **cubed**' or 'three to the power three'. Again, it is easy to generate cube numbers using a simple calculator; for example, to

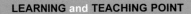

LEARNING and TEACHING POINT

Cube numbers can be explored by older and more able children in the primary school. Get them to construct cubes from cubic units. Connect the cube of a number with the volume of the cube, given by counting the number of cubic units used to construct it.

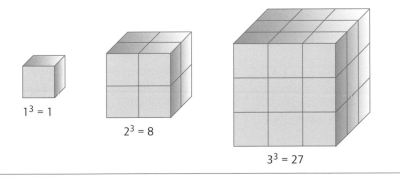

$1^3 = 1$

$2^3 = 8$

$3^3 = 27$

Figure 15.2 *Examples of cube numbers*

obtain 6 cubed, simply enter: 6, ×, =, =. By analogy with the square numbers above, we can construct the following pattern for the cube numbers:

$1 \times 1 \times 1 = 1^3 = 1$
$2 \times 2 \times 2 = 2^3 = 8$
$3 \times 3 \times 3 = 3^3 = 27$
$4 \times 4 \times 4 = 4^3 = 64$
$5 \times 5 \times 5 = 5^3 = 125$
$6 \times 6 \times 6 = 6^3 = 216$, and so on.

What are square roots and cube roots?

What is the length of the side of a square that has an area of 729 square units? Another way of asking the same question is: Which number when multiplied by itself gives 729? Or, which number has a square equal to 729? The answer (27) is called the **square root** of 729. (Strictly speaking, 27 is the *positive* square root of 729; you can also get 729 by multiplying the negative number, –27, by itself, but we are not concerned with negative numbers in this chapter.) The mathematical abbreviation for 'the (positive) square root of' is: $\sqrt{}$. So we could write, for example, $\sqrt{729} = 27$. Finding a square root is the *inverse* process of finding a square. This means that one process undoes the effect of the other, for example:

$2^2 = 4$ so $\sqrt{4} = 2$
$3^2 = 9$ so $\sqrt{9} = 3$
$4^2 = 16$ so $\sqrt{16} = 4$
$27^2 = 729$ so $\sqrt{729} = 27$

The recurrent mathematical idea of inverse was introduced in Chapter 7, where we saw addition and subtraction as inverse processes, and in Chapter 10 where we saw multiplication and division as inverse processes.

The idea of a **cube root** follows the same logic. In geometric terms the question would be: what is the length of the side of a cube with a total volume of 729 cubic units? Or, in arithmetic terms, what number has a cube equal to 729? The answer (9) is called the cube root of 729. As with square roots we can think in terms of an *inverse* process: finding the cube root is the inverse process of finding the cube. For example, the cube of 14 is 2744, so the cube root of 2744 is 14. The symbol for a cube root is: $\sqrt[3]{}$. So, for example, we could write: $\sqrt[3]{2744} = 14$.

How can you find square roots and cube roots?

Using a basic calculator, finding a square root may be very simple, since it will often have a square root key, with the symbol for square root ($\sqrt{}$) written on it. In this case, to find, for example, the square root of 361, you simply enter: 361, $\sqrt{}$. The calculator displays the answer, 19. The basic calculator on my desk has this function, but the one on my computer does not.

It is anyway instructive to try to find square roots without using the square root key, since this introduces a mathematical process, sometimes called **trial and improvement**, which can then be applied to other problems. For example, the problem might be to find the side of a square with a total area of 3844 square units. Using a calculator, we simply try various numbers, square them and decide whether the results are too high or too low, gradually refining our guesses so that we home in on the solution. Like this:

Try 50 ... square it (enter 50, ×, =) ... answer: 2500 ... too low.
Try 60 ... square it (enter 60, ×, =) ... answer: 3600 ... too low.
Try 70 ... square it (enter 70, ×, =) ... answer: 4900 ... too high.

So, the answer lies between 60 and 70.

Try 65 ... square it (enter 65, ×, =) ... answer: 4225 ... too high.
Try 63 ... square it (enter 63, ×, =) ... answer: 3969 ... too high.

Getting close!

Try 62 ... square it (enter 62, ×, =) ... answer: 3844 ... got it.

So the square root of 3844 is 62. This is really the only way to find a cube root using a simple calculator. For example, to find the cube root of 85184:

Try 50 ... cube it (enter 50, ×, =, =) ... answer: 125 000 ... too high.
Try 30 ... cube it (enter 30, ×, =, =) ... answer: 27 000 ... too low.
Try 40 ... cube it (enter 40, ×, =, =) ... answer: 64 000 ... too low.
Try 45 ... cube it (enter 45, ×, =, =) ... answer: 91 125 ... too high.
Try 43 ... cube it (enter 43, ×, =, =) ... answer: 79 507 ... too low.
Try 44 ... cube it (enter 44, ×, =, =) ... answer: 85 184 ... got it.

In the two examples above the numbers were chosen carefully so that the square root or the cube root was an exact whole number. In real situations where a square root or cube root is required, this is unlikely to be the case. For example, if I want to build a square patio with an area of 200 square metres, the length of the side in metres must be the square root of 200. However, my calculator tells me that $14^2 = 196$ (too low) and $15^2 = 225$ (too high). So the answer lies between 14 and 15. There is, in fact, no number that I can enter on a calculator that is the exact square root of 200. This is because $\sqrt{200}$ is an irrational number: see Chapter 6. But using the trial and improvement method, we can get an answer as close as we wish, by going into decimals. For example, since I find that $14.1^2 = 198.81$ (too low) and $14.2^2 = 201.64$ (too high), the answer must lie between 14.1 and 14.2. Readers confident in handling decimals may wish to pursue this in self-assessment questions 15.6 and 15.7 at the end of the chapter.

We should note here that the mathematical signs for **inequality** (> and <) can be used in this context for recording results rather more concisely. Some examples are given in the table below.

Statement of inequality	can be recorded as …
$\sqrt{200}$ is less than 15	$\sqrt{200} < 15$
15 is greater than $\sqrt{200}$	$15 > \sqrt{200}$
$\sqrt{200}$ is greater than 14	$\sqrt{200} > 14$
14 is less than $\sqrt{200}$	$14 < \sqrt{200}$
$\sqrt{200}$ lies between 14 and 15	$14 < \sqrt{200} < 15$

Note that the last statement in this table is saying effectively: 14 is less than $\sqrt{200}$ which is less than 15. It could also be written the other way round using greater-than signs: $15 > \sqrt{200} > 14$. Both express the fact that $\sqrt{200}$ **lies between** the natural numbers 14 and 15.

People with little experience of mathematics are often uneasy about the trial-and-improvement approach, feeling that it is not respectable mathematics. So let me assure you that it is! There are many problems in advanced mathematics which were at one time practically impossible, but which can now be solved by using numerical methods of this kind, employing a calculator or a computer to do the hard grind of the successive calculations involved.

How are squares and square roots used in applying the theorem of Pythagoras?

Pythagoras (569 to 500 BC) was a Greek mathematician and philosopher, most famous for the theorem about right-angled triangles that is attributed to him. In fact, there is evidence that the theorem had been discovered and used perhaps a thousand years earlier than Pythagoras by the ancient Chinese. Pythagoras's achievement was to put the proof of the theorem into a formal mathematical argument, which I do not intend to reproduce here. This theorem is anyway beyond the primary curriculum and I am only including it here because it gives the reader the chance to use and apply some of the mathematical content of this chapter!

The longest side of a right-angled triangle, the side opposite the right angle, is called the **hypotenuse**. The **theorem of Pythagoras** states that, for any right-angled triangle, the square of the length of the hypotenuse is equal to the sum of the squares of the lengths of the other two sides.

In relation to the right-angled triangle shown in Figure 15.3, the generalization that Pythagoras proved can be written as $c^2 = a^2 + b^2$ So if we know the lengths of the two shorter sides in a right-angled triangle, we can calculate the length of the hypotenuse, using our facility with squares and square roots. For example, if $a = 12$ units and $b = 16$ units, then $c^2 = 12^2 + 16^2 = 144 + 256 = 400$. Now, if $c^2 = 400$, then $c = \sqrt{400} = 20$ units.

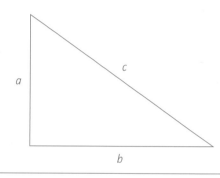

Figure 15.3   *The theorem of Pythagoras: $c^2 = a^2 + b^2$*

When the three sides of a right-angled triangle work out to be natural numbers, such as the numbers 12, 16 and 20 in the example above, they are called a **Pythagorean triple**. Other well-known examples of Pythagorean triples are 3, 4, 5 (because $9 + 16 = 25$) and 5, 12, 13 (because $25 + 144 = 169$). Most often though, when the lengths a and b are natural numbers the hypotenuse will not work out exactly. For example, if $a = 1$ unit and $b = 2$ units, then $c^2 = 1^2 + 2^2 = 1 + 4 = 5$, so $c = \sqrt{5}$. Using either a calculator key or a trial-and-improvement method to find the square root of 5, we get that c is approximately 2.236 units. (The length of c in this case, $\sqrt{5}$, is an irrational number: see Chapter 6.)

Are there any other geometric shapes, in addition to squares and cubes, which describe sets of numbers?

Almost any sequence of geometric shapes or patterns, such as those shown in Figure 15.4, can be used to generate a corresponding set of numbers. Exploring these kinds of sequences, trying to relate the geometric and numerical patterns, can produce some

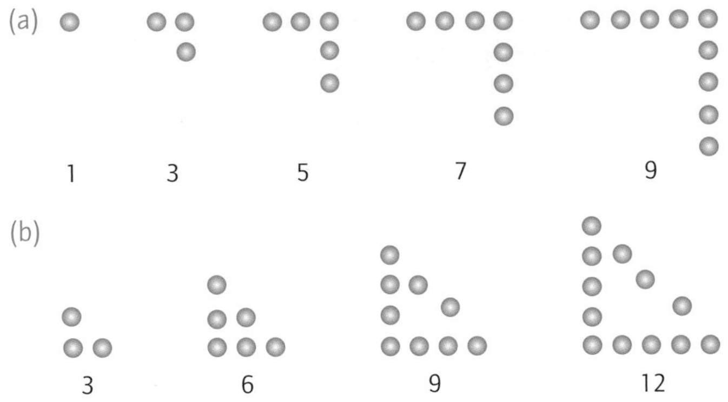

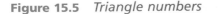

Figure 15.4 *Geometric patterns generating sets of numbers*

intriguing mathematics. For example, the reader might consider why the first sequence of patterns in Figure 15.4 generates the odd numbers: 1, 3, 5, 7, 9 and so on; and why the second sequence generates the multiples of 3: 3, 6, 9, 12, and so on.

Some of these patterns turn out to be particularly interesting and are given special names. For example, you may come across the so-called **triangle numbers**. These are the numbers that correspond to the particular pattern of triangles of dots shown in Figure 15.5: 1, 3, 6, 10, 15, and so on. Notice that you get the second triangle by adding two dots to the first; the third by adding three dots to the second; the fourth by adding four dots to the third; and so on. The geometric arrangements of dots show that these triangle numbers have the following numerical pattern:

$$1 = 1$$
$$3 = 1 + 2$$
$$6 = 1 + 2 + 3$$
$$10 = 1 + 2 + 3 + 4$$
$$15 = 1 + 2 + 3 + 4 + 5, \text{ and so on.}$$

A general formula for triangle numbers is given in Chapter 20. Self-assessment questions 15.3 and 15.8

LEARNING and TEACHING POINT

Give children opportunities to investigate the relationships between sequences of geometric patterns and numerical sequences. The kind of thinking involved is an introduction to algebraic reasoning, involving the recognition of and articulation of generalizations.

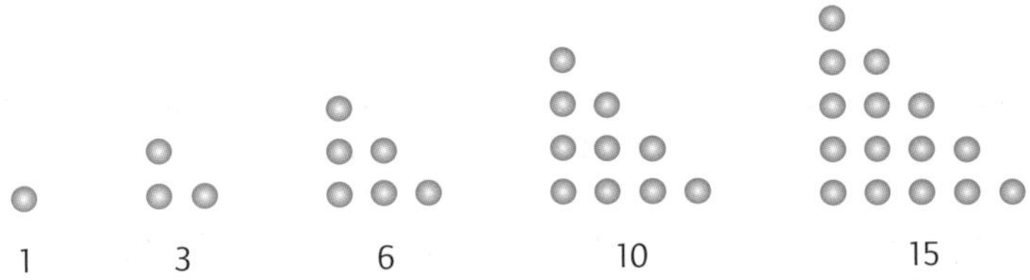

Figure 15.5 *Triangle numbers*

below provide two examples of explaining patterns in number sequences by thinking about the geometric patterns to which they correspond.

Research focus

Teachers of younger children may well wonder about the relevance of this chapter to their mathematics teaching. In this respect a paper by Fluellen (2008) makes intriguing reading. Working with children aged 4 and 5 years (USA kindergarten), using story and games as starting points, Fluellen enabled them to explore number, pattern and relationships in simple arrays, using objects and drawings. One of the games involved a story about a magic pot found in a garden that doubled everything that was put into it. The children were able to show what was happening by, for example, making a 2×5 array of pieces of chocolate on a chessboard. In the next story there was another pot that squared everything, so if the child put in 3 pieces of chocolate, 9 came out. Even children as young as these were able to engage with square numbers in this way, independently creating arrays for squares of natural numbers from 1 to 5. Examples are cited of children discussing the pattern of growth in the square numbers, connecting what the magic pot did and their square arrays by writing $5 \times 5 = 25$, and showing mathematical memory based on generalizations.

Suggestions for further reading

1. Beiler, A. (2000) is an entertaining and accessible exploration of many of the interesting puzzles in number theory. This is recommended for readers confident in mathematics who may have found the subject matter of the last two chapters particularly intriguing and who wish to explore these ideas further.
2. Williams and Shuard (1994) was a very influential book in the development of primary mathematics education in the UK. Chapter 22 ('Patterns among the natural numbers') covers similar material to that covered in this chapter on squares and cubes and the preceding chapter on multiples, factors and primes. It is particularly good at connecting numerical patterns with visual images.

Self-assessment questions

15.1: Drawing on the ideas of this and the previous chapter, find at least one interesting thing to say about each of the numbers from 20 to 29.

15.2: Find a triangle number that is also a square number.

15.3: Look at the sequence of square numbers: 1, 4, 9, 16, 25, 36, and so on. Find the differences between successive numbers in this sequence. What do you notice? Can you explain this in terms of patterns of dots?

15.4:   (a) Use a calculator. Choose a number. Square it, then cube the answer. Cube it, then square the answer. Are the results the same? (b) Can you find a whole number less than 100 that is both a cube number and a square number?

15.5:   Use the trial and improvement method to find: (a) the square root of 3249; (b) the cube root of 4913; and (c) a number which, when multiplied by 10 more than itself, gives the answer 2184.

15.6:   For those confident with decimals: continue with the trial and improvement method for finding the square root of 200, until you can give the length of the side of the square patio with area of 200 square metres to the nearest centimetre.

15.7:   To construct a cube with a volume of 500 cubic centimetres, what should be the length of the sides of the cube? Use a calculator and trial and improvement to answer this to a practical level of accuracy.

15.8:   List all the triangle numbers less than 100. Find the sums of successive pairs of triangle numbers, for example, $1 + 3 = 4, 3 + 6 = 9, 6 + 10 = 16$, and so on. What do you notice about the answers? Can you explain this numerical pattern by reference to the geometric patterns for these numbers?

15.9:   Use a calculator with a square-root key to help you to find a Pythagorean triple in which the smallest of the three natural numbers is 20.

15.10: What is the length of the diagonal of a square of side 10 cm?

15.11: Insert the correct inequality signs ($>$ or $<$) in the gaps in the following: (a) 10 ... $\sqrt{50}$; (b) $\sqrt[3]{100}$ ... 5; (c) 8 ... $\sqrt{70}$ ... 9.

Further practice

From the Student Workbook

Tasks 86–88: Checking understanding of squares, cubes and number shapes
Tasks 89–91: Using and applying squares, cubes and number shapes
Tasks 92–94: Learning and teaching of squares, cubes and number shapes

Glossary of key terms introduced in Chapter 15

Square (shape):   a rectangle (see Chapter 25) with all four sides equal in length.

Square number: a number that can be represented as a square array; a number that is obtained by multiplying a whole number by itself. Square numbers are 1, 4, 9, 16, 25, 36, 49, 64 ...

Square unit: a square shape used as a measure of area; for example, a square made up of 5 rows of 5 square units has an area of 25 square units.

Squared: 'to the power of 2'. For example, 'five squared' is written 5^2 and is equal to 5×5.

Cube (shape):   a solid shape with six square faces and all its edges equal in length.

Cube number: a number that can be represented as an arrangement of cubic units in the shape of a cube; a number that is obtained by multiplying a whole number by itself and by itself again. Cube numbers are 1, 8, 27, 64, 125, 216 ...

Cubic unit: a cube shape used as a measure of volume; for example, a cube made up of 5 layers of 5 rows of 5 cubic units has a volume of 125 cubic units.

Cubed: 'to the power of 3'. For example, 'five cubed' is written 5^3 and is equal to $5 \times 5 \times 5$.

Square root: the (positive) square root of a given number is the positive number which when squared gives that number; for example, because $5^2 = 25$, the (positive) square root of 25 is 5. In symbols, this is written $\sqrt{25} = 5$.

Cube root: the cube root of a given number is the number which when cubed gives that number; for example, because $5^3 = 125$, the cube root of 125 is 5. In symbols, this is written $\sqrt[3]{125} = 5$.

Trial and improvement: a procedure for finding the solution to a mathematical problem by means of successive approximations (trials) which gradually close in on the required solution.

Inequality: a statement that one number is greater than another ($>$) or less than another ($<$). For example, $80 < 87$ (80 is less than 87) and $100 > 87$ (100 is greater than 87).

Lies between: this phrase when used for comparing numbers or quantities can be expressed using two 'less than' symbols or two 'greater than' symbols. For example, '87 lies between 80 and 100' could be written $80 < 87 < 100$ or $100 > 87 > 80$.

Hypotenuse: the longest side of a right-angled triangle.

Theorem of Pythagoras: in a right-angled triangle, the square of the length of the hypotenuse is equal to the sum of the squares of the lengths of the other two sides.

Pythagorean triple: three natural numbers that could be the lengths of the three sides of a right-angled triangle. For example, 5, 12 and 13 form a Pythagorean triple because $5^2 + 12^2 = 13^2$.

Triangle numbers: numbers that can be arranged as triangles of dots in the way shown in Figure 15.5. The set of triangle numbers is 1, 3, 6, 10, 15, 21, 28, and so on. The eighth triangle number, for example, is the sum of the natural numbers from 1 to 8.

16
Integers: Positive and Negative

In this chapter there are explanations of

- how to make sense of negative numbers;
- situations in the contexts of temperatures and bank balances that are modelled by the addition and subtraction of positive and negative numbers; and
- how to enter negative numbers on a basic calculator.

How can we make sense of negative numbers?

Integers – positive and negative whole numbers and zero – were introduced in Chapter 6. Many people have difficulty with the concept of a negative number, mainly because we overemphasize the idea that a number represents a set of things. But this is not a difficult concept if we make strong connections between the number line and the ordinal aspect of number (numbers as labels for putting things in order). The number line, either drawn left to right (see Figures 6.2 and 6.3 in Chapter 6), or, preferably, drawn vertically with positive numbers going up and negative numbers going down, is the most straightforward image for us to associate with positive and negative integers. There are some other contexts that also help us to make sense of negative numbers.

The most familiar is probably the context of temperature. Quite young children can grasp the idea of the temperature falling below zero, associating this with feeling cold and icy roads, and are often familiar with the use of negative numbers to describe this. One small point about different uses of language should be made here. Mathematicians might prefer to refer to the integer, −5, as 'negative five' rather than 'minus five', using the word 'minus' as a synonym for the operation of subtraction.

But weather forecasters tend to say that the temperature is falling to 'minus five degrees'. Similarly, they might refer to a positive temperature as 'plus five' rather than 'positive five'. However, these are not serious difficulties and temperature is still one of the best contexts for experiencing positive and negative numbers.

We can also associate positive and negative integers with levels in, say, a multi-storey car park or department store, with, for example, 1 being the first floor, 0 being ground level, −1 being one floor below ground level, and −2 being two floors below ground level, and so on. We have a department store locally that has the buttons in the lift labelled in this way. Similarly, the specification of heights of locations above and below sea level provides another application for positive and negative numbers.

For some people the context of bank balances is one where negative numbers make real, if painful, sense. For example, being overdrawn by £5 at the bank can be represented by the negative number, −5.

Finally, in football league tables we find another application of positive and negative integers. If two teams have the same number of points, their order in the table is determined by their **goal difference**, which is 'the number of goals-for subtract the number of goals-against'. We should note that this is an unusual use of the word 'difference'. Usually the difference between two numbers is always given as a positive number. The difference between 23 and 28 is the same as the difference between 28 and 23, namely 5. But, in the context of football, a team with 28 goals-for and 23 goals-against has a goal difference of + 5. But a team with 23 goals-for and 28 goals-against has a goal difference of −5. Many children find this a relevant and realistic context for experiencing the process of putting in order a set of positive and negative numbers.

How do you explain addition involving negative integers?

The difficulty in making sense of the ways in which we manipulate positive and negative integers is that we really need to use different images to support different operations. With addition, we need contexts and problems that help us to make sense of such calculations as these:

Example 1.   10 + (−2).
Example 2.   2 + (−7).
Example 3.   (−3) + 4.
Example 4.   (−5) + (−3).

Let us try bank balances. We can interpret the addition as follows: the first number represents your starting balance, the second number represents either a credit (a positive number) or a debit (a negative number). So, with this interpretation, each of the examples 1–4 above can be seen as a mathematical model (see Chapter 5) for a real-life situation, as follows.

Example 1: We start with £10 and add a debit of £2. The result is a balance of £8. The corresponding mathematical model is: 10 + (−2) = 8.

Example 2: We start with a balance of £2 and add a debit of £7. The result is a balance of £5 overdrawn. The corresponding mathematical model is: 2 + (−7) = −5.

Example 3: We start with a balance of £3 overdrawn and add a credit of £4. The result is a balance of £1. The corresponding mathematical model is: (−3) + 4 = 1.

Example 4: We start with a balance of £5 overdrawn and add a debit of £3. The result is a balance of £8 overdrawn. The corresponding mathematical model is: (−5) + (−3) = −8.

LEARNING and TEACHING POINT

Use additions with positive and negative integers to model simple questions about temperatures falling and rising: with the first number representing a starting temperature and the second a rise or fall of so many degrees. Use parallel examples about bank balances, credits and debits.

We could also interpret these collections of symbols in the context of temperatures, with the first number being a starting temperature and the second being either a rise or a fall in temperature, or, on the number line, which, of course, is just like the scale on a thermometer, with the first number being the starting point and the second number a move in either the positive or the negative direction. The reader is invited to construct problems of this kind in self-assessment question 16.2 below.

What about subtraction involving negative integers?

The key to making sense of subtraction with positive and negative integers is to get out of our heads the idea that subtraction means 'take away'. This structure only applies to positive numbers: you cannot 'take away' a negative number. The calculation 6 − (−3), for example, cannot model a problem about having a set of 6 things and 'taking

away negative three things': the words here are just nonsense. We make sense of subtracting with negative numbers by drawing on situations that incorporate some of the
other structures for subtraction, notably the com-
parison and the inverse-of-addition structures (see
Chapter 7).

The kinds of calculations to which we need to
give meaning through experience in context
would include first examples where the first
number in the subtraction is greater than the
second, such as:

Example 5. $6 - (-3)$
Example 6. $(-3) - (-8)$

We will look at these in the context of temperatures, interpreting the subtractions in
terms of the comparison structure. In this structure, the subtraction $a - b$ is asking us
to compare a with b. It models a question of the form, 'How much greater is a than
b?' So the question in the context of temperature would be to find *how much higher*
is the first temperature than the second. In my experience surprisingly young children
can answer questions like, 'How much higher is a temperature of +16 degrees
inside than a temperature of −2 degrees outside?' although they would not necessarily
record this formally in symbols. Such questions become really straightforward
when we connect this language with the picture of the number line, as shown in
Figure 16.1.

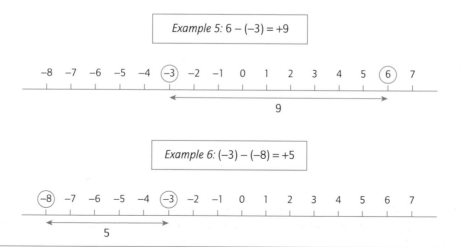

Figure 16.1 *Subtractions with integers: interpreted as comparison*

Example 5:   (i) Using the comparison structure, we could be looking at the difference between a temperature of 6 degrees at noon and a temperature of −3 degrees at midnight. The number line diagram for Example 5 in Figure 16.1 makes it clear that the temperature of 6 degrees is 9 degrees higher than that of −3. The corresponding mathematical model is: 6 − (−3) = +9.

Example 6:   (i) Using the idea of subtraction as comparison, we might be comparing a temperature of −3 degrees at noon with a temperature of −8 degrees at midnight, as shown in the number line diagram for Example 6 in Figure 16.1. It is clear from the diagram that the noon temperature is 5 degrees higher than the midnight temperature. The corresponding mathematical model is: (−3) − (−8) = +5.

This idea of comparison makes a lot of sense when we are using a subtraction to model a situation in which the first temperature is *higher* than the second. I would restrict primary school children's experience of subtracting with negative numbers to problems of this kind, namely, comparing two temperatures, one or both of which might be negative, to find the difference. This will always correspond then to a subtraction in which the first number is the higher temperature. We could just as easily interpret the subtractions in Examples 5 and 6 in terms of comparing bank balances. For Example 5, (6 − (−3)) we would compare a bank balance of £6 in credit with one that is £3 overdrawn. See self-assessment question 16.3.

LEARNING and TEACHING POINT

To enable children to experience subtractions with positive and negative integers informally, use questions about the comparison of two temperatures, finding how much higher is one temperature than another, or the difference in temperature. Also, use parallel examples comparing two bank balances.

For the sake of completeness, I will also discuss here examples where the first number in the subtraction is less than the second, such as these:

Example 7.   2 − 6
Example 8.   (−3) − 4.

I will explain these using the inverse-of addition structure for subtraction. In this structure, the subtraction $a − b$ models a question of the form, 'What must be added to b to give a?' So, in the context of temperatures, the question becomes: 'What change in temperature is required to get from b to a?' Note the order here: we are asking what *change in temperature* takes us from the *second* temperature to the *first*. In this structure, an increase in temperature is modelled by a positive integer and a decrease in temperature by a negative integer. So the arrows in Figure 16.2 indicate a movement from the second temperature in the subtraction to the first.

Example 7:   The subtraction 2 − 6 is related to the question: 'What change in temperature takes you from 6 degrees to 2 degrees?' Clearly this is a fall of 4 degrees, as shown in the number line diagram for Example 7 in Figure 16.2. This change is represented by the integer −4. The mathematical model is: 2 − 6 = −4.

Example 8:   The subtraction (−3) − 4 is related to the question: 'What change in temperature takes you from 4 degrees to −3 degrees?' Clearly this is a fall of 7 degrees, as shown in the number line diagram for Example 8 in Figure 16.2. This change is represented by the integer −7. The mathematical model is: (−3) − 4 = −7.

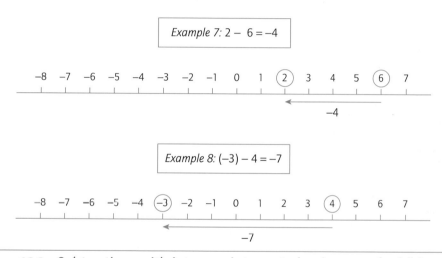

Figure 16.2   *Subtractions with integers: interpreted as inverse of addition*

It would be possible to pose exactly corresponding problems, modelled by the subtractions, with a starting and a finishing bank balance, and then to ask what credit or debit has been added. For Example 8, ((−3) − 4) we would be asking what has changed a bank balance from £4 in credit to £3 overdrawn. See self-assessment question 16.3.

I hope that these illustrations make it clear that we do not need a nonsense rule like, 'two minuses make a plus'. Apart from anything else, to be just a little pedantic, in a question such as 6 − (−3), the first '−' is a minus sign, indicating subtraction, and the second is a negative sign, indicating a negative number. If we simply interpret the subtraction as 'compare the first number with the second' or 'what must be added to the second to give the first?' and put these questions into contexts such as temperatures and bank balances, then there is some chance of actually understanding what is going on.

How do you put negative numbers on to a calculator?

Some calculators have a special key, usually labeled '+/−', which does this for you. To enter −78, for example, you press this key sequence: 78+/−. So to do a calculation such as, 184 − (−78), you could use this key sequence: 184, − ,78+/−, =.

Many basic calculators do not have this special key. But most of them do have a memory and a key labelled something like 'M−' that allows you to subtract a number from whatever is in the memory. This enables us very easily to put a number like −78 into the memory. First, ensure the memory is clear (on my calculator I do this by pressing a key labelled MRC twice), then press: 78, M−. This subtracts 78 from the zero in the memory, to give −78. There is then a key on the calculator that enables you to recall what is in the memory. This is often the same key as the one that clears the memory, for example, the MRC key. So, to do a calculation such as, 184 − (−78), you might use this key sequence: MRC, MRC (to clear the memory), 78, M− (puts −78 in the memory), 184, −, MRC (recalls the −78 from the memory), =. Try this on your own calculator: it is not nearly as complicated as it looks in print!

However, having explained all that, I should say that the context that gives rise to the problem will very often suggest that the actual calculation which you do makes no use of negative numbers whatsoever. For example, if the problem had been to find the difference in height between two points, one 184 metres above sea level and the other 78 metres below sea level, then the image formed in my mind by the context leads me simply to add 184 and 78.

> **LEARNING and TEACHING POINT**
>
> Make sure children know how to enter negative numbers on the basic calculators used in their school and that they know how they are displayed.

My conclusion therefore is that we rarely need to use calculations with negative numbers to solve real-life problems; but we do need the real-life problems to help to explain the way we manipulate positive and negative numbers when we are doing abstract mathematical calculations!

Research focus

Liebeck (1990) investigated an alternative to the traditional number-line approach to teaching additions and subtractions with positive and negative integers. As has been shown earlier in this chapter, the problem with subtraction of integers on the number line is that different interpretations have to be applied to different calculations in order for them to make any sense. Liebeck's intuitive model used a set of cards representing 'forfeits' and 'scores'. So, for example, one card might be a score of 3 (corresponding to +3) and another card a forfeit of 3 (corresponding to −3). Children played games in which they could win or lose these cards. Intuitively, losing a forfeit of 3 was easily perceived as a gain of 3. The approach, although limited in its scope, proved to be successful, with children doing better than those taught by the traditional number-line model in pure additions and subtractions with positive and negative numbers.

Suggestions for further reading

1. Chapter 14 ('Some types of numbers') of Williams and Shuard (1994) introduces the concept of negative number through the more general mathematical notion of vector. This book is recommended for any readers who want to put their own teaching of mathematics into a more secure and fundamental mathematical context.
2. There is plenty of good material to reinforce this chapter's explanation of integers in chapter 7 of Suggate, Davis and Goulding (2010).

Self-assessment questions

16.1: In a football league table, Arsenal, Blackburn and Chelsea (A, B and C) all have the same number of points. A has 18 goals for and 22 against, B has 32 for and 29 against, C has 25 for and 30 against. Work out the goal differences and put the teams in order in the table.

16.2: Make up situations about temperatures that are modelled by the additions: (a) 4 + (−12); and (b) (−6) + 10. Give the answers to the additions.

16.3: Give situations about bank balances that are modelled by the subtractions: (a) 20 − (−5); (b) (−10) − (−15); and (c) (−10) − 20. Give the answers to the subtractions.

16.4: Find how to enter the integer, −42, on your calculator, in the middle of a calculation. Note how your calculator displays this integer.

16.5: Yesterday I was overdrawn at the bank by £187.85. Someone paid a cheque into my account and this morning I am £458.64 in credit. Model this situation with a subtraction. Use a calculator to find out how much the cheque was that was paid in.

Further practice

From the Student Workbook

Tasks 95–96: Checking understanding of integers, positive and negative
Tasks 97–99: Using and applying integers, positive and negative
Tasks 100–102: Learning and teaching of integers, positive and negative

Glossary of key terms introduced in Chapter 16

Goal difference: in football, the number of goals scored by a team subtract the number of goals scored against them; this can therefore be either a positive integer or a negative integer. This is an unconventional use of the word 'difference', which is usually just given as a positive number.

17
Fractions and Ratios

In this chapter there are explanations of

- four different meanings of the fraction notation: a part of a unit, a part of a set, a division and a ratio;

- some of the traditional language of fractions;

- the important idea of equivalent fractions;

- equivalent ratios and their use in scale drawings and maps;

- simplifying fractions and ratios by cancelling;

- how to compare two simple fractions;

- how to add and subtract simple fractions; and

- how to find a simple fraction of a quantity.

I think of a fraction as representing a part of a whole. Is there any more to it than that?

In Chapter 6 we introduced the set of rational numbers. **Fraction** notation is one of the ways in which we can represent rational numbers. But what precisely is the meaning of a fraction such as $^3/_8$? Once again we encounter the special difficulty presented by mathematical symbols: that one symbol (or collection of symbols) can represent a number of different kinds of situation in the real world. The mathematical notation used for a fraction might, in fact, be used in at least four different ways:

- To represent a part of a whole or a unit.
- To represent a part of a set.

- To model a division problem.
- As a ratio.

How does a fraction represent a part of a whole or a unit?

Consider, for example, the fraction three-eighths, which in symbols is $^3/_8$. The commonest interpretation of these symbols is illustrated by the diagrams in Figure 17.1. I find the most useful everyday examples are chocolate bars (rectangles) and pizzas (circles). One item (sometimes called the 'whole'), such as a bar of chocolate or a pizza, is somehow subdivided into eight equal sections, called 'eighths', and three of these, 'three-eighths', are then selected.

Note that the word 'whole' does sound the same as 'hole'; this can be confusing for children in some situations. I recall one teacher tearing a sheet of paper into four quarters and then, in the course of her explanation, asking a child to show her 'the whole'; not surprisingly, the child kept pointing to the space in the middle. It is also not uncommon colloquially to hear someone talk about 'a whole half', as in 'I ate a whole half of a pizza'. Because of all this I prefer to talk about 'fractions of a unit'.

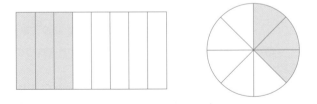

Figure 17.1 *The shaded sections are three-eighths of the whole shape*

How does a fraction represent a part of a set?

The idea of the fraction $^3/_8$ as meaning 3 parts selected from 8 parts of a unit can then be extended to situations where a set of items is subdivided into eight equal subsets and three of these subsets are selected. For example, the set of 40 dots in Figure 17.2(a) has been subdivided into eight equal subsets (of 5 dots each) in Figure 17.2(b). The 15 dots selected in Figure 17.2(c) can therefore be described as three-eighths of the set of 40.

LEARNING and TEACHING POINT

Build on the idea of a fraction as representing a number of equal parts of a unit to extend the meaning to include a number of equal parts of a set, for example, two-thirds of a set of 12.

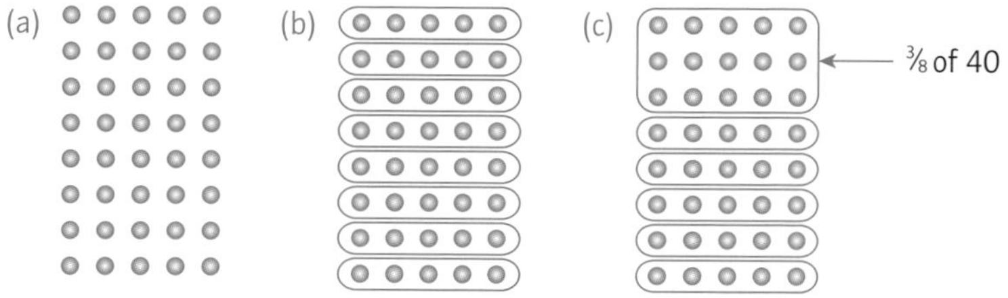

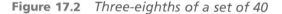

Figure 17.2 *Three-eighths of a set of 40*

How does a fraction represent a division?

The fraction $^3/_8$ can also be used to represent the division of 3 by 8, thinking of division as 'equal sharing between'. It might, for example, represent the result of sharing three bars of chocolate equally between eight people. Notice the marked difference here: in Figure 17.1, it was one bar of chocolate that was being subdivided; now we are talking about cutting up three bars. The actual process we would have to go through to solve this problem practically is not immediately obvious.

LEARNING and TEACHING POINT

Using simple examples with sharing pizzas and chocolate bars, establish the idea that $^p/_q$ can also mean 'p divided by q'. For example, 'three pizzas shared between four people' is '3 divided by 4' and this results in $^3/_4$ of a pizza each.

One way of doing it is to lay the three bars side by side, as shown in Figure 17.3, and then to slice through all three bars simultaneously with a knife, cutting each bar into eight equal pieces. The pieces then form themselves nicely into eight equal portions. Figure 17.3 shows that each of the eight people gets the equivalent of three-eighths of a whole bar of chocolate. (If you are doing this with pizzas you have to place them one on top of the other, rather than side by side, but otherwise the process is the same.)

So what we see here is, first, that the symbols $^3/_8$ can mean 'divide 3 units by 8' and, second, that the result of doing this division is 'three-eighths of a unit'. So the symbols $^3/_8$ represent both an *instruction* to perform an operation and the *result* of performing it! We often need the idea that the fraction $^p/_q$ means 'p divided by q' in

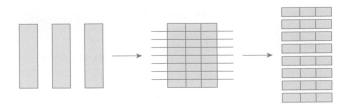

Figure 17.3   *Three shared between eight*

order to handle fractions on a calculator. Simply by entering $p \div q$ we can express the fraction as a decimal.

How does a fraction represent a ratio?

We have seen in Chapter 10 that one of the categories of problems modelled by division is where two quantities are compared by means of ratio. So, because the symbols $^3/_8$ can mean 'three divided by eight', we can extend the meanings of the symbols to include 'the ratio of three to eight'. This is written sometimes as 3:8. For example, in Figure 17.4(a), when comparing the set of circles with the set of squares, we could say that 'the ratio of circles to squares is three to eight'. This means that for every three circles there are eight squares. Arranging the squares and circles as shown in Figure 17.4(b) shows this to be the case. The reason why we also use the fraction notation ($^3/_8$) to represent the ratio (3:8) is simply that another way of expressing the comparison between the two sets is to say that the number of circles is three-eighths of the number of squares. The reader may recall from Chapter 6 that *rational* numbers are given that name because they can be expressed as the *ratio* of two integers. So, the principle that any fraction can be understood as a ratio is a really fundamental dea – mathematically, this is probably the most important meaning of a fraction.

> **LEARNING and TEACHING POINT**
>
> Introduce children to the use of fractions to compare one quantity with another (that is, finding the ratio) especially in the context of prices. For example, we can compare two prices of £9 and £12 by stating that one is three-quarters of the other.

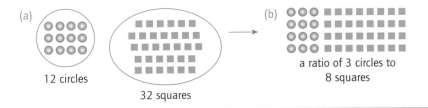

Figure 17.4   *A ratio of three to eight*

What about numerators, denominators, vulgar fractions, proper and improper fractions, mixed numbers, and so on?

These are all important ideas associated with learning about fractions but, in my view, it is quite acceptable to use more informal language to refer to them. For example, the **numerator** and the **denominator** are simply the top number and the bottom number in the fraction notation. So, for example, in the fraction $^3/_8$ the numerator is 3 and the denominator is 8. I prefer to call them simply the top number and the bottom number, but by all means use the technical terms if you wish!

The phrase '**vulgar fraction**', in which the word 'vulgar' actually means 'common' or 'ordinary', is archaic. It was used to distinguish between the kinds of fractions discussed in this chapter, such as $^3/_8$, written with a top number and a bottom number, and decimal fractions, such as 0.375, which are discussed in the next. (For those who are interested in the ways in which words shift their meaning, I have an arithmetic book dated 1886 in which the chapter on 'vulgar fractions' concludes with a set of 'promiscuous exercises'!)

> **LEARNING and TEACHING POINT**
>
> It is quite acceptable to use informal language such as *top number, bottom number* and *top-heavy fraction*, alongside or instead of formal language such as *numerator, denominator* and *improper fraction*.

The fraction notation for parts of a unit can also be used in a situation such as that shown in Figure 17.5, where there is more than one whole unit to be represented. Altogether here, there are eleven-eighths of a pizza, written $^{11}/_8$. Since eight of these make a whole pizza this quantity can be written as $1 + ^3/_8$, which is normally abbreviated to $1^3/_8$. This is sometimes called a **mixed number**.

A fraction in which the top number is smaller than the bottom number, such as $^3/_8$, is sometimes called a **proper fraction**, with a fraction such as $^{11}/_8$ being referred to as an **improper fraction**. Proper fractions are therefore those that are less than 1, with improper fractions being those greater than 1. We could refer to improper fractions more informally as 'top-heavy fractions'.

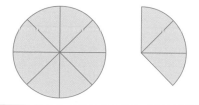

Figure 17.5   *A fraction greater than 1*

What are equivalent fractions?

The concept of equivalence – which we saw in Chapter 3 to be one of the fundamental processes for understanding mathematics – is one of the key ideas for children to grasp when working with fractions. Using the first idea of a fraction above, that it represents a part of a unit, it is immediately apparent from Figure 17.6, for example, that the fractions, three-quarters, six-eighths and nine-twelfths, all represent the same amount of chocolate bar. This kind of 'fraction chart' is an important teaching aid for explaining the idea of equivalence.

> **LEARNING and TEACHING POINT**
>
> Equivalence of fractions is one of the most important ideas to get across to primary children. Get them to make a variety of fraction charts like Figure 17.6 and find various examples of equivalent fractions.

Sequences of **equivalent fractions** follow a very straightforward pattern. For example, all these fractions are equivalent:

$^{3}/_{5}$, $^{6}/_{10}$, $^{9}/_{15}$, $^{12}/_{20}$, $^{15}/_{25}$, $^{18}/_{30}$, $^{21}/_{35}$, $^{24}/_{40}$, and so on.

The numbers on the top and bottom are simply the 3-times and 5-times tables, respectively. This means that, given a particular fraction, you can always generate an equivalent

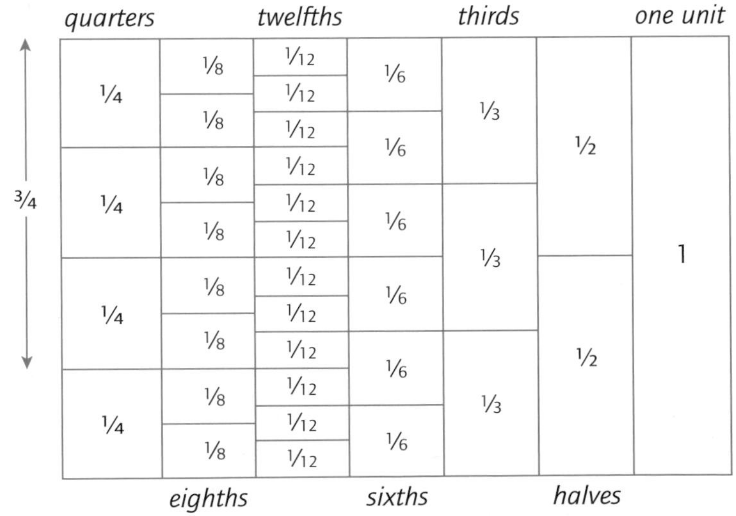

Figure 17.6 *A fraction chart showing some equivalent fractions*

fraction by multiplying the top and the bottom by the same number; or, vice versa, by dividing by the same number. So, for example:

$^4/_7$ is equivalent to $^{36}/_{63}$ (multiplying top and bottom by 9).
$^{40}/_{70}$ is equivalent to $^4/_7$ (dividing top and bottom by 10).

How do you simplify fractions?

If we remember that the fraction notation can also be interpreted as meaning division of the top number by the bottom number, the principle above is another version of stating the constant ratio principle explained in Chapter 11: that you do not change the answer to a division calculation if you multiply or divide both numbers by the same thing. This is an important method for simplifying fractions. By dividing the top and bottom numbers by any common factors we can reduce the fraction to its simplest form. This process is often called '**cancelling**'.

For example, $^6/_8$ can be simplified to the equivalent fraction $^3/_4$ by dividing top and bottom numbers by their highest common factor, 2 (cancelling 2). Similarly, $^{12}/_{18}$ can be simplified to the equivalent fraction $^2/_3$ by cancelling 6.

How does this work with ratios?

The principle used for simplifying fractions applies to ratios, of course, because fractions can be interpreted as ratios. If you multiply or divide two numbers by the same thing then the ratio stays the same.

For example, if I am comparing the price of two articles costing £28 and £32 by looking at the ratio of the prices, then the ratio 28:32 can be simplified to the **equivalent ratio** of 7:8 (dividing both numbers by 4). This means that one price is $^7/_8$ (seven-eighths) of the other.

Another example: if I am comparing a journey of 2.8 miles with one of 7 miles, then I could simplify the ratio, 2.8:7, by first multiplying both numbers by 10 (to get 28:70) and then dividing both numbers by 14 (to get 2:5), drawing the conclusion that one journey is $^2/_5$ (two-fifths) of the other.

Often it is particularly useful to express a ratio as an equivalent ratio in which the first number is 1. For example, the ratio 2:5 used to compare the two journeys in the previous paragraph can be written as the equivalent ratio 1:2.5 (dividing both numbers by 2). This can then be interpreted as 'for every mile in the first journey you have to travel 2.5 miles in the second' or 'the second journey is 2.5 times longer than the first'.

The commonest application of this kind of ratio is to scale-drawings and map scales. For example, if a scale drawing of the classroom represents a length of 2 metres by a length of 5 cm then the scale is the ratio of 5 cm to 2 metres, or, writing both lengths in centimetres, 5 cm to 200 cm. The ratio 5:200 can then be simplified to the equivalent ratio 1:40. This would be the conventional way of expressing the scale, indicating that each length in the original is 40 times the corresponding length in the scale drawing, or that each length in the scale drawing is $\frac{1}{40}$ of the length of the original. Scale factors for maps are usually much larger than this, of course. For example, the Ordnance Survey Landranger maps of Great Britain use a scale of 1:50 000. This means that a distance of 1 cm on the map represents a distance of 50 000 cm in reality. Since 50 000 cm = 500 m = 0.5 km, then we conclude that each centimetre on the map represents $\frac{1}{2}$ kilometre.

How do you compare one fraction with another?

LEARNING and TEACHING POINT

Explain to children, with concrete illustrations, why making the bottom number larger makes the fraction smaller, and vice versa.

The first point to notice here is that when you increase the bottom number of a fraction you actually make the fraction smaller, and vice versa. For example, $\frac{1}{2}$ is greater than $\frac{1}{3}$, which is greater than $\frac{1}{4}$, which is greater than $\frac{1}{5}$, and so on. This is very obvious if the symbols are interpreted in concrete terms, as bits of pizzas or chocolate bars, for example. It is possible to get this wrong, of course, if you simply look at the numbers involved in the fraction notation without thinking about what they mean.

Then, second, there is no difficulty in comparing two fractions with the same bottom number. Clearly, five-eighths of a pizza ($\frac{5}{8}$) is more than three-eighths ($\frac{3}{8}$), for example.

Generally, to compare two fractions with *different* bottom numbers we may need to convert them to equivalent fractions with the *same* bottom number. This will have to be a common multiple of the two numbers. It might be (but does not have to be) the lowest common multiple (see Chapter 14). For example, which is greater, seven-tenths ($\frac{7}{10}$) of a chocolate bar or five-eighths ($\frac{5}{8}$)? The lowest common multiple of 10 and 8 is 40, so convert both fractions to fortieths:

LEARNING and TEACHING POINT

With more able older children, introduce the procedure for finding which is the larger or which the smaller of two fractions, by changing them to equivalent fractions with the same bottom number.

$\frac{7}{10}$ is equivalent to $\frac{28}{40}$ (multiplying top and bottom by 4); and
$\frac{5}{8}$ is equivalent to $\frac{25}{40}$ (multiplying top and bottom by 5).

We can then see instantly that, provided you like chocolate, the seven-tenths is the better choice.

How do you add and subtract fractions?

To be honest I have to say that there are not many practical situations that genuinely require the addition or subtraction of fractions. In practice, most calculations, such as those arising from measurements, are done with decimals. Questions such as '$\frac{1}{6}$ of a class are 7 years of age and $\frac{1}{2}$ of the class are 8 years of age – what fraction of the class are 7 or 8 years of age?' do sound a bit contrived. However, just in case you find yourself in the situation where someone expects you to be able to do this kind of thing, here's how it's done.

To add or subtract two fractions:

(a) Change one or both of the fractions to equivalent fractions so that they finish up with the same bottom number – it's best to use the lowest common multiple for this.
(b) Add or subtract the top numbers.
(c) If possible, cancel down to an equivalent fraction.

So to add $\frac{1}{6}$ and $\frac{1}{2}$, as in the example above, we would first change the $\frac{1}{2}$ to $\frac{3}{6}$, because 6 is the lowest common multiple of 6 and 2. Then we simply add up how many sixths there are altogether (1 + 3 = 4) and finally cancel the $\frac{4}{6}$ to $\frac{2}{3}$. Written down, the calculation looks like this:

$$\frac{1}{6} + \frac{1}{2} = \frac{1}{6} + \frac{3}{6} = \frac{4}{6} = \frac{2}{3}$$

Here is an example with subtraction: how much more is $\frac{2}{3}$ of a litre than $\frac{1}{4}$ of a litre? This time we change both fractions to twelfths, because 12 is the lowest common multiple of 3 and 4, to determine that the answer is $\frac{5}{12}$ of a litre. Written down, the calculation looks like this:

$$\frac{2}{3} - \frac{1}{4} = \frac{8}{12} - \frac{3}{12} = \frac{5}{12}$$

What calculations with fractions do we have to do most often in everyday life?

The commonest everyday situations involving calculations with fractions are those where we have to calculate a simple fraction of a set or a quantity. For example, we might say, 'three-fifths of my class of 30 are boys'. If we see an article priced at £45 offered with one-third off, then the reduced price must be 'two-thirds of £45'. Or we might encounter fractions in measurements such as 'three-quarters of a litre' or 'two-fifths of a metre' and want to change these to millilitres and centimetres respectively.

The process of doing these calculations is straightforward. For example, to find $^3/_5$ of 30, first divide by the 5 to find one-fifth of 30, then multiply by the 3 to obtain three-fifths. Here are some example of the process:

LEARNING and TEACHING POINT

Explain to children the procedure for finding a fraction of a quantity, by dividing by the bottom number and then multiplying by the top number, applying this procedure to a range of everyday practical contexts, and using a calculator where necessary.

$^1/_5$ of 30 is 6, so $^3/_5$ of 30 is 18.

$^1/_3$ of £45 is £15, so $^2/_3$ of £45 is £30.

$^1/_4$ of 1000 ml is 250 ml, so $^3/_4$ of 1000 ml (a litre) is 750 ml.

$^1/_5$ of 100 cm is 20 cm, so $^2/_5$ of 100 cm (a metre) is 40 cm.

If the division and multiplication involved are difficult a calculator can be used. For example, if I am due to get three-sevenths of a legacy of £4500, then the calculation is performed on a calculator by entering: 4500, ÷ 7, × 3, =. The calculator display of 1928.5714 indicates that my entitlement is £1928.57. There is no need to go further than this in calculations with fractions in the primary school.

Research focus

A teaching experiment with children aged 9 years (Boulet, 1998) sheds light on many of the conceptual difficulties that children have with fraction notation. Difficulties were highlighted in what is termed 'equipartition'. In representing simple fractions such as $^1/_3$ by dividing up a given shape such as a rectangle or a circle, often children would use non-equal sections for thirds. The exception was when they could generate the fractions (such as quarters) by halving. Children had difficulty in 'reconstitution'; that is, they did not necessarily recognize that if you put all fractional parts back together again then you would have the 'whole' that you started with. Ordering fractions proved to be a real problem, with the expected error of deducing, for example, that $^1/_4 > ^1/_3$, simply because 4 > 3. Some children responded that which of $^1/_4$ and $^1/_3$ was the greater would depend on the size of the whole. You can see their point! This is an illuminating observation for teachers to note in teaching the ordering of fractions. Some interesting errors of 'quantification' were also noted. For example, to represent the fraction $^1/_7$ with counters, children might make an arrangement of 1 black counter placed above a line of 7 white counters. When given a rectangular strip of 5 squares, the association of the word 'fifth' with ordinal numbers led some children to reject the idea that one of the squares not at the end of the strip could be a 'fifth' of the rectangle.

Suggestions for further reading

1. Chapter 4 (Fractions) of Graham (2008) would be helpful for readers looking for an opportunity to reinforce their understanding of fractions and their skills in manipulating them.
2. Hart (1984) was at the time a seminal study of how children tackle mathematical questions involving ratio and reasons for the kinds of errors that they make. This was a continuation of an influential project called Concepts in Secondary Mathematics and Science. Although it draws on data from the early years of secondary school, the study contains material and significant insights that have impacted ever since on the teaching and learning of this area of mathematics at both primary and secondary levels.

Self-assessment questions

17.1: Give examples where $^4/_5$ represents: (a) a part of a whole unit; (b) a part of a set; (c) a division using the idea of sharing; and (d) a ratio.

17.2: Find as many different examples of equivalent fractions illustrated in the fraction chart in Figure 17.6 as you can.

17.3: Assuming you like pizzas, which would you prefer, three-fifths of a pizza ($^3/_5$) or five-eighths ($^5/_8$)? (Convert both fractions to fortieths.)

17.4: Put these fractions in order, from the smallest to the largest: ($^3/_4$, $^1/_6$, $^1/_3$, $^2/_3$, $^5/_{12}$).

17.5: Make up a problem about prices to which the answer is 'the price of A is three-fifths ($^3/_5$) of the price of B'.

17.6: Walking to work takes me 24 minutes, cycling takes me 9 minutes. Complete this sentence with an appropriate fraction: 'The time it takes to cycle is … of the time it takes to walk.'

17.7: Find: (a) three-fifths of £100, without using a calculator; and (b) five-eighths of £2500, using a calculator.

Further practice

From the Student Workbook
>Tasks 103–105: Checking understanding of fractions and ratios
>Tasks 106–109: Using and applying fractions and ratios
>Tasks 110–113: Learning and teaching of fractions and ratios

On the website (www.sagepub.co.uk/haylock)
>Check-Up 7: Finding a fraction of a quantity
>Check-Up 31: Simplifying ratios
>Check-Up 32: Sharing a quantity in a given ratio

Glossary of key terms introduced in Chapter 17

Fraction: a way of (a) representing a part of a whole or unit, (b) representing a part of a set, (c) modelling a division problem, (d) expressing a ratio.

Numerator: the top number in a fraction.

Denominator: the bottom number in a fraction.

Vulgar fraction: an archaic term for a 'common' fraction; in other words a fraction expressed as a numerator over a denominator (for example, $^3/_8$) rather than as a decimal (that is, 0.375).

Mixed number: a way of writing a fraction greater than 1 as a whole number plus a proper fraction. For example, $^{18}/_5$ as a mixed number is $3^3/_5$ (three and three-fifths).

Proper fraction: a fraction in which the top number is smaller than the bottom number; a fraction less than 1.

Improper fraction: a fraction in which the top number is greater than the bottom number; a fraction greater than 1; informally, a top-heavy fraction.

Equivalent fractions: two or more fractions that represent the same part of a unit or the same ratio. For example, $^2/_3$, $^4/_6$, $^6/_9$, $^8/_{12}$ are all equivalent fractions.

Cancelling: the process of dividing the top number and bottom number in a fraction by a common factor to produce a simpler equivalent fraction.

Equivalent ratios: different ways of expressing the same ratio; for example the ratio 30:50 can be written as the equivalent ratio 3:5.

18
Calculations with Decimals

Is there anything different about the procedures for addition and subtraction with decimals from those with whole numbers?

The procedures are effectively the same. Difficulties would arise only if you were to forget about the principles of place value outlined in Chapter 6. Provided you remember

LEARNING and TEACHING POINT

When adding or subtracting with decimals, show children how the principle of 'one of these can be exchanged for ten of these' works in the same way as when working with integers.

which digits are units, tens and hundreds, or tenths, hundredths, and so on, then the algorithms (and adhocorithms) employed for whole numbers (see Chapters 8 and 9) work in an identical fashion for decimals, with the principle that 'one of these can be exchanged for ten of these' guiding the whole process.

A useful tip with decimals is to ensure that the two numbers in an addition or a subtraction have the same number of digits after the decimal point. If one has fewer digits than the other then fill up the empty places with zeros, acting as 'place holders' (see Chapter 6). So, for example, 1.45 + 1.8 would be written as 1.45 + 1.80, 1.5 – 1.28 would be written as 1.50 – 1.28 and 10 – 4.25 would be written as 10.00 – 4.25. This makes the standard algorithms for addition and subtraction look just the same as when working with whole numbers, but with the decimal points in the two numbers lined up, one above the other, as shown in Figure 18.1.

(a)	(b)	(c)	(d)
2.86	1.45	1.50	10.00
+4.04	+1.80	−1.28	− 4.25
______	______	______	______

Figure 18.1 *Additions and subtractions with decimals*

LEARNING and TEACHING POINT

Locate calculations with decimals in realistic contexts where the decimals represent money or measurements. Emphasize the usefulness of having the same number of digits after the decimal point when adding or subtracting money or measurements written in decimal notation. Explain to children about putting in extra zeros as place holders where necessary.

In practice, additions and subtractions like these with decimals would usually be employed to model real-life situations related to money or measurement. In Chapter 6, I discussed the convention of putting two digits after the decimal point when recording money in pounds. We saw also that when dealing with measurements of length in centimetres and metres, with a hundred centimetres in a metre, it is often a good idea to adopt the same convention, for example, writing 180 cm as 1.80 m, rather than 1.8 m. Similarly, when handling liquid volume and capacity, where we have 1000 millilitres in a litre, or mass, where we have 1000 grams in a kilogram, the convention would often be to write measurements in litres or kilograms with three digits after the point. This means that, if this convention is followed, the decimal numbers will arrive for the calculation already written in the required form, that is with each of the two numbers in the addition or subtraction having the same number of digits after the point, with zeros used to fill up empty places.

For example, the four calculations shown in Figure 18.1 might correspond to the following real-life situations:

(a) If I save £2.86 one month and £4.04 the next month, how much have I saved altogether?
(b) Find the total length of wall space taken up by a cupboard that is 1.45 m wide and a bookshelf that is 1.80 m wide.
(c) What is the difference in height between a girl who is 1.50 m tall and a boy who is 1.28 m tall?
(d) What is the change from a ten-pound note (£10.00) if you spend £4.25?

How can you be confident you have not made an error with the decimal point in a calculation?

Always check the reasonableness of your answer with an estimate based on simple approximations. For example (a) above, the amounts of money could be approximated to £3 and £4, so we would expect an answer around £7. In example (b), the lengths are about 1 m and 2 m, so we expect an answer around 3 m. In example (c), we might approximate the heights to 150 cm and 130 cm, so an answer around 20 cm would be expected. And in example (d) we would expect the change to be around £6.

Notice how I have tended to round the numbers to the nearest something in these examples (see Chapter 13). A word of caution, however: when you are adding two numbers remember that you will be adding the rounding errors. If both numbers have been rounded up (or both down) then this could lead to quite a significant error in your estimate. A safer procedure is first to round both up and then to round both down, thus determining limits within which the sum must lie.

An addition example: $16.47 + 7.39$
Round both up: $17 + 8 = 25$
Round both down: $16 + 7 = 23$
So the answer lies between 23 and 25.

A similar comment applies when subtracting two numbers when one has been rounded up and the other rounded down. For subtraction, we obtain limits within which the answer must lie by rounding the first number up and the second one down (to get an answer which is clearly too large) and then rounding the first number down and the second one up (to get an answer which is clearly too small).

A subtraction example: $16.47 - 7.39$
Round first number up, second one down: $17 - 7 = 10$
Round second number up, first one down: $16 - 8 = 8$
So the answer lies between 8 and 10.

What about multiplications involving decimals?

I will discuss first the multiplication of a decimal number by a whole number. Once again, the key point is to think about the practical contexts that would give rise to the need to do multiplications of this kind. In the context of money we might need to find the cost of a number of articles at a given price. For example, find the cost of 12 rolls of sticky tape at £1.35 per roll. This problem in the real world is modelled by the multiplication, 1.35×12. On a calculator, we enter 1.35, ×, 12, =, read off the mathematical solution (16.2) and then interpret this as a total cost of £16.20.

> **LEARNING and TEACHING POINT**
>
> Realistic multiplication and division problems with decimals involving money or measurements can often be recast into calculations with whole numbers by changing the units (for example, pounds to pence, metres to centimetres). Teach children how to do this.

But there is some potential to get in a muddle with the decimal point when doing this kind of calculation by non-calculator methods. So a useful tip is, if you can, avoid multiplying the decimal numbers altogether! In the example above this is easily achieved, simply by rephrasing the situation as 12 rolls at 135p per roll, hence writing the cost in pence rather than in pounds. We then multiply 135 by 12, by whatever methods we prefer (see Chapters 11 and 12), to get the answer 1620, interpret this as 1620p and, finally, write the answer as £16.20.

Almost all the multiplications involving decimals we have to do in practice can be tackled like this. Here's another example: find the length of wall space required to display eight posters each 1.19 m wide. Rather than tackle 1.19×8, rewrite the length as 119 cm, calculate 119×8 and convert the result (952 cm) back to metres (9.52 m).

What about dividing a decimal by a whole number?

The same tip applies when dividing a decimal number by a whole number. The context from which the calculation has arisen will suggest a way of handling it without the use of decimals. For example, a calculation such as $3.45 \div 3$ could have arisen from a problem about sharing £3.45 between 3 people. We can simply rewrite this as the problem of sharing 345p between 3 people and deal with it by whatever division process is appropriate (see Chapters 11 and 12), concluding that each person gets 115p each. The final step is to put this back into pounds notation, as £1.15.

How do you explain the business about moving the decimal point when you multiply and divide by 10 or 100 and so on?

On a basic calculator enter the following key sequence and watch carefully the display: 10, ×, 1.2345678, =, =, =, =, =, =, =. This procedure is making use of the constant facility, which is built into most basic calculators, to multiply repeatedly by 10. (If this does not work on your calculator, try 1.2345678, ×, 10, =, =, =, =, =, =, =. The calculator on my desk requires the first option, the one on my computer the second!) The results are shown in Figure 18.2(a). It certainly looks on the calculator as though the decimal point is gradually moving along one place at a time to the right.

Now, without clearing your calculator, enter: ÷, 10, =, =, =, =, =, =, =. This procedure is repeatedly dividing by 10, thus undoing the effect of multiplying by 10 and sending the decimal point back to where it started, one place at a time. Because of this phenomenon we tend to think of the effect of multiplying a decimal number by 10 to be to move the decimal point one place to the right, and the effect of dividing by 10 to be to move the decimal point one place to the left. Since multiplying (dividing) by 100 is equivalent to multiplying (dividing) by 10 and by 10 again, this results in the point moving two places. Similarly multiplying or dividing by 1000 will shift it three places, and so on for other powers of 10.

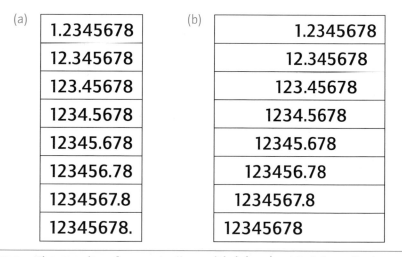

(a)

| 1.2345678 |
| 12.345678 |
| 123.45678 |
| 1234.5678 |
| 12345.678 |
| 123456.78 |
| 1234567.8 |
| 12345678. |

(b)

| 1.2345678 |
| 12.345678 |
| 123.45678 |
| 1234.5678 |
| 12345.678 |
| 123456.78 |
| 1234567.8 |
| 12345678 |

Figure 18.2 *The results of repeatedly multiplying by 10: (a) as displayed on a calculator, (b) arranged on the basis of place value*

However, to understand this phenomenon, rather than just observing it, it is more helpful to suggest that it is not the decimal point that is moving, but the digits. This is shown by the results displayed on the basis of place value, as shown in Figure 18.2(b). Each time we multiply by 10 the digits all move one place to the left. The decimal point stays where it is! To understand why this happens, trace the progress of one of the digits, for example the 3. In the original number it represents 3 hundredths. When we multiply the number by 10, each hundredth becomes a tenth, because ten hundredths can be exchanged for a tenth. This is, once again, the principle that 'ten of these can be exchanged for one of these', as we move right to left. So the 3 hundredths become 3 tenths and the digit 3 moves from the hundredths position to the tenths position. Next time we multiply by 10, these 3 tenths become three whole units, and the 3 shifts to the units position. Next time we multiply by 10, these 3 units become 3 tens, and so on. Because the principle that 'ten of these can be exchanged for one of these' as you move from right to left applies to any position, each digit moves one place to the left every time we multiply by 10.

Since dividing by 10 is the inverse of multiplying by 10 (in other words, one operation undoes the effect of the other), clearly the effect of dividing by 10 is to move each digit one place to the right.

How does all this help when you have to multiply together two decimal numbers?

Imagine we want to find the area in square metres of a rectangular lawn, 3.45 m wide and 4.50 m long. The calculation required is 3.45 × 4.50. For multiplications there is no particular value in carrying around surplus zeros, so we can rewrite the 4.50 as 4.5, giving us this calculation to complete, 3.45 × 4.5. This is a pretty difficult calculation. In practice, most people would sensibly do this on a calculator and read off the answer as 15.525 square metres. But it will be instructive to look at how to tackle it without a calculator. There are three steps involved:

1. Get rid of the decimals by multiplying each number by 10 as many times as necessary.
2. Multiply together the two integers.
3. Divide the result by 10 as many times in total as you multiplied by 10 in step 1.

So the first step is to get rid of the decimals altogether, using our knowledge of multiplying decimals repeatedly by 10, as follows:

$3.45 \times 10 \times 10 = 345$
$4.5 \times 10 = 45$

Hence, by doing '× 10' *three* times in total we have changed the multiplication into 345 × 45, a fairly straightforward calculation with integers. The second step is to work this out, using whatever method is preferred (see Chapters 11 and 12), to get the result 15 525. Finally, we simply undo the effect of multiplying by 10 three times, by dividing by 10 three times, shifting the digits three places to the right and producing the required result, 15.525.

To be honest, you do not really have to think in terms of multiplying and dividing by 10 like this, when doing an actual calculation, although you will probably not understand what you are doing without the explanation above. We can simply notice that the total number of times we have to multiply by 10 is determined by the total number of digits after the decimal points in the numbers we are multiplying. For example, in 3.45 × 4.5, there are two digits after the point in the first number and one in the second, giving a total of three: so we have to apply '× 10' three times in total to produce a multiplication of whole numbers. Then, when we apply '÷ 10' three times to our whole-number result, the effect is to shift three digits to positions after the decimal point. The upshot is that the total number of digits after the decimal points in the two numbers being multiplied is the same as the number of digits after the decimal point in the answer! So our procedure can be rewritten as follows:

1. Count the total number of digits after the decimal points in the numbers being multiplied.
2. Remove the decimal points from the two numbers and multiply them as though they were integers.
3. Put the decimal point back in the answer, ensuring that the number of digits after the point is the same as the total found in step 1.

For example:

1. Calculate 0.04 × 3.6 (three digits in total after the decimal points).
2. 4 × 36 = 144 (dropping the decimal points altogether).
3. 0.04 × 3.6 = 0.144 (with three digits after the decimal point).

Using this principle, Figure 18.3 shows how a whole collection of results can be deduced from one multiplication result with integers, using as examples: (a) 4 × 36 = 144; and (b) 5 × 44 = 220, to show that the procedure works just the same when there is a zero in the result. At an appropriate stage in the development of their work with decimals it can be instructive for children to use a calculator to compile various tables of this kind and to discuss the patterns that emerge.

(a)

×	36	3.6	0.36	0.036
4	144	14.4	1.44	0.144
0.4	14.4	1.44	0.144	0.0144
0.04	1.44	0.144	0.0144	0.00144
0.004	0.144	0.0144	0.00144	0.000144

(b)

×	44	4.4	0.44	0.044
5	220	22	2.2	0.22
0.5	22	2.2	0.22	0.022
0.05	2.2	0.22	0.022	0.0022
0.005	0.22	0.022	0.0022	0.00022

Figure 18.3 *Multiplication tables for decimal numbers derived from (a) 4 × 36 = 144; and (b) 5 × 44 = 220*

How do you check the reasonableness of the result of a multiplication?

As with addition and subtraction, we should always remember to check the reasonableness of our answers to multiplication calculations by using approximations. For example, 3.45×4.5 should give us an answer fairly close to $3 \times 5 = 15$. So the answer of 15.525 looks reasonable, whereas an answer of 1.5525 or 155.25 would suggest we had made an error with the decimal point.

We need to be particularly alert to the problems of multiplying rounding errors when estimating answers to multiplications. If both numbers are rounded up (or both down) then we can generate much more significant errors in our estimate than was the case with addition. Often it makes most sense to round one up and one down. So an estimate for 1.67×6.39 (which equals 10.6713) might be 2×6 (12). A more sophisticated procedure is to round both up (to get an answer clearly too large) and then round both down (to get an answer clearly too small), to determine limits within which the answer must lie.

A multiplication example: 1.67×6.39
Round both up: $2 \times 7 = 14$
Round both down: $1 \times 6 = 6$
So the answer lies between 6 and 14.

And what about dividing a decimal by a decimal?

As in the previous section, this is an area where the teacher's own level of skills should perhaps be markedly higher than those they have to teach to their children. I have four suggestions here for handling divisions by decimals:

Suggestion 1.   In measuring contexts you can often work with whole numbers by changing the units appropriately.

Suggestion 2. You can often transform a division question involving decimals into a much easier equivalent calculation by multiplying both numbers by 10 or 100 or 1000.

Suggestion 3. You can always start from a simpler example involving the same digits and work your way gradually to the required result by multiplying and dividing by 10s.

Suggestion 4. Remember to check whether the answers are reasonable by using approximation.

How does suggestion 1 help with dividing decimals?

The need to divide a decimal number by a decimal number might occur in a real-life situation with the inverse-of-multiplication division structure (see Chapter 10). This could be, for example, in the contexts of money or measurement. My first suggestion then is that in these cases we can usually recast the problem in units that dispense with the need for decimals altogether. For example, to find how many payments of £3.25 we need to make to reach a target of £52 (£52.00), we might at first be inclined to model the problem with the division, 52.00 ÷ 3.25. This would be straightforward if using a calculator. However, without a calculator we might get in a muddle with the decimal points. So what we could do is to rewrite the problem in pence, which gets rid of the decimal points altogether: how many payments of 325p do we need to reach 5200p? The calculation is now 5200 ÷ 325, which can then be done by whatever method is appropriate.

Similarly, to find how many portions of 0.125 litres we can pour from a 2.5-litre container, we could model the problem with the division, 2.500 ÷ 0.125. But it's much less daunting if we change the measurements to millilitres, so that the calculation becomes 2500 ÷ 125, with no decimals involved at all.

And what about suggestion 2?

In fact, what we are doing above, in changing, for example, 52.00 ÷ 3.25 into 5200 ÷ 325, is multiplying both numbers by 100. This is using the principle established in Chapter 11, that you do not change the result of a division calculation if you multiply both numbers by the same thing. This is my second suggestion: that we can often use this principle when we have to divide by a decimal number. Here are two examples:

1. To find 4 ÷ 0.8, simply multiply both numbers by 10, to get the equivalent calculation 40 ÷ 8: so the answer is 5.
2. To find 2.4 ÷ 0.08, multiply both numbers by 100, to get the equivalent calculation 240 ÷ 8: so the answer is 30.

And when does suggestion 3 help?

I find that an innocent-looking calculation like $0.46 \div 20$ can cause considerable confusion amongst students. Using the method suggested above, multiplying both numbers by 100 changes the question into the equivalent calculation $46 \div 2000$. But how do you deal with this? This is where my third suggestion comes to the rescue. I will first make one observation about division: *the smaller the divisor, the larger the answer (the quotient)*.

Notice the pattern in the results obtained when, for example, 10 is divided by 2, 0.2, 0.02, 0.002, and so on:

$10 \div 2$ $\quad = \quad 5$
$10 \div 0.2$ $\quad = \quad 50$
$10 \div 0.02$ $\quad = \quad 500$
$10 \div 0.002$ $\quad = \quad 5000$
$10 \div 0.0002$ $\quad = \quad 50000$, and so on.

Each time the divisor gets 10 times smaller the quotient gets 10 times bigger. This is such a significant property of division – which for some reason often surprises people – that it is worth drawing specific attention to it from time to time. It's easy enough to make sense of this property if you think of $a \div b$ as meaning 'how many bs make a?' Is it not obvious that the smaller the number b, the greater the number of bs that you can get from a?

And, of course, the reverse principle is true as well: *the larger the divisor the smaller the answer.*

So we could construct a similar pattern for dividing 10 successively by 2, 20, 200, 2000, and so on:

$10 \div 2$ $\quad = 5$
$10 \div 20$ $\quad = 0.5$
$10 \div 200$ $\quad = 0.05$
$10 \div 2000 = 0.005$, and so on.

Each time the divisor gets 10 times larger the answer gets 10 times smaller; in other words, it is divided by 10. So my third suggestion is that we can use these two principles to handle a division like the $0.46 \div 20$ above. Start with what you can do … $46 \div 2 = 23$. Then work step by step to the required calculation. Here are two examples:

(1) To calculate $0.46 \div 20$

$0.46 \div 20 = 46 \div 2000$ (multiplying both numbers by 100)
$46 \div 2$ $\quad = 23$

$46 \div 20\ \ \ = 2.3,$
$46 \div 200\ = 0.23,$
$46 \div 2000 = 0.023,$ so $0.46 \div 20 = 0.023.$

(2) To calculate $0.05 \div 25.$

$0.05 \div 25 = 5 \div 2500$ (multiplying both numbers by 100)
$5 \div 2.5\ \ \ = 2$
$5 \div 25\ \ \ \ = 0.2$
$5 \div 250\ \ \ = 0.02$
$5 \div 2500\ = 0.002,$ so $0.05 \div 25 = 0.002.$

And what about suggestion 4, checking the reasonableness of the answer?

My final suggestion for being successful at division with decimals, as with all calculations, is to remember to check the reasonableness of the answers by making estimates using approximations. For example, in working out how many payments of £3.25 are needed to reach £52 we should expect the answer to be somewhere between 10 and 20, since £3 × 10 = £30 and £3 × 20 = £60. So if we get the answer to be 160 or 1.6 rather than 16 we have obviously made a mistake with the decimal point. Similarly, for the calculation 4 ÷ 0.8, we would

expect the answer to be fairly close to 4 ÷ 1, which is 4. (In fact it should be greater than this, because the divisor is less than 1.) So, we are not surprised to get the answer 5. However, an answer of 0.5 or 50 would suggest again that we had made an error with the decimal point.

As with multiplication, we need to be particularly alert to the problems of compounding rounding errors when estimating answers to divisions. If one number in a division is rounded up and the other rounded down then we can generate significant errors in our estimate. Often it makes most sense to round both numbers up or to round both down. So an estimate for 20.67 ÷ 3.39 (which equals approximately 6.097) might be 20 ÷ 3 (which is 6.7 to one decimal place). A more sophisticated procedure is to find limits within which the answer must lie by rounding the first number up and the second one down (to get an answer which is clearly too large) and then rounding the first number down and the second one up (to get an answer which is clearly too small).

A division example: 20.67 ÷ 3.39
Round first number up, second one down: 21 ÷ 3 = 7

Round first number down, second one up: $20 \div 4 = 5$
So the answer lies between 5 and 7.

How do you change decimals into fractions?

First we recall that the decimal 0.3 means 'three-tenths', so it is clearly equivalent to the fraction $^3/_{10}$. Likewise, 0.07 means 'seven-hundredths' and is equivalent to the fraction $^7/_{100}$. Then to deal with, say, 0.37 (3 tenths and 7 hundredths), we have to recognize that the 3 tenths can be exchanged for 30 hundredths, which, together with the 7 hundredths, makes a total of 37 hundredths, which is the fraction $^{37}/_{100}$. The only slight variation in all this is that sometimes the fraction obtained can be changed to an equivalent, simpler fraction, by cancelling (dividing top and bottom numbers by a common factor). Here are a few examples:

0.6 becomes $^6/_{10}$ which is equivalent to $^3/_5$ (dividing top and bottom by 2)
0.04 becomes $^4/_{100}$ which is equivalent to $^1/_{25}$ (dividing top and bottom by 4)
0.45 becomes $^{45}/_{100}$ which is equivalent to $^9/_{20}$ (dividing top and bottom by 5)
0.44 becomes $^{44}/_{100}$ which is equivalent to $^{11}/_{25}$ (dividing top and bottom by 4).

How do you change fractions into decimals?

Fractions such as tenths, hundredths and thousandths, where the denominator (the bottom number) is a power of ten, can be written directly as decimals. Here are some examples to show how this works:

$^3/_{10}$ =   0.3 (0.3 means 3 tenths)
$^{23}/_{10}$ =   2.3 (23 tenths make 2 whole units and 3 tenths)
$^3/_{100}$ =   0.03 (0.03 means 3 hundredths)
$^{23}/_{100}$ =   0.23 (23 hundredths make 2 tenths and 3 hundredths)
$^{123}/_{100}$ =   1.23 (123 hundredths make 1 whole unit and 23 hundredths)
$^3/_{1000}$ = 0.003 (0.003 means 3 thousandths)
$^{23}/_{1000}$ = 0.023 (23 thousandths make 2 hundredths and 3 thousandths).

Then there are those fractions that we can readily change into an equivalent fraction (see Chapter 17) with a denominator of 10, 100 or 1000. For example, $^1/_5$ is equivalent to $^2/_{10}$ (multiplying top and bottom by 2), which, of course, is written as a decimal fraction as 0.2. Similarly, $^3/_{25}$ is equivalent to $^{12}/_{100}$ (multiplying top and bottom by 4), which then becomes 0.12. Here are some further examples, many of which should be memorized:

$\frac{1}{2}$	is equivalent to	$\frac{5}{10}$	which as a decimal is 0.5
$\frac{4}{5}$	is equivalent to	$\frac{8}{10}$	which as a decimal is 0.8
$\frac{1}{4}$	is equivalent to	$\frac{25}{100}$	which as a decimal is 0.25
$\frac{3}{4}$	is equivalent to	$\frac{75}{100}$	which as a decimal is 0.75
$\frac{1}{20}$	is equivalent to	$\frac{5}{100}$	which as a decimal is 0.05
$\frac{7}{20}$	is equivalent to	$\frac{35}{100}$	which as a decimal is 0.35
$\frac{1}{50}$	is equivalent to	$\frac{2}{100}$	which as a decimal is 0.02
$\frac{3}{50}$	is equivalent to	$\frac{6}{100}$	which as a decimal is 0.06
$\frac{1}{25}$	is equivalent to	$\frac{4}{100}$	which as a decimal is 0.04.

Otherwise, to change a fraction into an equivalent decimal, recall that one of the meanings of the fraction notation is division (see Chapter 17). So all you have to do is to divide the top number by the bottom number, preferably using a calculator. Sometimes the result obtained will be an exact decimal, but often it will be a recurring decimal that has been truncated by the calculator.

When is a fraction equivalent to a recurring decimal, and vice versa?

If the denominator of a fraction is a factor of 10, 100, 1000, or any power of 10, then it will work out exactly as a non-recurring decimal. For example, because 125 is a factor of 1000 we can be sure that any fraction with 125 as the denominator will be a non-recurring decimal. I will demonstrate why I am confident about this using as an example the fraction $\frac{7}{125}$:

$\frac{1000}{125} = 8$, so $\frac{7000}{125} = 56$ (multiplying by 7).
Dividing this by 1000, $\frac{7}{125} = 0.056$

If the fraction in its simplest form (after cancelling) has a denominator that does not divide exactly into 10 or a power of 10, then it is equivalent to a recurring decimal. This would include all fractions in their simplest form that have denominators 3, 6, 7, 9, 11, 12, 13, 14, 15, 17, 18, 19 and so on. At a glance, then, we can tell that all these fractions will give recurring decimals if we divide the bottom number into the top number: $\frac{1}{3}$, $\frac{2}{3}$, $\frac{1}{6}$, $\frac{5}{6}$, $\frac{1}{7}$, $\frac{2}{7}$, $\frac{3}{7}$, $\frac{4}{7}$, $\frac{5}{7}$, $\frac{6}{7}$, $\frac{1}{9}$, $\frac{2}{9}$, $\frac{4}{9}$, and so on.

Now here is a remarkable fact: all recurring decimals are actually rational numbers. In other words, they are equivalent to the ratio of two integers, a fraction. For example: 0.333333 ..., with the 3 recurring for ever, is $\frac{1}{3}$; 0.2792727 ..., with the 279 recurring for ever, is $^{31}/_{111}$. Demonstrating this is a really neat piece of mathematics. I will take this last example and show how we get $^{31}/_{111}$. The reader should be able to deduce how this process could be applied to any recurring decimal. If there were just one figure recurring we would start by multiplying the number by 10, and if two figures recurring by 100. In this case we have three figures recurring so we multiply by 1000:

$$1000 \times 0.279279279 \ldots = 279.279279279 \ldots$$
$$1 \times 0.279279279 \ldots = 0.279279279 \ldots$$

Subtracting: $999 \times 0.279279279 \ldots = 279$

So $0.279279279 \ldots$ must equal 279 divided by $999 = {}^{279}/_{999}$ which simplifies to $^{31}/_{111}$.

What is scientific notation?

The place-value system is a very powerful and concise way of representing numbers, but it can be difficult to appreciate at a glance the values of very large (and very small) numbers. To help us in this there is a convention of separating the digits in very large numbers into groups of three, usually with a space. For example, the number 'twenty-three million, six hundred and forty-eight thousand and twenty-six' is correctly written as 23 648 026. Sometimes we might use commas to separate the groups of three digits, but this is no longer the accepted convention, partly because some countries use the comma to represent the decimal point. **Scientific notation** (also called 'standard form') is a more sophisticated and very neat way of representing large numbers. Here is how it works.

Take, as an example, the number 37 600 000. To put this into scientific notation we first put the decimal point immediately after the first digit, reading from left to right. This gives us 3.76 (dropping the superfluous zeros, which are no longer needed as place holders). We then indicate how many times we have to multiply this by ten to get it back to the original number. In this case we have to multiply by ten 7 times, because the decimal point has moved 7 places. So our number is written as 3.76×10^7, meaning 3.76 multiplied by 10 seven times. Here are some other examples of large numbers written in scientific notation:

5600	$= 5.6 \times 10^3$
6 102 000	$= 6.102 \times 10^6$
60 000 000 000 000 000	$= 6 \times 10^{16}$

Scientific notation can also be used to represent very small numbers. For example, the number 0.000 003 would be written 3×10^{-6}. The negative power of 10 indicates how many times the 3 has to be *divided* by 10 to get the given number. Here are some other examples:

$$0.000\,56 \qquad = 5.6 \times 10^{-4}$$
$$0.000\,001 \qquad = 1 \times 10^{-6}$$
$$0.000\,000\,801 \ = 8.01 \times 10^{-7}$$

Scientific notation enables you quickly to compare the sizes of large or small numbers, because the most significant part of the number is the power of ten. So, for example, I can spot at a glance that 1.2×10^{8} is greater than 9.8×10^{7}; and that 1.8×10^{-6} is greater than 8.9×10^{-7}.

Scientific calculators use scientific notation to display numbers that are too large or too small to fit on the screen. Often they will do this using by a letter E (an abbreviation for exponent) to indicate the power of 10. For example, on many scientific calculators the number 9.8×10^{7} would be displayed as 9.8E7 and the number 8.9×10^{-7} as 8.9E−7.

Scientific notation would not usually be introduced in a primary school, but it is included here because primary teachers may need to understand the notation when accessing statistical or scientific data involving large or small numbers.

Research focus

Working with children aged 11 and 12 from a lower economic area in New Zealand, Irwin (2001) investigated the role of students' everyday knowledge of decimals in supporting the development of their knowledge of decimals. The children worked in pairs (one member of each pair a more able student and one a less able student) to solve problems related to common misconceptions about decimal fractions. Half the pairs worked on problems presented in familiar everyday contexts and half worked on problems presented without context. The children who worked on contextual problems made significantly more progress in their knowledge of decimals than did those who worked on non-contextual problems. Irwin also analysed the conversations between the pairs of students during problem solving. The pairs working on the contextualized problems worked much better together, because the less able students were able to contribute from their everyday knowledge and experience of decimals in the world outside the classroom.

Suggestions for further reading

1. For some clear and straightforward material to help understand how decimals work and how to do basic calculations involving decimals look at chapter 5 ('Decimals') in Graham (2008).
2. Chapter 27 ('Operations on decimal fractions') of Williams and Shuard (1994) contains further material on decimal notation, addition and subtraction with decimals, the importance of estimation in decimal calculations, and multiplication and division with decimals.

Self-assessment questions

18.1:   Complete the solution of the problems (a), (b), (c) and (d) modelled by the additions and subtractions in Figure 18.1.

18.2:   Pose a problem in the context of money that is modelled by 3.99×4. Solve your problem without using a calculator.

18.3:   Pose a problem in the context of length that might be modelled by $4.40 \div 8$. Solve your problem without using a calculator.

18.4:   Given that $4 \times 46 = 184$, find: (a) 4×4.6; (b) 0.4×46; and (c) 0.04×0.046.

18.5:   Given that $4 \times 45 = 180$, find: (a) 4×4.5; (b) 0.4×45; and (c) 0.04×0.045.

18.6:   What is the value of $(0.01)^2$? State a question about area that might be modelled by this calculation.

18.7:   Find: (a) $2 \div 0.5$ (hint: multiply both numbers by 10); and (b) $5.5 \div 0.11$ (hint: multiply both numbers by 100).

18.8:   You know that $2 \div 4 = 0.5$, so what is: (a) $2 \div 0.04$? (b) $2 \div 4000$? (c) $0.02 \div 4$?

18.9:   Express these fractions as equivalent decimals: (a) $^{17}/_{100}$; (b) $^3/_5$; (c) $^7/_{20}$; (d) $^2/_3$ (use a calculator); and (e) $^1/_7$ (use a calculator).

18.10: Express these decimals as fractions: (a) 0.09; (b) 0.79; and (c) 0.15.

18.11: Which of these would be equivalent to recurring decimals: $^7/_{20}$, $^7/_{24}$, $^7/_{25}$, $^7/_{27}$, $^7/_{28}$?

18.12: The populations of three states are given as 2.4×10^5, 1.2×10^6, and 9.8×10^5. Put these in order of size from largest to smallest.

18.13: Use approximations to spot the errors that have been made in placing the decimal points in the answers to the following calculations: (a) $2.8 \times 0.95 = 0.266$; (b) $12.05 \times 0.08 = 9.64$; and (c) $27.9 \div 0.9 = 3.1$.

Further practice

From the Student Workbook
Tasks 114–116: Checking understanding of calculations with decimals
Tasks 117–119: Using and applying calculations with decimals
Tasks 120–122: Learning and teaching of calculations with decimals

On the website (www.sagepub.co.uk/haylock)
Check-Up 8: Fractions to decimals and vice versa
Check-Up 17: Very large and very small numbers
Check-Up 22: Adding and subtracting decimals
Check-Up 26: Multiplication with decimals
Check-Up 27: Division with decimals

Glossary of key terms introduced in Chapter 18

Scientific notation (standard form):   representing a number, especially a very large or a very small one, as a number between 1 and 10 multiplied by a power of 10. For example, 7 654 000 would be written as 7.654×10^6 and 0.000 765 4 would be written as 7.654×10^{-4}.

19
Proportions and Percentages

In this chapter there are explanations of

- how to solve simple proportion problems;
- the meaning of per cent;
- the use of percentages to express proportions of a quantity or of a set;
- ad hoc and calculator methods for evaluating percentages;
- the usefulness of percentages for comparing proportions;
- equivalences between fractions, decimals and percentages;
- the meaning of percentages greater than 100;
- how to calculate a percentage of a given quantity or number, using ad hoc and calculator methods; and.
- percentage increases and decreases.

How do you solve proportion problems?

Consider the following five problems, all of which have exactly the same mathematical structure:

Recipe problem 1. A recipe for 6 people requires 12 eggs. Adapt it for 8 people.
Recipe problem 2. A recipe for 6 people requires 4 eggs. Adapt it for 9 people.
Recipe problem 3. A recipe for 6 people requires 120 g of flour. Adapt it for 7 people.
Recipe problem 4. A recipe for 8 people requires 500 g of flour. Adapt it for 6 people.
Recipe problem 5. A recipe for 6 people requires 140 g of flour. Adapt it for 14 people.

These have the classic structure of a problem of **direct proportion**. Such a problem involves four numbers, three of which are known and one of which is to be found. The structure can be represented by the four-cell diagram shown in Figure 19.1, in which it is assumed that the three numbers w, x and y are known and the fourth number z is to be found.

Variable A Variable B

w	x
y	$z?$

Figure 19.1   *The structure of a problem of direct proportion*

The problems always involve two **variables** (see Glossary at the end of this chapter), which I have called variable A and variable B in Figure 19.1. For example, in problem (1) above, variable A would be the number of people and variable B would be the number of eggs. The numbers w and y are values of variable A, and the numbers x and z are values of variable B. So, for example, in recipe problem (1) above $w = 6$ and $y = 8$, $x = 12$ and z is to be found. (See Figure 19.2(a).) In situations like the recipe problems above we say that the two variables are 'in direct proportion', meaning that the ratio of variable A to variable B (for example, the ratio of people to eggs) is always the same. This means that the ratio w:x must be equal to the ratio y:z. It is also true that the ratio w:y is equal to the ratio x:z. As a consequence, when it comes to solving problems of this kind you can work with either the left-to-right ratios or the top-to-bottom ratios, depending on the numbers involved. It is important to note therefore that the most efficient way of solving one of these problems will be determined by the numbers involved, as is illustrated in Figure 19.2(a), (b), (c) and (d).

> **LEARNING and TEACHING POINT**
>
> Use the four-cells diagram to make clear the structure of direct proportion problems and encourage children to use the most obvious relationships between the given three numbers to find the fourth number.

Recipe problem (1) (Figure 19.2a)
Here I am attracted immediately by the simple relationship between 6 and 12. Double 6 gives me 12. So, I work from left to right, doubling the 8, to get 16. Answer: 16 eggs.

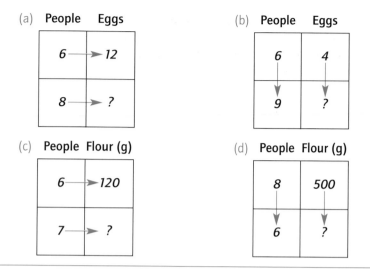

Figure 19.2 *Solving the recipe problems*

Recipe problem (2) (Figure 19.2b)
This time it's the relationship between the 6 and the 9 that attracts me. Halving 6 and multiplying by 3 gives 9. So, I work from top to bottom, and do the same thing to the 4, halving it and multiplying by 3, to get 6. Answer: 6 eggs.

Recipe problem (3) (Figure 19.2c)
The left to right relationship is the easier to work with here: multiplying 6 by 20 gives 120. So, do the same to the 7, to get 140. Answer: 140 g of flour.

Recipe problem (4) (Figure 19.2d)
I think it's easier to use the ratio of 8 to 6 than 8 to 500. So I'll work from top to bottom, going from 8 people to 4 to 2, and then to 6. Now, 8 people need 500 g, so 4 people need 250 g, so 2 people need 125 g. Adding the results for 4 people and 2 people, 6 people need 375 g.

These informal, ad hoc approaches are the ways in which most people solve the problems of ratio and direct proportion that they encounter in everyday life, including problems involving percentages such as those discussed below. We should encourage their use by children. The four-cell diagrams used in Figures 19.1 and 19.2 provide a useful starting point for organizing the data in a structured way that makes the relationships between the numbers more transparent. However, sometimes there is no easy or obvious relationship between the numbers in the problem. In such a case we may call on a calculator to help us in using the method shown below.

Recipe problem (5)
6 people require 140 g
So, 1 person requires 140 ÷ 6 = 23.333 g (using a calculator)
So, 14 people require 23.333 × 14 = 326.662 g (using a calculator)
Answer: approximately 327 g.

What does 'per cent' mean?

Per cent means 'in (or 'for') each hundred'. The Latin root *cent*, meaning 'a hundred', is used in many English words, such as 'century', 'centurion', 'centigrade' and 'centipede'. We use the concept of 'per cent' to describe a **proportion** of a quantity or of a set. So, for example, if there are 300 children in a school and 180 of them are girls, we might describe the proportion of girls as 'sixty per cent' (written as 60%) of the school population. This means simply that there are 60 girls for each 100 children. If on a car journey of 200 miles a total of 140 miles is single carriageway, we could say that 70% (seventy per cent) of the journey is single carriageway, meaning 70 miles for each 100 miles. In effect, we have here the structure shown in Figure 19.1 for a direct proportion problem, but where one of the numbers must be 100, as shown in Figure 19.3.

> **LEARNING and TEACHING POINT**
>
> Repeatedly emphasize the meaning of *per cent* as 'for each hundred' and show how percentages are used to describe a fraction of a quantity or of a set.

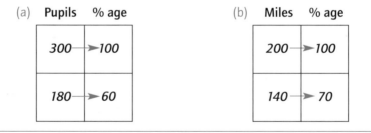

Figure 19.3 *Percentage seen as direct proportion*

What we are doing in these examples is also just what we did with fractions in Chapter 17, when we used them to represent a part of a unit or a part of a set. The concept of a percentage is simply a special case of a fraction, with 100 as the bottom number. So 60% is an abbreviation for $^{60}/_{100}$ and 70% for $^{70}/_{100}$.

How do you use ad hoc methods to express a proportion as a percentage?

In the examples above it is fairly obvious how to express the proportions involved as 'so many per hundred'. This is not always the case. The following examples demonstrate a number of approaches to expressing a proportion as a percentage, using ad hoc methods, when the numbers can be related easily to 100. The trick is to find an equivalent proportion for a population of 100, by multiplying or dividing by appropriate numbers.

1. In a school population of 50, there are 30 girls. What percentage are girls? What percentage are boys?
    30 girls out of 50 children is the same proportion as 60 out of 100.
    So, 60% of the population are girls.
    This means that 40% are boys. (Since the total population must be 100%.)

2. In a school population of 250, there are 130 girls. What percentage are girls? What percentage are boys?
    130 girls out of 250 children is the same proportion as 260 out of 500.
    260 girls out of 500 children is the same as 52 per 100 (dividing 260 by 5).
    So, 52% of the population are girls.
    This means that 48% are boys. (52% + 48% = 100%)

3. In a school population of 75, there are 30 girls. What percentage are girls? What percentage are boys?
    30 girls out of 75 children is the same proportion as 60 out of 150.
    60 girls out of 150 children is the same proportion as 120 out of 300.
    120 girls out of 300 children is the same as 40 per 100 (dividing 120 by 3).
    So, 40% of the population are girls, and therefore 60% are boys.

4. In a school population of 140, there are 77 girls. What percentage are girls? What percentage are boys?
    77 girls out of 140 children is the same proportion as 11 out of 20 (dividing by 7).
    11 girls out of 20 children is the same proportion as 55 per 100 (multiply by 5).
    So, 55% of the population are girls, and therefore 45% are boys.

How do you use a calculator to express a proportion as a percentage?

When the numbers do not relate so easily to 100 as in these examples, the procedure is more complicated and is best done with the aid of a calculator, as in the following example:

5. In a school population of 140, there are 73 girls. What percentage are girls? What percentage are boys?
    73 girls out of 140 children means that $^{73}/_{140}$ are girls.
    The equivalent proportion for a population of 100 children is $^{73}/_{140}$ of 100.
    Work this out on a calculator. (Key sequence: 73, ÷, 140, ×, 100, =.)

Interpret the display (52.142857): just over 52% of the population are girls.
This means that just under 48% are boys.

Most calculators have a percentage key (labelled %) which enables this last example to be done without any complicated reasoning at all. On my calculator, for example, I could use the following key sequence: 73, ÷, 140, %. This makes finding percentages with a calculator very easy indeed.

Why are percentages used so much?

They certainly are used extensively, in newspapers, in advertising, and so on. We are all familiar with claims such as '90% of cats prefer Kittymeat' and '20% of 7-year-olds cannot do subtraction'. There is certainly no shortage of material in the media for us to use with children to make this topic relevant to everyday life. Teachers will also find that they require considerable facility with percentages to make sense of such areas of their professional lives as assessment data, inspection reports and salary claims.

The convention of always relating everything to 100 enables us to make comparisons in a very straightforward manner. It is much easier, for example, to compare 44% with 40%, than to compare $\frac{4}{9}$ with $\frac{2}{5}$. This is why percentages are used so much: they provide us with a standard way of comparing various proportions. Consider this example.

School A spends £190 300 of its annual budget of £247 780 on teaching-staff salaries.
School B is larger and spends £341 340 out of an annual budget of £450 700.

It is very difficult to take in figures like these. The standard way of comparing these would be to express the proportions of the budget spent on teaching-staff salaries as percentages.

School A spends about 76.80% of its annual budget on salaries.
School B spends about 75.74% of its annual budget on salaries.

Now we can make a direct comparison: school A spends about £76.80 in every £100; school B spends about £75.74 in every £100. There are other occasions, however, when the tendency always to put proportions into percentage terms seems a bit daft, particularly when the numbers involved are very small. For example, I come from a family of 3 boys and 1 girl. I could say that 75% of the children in my family are boys. I suppose there's no harm in this, but remember that what this is saying is effectively: '75 out of every 100 children in my family are boys'!

How do percentages relate to decimals?

In the previous chapter we saw how a decimal such as 0.37 means 37 hundredths. Since 37 hundredths also means 37 per cent, we can see a direct relationship between decimals with two digits after the point and percentages. So, 0.37 and 37% are two ways of expressing the same thing. Here are some other examples: 0.50 is equivalent to 50%, 0.05 is equivalent to 5%, 0.42 is equivalent to 42%. It really is as easy as that: you just move the digits two places to the left, because effectively what we are doing is multiplying the decimal number by 100. It's just like changing pennies into pounds and vice versa. This works even if there are more than two digits, for example, 0.125 = 12.5% and 1.01 = 101%.

This means that we have effectively three ways of expressing proportions of a quantity or of a set: using a fraction, using a decimal or using a percentage. It is useful to learn by heart some of the most common equivalences, such as the following:

Fraction	Decimal	Percentage
$1/2$	0.5 (0.50)	50%
$1/4$	0.25	25%
$3/4$	0.75	75%
$1/5$	0.2 (0.20)	20%
$2/5$	0.4 (0.40)	40%
$3/5$	0.6 (0.60)	60%
$4/5$	0.8 (0.80)	80%
$1/10$	0.1 (0.10)	10%
$3/10$	0.3 (0.30)	30%
$7/10$	0.7 (0.70)	70%

$\frac{9}{10}$	0.9 (0.90)	90%
$\frac{1}{20}$	0.05	5%
$\frac{1}{3}$	0.33 (approximately)	33% (approximately)

Knowledge of these equivalences is useful for estimating percentages. For instance, if 130 out of 250 children in a school are girls, then because this is just over half the population, I would expect the percentage of girls to be just a bit more than 50% (it is 52%). If the proportion of girls is 145 out of 450 children, then because this is a bit less than a third, I would expect the percentage of girls to be around 33% (it is about 32.22%).

LEARNING and TEACHING POINT

Encourage children to memorize common equivalences between fractions, decimals and percentages and reinforce these in question-and-answer sessions with the class.

Also, because it is so easy to change a decimal into a percentage, and since we can convert a fraction to a decimal (see Chapter 18) just by dividing the top number by the bottom number, using a calculator, this gives us another direct way of expressing a fraction or a proportion as a percentage. For example, 23 out of 37 corresponds to the fraction $\frac{23}{37}$. On a calculator enter: 23, ÷, 37, =. This gives the approximate decimal equivalent, 0.6216216. Since the first two decimal places correspond to the percentage, we can just read this straight off as 'about 62%'. If we wish to be more precise, we could include a couple more digits, such as 62.16%. (See Chapter 13 for a discussion of rounding.)

So, in summary, we now have these four ways of expressing a proportion of '*A* out of *B*' as a percentage:

1. Use ad hoc multiplication and division to change the proportion to an equivalent number out of 100.
2. Work out $^A/_B \times 100$, using a calculator, if necessary.
3. Enter on to a calculator: *A*, ÷, *B*, % (but note that calculators may vary in the precise key sequence to be used).
4. Use a calculator to find $A \div B$ and read off the decimal answer as a percentage, by shifting all the digits two places to the left.

How can you have a hundred and one per cent?

Since 100% represents the whole quantity being considered, or the whole population, it does seem a bit odd at first to talk about percentages greater than 100. Football managers are well known for abusing mathematics in this way, for example, by talking about their team having to give a hundred and one per cent – meaning, presumably, everything they have plus a little more.

However, there are perfectly correct uses of percentages greater than 100, not for expressing a proportion of a whole unit but for comparing two quantities. Just as we use fractions to represent the ratio of two quantities, we can also use percentages in this way. So, for example, if in January a window-cleaner earns £2000 and in February he earns only £1600, one way of comparing the two months' earnings would be to say that February's were 80% of January's. The 80% here is simply an equivalent way of saying four-fifths ($^4/_5$). If then in March he was to earn £2400 then we could quite appropriately record that March's earning were 120% of January's. This is equivalent to saying 'one and a fifth' of January's earnings.

How do you use ad hoc methods to calculate a percentage of a quantity?

The most common calculation we have to do with percentages is to find a percentage of a given quantity, particularly in the context of money. In cases where the percentage can be converted to a simple equivalent fraction, there are often very obvious ad hoc methods of doing this. For example, to find 25% of £48, simply change this to $^1/_4$ of £48, which is £12.

Then when the quantity in question is a nice multiple of 100, we can often find easy ways to work out percentages. First, let us note that, for example, 37% of 100 is 37. So, if I had to work out 37% of £600, we could reason that, since 37% of £100 is £37, we simply need to multiply £37 by 6 to get the answer required, namely, £222.

It is also possible to develop ad hoc methods for building up a percentage, using easy components. One of the easiest percentages to find is 10% and most people intuitively start with this. (Note, however, that the fact that 10% is the same as a tenth makes it a very special case: 5% is not a fifth, 7% is not a seventh, and so on.) So to find, say, 35% of £80, I could build up the answer like this:

> **LEARNING and TEACHING POINT**
>
> Make a special point of explaining to children that 10% being equivalent to $^1/_{10}$ is a special case and warn them not to fall into the trap of thinking that, for example, 20% is equal to $^1/_{20}$.

	10% of £80 is £8	
so	20% of £80 is £16	(doubling the 10%)
and	5% of £80 is £4	(halving the 10%).

Adding the 10%, 20% and 5% gives me the 35% required: £28.

> **LEARNING and TEACHING POINT**
>
> In your teaching show that you value informal, intuitive methods for finding a percentage of a quantity; teach children some of these strategies, particularly building up a percentage using easy proportions such as 10% and 5%.

It is often the case that 'intuitive' approaches to finding percentages, such as this one, are neglected in schools, in favour of more formal procedures. This is a pity, since success with this kind of manipulation contributes to greater confidence with numbers generally.

What about using a calculator to find a percentage of a quantity?

When the numbers are too difficult for intuitive methods such as those described above, then we should turn to a calculator. For example:

To find 37% of £946.
We need to find $^{37}/_{100}$ of 946.
On a calculator enter: 37, ÷, 100, ×, 946, =.
This gives the result, 350.02, so we conclude that 37% of £946 is £350.02.

Personally, I use a more direct method on the calculator. Since 37% is equivalent to 0.37, I just enter the key sequence: 0.37, ×, 946, =. There is another way, of course, using the percentage key. On my calculator the appropriate key sequence is: 946, ×, 37, %.

What about percentage increases and decreases?

One of the most common uses of percentages is to describe the size of a change in a given quantity, by expressing it as a proportion of the starting value in the form of a **percentage increase or percentage decrease**. We are familiar with percentage increases in salaries, for example. So if your monthly salary of £1500 is increased by 5%, to find your new salary you would have to find 5% of £1500 (£75) and add this to the existing salary.

There is a more direct way of doing this: since your new salary is the existing salary (100%) plus 5%, it must be 105% of the existing salary. So you could get your new salary by finding 105% of the existing salary, that is, by multiplying by 1.05 (remember that 105% = 1.05 as a decimal).

Similarly, if an article costing £200 is reduced by 15%, then to find the new price we have to find 15% of £200 (£30) and deduct this from the existing price, giving the new price as £170. More directly, we could reason that the new price is the existing price (100%) less 15%, so it must be 85% of the existing salary. Hence we could just find 85% of £200, for example, by multiplying 200 by 0.85.

The trickiest problem (too tricky for primary school children) is when you are told the price *after* a percentage increase or decrease and you have to work backwards to get the original price. For example, if the price of an article has been reduced by 20% and now costs £44, what was its original price? This problem is represented in Figure 19.4. The £44 must be 80% of the original price. We have to find what is 100% of that original price. It's fairly easy now to get from 80% (£44) to 20% (£11) and then to 100% (£55).

% age	Price (£)
80	44
100	?

Figure 19.4   *If 80% is £44 find 100%*

There is an interesting phenomenon, related to percentage increases and decreases, that often puzzles people. If you apply a given percentage increase and then apply the same percentage decrease, you do not get back to where you started! For example, the price of an article is £200. The price is increased one month by 10%. The next month the price is decreased by 10%. What is the final price? Well, after the 10% increase the price has gone up to £220. Now we apply the 10% decrease to this. This is a decrease of £22, not £20, because the percentage change always applies to the existing value. So the article finishes up costing £198.

Research focus

Carraher, Carraher and Schliemann (1985) report a fascinating study of the extraordinary ability of Brazilian street children with little or no formal education to perform complicated calculations, which they had learnt from necessity in the meaningful context of their work as street vendors. In particular, some of these children handled proportional reasoning with a startling facility. For example, one 9-year-old child (who apparently did not know that 35×10 was 350) nevertheless worked out the cost of 10 coconuts from knowing that 3 cost 105 cruzerios, reasoning as follows: 'Three will be a hundred and five. With three more that will be two hundred and ten … I need four more. That is … three hundred and fifteen … I think it is three hundred and fifty' (ibid.: 23). This child shows a grasp of the principles of proportion, simultaneously co-ordinating the pro rata increases in the two variables involved, the number of coconuts and the cost, using a combination of adding and doubling. This research is one of the most significant pieces of evidence for the effectiveness of children learning mathematics through purposeful activity in meaningful contexts.

Suggestions for further reading

1. Chapter 6 of Graham (2008) deals with percentages. The material here is easily understood and will help readers who need to reinforce their understanding and basic calculation skills in this area.

2. Chapter 7 of Anghileri (2007) is a thoughtful chapter on decimals, fractions and percentages.
3. Singer, Kohn and Resnick provide a fascinating study of the intuitive bases for ratio and proportion that are available to young children in a chapter entitled 'Knowing about proportions in different contexts', in Nunes and Bryant (1996). The study addresses the question of how children can be helped to build on this informal grasp of these ideas in the context of formalizing mathematical concepts and procedures.

Self-assessment questions

19.1: If you can exchange 100 Danish kroner for 15 euros, what would be the equivalent cost in euros of an article costing 60 kroner?

19.2: A rise in temperature of 9 °F is equivalent to a rise of 5 °C. What is the equivalent in °C of a rise of 45 °F?

19.3: A department store is advertising '25% off' for some items and 'one-third off' for others. Which is the greater reduction?

19.4: Use ad hoc methods to find what percentage of children in a year group achieve level 5 in a mathematics test, if there are:

(a) 50 children in the year group and 13 achieve level 5;
(b) 300 in the year group and 57 achieve level 5;
(c) 80 in the year group and 24 achieve level 5; and
(d) 130 in the year group and 26 achieve level 5.

In each case, state what percentage does not achieve level 5.

19.5: On a page of an English textbook there are 1249 letters, of which 527 are vowels. In an Italian text it is found that there are 277 vowels in a page of 565 letters. Use a calculator to determine approximately what percentage of letters are vowels in each case.

19.6: Change: (a) $^3/_{20}$ into a percentage; and (b) 65% into a fraction.

19.7: Use informal, intuitive methods to find: (a) 30% of £120; and (b) 17% of £450.

19.8: The price of a television costing £275 is increased by 12% one month and decreased by 12% the next. What is the final price? Use a calculator, if necessary.

19.9: The price of a television licence is increased by 14% to £171. How much was it before the increase?

Further practice

From the Student Workbook

Tasks 123–125: Checking understanding of proportions and percentages
Tasks 126–128: Using and applying proportions and percentages
Tasks 129–131: Learning and teaching of proportions and percentages

On the website (www.sagepub.co.uk/haylock)

Check-Up 1:   Mental calculations, changing proportions to percentages
Check-Up 2:   Mental calculations, changing more proportions to percentages
Check-Up 3:   Decimals and percentages
Check-Up 9:   Expressing a percentage in fraction notation
Check-Up 15: Using a calculator to express a proportion as a percentage
Check-Up 20: Mental calculations, finding a percentage of a quantity
Check-Up 21: Finding a percentage of a quantity using a calculator
Check-Up 33: Increasing or decreasing by a percentage
Check-Up 34: Expressing an increase or decrease as a percentage
Check-Up 35: Finding the original value after a percentage increase or decrease

Glossary of key terms introduced in Chapter 19

Direct proportion: the relationship between two variables where the ratio of one to the other is constant. For example, the number of cows' legs in a field and the number of cows would normally be in direct proportion.

Variable: a quantity the value or size of which can vary; for example, the number of children in a school is a variable, whereas the number of letters in the word 'school' is not.

Per cent (%):   in (or 'for') each hundred; for example, 87% means 87 in each hundred.

Proportion: a comparative part of a quantity or set. A proportion (such as 4 out of 10) can be expressed as a fraction ($^2/_5$), as a percentage (40%) or as a decimal (0.4).

Percentage increase or percentage decrease: an increase or decrease expressed as a percentage of the original value.

20
Algebra

 In this chapter there are explanations of

- the nature of algebraic thinking and the central idea of making generalizations;
- the difference in the meaning of letters used as abbreviations in arithmetic and as used in algebra;
- the idea of a letter representing a variable;
- some other differences between arithmetic thinking and algebraic thinking;
- precedence of operators;
- ways of introducing children to the idea of a letter as a variable;
- the important role played by tabulation;
- the ideas of sequential and global generalization;
- independent and dependent variables;
- the meaning of the word 'mapping' in an algebraic context; and
- using spreadsheets for trial and improvement and budgeting.

Algebra? Isn't that secondary school mathematics?

My main aim in writing this chapter is to disabuse the reader of this notion! By the time you get to the end I hope you will have a better understanding of the true nature of algebraic thinking. It's not just about simplifying expressions like $2x + 3x$ to get $5x$, rearranging formulas and solving quadratic equations. Genuine algebraic thinking starts in the exploration of number patterns in the early years of primary school. Below are some examples of things that children up to the age of 7 years might do that are the beginnings of thinking algebraically.

- Explore and discuss patterns in odd and even numbers.
- Understand a statement like 'all numbers ending in 5 or 0 can be grouped into fives' and check whether this is true in particular cases, using counters.
- On a grid 3 squares wide, colour in the numbers 1, 4, 7, 10, 13, 16 … and describe the pattern that emerges (see Figure 20.1).
- Recognize the relationship between doubling and halving.
- Put the numbers from 1 to 10 into a 'double and add 1' rule and discuss the pattern of numbers that emerges.

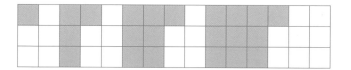

Figure 20.1 *The pattern for the sequence 1, 4, 7, 10 …*

Examples such as these, none of which uses letters for numbers, are about making *generalizations*. This, as we shall see, is the essence of algebraic thinking.

So what do the letters used in algebra, like *x* and *y*, actually mean?

To answer this important question I will pose the reader two problems, using letters as symbols. First, the reader is invited to write down his or her answer to problem 1 before reading on:

Problem 1:   You can exchange 7 kroner for 1 euro. You have *e* euros.
You exchange this money for *k* kroner.
What is the relationship between *e* and *k*?

Most people I give this problem to write down $7k = e$ (or $7k = 1e$ or $e = 7k$ or $1e = 7k$, which are all different ways of saying the same thing). If you have done that, then please forgive me for deliberately leading you astray! The correct answer is actually $k = 7e$. Let me explain. Figure 20.2 shows various values for e and k. For example, if I have 1 euro ($e = 1$) I can exchange this for 7 kroner ($k = 7$); if I have 2 euros ($e = 2$) I can exchange them for 14 kroner ($k = 14$); similarly, when $e = 3$, $k = 21$, and so on. The table in Figure 20.2 makes it clear that whatever number is chosen for e (1, 2, 3, …) the value of k is 7 times this number (7, 14, 21, …). This is precisely what is meant by the algebraic statement, $k = 7e$.

No. of euros e	No. of kroner k
1	7
2	14
3	21
4	28
5	35

Figure 20.2   *Tabulating values for problem 1*

Many people who are quite well qualified in mathematics get this answer the wrong way round when this problem is given to them, so you need not feel too bad if you did as well. It is instructive to analyse the thinking which leads to this misunderstanding. When we wrongly write down $7k = e$ what we are thinking, of course, is that we are writing a statement that is saying '7 kroner make a euro'. The k and e are being used as abbreviations for 'kroner' and 'euro'. This is, of course, how we use letters in *arithmetic*, when they are actually abbreviations for fixed quantities or measurements. When we write 10p for ten pence or 5 m for five metres the p stands for 'a penny' and the m stands for 'a metre'. But this is precisely what the letters do *not* mean in **algebra**. They are not abbreviations for measurements. They do not represent 'a thing' or an object. They usually represent *variables*. The letter e in problem 1 stands for 'whatever number of euros you choose'. It does not stand for a euro, but for the *number* of euros. Now, try problem 2:

Problem 2:   The number of students in a school is s and the number of teachers is t. There are 20 times as many students as teachers. Write down an equation using s and t.

The temptation here is to write down the relationship between s and t incorrectly as $20s = t$. When we do this we think that what we are saying is, '20 students for 1 teacher'.

Here we are thinking that the *s* stands for 'a student' and the *t* stands for 'a teacher'. Again, we see the same misunderstanding. In problem 2 the symbols *s* and *t* are not abbreviations for a student and a teacher. They stand for 'the number of students' and 'the number of teachers'. They are variables. The value of *t* can be any number and whatever number is chosen, the value of *s* is 20 times this. So the relationship is $s = 20t$. This means 'the number of students is 20 times the number of teachers' or, referring to the tabulation of values in Figure 20.3, 'the number in column *s* is 20 times whatever number is in column *t*'.

LEARNING and TEACHING POINT

If you introduce older primary children to the use of letters to express general statements emphasize the idea that a letter in algebra stands for 'whatever number is chosen', that is, a variable.

No. of teachers *t*	No. of students *s*
1	20
2	40
3	60
4	80
5	100

Figure 20.3 *Tabulating values for problem 2*

It is understandable that so many people get the algebraic statements in these problems the wrong way round. First, the choice of *e*, *k*, *s*, *t* as letters to represent the variables in the problems is actually unhelpful (deliberately, I have to admit: sorry!). Using the first letters of the words 'euro', 'krone', 'student' and 'teacher' does rather suggest that they are abbreviations for these things. (Fewer people get these relationships the wrong way round if other letters are used for the variables, such as *n* and *m*.) Then, so many of us have been subjected to explanations in 'algebra lessons' that reinforce this misconception that the letters stand for things. For example, it does not help to explain $2a + 3a = 5a$ by saying '2 apples plus 3 apples makes 5 apples'. This again makes us think of *a* as an abbreviation for apples. What this statement means is: whatever number you choose for *a*, then '*a* multiplied by 2' plus '*a* multiplied by 3' is the same as '*a* multiplied by 5'.

LEARNING and TEACHING POINT

Avoid the fruit-salad approach to explaining algebraic statements, for example, referring to 3*a* as '3 apples' and 5*b* as '5 bananas', or anything that reinforces the ideas that the letters stand for objects or specific numbers.

Are there other differences between arithmetic and algebra in the way symbols are used that I should be aware of?

The distinction between the meaning of letters used in algebra (as variables) and in arithmetic (as abbreviations) is undoubtedly one of the most crucial differences between these two branches of mathematics. But there are a number of other significant differences of which teachers should be aware:

- the use of the equals sign and lack of closure;
- the need to recognize the mathematical structure of a problem;
- the distinction between solving a problem and representing it; and
- the need to recognize 'precedence of operators'.

Surely the equals sign always means the same thing, doesn't It?

What the equals sign means strictly in mathematical terms is not the same thing necessarily as the way it is interpreted in practice. When doing arithmetic, that is manipulating numbers, most children (and especially younger children) think of the equals sign as an instruction to do something with some numbers, to perform an operation. They see '3 + 5 =' and respond by doing something: adding the 3 and the 5 to get 8. So, given the question, 3 + □ = 5, many younger children put 8 in the box; they see the equals sign as an instruction to perform an operation on the numbers in the question, and naturally respond to the '+' sign by adding them up.

Children also use the equals sign simply as a device for connecting the calculation they have performed with the result of the calculation. It means simply, 'This is what I did and this is what I got …'. Given the problem, 'You have £28, earn £5 and spend £8, how much do you have now?' children will quite happily write something like: 28 + 5 = 33 – 8 = 25. This way of recording the calculation is mathematically incorrect, because 28 + 5 does not equal 33 – 8. But this is not what the child means, of course. What is written down here represents the child's thinking about the problem, or the buttons he or she has pressed on a calculator to solve it. It simply means something like, 'I added 28 and 5, and got the answer 33, and then I subtracted 8 and this came to 25'.

In algebra, however, the equals sign must be seen as representing *equivalence*. It means that what is written on one side 'is the same as' what is written on the other side. Of course, it has this meaning in arithmetic as well: 3 + 5 = 8 does mean that 3 + 5 is the same as 8. But children rarely use it to mean this; their experience reinforces the perception of the equals sign as an instruction to perform an operation with some numbers. In algebraic statements it is the idea of equivalence that is strongest in the way the equals sign is used. For example, when we write $p + q = r$, this is not actually an instruction to add p and q. In fact, we may not have to do anything at all with the statement. It is simply a statement of equivalence between one variable and the sum of two others. This apparent lack of closure is a cause of consternation to some children. If the answer to an algebra question is $p + q$, they will have the feeling that there is still something to be done, because they are so wedded to the idea that the addition sign is an instruction to do something to the p and the q.

What is different about arithmetic and algebra in relation to recognizing the mathematical structure of a problem?

In arithmetic, children often succeed through adopting informal, intuitive, context-bound approaches to solving problems. Often they do this without having to be aware explicitly of the underlying mathematical structure. For example, many children will be able to solve, 'How much for 10 grams of chocolate if you can get 2 grams per penny?' without recognizing the formal

structure of the problem as that of division. So, even with a calculator, they may then be unable to solve the same problem with more difficult numbers: 'How much for 75 grams of chocolate if you can get 1.35 grams per penny?'

The corresponding algebraic problem is a generalization of all problems with this same structure: 'How much for p grams of chocolate if you can get q grams per penny?' It is often no use in trying to explain this by just putting in some simple numbers for p and q and asking what you do to these numbers to answer the question if the children do not recognize the existence of a division structure here at all. The primitive, intuitive thinking about the arithmetic problem with simple numbers does not make the mathematical structure explicit in a way that supports the algebraic generalization, $p \div q$. It is partly because of this that I have put so much stress on the *structures* of addition, subtraction, multiplication and division in Chapters 7 and 10.

Can you explain the distinction between solving a problem and representing it?

The discussion above leads to a further significant difference between arithmetic and algebra. Given a problem to solve in arithmetic involving more than one operation, the question we ask ourselves is, 'What sequence of operations is needed to *solve* this problem?' In algebra, the question is, 'What sequence of operations is needed to *represent* this problem?' For example, consider this problem:

> Problem 3:   A plumber's call-out charge is £15; then you pay £12 an hour. How many hours' work would cost £75?

The arithmetic thinking might be: $75 - 15 = 60$, then $60 \div 12 = 5$. This is the sequence of operations required to *solve* the problem. But the algebraic approach would be to let *n* stand for the number of hours (which is therefore a variable and can take any value) and then to write down: $12n + 15 = 75$. This is the sequence of operations that *represents* the problem. (Then to solve the problem we have to find the value of *n* that makes this algebraic equation true.)

It is quite possible, therefore, that the two approaches, as illustrated here, result in the use of inverse operations. To solve the problem we think: subtraction, then division; but to represent the problem algebraically we think: multiplication, then addition. It is this kind of difference in the thinking involved which makes it so difficult for many children to make generalized statements using words or algebraic symbols, even of the simplest kind.

What is meant by 'precedence of operators'?

An expression like $3 + 5 \times 2$ is potentially ambiguous. If you do the addition first the answer is 16. But if you do the multiplication first the answer is 13. Which is correct?

Well, if you enter this calculation as it stands on to the kind of basic calculator used in primary schools (using the key sequence: $3, +, 5, \times, 2, =$), you get 16. The calculator does the operations in the order they are entered. However, if you use a more advanced, scientific calculator, with the same key sequence, you will probably get the answer 13. These calculators use what is called an **algebraic operating system** (as do many computer applications, such as spreadsheet programs). This means that they adopt the convention of giving precedence to the operations of multiplication and division. So, when you enter 3, 5, the calculator waits to determine whether there is a multiplication or a division following the 5; if there is, this is done first. If you actually mean to do the addition first, you would have to use brackets to indicate this: for example, $(3 + 5) \times 2$.

Now this convention of **precedence of operators** (sometimes called 'the hierarchy of operations') is always applied strictly in algebra and is essential for avoiding ambiguity, particularly because of the way symbols are used in algebra to represent problems not just to solve them. So, for example, $x + y \times z$ definitely stands for 'x added to the product of y and z'; to represent 'x added to y, then multiply by z' we would write $(x + y) \times z$.

But in arithmetic – and therefore in number work in primary schools – we do not usually need this convention. The calculations we have to do would normally arise from a practical context which will naturally determine the order in which the various operations have to be performed, so there is not usually any ambiguity. Since the basic calculators we use in primary schools deal with operations in the order they arrive, there is little point in giving children calculations like $32 + 8 \times 5$ and insisting that this means you do the multiplication first. If that is what we want, then write either $8 \times 5 + 32$ or $32 + (8 \times 5)$. But as soon as we get into using algebra to express generalizations, we need this convention for precedence of operators. At this stage children will have to learn to recognize it and to use brackets as necessary to override it.

This is an opportune moment to mention the convention of dropping the multiplication sign in algebraic expressions and sometimes in arithmetic calculations where brackets remove any ambiguity. For example, the calculation $(3 + 5) \times 2$, using the commutative law, can be written as $2 \times (3 + 5)$; and then, using the convention, this could be written as $2(3 + 5)$. The multiplication sign is omitted but understood. Similarly, $(x + y) \times z$ would normally be written as $z(x + y)$ and $x + y \times z$ would normally be written as $x + yz$.

How can the idea of a letter being a variable be introduced to children?

The central principle in algebra is the use of letters to represent *variables*, which enable us to express *generalizations*. Children should therefore first encounter the use of letters as algebraic symbols for this purpose. The most effective way of doing this is through the tabulation of number patterns in columns, with the problem being to express the pattern in the numbers, first in words and later in symbols. A useful game in this context is *What's my rule?*

Figure 20.4 shows some examples of this game. In each case the children are challenged to say what is the rule that is being used to find the numbers in column B and then to use this rule to find the number in column B when the number in column A is 100. In example (a), children usually observe first that the rule is 'adding 2'. Here they have spotted what I refer to when talking to children as the 'up-and-down rule'. When talking to teachers I call it the **sequential generalization**. This is the pattern that determines how to continue the sequence.

Asking what answer do you get when the number in A is 100, or some other large number, makes us realize the inadequacy of the sequential generalization. We need a 'left-to-right rule': a rule that tells us what to do to the numbers in A to get the numbers in B. This is what I shall refer to as the **global generalization**. Many children towards the top end of the primary range can usually determine that when the number in A is

(a)			(b)			(c)			(d)		
	A	B		A	B		A	B		A	B
	1	3		1	3		1	3		1	99
	2	5		2	7		2	8		2	98
	3	7		3	11		3	13		3	97
	4	9		4	15		4	18		4	96
	5	11		5	19		5	23		5	95
	6	13		6	23		6	28		6	94
	7	15		7	27		7	33		7	93
	8	17		8	31		8	38		8	92
	9	19		9	35		9	43		9	91
	10	21		10	39		10	48		10	90
	100	?		100	?		100	?		100	?

Figure 20.4   *What's my rule?*

100, the number in B is 201, and this helps them to recognize that the rule is 'double and add 1'.

Later this can be expressed algebraically. If we use x to stand for 'any number in column A' and y to stand for the corresponding number in column B, then the generalization is $y = x \times 2 + 1$, or $y = 2x + 1$. This clearly uses the idea of letters as variables, expressing generalizations. The statement means essentially, 'The number in column B is whatever number is in column A multiplied by 2, add one'.

Similarly, in Figure 20.4(b), the sequential generalization, 'add 4', is easily spotted. More difficult is the global generalization, 'multiply by 4 and subtract 1', although again working out what is in B when 100 is in A helps to make this rule explicit. This leads to the algebraic statement, $y = x \times 4 - 1$, or $y = 4x - 1$.

In these kinds of examples, where x is chosen and a rule is used to determine y, x is called the **independent variable** and y is called the **dependent variable**.

LEARNING and TEACHING POINT

The *What's my rule?* game can be used in simple examples with quite young children to introduce them to algebraic thinking through making generalizations in words. Use the game with older, more able children to express their generalizations in symbols.

Where else are tabulation and algebraic generalization used?

This experience of tabulation and finding generalizations to describe the patterns that emerge occurs very often in *mathematical investigations*, particularly those involving a sequence of geometric shapes. An example is the investigation of square picture frames in

Chapter 4 (see Figure 4.1 and the associated text), where the global generalization was given as $f = 4n - 4$. Other examples would be the patterns of shapes discussed in Chapter 15. For example, an investigation into the pattern in the triangle numbers shown in Figure 15.5 could lead to the generalization that the nth triangle number, which is the sum of $1 + 2 + 3 + 4 + 5 \ldots + n$, is equal to $\frac{1}{2}n(n + 1)$. The reader is invited to confirm this in self-assessment question 20.8 below.

LEARNING and TEACHING POINT

Encourage children to tabulate results from investigations, to enable them to find and articulate patterns in the sequence of numbers obtained.

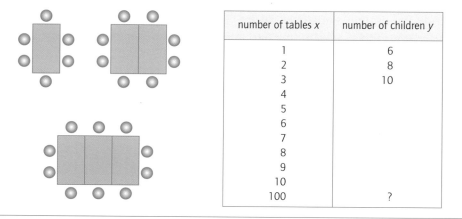

number of tables x	number of children y
1	6
2	8
3	10
4	
5	
6	
7	
8	
9	
10	
100	?

Figure 20.5 *An investigation leading to a generalization*

Figure 20.5 provides another example: the problem is to determine how many children can sit around various numbers of tables, arranged side by side, if six children can sit around one table. The number of tables here is the independent variable and the number of children the dependent variable.

With 2 tables we can seat 8 children; with 3 tables we can seat 10. These results are already tabulated. The tabulation can then be completed for other numbers of tables, the sequential generalization can be articulated, the answer for 100 tables can be predicted and finally the global generalization can be formulated. This will be first in words ('the

LEARNING and TEACHING POINT

Take children through this procedure, allowing children of differing abilities to reach different stages: tabulate results in an orderly fashion; articulate the up-and-down rule; check this with a few more results; predict the result for a big number, such as 100; articulate the left-to-right rule in words; check this on some results you know; and, for the most able children, express the left-to-right rule in symbols.

number y is equal to the number x multiplied by …') and then in symbols ($y = \ldots$), with x being the independent variable (the number of tables) and y the dependent variable (the corresponding number of children). This is left as an exercise for the reader, in self-assessment question 20.6 below.

So what is a mapping?

In the examples of tabulation used above there have always been the following three components: a set of input numbers (the values of the independent variable), a rule for doing something to these numbers and a set of output numbers (the values of the dependent variable). These three components put together – input set, rule, output set – constitute what is sometimes called a **mapping**. It is also sometimes called a *functional relationship* and the dependent variable is said to be a **function** of the independent variable.

This idea of a mapping, illustrated in Figure 20.6, is an all-pervading idea in algebra. In fact, most of what we have to learn to do in algebra fits into this simple structure of input, rule and output. Sometimes we are given the input and the rule and we have to find the output: this is substituting into a formula. Then sometimes we are given the input and the output and our task is to find the rule: this is the process of generalizing (as in the examples of tabulation above). Then, finally, we can be given the output and the rule and be required to find the input: this is the process of solving an **equation**. That just about summarizes the whole of algebra!

Figure 20.6   *A mapping*

Is solving equations something to introduce in primary schools?

As a formal algebraic process, I would not usually introduce solving equations in primary schools, especially since the techniques involved can so easily reinforce the idea that the letters stand for 'things', or even specific numbers, rather than variables. What is appropriate, however, is to introduce children to the algebraic thinking involved in solving problems through the *trial and improvement* approach (see Chapter 15) using a calculator or a computer spreadsheet. These can be purely numerical problems that cannot be solved by a simple arithmetic procedure, such as finding square roots and cube roots, as explained in Chapter 15, or they can be practical problems.

Simple problems about area and perimeter and budgeting are particularly useful here. I will demonstrate with a fairly challenging problem about area. In Figure 20.7, the problem posed is:

'What should be the length of the side of a square lawn if the area of the whole garden is to be 200 square metres?' The width of the patio is fixed as 5 metres.

This is approached by trying various inputs (for the side of the square) and using an appropriate rule to determine the outputs (the corresponding area of the garden). One possible rule is 'add 5 to the side of the square and multiply by the side of the square'. Expressing this in symbols: the area $= x(x + 5)$. So we are actually solving the equation, $x(x + 5) = 200$. The first trial is $x = 20$. This gives an area of 500,

which is too large. Next we try 10, which gives an area of 150, which is too small. So we try something in between, say, $x = 13$. This gives an area of 234, too large ... and so on, until we get an answer to whatever level of accuracy we require.

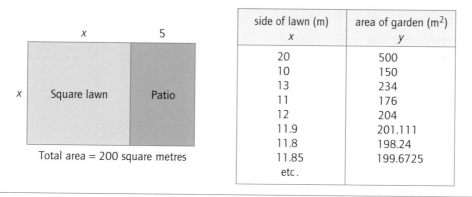

side of lawn (m) x	area of garden (m²) y
20	500
10	150
13	234
11	176
12	204
11.9	201.111
11.8	198.24
11.85	199.6725
etc.	

Total area = 200 square metres

Figure 20.7 *A problem solved by trial and improvement*

The calculations here can be done with a calculator, as they have been in the table in Figure 20.7. Alternatively, this kind of problem provides a good application of a computer spreadsheet package.

How would this problem be solved on a spreadsheet?

Figure 20.8 shows how this might work. In column A are entered the various trials used for the values of x. **Formulas** are entered into the cells in column B which calculate automatically the areas for the corresponding garden. Figure 20.8(a) shows what a typical **spreadsheet** might look like on the computer screen, with the areas in column B given to one decimal place. The solution found here is that (to 2 decimal places) a side of length 11.86 m gives the required area of 200 square metres.

The beauty of using a spreadsheet is that the formula for the area has to be entered only once. This can be explained with Figure 20.8 (b), which reveals the formulas that have been entered in the spreadsheet to produce the numbers in Figure 20.8(a). We

(a)

	A	B
1	x: Side of square (m)	Area of garden (m²)
2	20	500.0
3	10	150.0
4	13	234.0
5	11	176.0
6	12	204.0
7	11.8	198.2
8	11.9	201.1
9	11.88	200.5
10	11.87	200.2
11	11.86	200.0

(b)

	A	B
1	x: Side of square (m)	Area of garden (m²)
2	20	= A2*(A2+5)
3	10	= A3*(A3+5)
4	13	= A4*(A4+5)
5	11	= A5*(A5+5)
6	12	= A6*(A6+5)
7	11.8	= A7*(A7+5)
8	11.9	= A8*(A8+5)
9	11.88	= A9*(A9+5)
10	11.87	= A10*(A10+5)
11	11.86	= A11*(A11+5)

Figure 20.8   *Using a spreadsheet to solve x(x + 5) + 200*

first enter the appropriate formula in cell B2. This is '= A2*(A2 + 5)'. This means: take the number in cell A2 and multiply by the sum of the number in A2 plus 5. Note that the asterisk is used for multiplication. We then simply instruct the computer to fill this formula down the column – all spreadsheet packages have a simple procedure for doing this – and the computer automatically modifies the formula for each row, as shown. Then we can enter our various trials in column A and home in on the solution. The reader should note that it is a small step from entering a series of formulas like B2 = A2*(A2 + 5) to the algebraic generalization $y = x(x + 5)$.

The point about solving equations this way is that the letter involved (x metres standing for the length of the side of the square) is genuinely perceived as a variable – and our task is to find the value of this independent variable which generates the required value for the dependent variable (the total area). In this case we are finding the value of x for which $x(x + 5) = 200$. This idea of x being a variable is much more sophisticated and powerful than the idea that 'x stands for an unknown number'. I remember being told this at school and spending a whole year doing things like $2x + 3x = 5x$, all the time believing that the teacher actually knew what this unknown number was and that one day he would tell us.

How would spreadsheets be used in a problem about budgets?

The example I have used above is intended to be instructive for primary school teachers or trainees, to show the potential of spreadsheets. It is clearly at a fairly advanced level for most primary school children. So here's a simpler example of spreadsheets being used for a budget. The problem is:

> Drinks cost 35p, muffins cost 69p. John has some friends coming for a sleepover. How many drinks and muffins can he buy with a budget of £5?

	A	B	C	D	E
1	No. of drinks	Cost of drink (pence)	No. of muffins	Cost of a muffin (pence)	Total cost (pence)
2	8	35	4	69	556

Figure 20.9 *A budget problem set up on a spreadsheet*

A simple spreadsheet can be set up, as shown in Figure 20.9. Entered in cells B2 and D2 are costs of a drink and a muffin in pence. Entered in cells A2 and C2 are some initial guesses for how many drinks and how many muffins might be bought. In cell E2 is entered the formula for working out the total cost in pence: = A2*B2 + C2*D2. Note that no brackets are needed because the spreadsheet automatically gives precedence to multiplication over division. The answer for the total cost of 8 drinks and 4 muffins (566 pence) appears in cell E2. This is clearly over budget. All John has to do now is to change the values of the variables in cells A2 and C2. For example, John might change the number of drinks in cell A2 to 4; immediately the number in cell E2 changes to 416, well under the budget. He then might increase the number of muffins by changing the number in cell C2 to 5; now the number in cell E2 becomes 485, still under budget. And so on! This kind of problem set up on a spreadsheet is a very accessible introduction to the ideas of independent and dependent variables and therefore to genuine algebraic thinking.

Research focus

The use of spreadsheets for encouraging algebraic thinking is supported by research. Tall and Thomas (1991) identified three obstacles in learning algebra. The *parsing obstacle* refers to the conflict with the natural language process of reading from left to right; this is the basis of the error that translates, for example, $2 + 3a$ into $5a$. The *lack of closure obstacle* is the problem caused by the fact that, say, $2 + 3a$ cannot be simplified any further. The *process–product* obstacle is the fact that an expression such as $2 + 3a$ represents both the process by which a computation might be carried out and the product of that computation. These are some of the conflicts with arithmetic thinking identified earlier in this chapter. Tall and Thomas demonstrated that children who had a three-week programme called 'The Dynamic Algebra Module' were better able to cope with all three of these obstacles than their peers. The module consisted of computer-based activities that involved the use of letters to label cells, and values and formulas assigned to these cells, rather like the spreadsheet approach advocated towards the end of this chapter. In another piece of research, Ainley (2001) interviewed Year 6 children who had used spreadsheets to solve problems, such as 'guess my rule' activities, and found that they were beginning to show a grasp of the notion of variables, could reason with unknown quantities and were not confused by algebraic notation.

Suggestions for further reading

1. Chapter 7 on algebra in Brown (2003) will provide the reader with a comprehensive coverage of all the algebra they will ever need and more. It is written from the perspective of primary school teaching and raises important issues about teaching this area of mathematics. The reader is enabled to see how formal algebra evolves developmentally from early experiences of sorting and patterns.
2. Chapter 7 of Orton (2004), written by Orton and Orton, is entitled 'Pattern and the approach to algebra'. They discuss the use of number patterns as a route into algebra and explore children's approaches to identifying and articulating simple patterns. It includes a study of the performance of 10–13-year-old children on tasks involving the recognition and formulation of simple generalizations from number patterns.

Self-assessment questions

20.1: The length of a garden is f feet. Measured in yards, it is y yards long. What is the relationship between f and y? (There are three feet in one yard.) What criticism could you make of this question?

20.2: If I buy a apples at 10p each and b bananas at 12p each, what is the meaning of: (a) $a + b$; (b) $10a$; (c) $12b$; and (d) $10a + 12b$? What criticism could you make of this question?

20.3: The first 5 rides in a fair are free. The charge for all the other rides is £2 each. If Jenny has £12 to spend, how many rides can she have? What are the arithmetic steps you used in answering this question? How would you *represent* the problem algebraically, using n to stand for the number of rides?

20.4: What answer would you get if you entered $25 - 5 \times 3$ on to: (a) a basic calculator; and (b) a scientific calculator using an algebraic operating system?

20.5: For each of Figures 20.4(c) and 20.4(d), using x for any number in column A and y for the corresponding number in column B, write down:

(a) the sequential generalization;
(b) the value of *y* when *x* is 100;
(c) the global generalization in words; and
(d) the global generalization in symbols (*y* = …).

20.6: Complete the tabulation of results in Figure 20.5. Then write down:

(a) the sequential generalization;
(b) the number of children if there are 100 tables;
(c) the global generalization in words; and
(d) the global generalization in symbols (*y* = …).

Now repeat this investigation with the tables arranged end to end, rather than side by side (for 2 tables the number of children is 10).

20.7: I choose a number, double it, add 3 and multiply the answer by my number. The result is 3654. What is my number? Use a calculator or spreadsheet and the trial and improvement method to answer this. What equation have you solved?

20.8: List the first 10 triangle numbers: 1, 3, 6, 10, and so on. Now double these to get 2, 6, 12, 20, and so on. Express each of these numbers as products of two factors, starting with 1×2, 2×3, 3×4. Hence obtain a generalization for the *n*th triangle number (the sum of the first *n* natural numbers). What is the one-hundredth triangle number (that is, the sum of all the natural numbers from 1 to 100)?

Further practice

From the Student Workbook

Tasks 132–134: Checking understanding of mental strategies for algebra
Tasks 135–137: Using and applying algebra
Tasks 138–139: Learning and teaching of algebra

On the website (www.sagepub.co.uk/haylock)

Check-Up 13: Using a four-function calculator, precedence of operators
Check-Up 44: Substituting into formulas

Glossary of key terms introduced in Chapter 20

Algebra: a branch of mathematics in which letters are used to represent variables in order to express generalizations.

Algebraic operating system: a system used by scientific calculators and spreadsheet software that follows the algebraic conventions of precedence of operators.

Precedence of operators: a convention that, unless otherwise indicated by brackets, the operations of multiplication and division should have precedence over addition and subtraction. This convention is always used in algebraic expressions.

Sequential generalization: when the input and output sets of a mapping are tabulated, a rule for getting the next value of the dependent variable from the previous one(s); the up-and-down rule.

Global generalization: when the input and output sets of a mapping are tabulated, a rule for getting the value of the dependent variable from any value of the independent variable; the left-to-right rule.

Independent variable: in a relationship between two variables, the variable whose values may be chosen freely from the given input set, and are then put into the rule to generate the values of the dependent variable in the output set.

Dependent variable: in a relationship between two variables, the one whose values are determined by the value of the independent variable and the rule.

Mapping: a system consisting of an input set, a rule and an output set.

Function: in a mapping, the relationship between the dependent variable and the independent variable. For example, if $y = 2x + 1$, then y is a function of x.

Equation: a statement of equivalence involving one or more variables, which may or may not be true for any particular value of the variable(s). To solve an equation is to find all the values of the variable(s) that make the equivalence true. For example, $2x + 1 = 16 - x$ is an equation with the solution $x = 5$.

Formula: an algebraic rule involving one or more independent variables, used to determine the value of a dependent variable; also a rule entered into a cell in a spreadsheet to determine its value.

Spreadsheet: on a computer, a rectangular array of cells, labelled by rows and columns (for example, cell B3 is in column B and row 3), into which data can be entered; the data can be words, numbers or formulas.

21
Coordinates and Linear Relationships

In this chapter there are explanations of

- how the coordinate system enables us to specify location in a plane;
- axis, *x*-coordinate and *y*-coordinate, origin;
- the meaning of 'quadrant' in the context of coordinates;
- the difference between the coordinate system for labelling points in a plane and other systems which label spaces;
- how to plot an algebraic relationship as a graph;
- linear relationships, including those where one variable is directly proportional to another; and
- how coordinates can be used to investigate geometric properties.

How does the coordinate system work and what are quadrants?

The coordinate system is a wonderfully simple but elegant device for specifying location in two dimensions. Two number lines are drawn at right angles to each other, as shown in Figure 21.1. These are called **axes** (pronounced *ax-eez*, the plural of *axis*). Of course, the lines can continue as far as we wish at either end. The point where the two lines meet (called the **origin**) is taken as the zero for both number lines. The vertical line is called the *y*-axis, and the horizontal line the *x*-axis. Then any

LEARNING and TEACHING POINT

There is actually no need to limit primary-school children's experience of coordinates to the first quadrant, since the principles are the same in the other quadrants and these provide some useful experience of interpreting and applying negative numbers.

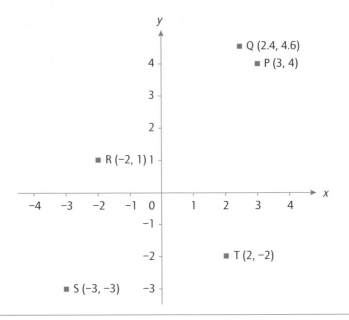

Figure 21.1   *The coordinate system*

point in the plane can be specified by two numbers, called its **coordinates**. The x-coordinate of a point is the distance moved along the x-axis, and the y-coordinate is the distance moved vertically, in order to get from the origin to the point in question. For example, to reach the point P shown in Figure 21.1 we would move 3 units along the x-axis and then 4 units vertically, so the x-coordinate of P is 3 and the y-coordinate is 4. We then state that the coordinates of P are (3, 4). The convention is always to give the x-coordinate first and the y-coordinate second.

The axes divide the plane into four sections, called **quadrants**. The **first quadrant** consists of all the points that have a positive number for each of their two coordinates. The points P and Q in Figure 21.1 are in the first quadrant. The point R (−2, 1) is in the second quadrant, S (−3, −3) in the third quadrant and T (2, −2) in the fourth quadrant.

The beauty of this system is that we can now refer specifically to any point in the plane. And, of course, we are not limited to integers, as is shown by the point Q, with coordinates (2.4, 4.6). We can also use the coordinate system to describe the movement from one point to another. For example, from R to P is a movement of 5 units in the x-direction and 3 units in the y-direction; from T to S is a movement of −5 in the x-direction and −1 in the y-direction.

LEARNING and TEACHING POINT

Give children the chance to play simple games where they use the coordinate system to describe movements from one point to another.

An important feature of this system is that it is the points in the plane that are labelled by the coordinates, not the *spaces*. This is an important teaching point, because there are a number of situations that children will encounter which use coordinate systems based on the idea of labelling the spaces – for example, a number of board games and computer games, city street maps, and computer spreadsheets. A common system employed in these and other similar examples is to use the labels for the columns (for example, A, B, C ...) and the labels for the rows (for example, 1, 2, 3 ...) to specify individual cells or squares (for example, B3), as we saw in the preceding chapter when labelling the cells in a spreadsheet.

What are linear relationships?

The system described above is sometimes called the *Cartesian coordinate system.* It takes its name from René Descartes (1596–1650), a prodigious French mathematician, who first made use of the system to connect geometry and algebra. He discovered that by interpreting the inputs and outputs from an algebraic mapping (see Chapter 20) as coordinates, and then plotting these as points, you could generate a geometric picture of the relationship. Then by the reverse process, starting with a geometric picture drawn on a coordinate system, you can generate an algebraic representation of the geometric properties. At primary school level, we can only just touch on these massive mathematical ideas, so a couple of simple examples will suffice here.

First, we can take any simple algebraic relationship of the kind considered in Chapter 20 and explore the corresponding geometric picture. The convention is to use the x-axis for the independent variable. For example, the table shown in Figure 20.4(a) is generated by the algebraic rule, $y = 2x + 1$. In this case, x is the independent variable and is represented by the x-axis, and y, the dependent

variable, is represented by the y-axis. The pairs of values in the table can be written as coordinates, as follows: (1, 3), (2, 5), (3, 7), and so on. When these are plotted, as shown in Figure 21.2(a), it is clear that they lie on a straight line. These points can then be joined up and the line continued indefinitely, as shown in Figure 21.2(b). This straight line is a powerful geometric image of the way in which the two variables are related. An algebraic rule like $y = 2x + 1$ which produces a straight-line graph is called a **linear relationship**.

(a)   (b)

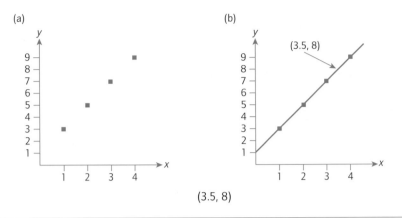

(3.5, 8)

Figure 21.2   *The rule y = 2x + 1 represented by coordinates*

We can use the straight-line graph to read off
related values of x and y other than those plotted;
for example, the arrow in Figure 21.2(b) shows
that when $y = 8$, $x = 3.5$. What we have done
here is to find the value of the variable x for which
$2x + 1 = 8$; in other words, we have *solved the
equation* $2x + 1 = 8$. This can be an early introduction to the important mathematical method
of solving equations by drawing graphs and
reading off values.

Exploring the graphs of different algebraic rules leads us to recognize a linear relationship as one in which the rule is simply a combination of multiplying or dividing by
a fixed number and addition or subtraction. For example, all these rules are linear
relationships:

divide by 6 and add 4 $(y = {}^{x}/_{6} + 4)$
multiply by 7 and subtract 5 $(y = 7x - 5)$
multiply by 3 and subtract from 100 $(y = 100 - 3x)$
add 1 and multiply by 2 $(y = 2(x + 1))$

There are, of course, relationships that are non-linear. These have other kinds of rules,
for example, those involving squares (multiply the input by itself) and other powers
(cubes, and so on), which produce sets of coordinates that do not lie on straight lines.
Typically these kinds of relationships produce curved graphs. Non-linear relationships
are beyond the scope of this book.

What happens when *y* is directly proportional to *x*?

The simplest kind of linear relationship is where *y* is *directly proportional* to *x* (see Chapter 19). This means that the ratio of *y* to *x* is constant, or, to put it another way, *y* is obtained by multiplying *x* by a constant factor. Examples of this kind of relationship abound in everyday life.

If a bottle of wine costs £3, *x* is the number of bottles I buy and *y* is the total cost in pounds, then the rule for finding *y* is 'multiply *x* by 3' or $y = 3x$.

This rule generates the coordinates, (1, 3), (2, 6), (3, 9), and so on, and, including the possibility that I do not buy any bottles, (0, 0). As shown in Figure 21.3, this rule produces a straight-line graph, which passes through the origin, (0, 0).

Here are two simple tips for spotting that two variables are directly proportional:

1. If one variable takes the value 0, so does the other one.
2. If you double one variable, you double the other one.

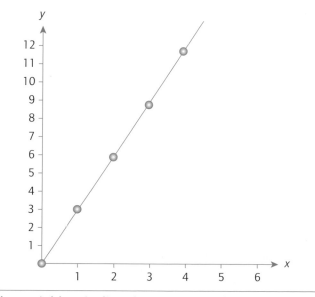

Figure 21.3 *The variable y is directly proportional to x*

Any rule of this kind, in which y is directly proportional to x, such as $y = 7x$, $y = 0.5x$, $y = 2.75x$, will produce a straight-line graph passing through the origin. An interesting point for discussion in the example above relates to the fact that the number of bottles bought can only be a whole number: you cannot buy 3.6 bottles, for example. (In Chapter 27 we refer to such a variable as a 'discrete variable'.) This means that the points on the line between the whole number values do not actually have any meaning. By contrast, if x had been the number of litres of petrol being bought at £3 per litre (price used for demonstration purposes only), then the rule would have been the same, $y = 3x$, but this time x would be a continuous variable and all the points on the straight-line graph in the first quadrant would have meaning. For example, when x is 3.6, y is 10.8, corresponding to a charge of £10.80 for 3.6 litres of petrol.

This provides us with a practical method for solving direct proportion problems. For example, most conversions from one unit of measurement to another provide examples of two variables that are directly proportional and will therefore generate a straight-line graph passing through the origin. This will always be the case where zero of one kind of unit of measurement corresponds to zero of the other kind. So, an exception, for example, would be converting temperatures between °F and °C; the relationship between these two temperature scales is not linear.

Consider exchanging British pounds for US dollars, for example, assuming the tourist exchange rate is given as $1.45 dollars to the pound. A quick bit of mental arithmetic tells us that $29 is equivalent to £20. Plotting this as the point with coordinates (29, 20) and drawing the straight line through this point and the origin produces a standard conversion graph, as shown in Figure 21.4. This can then be

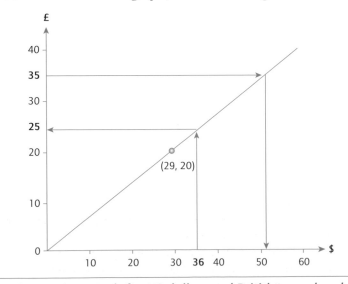

Figure 21.4 *Conversion graph for US dollars and British pounds, where $29 = £20*

used to do other conversions. The arrows, for example, show (a) how you would convert $36 to just under £25, and (b) £35 to just over $50. All problems of direct proportion, such as those tackled by arithmetic methods in Chapter 19, can also be solved by this graphical method (see, for example, self-assessment question 21.6 below).

Can you give an example of an investigation using coordinates?

Using coordinates we can easily communicate a geometric shape, made up of straight lines, to someone else. For example, I could ask a class of children to plot the points (1, 2), (3, 2), (3, 6) and (1, 6) and to join these points up in the order given, to produce the rectangle ABCD in Figure 21.5. The corners A, B, C and D are called the *vertices* of the rectangle (each one is a **vertex**). Similarly, rectangle PQRS is produced by plotting (5, 2), (9, 4), (8, 6) and (4, 4).

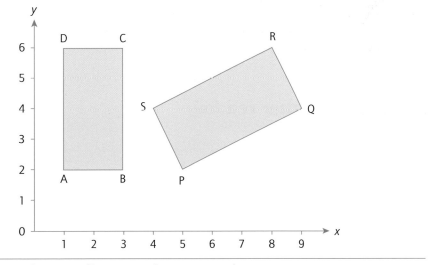

Figure 21.5 *Using coordinates to draw rectangles*

An interesting question can now be investigated: what rules or numerical patterns determine the coordinates of the four vertices of a rectangle? For example, we might notice that the movement from P to S (−1 in the *x*-direction, 2 in the *y*-direction) is the same as that from Q to R; and similarly for S to R and P to Q. A particularly interesting rule relates the coordinates of opposite vertices. I will leave readers to discover this for themselves (see self-assessment question 21.4 below). In this way we can analyse geometric properties, such as the characteristics of a rectangle, by means of algebraic relationships. It is the potential for exploring the connection between algebraic and geometric relationships that makes the coordinate system such a fundamental part of mathematics at every level.

Research focus

The axes used in the Cartesian coordinate system are number lines. When the axes are used in plotting graphs the position on the number line represents a variable, the fundamental idea of algebra. In a fascinating study Carraher et al. (2006) provide evidence that primary school children can make use of algebraic representations like this that we might imagine to be beyond their reach. For example, some children aged 9–10 years were told a story that involved the differences in heights between three children. They were able to relate these differences to a number line with a central point labelled N, to represent the unknown height of one of the children, and other points labelled $N - 1$, $N - 2, N - 3, \ldots$, to the left, and $N + 1, N + 2, N + 3, \ldots$, to the right. The children were able to locate correctly the positions on this number line representing the other two children. In fact most of them could successfully complete this task using N to represent the unknown height of any of the three children in the story. The researchers conclude from their research that the children's understanding of simple linear functions such as $y = x + b$ and the use of position on a number line to represent an unknown value was robust and flexible.

Suggestions for further reading

1. Chapter 21 of Williams and Shuard (1994) explains how the idea of using coordinates builds on early forms of pictorial representation. The limitation of bar charts for showing a linear relationship is used as the rationale for introducing a coordinate system. The authors show also how the graphical ideas introduced in this chapter can be extended to explore a range of mathematical relationships.
2. To take the material in this chapter further, you could look at chapter 10 of Suggate, Davis and Goulding (2010), which deals with graphs and functions.

Self-assessment questions

21.1: A knight's move in chess is two units horizontally (left or right) and one unit vertically (up or down), or two units vertically and one unit horizontally. Starting at (3, 3), which points can be reached by a knight's move? Plot them and join them up.

21.2: On squared paper, plot some of the points corresponding to each of the tables (b), (c) and (d) in Figure 20.4. Are the algebraic rules here linear relationships?

21.3: Give an example of a variable which is directly proportional to each of the following independent variables: (a) the number of boxes of six eggs bought by a shopper; (b) the number of bars of a piece of music in waltz time that someone plays on the piano; and (c) the bottom number in a set of equivalent fractions.

21.4: Plot the three points, (1, 2), (0, 3) and (3, 6), on squared paper. Join them up in this order and find the fourth point needed to complete a rectangle. Looking at this example and the two rectangles in Figure 21.5, what is the rule connecting the coordinates of opposite vertices of a rectangle? Use this rule to determine the fourth vertex of a rectangle, if the first three vertices are (4, 4), (5, 8), (13, 6). Check your answer by plotting the points and joining them up.

21.5: Use Figure 21.2(b) to solve the equation $2x + 1 = 6$.

21.6: Use the fact that 11 stone is about the same as 70 kilograms to draw a conversion graph for stones and kilograms. Convert your personal weight from one to the other.

Further practice

From the Student Workbook

Tasks 140–142: Checking understanding of coordinates and linear relationships
Tasks 143–145: Using and applying coordinates and linear relationships
Tasks 146–148: Learning and teaching of coordinates and linear relationships

On the website (www.sagepub.co.uk/haylock)

Check-Up 42: Conversion graphs

Glossary of key terms introduced in Chapter 21

Axes (plural of axis): in a two-dimensional coordinate system, two number lines drawn at right angles to represent the variables x and y. Conventionally, the horizontal axis represents the independent variable (x) and the vertical axis the dependent variable (y).

Origin: the point where the axes in a coordinate system cross; the point with coordinates (0, 0).

Coordinates: starting from the origin, the distance moved in the x-direction followed by the distance moved in the y-direction to reach a particular point; recorded as (x, y).

Quadrant: One of the four regions into which the plane is divided by the two axes in a coordinate system.

First quadrant: the quadrant consisting of all those points with positive coordinates.

Linear relationship: a relationship between two variables that produces a straight-line graph. If the two variables are directly proportional the straight line passes through the origin.

Vertex (plural vertices):   in a plane geometric shape with straight sides, a point where two sides meet; similarly, for a three-dimensional shape, a point where three or more edges meet.

SECTION D
SHAPE, SPACE AND MEASURES

22
Measurement

> **In this chapter there are explanations of**
>
> - the distinction between mass and weight;
> - the distinction between volume and capacity;
> - two aspects of the concept of time: time interval and recorded time;
> - the role of comparison and ordering as a foundation for measurement;
> - the principle of transitivity in the context of measurement;
> - some principles of inequalities, using the signs < and >;
> - conservation of length, mass and liquid volume;
> - non-standard and standard units;
> - the idea that all measurement is approximate;
> - the difference between a ratio scale and an interval scale;
> - SI and other metric units of length, mass and time, including the use of prefixes;
> - the importance of estimation and the use of reference items; and
> - imperial units still in use and their relationship to metric units.

What is the difference between mass and weight?

There is a real problem here about the language we use to describe what we are measuring when, for example, we put a book in one pan of a balance and equalize it with, say, 200 grams in the other. Colloquially, most people say that what we have found out is that the book *weighs* 200 grams, or that its **weight** is 200 grams. This is technically incorrect. What we have discovered is that the book *weighs the same as* a mass of 200 grams, or that the **mass** of the book is 200 grams. This conflict between everyday language usage and the scientifically correct usage is not resolved simply by using the two words, mass and weight, interchangeably.

The units we use for weighing, such as grams and kilograms, or pounds and ounces, are actually units for measuring the mass of an object, not its weight. The mass is a measurement of the quantity of matter there is in the object. Note that this is not the same thing as the amount of space it takes up – that is, the volume of the object. A small lump of lead might have the same mass as the 200-gram book, but it would take up much less space, because the molecules making up the piece of lead are much more tightly packed together than those in the book.

The problem with the concept of mass is that we cannot actually experience mass directly. I cannot see the mass of the book, feel it or perceive it in any way. When I hold the book in my hand what I experience is the weight of the book. The weight is the force exerted on the book by the pull of gravity. I can feel this, because I have to exert a force myself to hold the book up.

Of course, the weight and the mass are directly related: the greater the mass, the greater the weight, and therefore the heavier the object feels when I hold it in my hand. However, the big difference between the two is that, whereas the mass of an object is invariant, the weight changes depending on how far you are from the centre of the Earth (or whatever it is that is exerting the gravitational pull on the object).

We are all familiar with the idea that an astronaut's weight changes in space, or on the Moon, because the gravitational pull being exerted on the astronaut is less than it is on the Earth's surface. In some circumstances, for example when in orbit, this gravitational pull can effectively be cancelled out and the astronaut experiences 'weightlessness'. The astronaut can then place a book on the palm of his or her hand and it weighs nothing. On the Moon's surface the force exerted on the book by gravity, that is, the weight of the book, is about one-sixth of what it was back on the Earth's surface. But throughout all this the mass of the astronaut and the mass of the book remain unchanged. The book is still 200 grams, as it was on Earth, even though its weight has been changing constantly. (So a good way of losing weight is to go to the Moon, but this does not affect your waist size because what you really want to do is lose mass!)

An important point to note is that the balance-type weighing devices do actually measure mass. We put the book in one pan, balance it with a mass of 200 grams in the other pan, and because the book 'weighs the same as' a mass of 200 grams we conclude that it also has a mass of 200 grams. Note that we would get the same result using the balance on the Moon. However, the pointers on spring-type weighing devices, such as many kitchen scales and bathroom scales, actually respond directly to weight. This means that they would give a different reading if we took them to the Moon, for example. But, of course, they are calibrated for use on the Earth's surface, so when I stand on the bathroom scales and the pointer indicates 72 kilograms I can rely on that as a measurement of my mass. On the Moon it would point to 12 kilograms; this would just be wrong.

Because weight is a force, it should be measured in the units of force. The standard unit of force in the metric system is the **newton**, appropriately named after Sir Isaac Newton (1642–1727), the mathematical and scientific genius who first articulated this distinction between mass and weight. A newton is defined as the force required to increase the speed of a mass of 1 kilogram by 1 metre per second every second. A newton is actually about the weight of a small apple (on Earth) and a mass of a kilogram has a weight of nearly 10 newtons. You probably do not need to know this, although you may come across spring-type weighing devices with a scale graduated in newtons.

One way to introduce the word 'mass' to primary school children is to refer to those plastic or metal things we use for weighing objects in a balance as 'masses' (rather than 'weights'). So we would have a box of 10-gram masses and a box of 100-gram masses, and so on. Then when we have balanced an object against some masses, we can say that the object weighs the same as a mass of so many grams, as a step towards using the correct language, that the mass of the object is so many grams.

Can you explain the distinction between volume and capacity?

The **volume** of an object is the amount of three-dimensional space that it occupies. By historical accident, liquid volume and solid volume are conventionally measured in different units, although the concepts are exactly the same. Liquid volume is measured in litres and millilitres, and so on, whereas solid volume would have to be measured in units such as cubic metres and cubic centimetres. In the metric system the units for liquid and solid volume are related in a very simple way: 1 millilitre is the same volume as 1 cubic centimetre; or 1 litre is the same volume as 1000 cubic centimetres (see Figure 22.1).

Only containers have **capacity**. The capacity of a container is the maximum volume of liquid that it can hold. Hence capacity is measured in the same units as liquid volume. For example, if a wine glass holds 180 millilitres of wine when filled to the brim then its capacity is 180 millilitres.

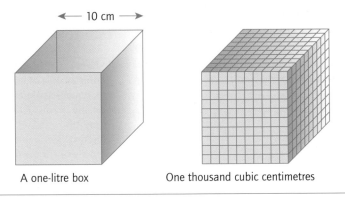

A one-litre box   One thousand cubic centimetres

Figure 22.1   *A litre is the same volume as 1000 cubic centimetres*

What about measuring time?

There are two quite different aspects of time that children have to learn to handle. First, there is the idea of a *time interval*. This refers to the length of time occupied by an activity, or the time that passes from one instant to another. Time intervals are measured in units such as seconds, minutes, hours, days, weeks, years, decades, centuries and millennia.

Then there is the idea of *recorded time*, the time at which an event occurs. To handle recorded time, we use the various conventions for reading the time of day, such as o'clocks, a.m. and p.m., the 24-hour system, together with the different ways of recording the date, including reference to the day of the week, the day in the month and the year. So, for example, we might say that the meeting starts at 1530 on Monday, 17 October 2011, using the concept of 'recorded time', and that it is expected to last for 90 minutes, using the concept of 'time interval'.

Time is one aspect of measurement that has not gone metric, so the relationships between the units (60 seconds in a minute, 60 minutes in an hour, 24 hours in a day, and so on) are particularly challenging. This makes it difficult, for example, to use a subtraction algorithm for finding the time intervals from one time to another. I strongly recommend that problems of this kind are done by an ad hoc process of adding-on. For example, to find the length of time of a journey starting at 10.45 a.m. and finishing at 1.30 p.m., reason like this:

From 10.45 a.m.:
15 minutes to 11 o'clock,
then 2 hours to 1 o'clock,
then a further 30 minutes to 1.30 p.m.
making a total of 2 hours and 45 minutes.

Setting this out as a formal subtraction would be inadvisable. But representing it as a calculation on a number line as shown in Figure 22.2 would be highly advisable.

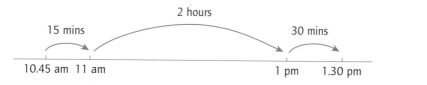

Figure 22.2   *Finding the time interval from 10.45 a.m. to 1.30 p.m. on a number line*

Learning about time is also complicated by the fact that the hands on a conventional dial-clock go round twice in a day; it would have been so much more sensible to go round once a day! Because of the association of a circle with 12 hours on a clock face, I always avoid using a circle to represent a day. For example, I would avoid a pie chart for 'how I spend a day' or a circular diagram showing the events of a day. For this last illustration I would recommend a diagram like that shown in Figure 22.3. Children can add to this pictures or verbal descriptions of what they are doing at various times of day.

Then there are the added complications related to the variety of watches and clocks that children may use, as well as the range of ways of saying the same time. For example, as well as being able to read a conventional dial-clock and a digital display in both 12-hour and 24-hour versions, children have to learn that the following all represent the same time of day: twenty to four in the afternoon, 3.40 p.m., 1540 (also written sometimes as 15:40 or 15.40). Incidentally, the colloquial use of, for example, 'fifteen hundred' to refer to the time 1500 in the 24-hour system is an unhelpful abuse of mathematical language. It reinforces the misunderstanding,

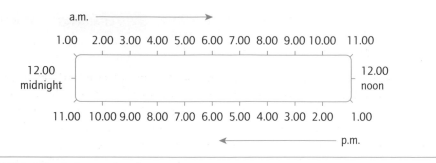

Figure 22.3 *A picture of a day*

mentioned in Chapter 6, of thinking that '00' is an abbreviation for 'hundred'. I prefer the BBC World Service convention: 'The time is fifteen hours.'

A couple of further small points relate to noon and midnight. First, note that 'a.m.' and 'p.m.' are abbreviations for **ante meridiem** and **post meridiem**, meaning 'before noon' and 'after noon', respectively. This means that 12 noon is neither a.m. nor p.m. It is just 12 noon. Similarly, 12 o'clock midnight is neither a.m. nor p.m. Then, in the 24-hour system, midnight is the moment when the recorded time of day starts again, so it is not 2400, but 0000, **'zero hours'**.

What principles are central to teaching measurement in the primary age range?

Some of the central principles in learning about measurement relate to the following headings:

- comparison and ordering;
- transitivity;
- conservation;
- non-standard and standard units;
- approximation;
- a context for developing number concepts; and
- the meaning of zero.

What have comparison and ordering to do with measurement?

The foundation of all aspects of measurement is direct comparison, putting two and then more than two objects (or events) in order according to the attribute in question. The language of comparison, discussed in relation to subtraction in Chapter 7, is of central importance here. Two objects are placed side by side and children determine which is the longer, which is the shorter. Two items are placed in the pans of a balance and children determine which is the heavier, which is the lighter. Water is poured from one container to another to determine which holds more, which holds less. Two children perform specified tasks, starting simultaneously, and observe which takes a longer time, which takes a shorter time. No units are involved at this stage, simply direct comparison leading to putting two or more objects or events in order.

Recording the results of comparison and ordering can be an opportunity to develop the use of the *inequality signs* (see Chapter 15). So, for example, 'A is longer than B' can be recorded as A > B, and 'B is shorter than A' as B < A. This introduces in a practical context the important principle of inequalities that can be expressed formally as follows:

> **LEARNING and TEACHING POINT**
>
> Always introduce new aspects of measurement through direct comparison and activities involving ordering.

If A > B, then B < A.
If A < B, then B > A.

How does transitivity apply to measurement?

In Chapter 14 we saw that the mathematical property of *transitivity* applied to the relationships 'is a multiple of' (illustrated in Figure 14.1) and 'is a factor of' (illustrated in Figure 14.4). The principle of transitivity is shown in Figure 22.4. If we know that A is related to B (indicated by an arrow) and B is related to C, the question is whether A is related to C as a logical consequence. With some relations (such as 'is a factor of') it does follow logically and we can draw in the arrow connecting A to C. In other cases it does not. For example, the relationship 'is a mirror image of' can be applied to a set of shapes: if shape A is a mirror image of shape B, and B is a mirror image of shape C, then it is *not* true that A must automatically be a mirror image of C. So this is not a transitive relationship.

We can now see that whenever we compare and order three or more objects (or events) using a *measuring* attribute such as their lengths, their masses, their capacities or the length of time (for events), then we are again making use of a transitive relationship.

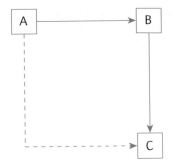

Figure 22.4   *The transitive property*

The arrow used in Figure 22.4 could represent any one of the measuring relationships used to compare two objects or events, such as: 'is longer than', 'is lighter than', 'holds more than' or 'takes less time than'. In each case, because A is related to B and B is related to C, then it follows logically that A is related to C. This principle is fundamental to ordering a set of more than two objects or events: once we know A is greater than B and B is greater than C, for example, it is this principle which allows us not to have to check A against C. Grasping this is a significant step in the development of a child's understanding of measuring.

The transitive property of measurement can be expressed formally using inequality signs as follows:

If A > B and B > C then A > C.
If A < B and B < C then A < C.

What is conservation in measurement?

Next we should note the principle of **conservation**, another fundamental idea in learning about measurement of length, mass and liquid volume. Children meet this principle first in the context of conservation of number, as discussed in Chapter 3 (see Figure 3.3 and accompanying text). They have to learn, for example, that if you rearrange a set of counters in different ways you do not alter the number of counters. Similarly, if two objects are the same length, they remain the same length when one is moved to a new position: this is the principle of conservation of length. Conservation of mass is experienced when children balance two lumps of dough, then rearrange each lump in some way, such as breaking one up into small pieces and moulding the other into some shape or other, and then checking that they still balance.

Conservation of liquid volume is the one that catches many children out. When they empty the water from one container into another, differently shaped container, as shown in Figure 22.5, by focusing their attention on the heights of the water in the containers, children often lose their grip on the principle that the volume of water has actually been unchanged by the transformation.

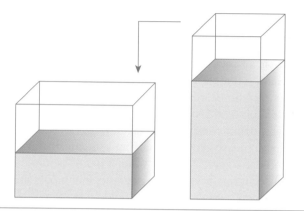

Figure 22.5   *Conservation of liquid volume*

How might children learn about using units in measurement?

Fundamental to the idea of measuring is the use of a 'unit'. The use of non-standard units to introduce to children the idea of measuring in units is a well-established tradition in primary school mathematics teaching. For example, they might measure the length of items of furniture in spans, the length of a wall in cubits (a cubit is the length of your forearm), the mass of a book in conkers, the capacity of a container in egg-cups.

Many adults make use of non-standard units of length in everyday life, especially, for example, when making rough-and-ready measurements for practical jobs around the house and garden. The value of this approach is that children get experience of the idea of measuring in units through familiar, unthreatening objects first, rather than going straight into the use of mysterious things called millilitres and grams, and so on.

Also, it is often the case that the non-standard unit is a more appropriate size of unit for early measuring experiences. For example, most of the things around the classroom the children might want to weigh will have a mass of several hundred grams. The gram is a very small mass for practical purposes to begin with, and the kilogram is far too large; conkers and glue-sticks are much more appropriate sizes of units for measuring mass in the early stages. Eventually, of

LEARNING and **TEACHING POINT**

Introduce the idea of measuring in units via non-standard units that are familiar and appropriately sized, and use these experiences to establish the need for a standard unit.

course, we must learn that there is a need for a standard unit. The experience of working with non-standard units often makes this need explicit, as, for example, when two children measure the length of the hall in paces and get different answers.

What is there to know about approximation?

The next major principle of measurement is that nearly all measurements are *approximate*. If you are measuring length, mass, time or capacity, all you can ever achieve is to make the measurement to the nearest something, depending on the level of accuracy of your measuring device. The reader may have noticed that against the stated mass or volume on many food and drink packages there is a large 'e'. This is a European symbol indicating that the stated measurement is only an estimate within mandatory limits. So when we say that a bottle contains 750 ml of wine, it has to be understood that this statement is an approximation. It might mean, for example, that it contains 750 ml if measured to the nearest 5ml, in which case the volume would lie between 747.5 ml and 752.5 ml. When I say below that a child is 90 cm tall, you have to realize that what I mean is that the child is 90 cm tall if measured to the nearest centimetre. This is particularly important when we do calculations with measurements, because of the problems of compounding rounding errors (see the discussion of rounding errors in Chapter 18). For example, when we calculate that 10 bottles containing 750 ml (to the nearest 5 ml) will provide 7.5 litres in total, by multiplying 750 ml by 10, this answer is correct only to the nearest 50 ml.

The principle of measuring to the nearest something and the associated language should be introduced to primary school children from the earliest stages (see Chapter 13 for a discussion on rounding). Even when measuring in non-standard units they will encounter this idea, as, for example, when determining that the length of the table is 'nearly 9 spans' or 'about 9 spans' or 'between 8 and 9 spans'.

How is measurement a context for developing number concepts?

LEARNING and TEACHING POINT

Make collections and displays of packages or labels, discussing which items are sold by mass or by volume, and note the units used. Challenge children to find as many different masses and volumes as they can and display these in order. Discuss the significance of the large 'e' that occurs next to most measurements on food packages and labels.

In discussing the principles of measurement, we should stress the central importance of measurement experiences as a context for developing number concepts. Throughout this book I have used measurement problems and situations to reinforce ideas such as place value (Chapter 6), the various structures for the four operations (Chapters 7 and 10) and calculations with decimals (Chapter 18). For example, the key idea of comparison in understanding subtraction is best experienced in practical activities comparing heights, masses, capacities and time; and the key structure of division as the inverse of multiplication can be connected with finding how many small containers can be filled from a large container.

Doesn't zero just mean 'nothing'?

Finally in this section on principles of measurement, a comment on the meaning of zero. Measurements such as length, mass, liquid volume and capacity, and time intervals, are examples of what are called **ratio scales**. These are scales where the ratio of two quantities has a real meaning. For example, if a child is 90 cm tall and an adult is 180 cm tall, we can legitimately compare the two heights by means of ratio, stating that the adult is twice as tall as the child. Similarly, we can compare masses, capacities and time intervals by ratio.

However, recorded time, for example, is not like this: it would make no sense to compare, say, 6 o'clock with 2 o'clock by saying that one is three times the other. This is an example of what is called an **interval scale**. Comparisons can only be made by reference to the difference (the interval) between two measurements, for example, saying that 6 o'clock is 4 hours later than 2 o'clock. Of course, you can compare the measurements in a ratio scale by reference to difference (for example, the adult is 90 cm taller than the child), but the point about an interval scale is that you *cannot* do it by ratio, you can only use difference. Temperature measured in °C (the **Celsius scale**) or °F (the **Fahrenheit scale**) is another example of an interval scale. It would be meaningless to assert that 15 °C is three times as hot as 5 °C; the two temperatures should be compared by their difference.

The interesting mathematical point here is that the thing that really distinguishes a ratio scale from an interval scale is that in a ratio scale the zero means *nothing*, but in an interval scale it does not! When the recorded time is 'zero hours', time has not disappeared. When the temperature is 'zero degrees', there is still a temperature out there and we can feel it! But a length of 'zero metres' is no length; a mass of 'zero grams' is nothing; a bottle holding 'zero millilitres' of wine is empty; a time interval of 'zero seconds' is no time at all.

What metric units and prefixes do I need to know about?

There is an internationally accepted system of metric units called **SI units** (Système International). This system specifies one base unit for each aspect of measurement. For length the SI unit is the **metre**, for mass it is the **kilogram** (not the gram), for time it is the *second*. There is not a specific SI unit for liquid volume, since this would be measured in the same units as solid volume, namely,

cubic metres. However, the **litre** is a standard unit for liquid volume and capacity that is used internationally.

Other units can be obtained by various prefixes being attached to these base units. There is a preference for those related to a thousand: for primary school use this would be just **kilo** (k), meaning 'a thousand', and **milli** (m), meaning 'a thousandth'. So, for example, throughout this book we have used kilograms (kg) and grams (g), where 1 kg = 1000 g, and litres (l) and millilitres (ml), where 1 litre = 1000 ml.

Similarly, we can have kilometres (km) and metres (m), with 1 km = 1000 m, and metres and millimetres (mm), with 1 m = 1000 mm. These are the only uses of the prefixes kilo and milli likely to be needed in the primary school.

LEARNING and TEACHING POINT

Restrict the range of metric units used for practical work in the primary school to metre, centimetre, millimetre, litre, millilitre, kilogram, gram. Reference may also be made to kilometre and decimetre.

For practical purposes we will need other prefixes, especially **centi** (c), meaning 'a hundredth'. This gives us the really useful unit of length, the **centimetre** (cm), where 1 m = 100 cm. We might also find it helpful, for example when explaining place value and decimals with length (see Chapter 6), to use the prefix **deci** (d), meaning 'a tenth', as in decimetre (dm), where 1 m = 10 dm. We might also note that some wine bottles are labelled 0.75 litres, others are labelled 7.5 dl (decilitres), others 75 cl (centilitres) and others 750 ml (millilitres). These are all the same volume of wine.

How can I get better at handling units of measurement?

Take every opportunity to practise *estimation* of lengths, heights, widths and distances, liquid volume and capacity, and mass. In the supermarket, take note of which items are sold by mass (although they will call it weight) and which by volume; estimate the mass or volume of items you are purchasing and check your estimate against what it says on the packet or the scales. This all helps significantly to build up confidence in handling less familiar units.

One way of becoming a better estimator is to learn by heart the sizes of some specific **reference items**. Children should be encouraged to do this for length, mass and capacity, and then to relate other estimates to these. Here are some that I personally use:

LEARNING and TEACHING POINT

Make considerable use of estimation as a class activity, encouraging children to learn by heart the measurements of specific reference items such as those given here.

- A child's finger is about 1 cm wide.
- The children's rulers are 30 cm long.
- A sheet of A4 paper is about 21 cm by 30 cm.

- The distance from my nose to my outstretched fingertip is about one metre (100 cm).
- The classroom door is about 200 cm or 2 m high.
- The mass of an individual packet of crisps is 30 g.
- The mass of a standard packet of tea is 125 g.
- The mass of a standard-size tin of baked beans is about 500 g (including the tin).
- A standard can of drink has a capacity of 330 ml.
- A wine bottle holds 750 ml of wine.
- Standard cartons of milk or fruit juice are 1 litre (1000 ml).
- A litre of water has a mass of a kilogram (1000 g).

What imperial units are still important?

The attempt to turn the UK into a fully metricated country has not been entirely successful. A number of popular units of measurement stubbornly refuse to go away. For example, some people still find temperatures given in degrees Fahrenheit to be more meaningful than those in degrees Celsius (also known as centigrade).

> **LEARNING and TEACHING POINT**
>
> To be realistic, work on journey distances and average speeds (see Chapter 28) is most appropriately done in miles and miles per hour.

The prime candidate for survival would seem to be the *mile*: somehow I cannot imagine in the foreseeable future all the road signs and speed limits in the UK being converted to kilometres. Unfortunately children cannot possibly have practical experience of measuring distances in kilometres in the classroom to compensate for the lack of experience of this metric unit in everyday life.

For those who wish to relate miles to kilometres the most common equivalence used is that 5 miles is about 8 kilometres. A simple method for doing conversions is to read off the corresponding speeds on the speedometer in a car, most of which are given in both miles per hour and kilometres per hour. For example, you can read off that 30 miles is about 50 km, 50 miles is about 80 km, 70 miles is about 110 km.

There is also an intriguing connection between this conversion and a sequence of numbers called the **Fibonacci sequence**, named after Leonardo Fibonacci, a twelfth/thirteenth-century Italian mathematician: 1, 2, 3, 5, 8, 13, 21, 34, 55, 89, and so on. The sequential generalization here is to add the two previous numbers to get the next one. So, for example, the next number after 89 is 144 (55 + 89). Now, purely coincidentally, it happens that one of these numbers in miles is approximately the same as the next one in kilometres. For example, 2 miles is about 3 km, 3 miles is about 5 km, 5 miles is about 8 km, 8 miles is about 13 km, and so on. This works remarkably well to the nearest whole number for quite some way! (See self-assessment question 22.1 below.)

Other common measurements of length still surviving in everyday usage, together with an indication of the kinds of equivalences that might be useful to learn, are:

- the inch (about the width of an adult thumb, about 2.5 cm);
- the foot (about the length of a standard class ruler or a sheet of A4 paper, that is, about 30 cm); and
- the yard (about 10% less than a metre, approximately 91 cm).

Imperial units of mass still used occasionally and unofficially in some markets are:

- the ounce (about the same as a small packet of crisps, that is, about 30 g);
- the pound (getting on for half a kilogram, about 450 g).

Many people still like to weigh themselves in stones: a stone is a bit more than 6 kg (about 6.35 kg). I find it useful to remember that 11 stone is about 70 kg: see self-assessment question 21.6 in the previous chapter. And, for those who enjoy this kind of thing, a hundredweight is just over 50 kg, and a metric tonne (1000 kg) is therefore just a little more than an imperial ton (20 hundredweight).

Gallons have disappeared from the petrol station, but still manage to survive in common usage; for example, people still tell me how many miles per gallon their car does, even though petrol is almost universally sold in litres. My (very economical) car does 11 miles to the litre. A gallon is about 4.5 litres. Given the drinking habits of the British public, another contender for long-term survival must be the pint. I have noticed that some primary school children and their parents refer to any carton of milk as 'a pint of milk', regardless of the actual volume involved. A pint is just over half a litre (568 ml).

Conversion between metric and imperial units can be done using the methods described in Chapter 19 for direct proportion problems or using conversion graphs as described in Chapter 21, so it provides a realistic context for some genuine mathematics.

Research focus

How might you recognize that children can reason using the transitive principle in the context of time? Long and Kamii (2001) played two extracts of music to children in grades 2, 4 and 6 (in the UK, Years 2, 4 and 6) and asked them how they could work out which one took longer. They made available to the children the following equipment: a supply of water, a tray, a clear bottle, a marker pen and a bottle fitted with a funnel and a tube. The children who showed the highest level of understanding of transitivity were reckoned to be those who would start and stop the water flowing from the funnel and tube into the clear bottle when the first piece of music started and stopped, mark the height, empty the bottle, then repeat for the second piece of music. Symbolically what these children were reasoning was that A = B > C = D implies A > D. About half of the grade 2 children showed this level of understanding. By grade 4, the proportion had risen to 90%, and by grade 6 to 96%.

Suggestions for further reading

1. Ainley, in chapter 7 of Pimm and Love (1991), describes how she observed a lesson on measurement and was struck by how little mathematics was involved. However, analysis of the topic persuades her that there is potential for considerable genuine mathematics in this topic, if it is taught appropriately and with more awareness by teachers of what is important in what they are doing with children in measurement.
2. Have a look at Blinko and Slater (1996): chapter 4, 'Length'; chapter 6, 'Mass'; chapter 7, 'Capacity/Volume'; chapter 8, 'Time'. These chapters contain many interesting suggestions for enjoyable practical activities to promote children's awareness of and understanding of the key measurement concepts and skills.
3. Fenna (2002) is a comprehensive and authoritative dictionary providing clear definitions of units, prefixes, and styles of weights and measures within the Système International (SI), as well as traditional, and industry-specific units. It also includes fascinating material on the historical and scientific background of units of measurement.
4. Chapter 7 of Haylock and Cockburn (2008) is on understanding measurement. We cover in this chapter the material on measurement particularly from the perspective of teaching the topic to younger children. The chapter concludes with a number of suggestions for classroom activities designed to promote understanding of the key ideas involved.

Self-assessment questions

22.1: Given that 1 mile is 1.6093 km (to four decimal places), use a calculator to find how far the rule for changing miles to kilometres based on the Fibonacci sequence is correct to the nearest whole number.

22.2: The mass of a litre of water is 1 kg (1000 g). What will it be on the Moon?

22.3: Are these relationships transitive?

(a) 'Is earlier than' applied to times of the day; and
(b) 'Is half of' applied to lengths.

22.4: Measure the length of a sheet of A4 paper to the nearest millimetre. Give the answer:

(a) in millimetres;
(b) in centimetres;
(c) in decimetres; and
(d) in metres.

22.5: Which is the greater:

(a) half a pound or 250 grams;
(b) 2 pints or a litre;
(c) 6 feet or 2 metres;
(d) 50 miles or 100 kilometres;
(e) 4 ounces or 100 grams;
(f) 10 stone or 50 kilograms; and
(g) 9 miles to the litre or 35 miles to the gallon?

22.6: Classify each of these statements as possible or impossible:

(a) An elephant has a mass of about 7000 kg.
(b) A standard domestic bath filled to the brim contains about 40 litres of water.
(c) Yesterday I put exactly 20 litres of petrol in the tank of my car.
(d) A normal cup of coffee is about 2 decilitres.
(e) It takes me about a week to complete a walk of 1000 km.
(f) An envelope containing 8 sheets of standard A4 photocopier paper does not exceed 60 g in mass.

Further practice

From the Student Workbook
Tasks 149–151: Checking understanding of measurement
Tasks 152–154: Using and applying measurement
Tasks 155–157: Learning and teaching of measurement
On the website (www.sagepub.co.uk/haylock)
Check-Up 28: Knowledge of metric units of length and distance
Check-Up 30: Knowledge of other metric units

Glossary of key terms introduced in Chapter 22

Weight: the force of gravity acting upon an object and therefore properly measured in newtons; colloquially used incorrectly as a synonym for mass.

Mass: a measurement of the quantity of matter in an object, measured, for example, in grams and kilograms; technically not the same thing as weight.

Newton: the SI unit of force (and therefore of weight); a newton is the force required to make a mass of 1 kg accelerate at the rate of one metre per second per second; named after Sir Isaac Newton, 1642–1727, English scientist and mathematician.

Volume: the amount of three-dimensional space taken up by an object; measured in cubic units, such as cubic centimetres or cubic metres.

Capacity: the volume of liquid that a container can hold; usually measured in litres and millilitres; only containers have capacity.

Ante meridiem and post meridiem: abbreviated to a.m. and p.m., before noon and after noon respectively.

Zero hours: midnight on the 24-hour clock.

Conservation in measurement: the principle that a measurement remains the same under certain transformations. For example, the length of an object is conserved when its position is altered; the volume of water is conserved when it is poured from one container to another.

Ratio scale: a measuring scale in which two measurements can be meaningfully compared by ratio; for example, if the mass of one object is 30 kg and the mass of another is 10 kg then it makes sense to say that one is 3 times heavier than the other.

Interval scale: a measuring scale in which two measurements can be meaningfully compared only by their difference, not by their ratio; for example, if the temperature outside is −3 °C and the temperature inside is +15 °C then the temperature difference of 18 °C is the only sensible comparison to make.

Celsius scale (°C):   a metric scale for measuring temperature, also called the centigrade scale, where water freezes at 0 degrees and boils at 100 degrees under standard conditions; named after Anders Celsius, 1701–44, Swedish astronomer, physicist and mathematician, who devised the scale.

Fahrenheit scale (°F):   a non-metric scale for measuring temperature, where water freezes at 32 degrees and boils at 212 degrees under standard conditions; named after the inventor, Gabriel Fahrenheit, 1686–1736, a German physicist.

SI units: an agreed international system of units for measurement, based on one standard unit for each aspect of measurement.

Metre (m):   the SI unit of length; about the distance from my nose to my fingertip when my arm is outstretched.

Kilogram (kg):   the SI unit of mass; equal to 1000 grams.

Cubic metre (m³):   the SI unit of volume; the volume of a cube of side 1 metre; written $1m^3$ but read as 'one cubic metre'.

Litre: a unit used to measure liquid volume and capacity; equal to 1000 cubic centimetres. The mass of a litre of water is 1 kilogram.

Kilo: a prefix (k) denoting a thousand; for example, a kilometre (km) is one thousand metres.

Milli: a prefix (m) denoting one thousandth; for example, a millilitre (ml) is one thousandth of a litre.

Centi: a prefix (c) denoting one hundredth; for example, a centilitre (cl) is one hundredth of a litre.

Centimetre (cm): one hundredth of a metre; 100 cm = 1 m; about the width of a child's little finger.

Deci: a prefix (d) denoting one tenth; for example, a decilitre (dl) is one tenth of a litre.

Reference item: a measurement that is memorized and used as a reference point for estimating other measurements; for example, the capacity of a wine bottle is 750 ml.

Fibonacci sequence: a sequence of numbers in which each term is obtained by the sum of the two previous terms. Starting with 1, the sequence is 1, 1, 2, 3, 5, 8, 13, 21 ...

Imperial units: units of measurement that were at one time statutory in the UK, most of which have now been officially replaced by metric units.

23
Angle

In this chapter there are explanations of

- the dynamic and static views of angle;
- comparison and ordering of angles;
- the use of turns and fractions of a turn for measuring angle;
- degrees;
- acute, right, obtuse, straight, reflex angles; and
- the sum of the angles in a triangle, a quadrilateral, and so on.

What is the dynamic view of angle?

An **angle** is a measurement. When we talk about the angle between two lines we are not referring to the shape formed by the two lines, nor to the point where they meet, nor to the space between the lines, but to a particular kind of measurement.

There are two ways we can think of what it is that is being measured. First, there is the *dynamic* view of angle: the angle between the lines is a measurement of the size of the *rotation* involved when you point along one line and then turn to point along the other. This is the most useful way of introducing the concept of angle to children, because it lends itself to practical experience, with the children themselves pointing in one direction and then turning themselves through various angles to point in other directions. Also, when it comes to

> **LEARNING and TEACHING POINT**
>
> Emphasize especially the dynamic view of angle, giving plenty of practical experience of rotating objects, the children themselves and pointers (such as fingers and pencils).

measuring angles between lines drawn on paper, children can physically point something, such as a pencil or a finger, along one line and rotate about the intersection of the
lines to point along the other line.

   We should note that there are always two angles involved when turning from one
direction to another, depending on whether you choose to rotate clockwise or anticlockwise, as shown in Figure 23.1.

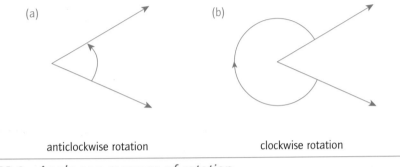

anticlockwise rotation   clockwise rotation

Figure 23.1   *Angle as a measure of rotation*

What is the static view of angle?

As well as the idea of an angle as a rotation there is also the *static* view of angle. This is
where we focus our attention on how pointed is the shape formed by the two lines. But
the angle is still a measurement: we can think of it as a measurement of the difference
in direction between the two lines. So, for example, in Figure 23.2, the angle marked in
(a) is greater than that marked in (b). This is because the two lines in (b) are pointing
in nearly the same direction, whereas the difference in the direction of the two lines in
(a) is much greater. Thinking of angle as the difference in direction between two lines
helps to link the static view of angle with the dynamic one of rotation, because the obvious way to measure the difference in two directions is to turn from one to the other and
measure the amount of turn.

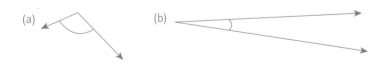

Figure 23.2   *Angle as a measure of the difference in direction*

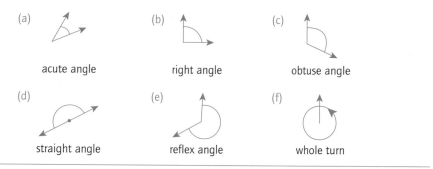

Figure 23.3 *A set of angles in order from smallest (a) to largest (f)*

How are angles measured?

Figure 23.2 illustrates that, like any aspect of measurement, the concept of angle enables us to make comparisons and to order (see Chapter 22). This can be dynamically, by physically doing the rotations involved (for example, with a pencil) and judging which is the greater rotation, which the smaller. It can also be experienced more statically, by cutting out one angle and placing it over another to determine which is the more pointed (the smaller angle). Figure 23.3 shows a set of angles, (a) – (f), ordered from smallest to largest.

The equivalent to making measurements of length, mass and capacity in non-standard units is to measure angle in turns and fractions of a turn, using the dynamic view. Figure 23.3(f) shows a whole turn, pointing in one direction and rotating until you point again in the same direction. Then, for example, if a child points North and then turns to point South they have moved through an angle that can be called a half-turn. Similarly, rotating from North, clockwise, to East is a quarter-turn. Figure 23.3(b) shows a quarter-turn from a horizontal position to a vertical position. This explains why a quarter-turn is also called a **right angle**: it is an *upright* angle. Figure 23.3(d) illustrates why a half-turn, formed by two lines pointing in opposite directions, is also called a **straight angle**.

The next stage of development is to introduce a standard unit for measuring angles. For primary school use this unit is the **degree**, where 360 degrees (360°) is equal to a complete turn. Hence a right angle (quarter-turn) is 90° and a straight

> **LEARNING and TEACHING POINT**
>
> Include the important stages of developing any measurement concept when teaching angle: comparison, ordering and the use of non-standard units (turns and fractions of turns). Get children to compare and order angles by cutting them out and placing them on top of each other.

> **LEARNING and TEACHING POINT**
>
> When explaining about angles, do not always draw diagrams or give examples in which one of the lines is horizontal.

angle (half-turn) is 180°. There is evidence that this system of measuring angles in degrees based on 360 was used as far back as 2000 BC by the Babylonians, and it is thought that it may be related to the Babylonian year being 360 days.

So we have here another example of a non-metric measurement scale in common use. There is actually a metric system for measuring angle, used in some European countries, in which '100 grades' is equal to a right angle, but this has never caught on in the UK. Interestingly, it is because 'centigrade' would then be one-hundredth of a grade, and therefore a measure of angle, that the 'degree centigrade' as a measure of temperature is officially called the 'degree Celsius', to avoid confusion.

The device used to measure angles in degrees is the **protractor**. I personally recommend the use of a 360° protractor, preferably marked with only one scale and with a pointer which can be rotated from one line of the angle being measured to the other, thus emphasizing the dynamic view of angle. Even if there is not an actual pointer, children can still be encouraged to imagine the rotation always starting at zero on one line and rotating through 10°, 20°, 30° … to reach the other.

Can you remind me about acute, obtuse and reflex angles?

Mathematicians can never resist the temptation to put things into categories, thus giving them the opportunity to invent a new collection of terms. Angles are classified, in order of size, as: acute, right, obtuse, straight, reflex, as illustrated in Figure 23.3.

An **acute angle** is an angle less than a right angle. An **obtuse angle** is an angle between a right angle and a straight angle.

A **reflex angle** is an angle greater than a straight angle, but less than a whole turn.

How can you show that the three angles in a triangle add up to 180 degrees?

A popular way of seeing this property of the angles of a **triangle** is to draw a triangle on paper, mark the angles, tear off the three corners and fit them together, as shown in Figure 23.4, to discover that together they form a straight angle, or two right angles (180°).

Figure 23.4   *The three angles of a triangle fitted together to make a straight angle*

This illuminative experience uses the static view of angle. It is also possible to illustrate the same principle using the dynamic view, as shown in Figure 23.5, by taking an arrow (or, say, a pencil) for a walk round a triangle. Step 1 is to place an arrow (or the pencil) along one side of the triangle, for example on AC. Step 2 is to slide the arrow along until it reaches A, then rotate it through the angle at A. It will now lie along AB, pointing towards A. Now, for step 3, slide it up to B and rotate through that angle. Finally, step 4, slide it down to C and rotate through that angle. The arrow has now rotated through the sum of the three angles and is facing in the opposite direction to which it started! Hence the three angles together make a half-turn, or two right angles. Clearly this will work for any triangle, not just the one shown here.

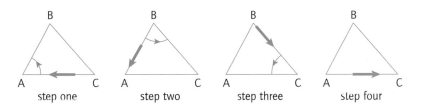

Figure 23.5   *The three angles of a triangle together make a half-turn*

What about the sum of the angles in shapes with more than three sides?

This is going beyond primary school mathematics, but teachers should know where the mathematics is heading. The four corners of any **quadrilateral** (a plane shape with four straight sides) can be torn off and fitted together in the same way as was done with a triangle in Figure 23.4. It is pleasing to discover this way that they always fit together to make a whole turn, or four right angles (360°).

But also the procedure used in Figure 23.5 can be applied to a four-sided figure, such as that shown in Figure 23.6. Now we find that the arrow does a complete rotation, finishing up pointing in the same direction as it started, so we conclude that the sum of the four angles in a four-sided figure is four right angles.

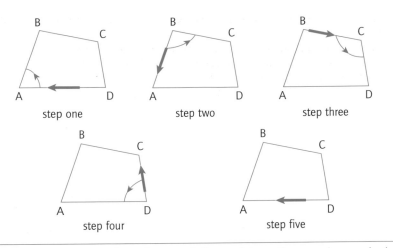

Figure 23.6   *The four angles of a quadrilateral together make a whole turn*

The delight of this experience of taking an arrow for a walk round a triangle or quadrilateral is that it can easily be extended to five-sided figures, six-sided, seven-sided, and so on. The results can then be tabulated, using the approach given in Chapter 20, to formulate a sequential generalization and a global generalization. This is left as an exercise for the reader in self-assessment question 23.2 below.

Research focus

In the early 1980s, in England, the Assessment of Performance Unit undertook a nation-wide survey of the performance of children aged 11 on a series of mathematical tasks across the curriculum (DES/APU, 1981). One question asked which was the biggest of a set of five angles, similar to those shown in Figure 23.2. Over 40% of the children were misled either by the lengths of the lines or by the distance of the arc indicating the angle from the point where the lines met. This finding underlines the importance of giving children plenty of experience of the dynamic view of angle described in this chapter.

Suggestions for further reading

1. Chapter 5 of Blinko and Slater (1996) is about teaching the concept and skills of angle. This chapter provides a set of enjoyable and well-focused classroom activities to promote children's learning about angle. The authors tell you what you need, what to do, and how

to manage the classroom organization, as well as suggesting preparatory and follow-up activities.

2. A sound explanation of the key mathematical ideas of angle can be found in Chapter 15 ('Angles and compass directions') of Suggate, Davis and Goulding (2010).

3. A chapter by Hejny and Slezáková entitled 'Investigating mathematical reasoning and decision making' in Cockburn (2007) provides an interesting range of activities to encourage classification, including that of shapes.

Self-assessment questions

23.1: Put these angles in order and classify them as acute, right, obtuse, straight or reflex: 89°, $\frac{1}{8}$ of a turn, 150°, 90°, $\frac{3}{4}$ of a turn, 200°, 2 right angles, 95°.

23.2: Use the idea of taking an arrow round a shape, rotating through each of the angles in turn, to find the sum of the angles in: (a) a five-sided figure (a pentagon); (b) a six-sided figure (a hexagon); and (c) a seven-sided figure (a heptagon). Give the answers in right angles, tabulate them and formulate both the sequential and the global generalizations. What would be the sum of the angles in a figure with 100 sides?

23.3: Which of the following are possible? Which are impossible?

(a) a triangle with two obtuse angles;
(b) a triangle with a right angle and two other equal angles;
(c) a quadrilateral with two obtuse angles;
(d) a quadrilateral with a reflex angle;
(e) a quadrilateral with four acute angles.

Further practice

From the Student Workbook

Tasks 158–160: Checking understanding of angle
Tasks 161–163: Using and applying angle
Tasks 164–166: Learning and teaching of angle

Glossary of key terms introduced in Chapter 23

Angle: dynamically, a measure of the amount of turn (rotation) from one direction to another; statically, the difference in direction between two lines meeting at a point.

Right angle: an upright angle, a quarter-turn, 90°.

Straight angle: a half-turn, 180°.

Degree: a measure of angle; 360 degrees (360°) is a complete turn.

Protractor: a device for measuring angles.

Acute angle: an angle between 0° and 90°.

Obtuse angle: an angle between 90° and 180°.

Reflex angle: an angle between 180° and 360°.

Triangle: a plane shape with three straight sides and three interior angles. The three angles of any triangle add up to 180°.

Quadrilateral: a plane shape with four straight sides and four interior angles. The four angles of any quadrilateral add up to 360°.

24
Transformations and Symmetry

In this chapter there are explanations of

- transformation, equivalence and congruence in the context of shape;
- translation, reflection and rotation as types of congruence;
- scaling up and down by a scale factor in the context of shape;
- similar shapes; and
- reflective and rotational symmetry for two-dimensional shapes.

How are the ideas of transformation and equivalence important in understanding shape and space?

The two basic processes in geometry are (a) moving or changing shapes, and (b) classifying shapes. These involve the fundamental concepts of transformation and equivalence. In Chapter 3 we saw that these two concepts are key processes in understanding mathematics in general. In this chapter we shall see how important they are in terms of understanding shapes in particular. The reader may recall from Chapter 3 (see, for example, Figure 3.2) that there are two fundamental questions when considering two mathematical entities: How are they the same? How are they different? The first question directs our attention to an *equivalence*, the second to a *transformation*. Much of what we have to understand in learning geometry comes down to recognizing the equivalences that exist within various transformations of shapes, which transformations preserve which equivalences, and how shapes can be different yet the same.

> **LEARNING and TEACHING POINT**
>
> Frequently use the two questions about transformation and equivalence to promote useful discussion in work with shapes: (a) How are they the same? (b) How are they different?

For example, if I draw a large rectangle on the board and ask the class to copy it onto their paper, they all dutifully do this, even though none of them has a piece of paper anything like large enough to produce a diagram as big as mine. Their rectangles are different from mine, that is, different in size, whilst in many respects they might be the same as mine. They have transformed my diagram, but produced something, which, I hope, is in some way equivalent. The diagrams are the same, but different.

In a mathematics lesson Cathy was asked to draw on squared paper as many different shapes as possible that are made up of five square units. Figure 24.1 shows four of the shapes that she drew. Her teacher told her that they were all the same shape. Cathy insisted they were all different. Who was right? The answer is, of course, that they are both right. The shapes are all the same in some senses and different in others.

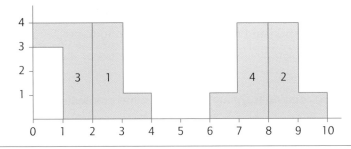

Figure 24.1   *The same but different*

What is a congruence?

Consider how the shapes in Figure 24.1 are the same. All four shapes are made up of five square units; they have the same number of sides (six); each shape has one side of length four units, one side of length three units, one side of length two units and three sides of length one unit; each shape has five 90° angles and one 270° angle; and the sides and the angles are arranged in the same way in each of the shapes to make what we might recognize as a letter 'L'. Surely they are identical, the same in every respect?

Well, they certainly are **congruent**. This word describes the relationship between two shapes that have sides of exactly the same length, angles of exactly the same size, with all the sides and angles arranged in exactly the same way, as in the four shapes shown in Figure 24.1. A practical definition would be that you could cut out one shape and fit it exactly over the other one. The pages in this book are congruent: as you can see, one page fits exactly over the next.

A transformation of a shape that changes it into a congruent shape is called a **congruence**. Three types of congruence are explained below: translation, rotation and reflection.

What is a translation?

So, how are the shapes in Figure 24.1 different? Figure 24.2 shows just the two shapes, 1 and 2. How is shape 2 different from shape 1? Cathy's argument is that they are in different positions on the paper: shape 1 is here and shape 2 is over there, so they are not the same shape. Surely every time I draw the shape in a different position I have drawn a different shape, in a sense. So the shapes are different if you decide to take *position* into account.

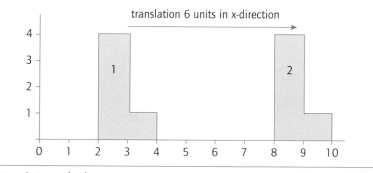

Figure 24.2   *A translation*

In order to do this we need a system of coordinates, as outlined in Chapter 21. The transformation that has been applied to shape 1 to produce shape 2 is called a **translation**. We saw in Chapter 21 that we can use the coordinate system to describe movements. So this translation can be specified by saying, for example, that to get from shape 1 to shape 2 you have to move 6 units in the x-direction and 0 units in the y-direction. Any movement of our shape like this, so many units in the x-direction and so many in the y-direction, without turning, is a translation. Note that every point in shape 1 moves the same distance in the same direction to get to the corresponding point in shape 2.

What is a rotation?

If we now decide that, for the time being, we will not count translations as producing shapes which are different, what about shape 3? Is that different from shape 1? These two shapes are shown in Figure 24.3. Cathy's idea is that shape 1 is an L-shape the right way up, but shape 3 is upside down, so they are different. So the shapes are different if you decide to take their orientation on the page into account. In order to take this into account we need the concept of direction, and, as we saw in Chapter 23, to describe a difference in direction we need the concept of *angle*. So, to transform shape 1 into shape 3 we can apply a **rotation**.

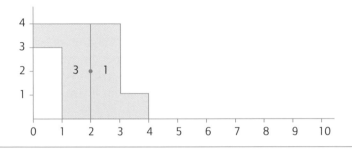

Figure 24.3   *A rotation*

To specify a rotation we have to indicate the point about which the rotation occurs and the angle through which the shape is rotated. If shape 1 is rotated through an angle of 180° (either clockwise or anticlockwise), about the middle of its left-hand side – the point with coordinates (2, 2) – then it is transformed into shape 3. Imagine copying shape 1 on to tracing paper, placing a pin in the point (2, 2) and rotating the tracing paper through 180°. The shape would land directly on top of shape 3. Any movement of our shape like this, turning through some angle about a given centre, is a rotation. Note that every line in shape 1 is rotated through this angle of 180° to get to the corresponding line in shape 2.

What is a reflection?

Now, if we decide that, for the time being, we will not count rotations or translations as producing shapes which are different, what about shape 4? Is that different from shape 1? These two shapes are shown in Figure 24.4. Cathy's idea is that they are actually mirror images of each other and this makes them different. This difference can be made explicit by colouring the shapes, say, red, before cutting them out. Shapes 1, 2 and 3 can all be placed on top of each other and match exactly, with the red faces uppermost. But shape 4 only matches if we turn it over so that it is red face down. This surely makes it different from all the others? The transformation that has been applied now to shape 1 to produce shape 4 is a **reflection**.

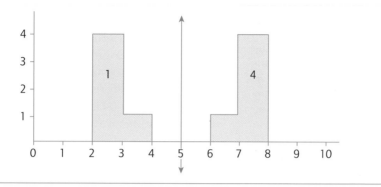

Figure 24.4 *A reflection*

To specify a reflection all you have to do is to identify the mirror line. In the case of shapes 1 and 4 the mirror line is the vertical line passing through 5 on the *x*-axis, shown as a double-headed arrow in Figure 24.4. Each point in shape 1 is matched by a corresponding point in shape 4, the other side of the mirror line and the same distance from it. For example, the point (3, 1) in shape 1 is 2 units to the left of the mirror line, and the corresponding point in shape 4, (7, 1), is 2 units to the right of the mirror line. Any transformation of our shape like this, obtained by producing a mirror image in any given mirror line, is a reflection.

Are there other transformations of shapes I should know about?

There are many ways in which a two-dimensional shape can be transformed yet still remain in some sense 'the same'. Perhaps the most extreme example you will come across is the kind of transformation that changes a network of railway lines into the familiar London Underground map. This is an example of what is called a *topological* transformation, in which all the lengths and angles can change, and curved lines can become straight lines, or vice versa; but the map still retains significant features of the original network to enable you to determine a route from one station to another. Then there is the kind of *perspective* transformation that we make when we draw, for example, the side of a building as seen at an angle, in which a rectangle might be transformed into a trapezium (see Chapter 25). Other transformations we might encounter are those that change a square into an oblong rect-angle or a rectangle into a parallelogram (see Chapter 25). These are examples of what are called *affinities*. The mathematics of topological and perspective transformations and affinities is beyond the scope of this book, although all these transformations are used by children intui-tively as they develop their understanding of space and shape (see Haylock and Cockburn, in the suggestions for further reading at the end of this chapter).

LEARNING and TEACHING POINT

Primary school children can have experi-ence of scaling in practical contexts by making scale drawings for a purpose. For example: they can scale material up or down on a photocopier for display; they can make a scale drawing of the class-room to redesign the layout of the furni-ture; they can make a scale drawing of the playground to solve a problem of where visitors park their cars.

But there is one other way in which shapes can be transformed and yet remain in some sense 'the same', which is taught directly in the primary cur-riculum. This is by **scaling the shape** up or down by a scale factor. This idea is illus-trated in Figure 24.5. Shape P is scaled up into shape Q by applying a scale factor of 3. This means that the lengths of all the lines in shape P are multiplied by 3 to produce shape Q. Each length in shape Q is three times the corresponding length in shape P. It is significant that we multiply here, because, as we saw in Chapter 10, scaling is one of the most important structures of multiplication. We should note also the connection with ratio. In Chapter 17 we discussed scale drawings and maps as an application of ratio. So, we could express the relationship between shapes P and Q in Figure 24.5 by

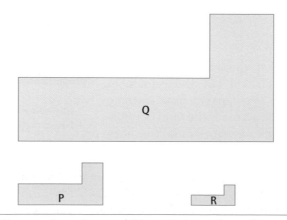

Figure 24.5   *Scaling up by a factor of 3 and down by a factor of $^1/_2$*

saying that the ratio of any length in P to the corresponding length in Q is 1:3; or that P is a scale drawing of Q using a scale of 1:3.

Scaling up is achieved by a scale factor greater than 1. When the scale factor is less than 1 the shape is **scaled down** and so made smaller. Scaling by a factor of 1 leaves a shape unchanged, of course. Shape R is a scaling of shape P; this is clearly a scaling down, rather than a scaling up, because R is smaller than P. The scale factor here is $^1/_2$. In this case, each length in R is a half of the corresponding length in P. The ratio of a length in P to the corresponding length in R is 1: $^1/_2$, although we should note that this could be expressed by the equivalent ratio 2:1.

Notice also how the concept of *inverse processes* (see Chapter 7's glossary) applies to scalings. Shape P is transformed into shape Q by scaling by a factor of 3; shape Q is transformed into shape P by scaling by a factor of $^1/_3$. Shape P is transformed into shape R by scaling by a factor of $^1/_2$; shape R is transformed into shape P by scaling by a factor of 2. In general, scalings by factors of n and $^1/_n$ are inverse transformations: one undoes the effect of the other. So, for example, on a photocopier,

enlarging something by a factor of 1.25 and then reducing this by a factor of 0.8 would get you back to what you started with.

What is meant by 'similar' shapes?

A scaling certainly changes a shape. It changes it by scaling up or down all the lengths by a given scale factor. But shapes P, Q and R in Figure 24.5 are still 'the same shape' in many ways, even though they are not congruent. In technical mathematical language we say they are **similar**. This does not just mean that they look a bit like each other. The word has a very precise meaning in this context. If shape P is similar to shape Q, then:

- for each line, vertex and angle in P there is a corresponding line, vertex and angle in Q;
- the length of each line in Q is in the same ratio to the length of the corresponding line in P; and
- each angle in P is equal to the corresponding angle in Q.

This last point is particularly significant. The lengths of the lines change – they are scaled up or down – but the angles do not change. This is why the shapes still look the same. Self-assessment question 24.2 provides the opportunity to discover some other interesting properties of scalings.

What is reflective symmetry?

Sometimes when we reflect a shape in a particular mirror line it matches *itself* exactly, in the sense that the mirror image coincides precisely with the original shape. Shape A in Figure 24.6 is an example of this phenomenon. The mirror line is shown as a double-headed arrow. This divides the shape into two identical halves that are mirror images of each other. If we cut the shape out we could fold it along the mirror line and the two halves would match exactly.

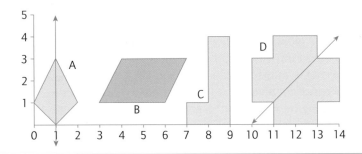

Figure 24.6   *Are these shapes symmetrical?*

Another approach is to colour the shape (so you can remember which way was face up to start with), cut it out and turn it face down: we find that the shape turned face down could still fit exactly into the hole left in the paper. The shape is said to have **reflective symmetry** (sometimes called *line symmetry*) and the mirror line is called a **line of symmetry**.

Shape D in Figure 24.6 also has reflective symmetry. There are actually four possible lines that divide this shape into two matching halves with one half the mirror image of the other, although only one of these is shown in the diagram. Finding the other three lines of symmetry is an exercise for the reader (self-assessment question 24.3). Again, notice that if you coloured the shape, cut it out and turned it face down, it could fit exactly into the hole left in the paper.

Shape C in Figure 24.6 does not have reflective symmetry. The colouring, cutting out and turning face down routine demonstrates this nicely, since it is clear that we would not then be able to fit the shape into the hole left in the paper.

> **LEARNING and TEACHING POINT**
>
> Use the colouring, cutting out, turning face down approach to explore the ideas of reflection and reflective symmetry – as well as folding shapes along potential mirror lines, and looking at shapes and their images in mirrors.

What is rotational symmetry?

Shape B (a parallelogram) in Figure 25.6 is perhaps a surprise, because this too does *not* have reflective symmetry. If you think, for example, that one of the diagonals is a line of symmetry, copy the shape onto paper and use the colouring, cutting out and turning face-down procedure; or try folding it in half along the diagonal. But it does have a different kind of symmetry. To see this, trace the shape onto tracing paper and then rotate it around the centre point through a half-turn. The shape matches the original shape exactly. A shape that can be rotated on to itself like this is said to have **rotational symmetry**. The point about which we rotate it is called the **centre of rotational symmetry**.

Another practical way of exploring rotational symmetry is to cut out a shape carefully and see how many ways it can be fitted into the hole left in the paper, by rotation. For example, if we coloured shape B in Figure 24.6 and cut it out, there would be two ways in which we could fit it into the hole left in the paper, by rotating it, without turning the shape face down. We therefore say that the **order of rotational symmetry** for this shape is *two*. Shape D also has rotational symmetry (see self-assessment question 24.3 below).

Shapes A and C do not have rotational symmetry. Well, not really. I suppose you could say that they have rotational symmetry of order one, since there is *one* way in which their cut-outs could fit into the hole left in the paper, without turning them face down. In this sense all two-dimensional shapes would have rotational symmetry of at least order one. While recognizing this, it is usual to say that shapes like A and C do *not* have rotational symmetry.

The ideas of reflective and rotational symmetry are fundamental to the creation of attractive designs and patterns, and are employed effectively in a number of cultural traditions, particularly the Islamic. Children can learn first to recognize these kinds of symmetry in the world around them, and gradually to learn to analyse them and to employ them in creating designs of their own.

Research focus

One of the findings of the Assessment of Performance Unit survey in the 1980s (DES/APU, 1980) was that 80% of 11-year-old children in English primary schools could successfully draw the reflection in a vertical mirror line of a shape drawn on squared paper. However, only 14% could do this when the mirror line was a 45° diagonal line. This marked difference reinforces the importance of children experiencing geometric concepts outside of the usual horizontal and vertical frame of reference.

Suggestions for further reading

1. Although the 'recent' research referred to in the title of Dickson, Brown and Gibson (1984) is now far from recent, Section 1 ('Spatial thinking') is a very interesting and comprehensive summary of how spatial concepts develop and the kinds of misconceptions that children can have.
2. Chapter 8 of Haylock and Cockburn (2008) is on understanding shape and space. In this chapter we show how all the different ways in which shapes can be transformed and all the geometric language used to describe shapes can be put into an analytic framework of transformations and equivalences.
3. Section 4.3 ('Position and movement') of Hopkins, Pope and Pepperell (2004) provides a very clear explanation of the basic kinds of geometric transformations.

Self-assessment questions

24.1:   Describe the congruences that transform shape 2 in Figure 24.1 into: (a) shape 1; (b) shape 4; and (c) shape 3.

24.2:   These questions refer to Figure 24.5.

    (a)   Shape P can be constructed from 5 square units. How many times greater than this is the number of these square units needed to construct shape Q? What might you infer from this result?

    (b)   Scaling by what factor transforms shape R into shape Q? Scaling by what factor transforms shape Q into shape R?

    (c)   With a pencil and a ruler, lightly draw a straight line connecting the top right hand corner of shape Q with the corresponding point in shape P; continue the line beyond shape P. Do the same for other pairs of corresponding points. What do you discover?

24.3:   In shape D in Figure 24.6, where are the other three lines of symmetry? What is the order of rotational symmetry of this shape?

24.4:   Is it possible to draw a two-dimensional shape with exactly two lines of symmetry without the lines of symmetry being at right angles to each other?

24.5:   Is it possible to draw a shape with exactly two lines of symmetry that does not have rotational symmetry?

24.6:   Describe all the symmetries of shapes E, F and G in Figure 24.7.

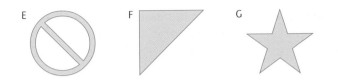

Figure 24.7 *Identify the symmetries in these shapes*

Further practice

From the Student Workbook

Tasks 167–169: Checking understanding of transformations and symmetry

Tasks 170–173: Using and applying transformations and symmetry

Tasks 174–176: Learning and teaching of transformations and symmetry

Glossary of key terms introduced in Chapter 24

Congruent shapes: two or more shapes that can be transformed into each other by congruences.

Congruence: any transformation of a shape that leaves unchanged the lengths and angles; congruences are translations, rotations, reflections and combinations of these.

Translation: a transformation in which a shape is slid from one position to another, without turning.

Rotation: a transformation in which a shape is rotated through an angle about a centre of rotation; every line in the shape turns through the same angle.

Reflection: a transformation in which a shape is reflected in a mirror line and changed into its mirror image.

Scaling of shape: a transformation in which all the lengths in a shape are multiplied by the same factor, called the scale factor; the angles remain unchanged.

Scaling up: scaling by a factor greater than 1.

Scaling down: scaling by a factor less than 1 (but greater than zero).

Similar shapes: two shapes either one of which is a scaling of the other. In similar shapes, corresponding lines are in the same ratio and corresponding angles are equal.

Reflective symmetry: the property possessed by a shape that is its own mirror image; also called line symmetry.

Line of symmetry: the mirror line in which a shape with reflective symmetry is reflected onto itself.

Rotational symmetry: the property possessed by a shape that can be mapped exactly onto itself by a rotation (other than through a multiple of 360°).

Centre of rotational symmetry: the point about which a shape with rotational symmetry is rotated in order to map onto itself.

Order of rotational symmetry: the number of ways in which a shape can be mapped onto itself by rotations of up to 360°. For example, a square has rotational symmetry of order 4.

25
Classifying Shapes

In this chapter there are explanations of

- the importance of classification as a process for making sense of the shapes in the world around us;
- polygons, including the meaning of 'regular polygon';
- different kinds of triangles;
- different kinds of quadrilaterals;
- tessellations;
- polyhedra, including the meaning of 'regular polyhedron';
- various three-dimensional shapes, including prisms and pyramids; and
- reflective symmetry applied to three-dimensional shapes.

Why are there so many technical terms to learn in geometry?

We need the special language of geometry in order to classify shapes into categories. In Chapter 3 I explained how classification is a key intellectual process that helps us to make sense of our experiences and one that is central to understanding mathematics. By coding information into categories we condense it and gain some control over it. We form categories in mathematics by recognizing attributes shared by various elements (such as numbers or shapes). These elements are then formed into a set. Although the elements in the set are different they have something the same about them, they are in some sense equivalent. When it is a particularly interesting or significant set we give it a name. Because it is important that we should be able to determine definitely whether or not a particular element is in the set, the next stage of the

LEARNING and TEACHING POINT

Children will develop geometric concepts, such as those discussed in this chapter, by experiences of classifying, using various attributes of shapes, informally in the first instance, looking for exemplars and non-exemplars, and discussing the relationships between shapes in terms of samenesses and differences.

process is often to formulate a precise definition. This whole process is particularly significant in making sense of shapes and developing geometric concepts.

The learner will recognize an attribute common to certain shapes (such as having three sides), form them into a category, give the set a name (for example, the set of triangles) and then, if necessary, make the classification more explicit with a precise definition. This process of classifying and naming leads to a greater confidence in handling shapes and a better awareness of the shapes that make up the world around us.

So, to participate in this important process of classification of shapes, we need first a whole batch of mathematical ideas related to the significant properties of shapes that are used to put them into various categories. This will include, for example, reference to whether the edges of the shape are straight, the number of sides and angles, whether various angles are equal or right angled, and whether sides are equal in length or parallel. Second, we need to know the various terms used to name the sets, supported where necessary by a definition. My experience is that many primary teachers and trainee teachers have a degree of uncertainty about some of these terms that undermines their confidence in teaching mathematics. For their sake the following material is provided for reference purposes.

LEARNING and TEACHING POINT

The role of a definition in teaching and learning is not to enable children to formulate a concept, but to sharpen it up once the concept has been formed informally through experience and discussion, and to deal with doubtful cases.

What are the main classes of two-dimensional shapes?

The first classification of two-dimensional shapes we should note separates out those with only straight edges from those, such as circles, semicircles and ellipses, which have curved edges. A two-dimensional closed shape made up entirely of straight edges is called a **polygon**. The straight edges are called *sides*. In discussing shapes we should restrict the use of the word 'side' to the straight edges of a polygon. It is not appropriate, for example, to refer to the circumference of a circle as a 'side'; I am perplexed when a circle is referred to in some texts as a shape 'with one side'.

Polygons can then be further classified depending on the number of sides: *triangles* with three sides, *quadrilaterals* with four, **pentagons** with five, **hexagons** with six, **heptagons** with seven, **octagons** with eight, **nonagons** with nine, **decagons** with ten, and so on.

What are regular polygons?

An important way in which we can categorize polygons is by recognizing those that are *regular* and those that are not, as shown in Figure 25.1. A **regular polygon** is one in which all the sides are the same length and all the angles are the same size. For example, a regular octagon has eight equal sides and eight angles, each of which is equal to 135°. To work out the angles in a regular polygon, use the rule ($2n - 4$ right angles) deduced in self-assessment question 23.2 (Chapter 23) to determine the total of the angles in the polygon (for example, for an octagon the sum is $2 \times 8 - 4 = 12$ right angles, that is, 1080°), then divide this by the number of angles (for example, for the octagon, 1080° ÷ 8 = 135°).

LEARNING and TEACHING POINT

Give children opportunity to explore the properties of various shapes, including the different kinds of triangles and quadrilaterals, and regular and irregular shapes, by folding, tracing, matching, looking for reflective and rotational symmetries, and drawing out the implications of these.

The word 'regular' is often misused when people talk about shapes, as though it were synonymous with 'symmetric' or even 'geometric'. For example, the rectangular shape of the cover of this book is *not* a regular shape, because two of the sides are longer than the other two – unless my publishers have decided to surprise me and produce a square book. I'm also a bit

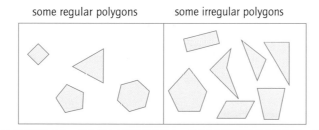

some regular polygons   some irregular polygons

Figure 25.1 *Regular and irregular polygons*

disappointed when every time you see an example of, say, a pentagon (or a hexagon) used in material for primary children it seems to be a regular one. This seems to me to confuse the distinction between a pentagon in general and a regular pentagon.

What are the different categories of triangles that I should know about?

There are basically two ways of categorizing triangles. The first is based on their angles, the second on their sides. Figure 25.2 shows examples of triangles categorized in these ways.

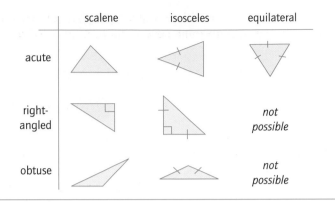

Figure 25.2   *Categories of triangles*

First, we can categorize a triangle as being *acute angled*, *right angled* or *obtuse angled*. (See Chapter 23 for the classification of angles.) An *acute-angled triangle* is one in which all three angles are acute, that is, less than 90°. A *right-angled triangle* is one in which one of the angles is a right angle; it is not possible, of course, to have two right angles since the sum of the three angles has to be 180°, and this would make the third angle zero! The right angles are indicated in the triangles in Figure 25.2 in the conventional fashion. An *obtuse-angled triangle* is one with an obtuse angle, that is, one angle greater than 90° and less than 180°; again it is possible to have only one such angle because of the sum of the three angles having to equal 180°. This condition also makes it impossible to have a triangle containing a reflex angle.

Second, looking at the sides, we can categorize triangles as being *equilateral*, *isosceles* or *scalene*. An **equilateral** (equal-sided) **triangle** is one in which all three sides are equal. Because of the rigid nature of triangles, the only possibility for an equilateral triangle is one in which the three angles are also equal (to 60°). So an equilateral triangle must be a regular triangle. This is only true of triangles. For example, you can have an equilateral octagon (with eight equal sides) in which the angles are not equal: just imagine joining eight equal strips of card with paper fasteners and manipulating the structure into many different shapes, all of which are equilateral octagons but only one of which is a regular octagon.

An **isosceles triangle** is one with two sides equal. In Figure 25.2 the equal sides are those marked with a small dash. An isosceles triangle has a line of symmetry passing through the middle of the angle formed by the two equal sides. If the triangle is cut out and folded in half along this line of symmetry the two angles opposite the equal sides match each other. In this way we can discover practically that a triangle with two equal sides always has two equal angles.

Finally, a **scalene triangle** is one with no equal sides. Using these different categorizations it is then possible to determine seven different kinds of triangle, as shown in Figure 25.2.

What are the different categories of quadrilaterals that I should know about?

The most important set of quadrilaterals is the set of **parallelograms**, that is, those with two pairs of opposite sides parallel. Figure 25.3 shows some examples of parallelograms. Two lines drawn in a two-dimensional plane are said to be **parallel** if theoretically they would never meet if continued indefinitely. This describes the relationship between the opposite sides in each of the shapes drawn in Figure 25.3. In Chapter 24 we saw that not all parallelograms have reflective symmetry; in Figure 25.3 only the special parallelograms A, B and C have reflective symmetry. But they do all have rotational symmetry at least of order two. This means that the opposite angles match onto each other, and the opposite sides match onto each other, when the shape is rotated through a half-turn. In other words, the opposite angles in a parallelogram are always equal and the opposite sides are always equal. There are then two main ways of classifying parallelograms. One of these is based on the angles, the other on the sides.

The most significant aspect of the angles of a parallelogram concerns whether or not they are right angled. If they are, as, for example, in shapes B and C in Figure 25.3, the shape is called a **rectangle**. Note that if one angle in a parallelogram is a right angle, because opposite angles are equal and the four angles add up to four right angles, all the angles

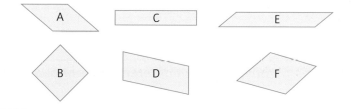

Figure 25.3   *Examples of parallelograms*

must be right angles. The rectangle is probably the most important four-sided shape from a practical perspective, simply because our artificial world is so much based on the rectangle. It is almost impossible to look anywhere and not see rectangles. Interestingly, however, there are children who grow up in rural areas of some African countries where their environment is based on the circle – they sit on circular stools in circular houses in circular villages – and this is often reflected in their relative confidence in handling the mathematics of circles and rectangles, compared with, say, British children.

Then, a **rhombus** is a parallelogram in which all four sides are equal, as, for example, in shapes A and B in Figure 25.3. A *square* (shape B) is therefore a rhombus that is also a rectangle, or a rectangle that is also a rhombus. It is, of course, a quadrilateral with all four sides equal and all four angles equal (to 90˚), so 'square' is another name for a regular quadrilateral.

There is an important point about language to make here. A square is a rectangle (a special kind of rectangle) and a rectangle is a parallelogram (a special kind of parallelogram). Likewise, a square is a rhombus (a special kind of rhombus) and a rhombus is a parallelogram (a special kind of parallelogram). Sometimes one hears teachers talking about 'squares or rectangles', for example, as though they were different things, overlooking the fact that squares are a subset of rectangles. If you need to distinguish between rectangles that are squares and those that are not, then you can refer to *square rectangles* (such as B in Figure 25.3) and **oblong rectangles** (such as C). Figure 25.4 summarizes the relationships between different kinds of quadrilaterals, using an arrow to represent the phrase 'is a special kind of'.

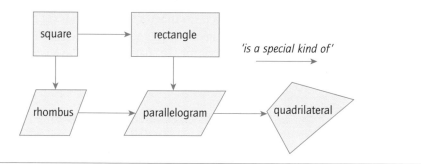

Figure 25.4   *The relationships between different kinds of quadrilaterals*

What is a tessellation?

One further way of classifying two-dimensional shapes is to distinguish between those that *tessellate* and those that do not. A shape is said to tessellate if it can be used to make a tiling pattern, or a **tessellation**. This means that the shape can be used over and over again to cover a flat surface, the shapes fitting together without any gaps. In practical terms we are asking whether the shape can be used as a tile to cover the kitchen floor (without worrying about what happens when we reach the edges).

The commonest shapes used for tiling are, of course, squares and other rectangles, which fit together so neatly without any gaps, as shown in Figure 25.5(a). This is no doubt part of the reason why the rectangle is such a popular shape in a technological world. Figure 25.5(b) demonstrates the remarkable fact that *any* triangle tessellates. If the three angles of the triangle are called A, B and C, then it is instructive to identify the six angles that come together at a point where six triangles meet in the tessellation, as shown. Because A, B and C add up to 180°, a straight angle, we find that they fit together at this point, neatly lying along straight lines. By repeating this arrangement in all directions the triangle can clearly be used to form a tessellation.

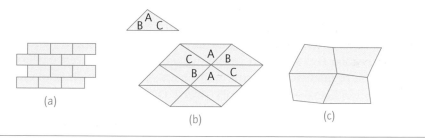

(a)

(b)

(c)

Figure 25.5 *Tessellations*

It is also true that *any* quadrilateral tessellates, as illustrated in Figure 25.5(c). Because the four angles add up to 360°, we can arrange for four quadrilaterals to meet at a point with the four different angles fitting together without any gaps. This pattern can then be continued indefinitely in all directions. Interestingly, apart from the equilateral triangle and the square, the only other regular polygon that tessellates is the regular hexagon, as seen in the familiar honeycomb pattern.

What are the main classes of three-dimensional shapes?

The first classification of three-dimensional shapes is to separate out those that have curved surfaces, such as a **sphere** (a perfectly round ball), a hemisphere (a sphere cut in half), a **cylinder** (like a baked-bean tin) and a **cone** (see the nearest motorway). A shape that is made up entirely of flat surfaces (also called **plane surfaces**) is called a **polyhedron** (plural: *polyhedra*). How can you tell that a surface is a plane surface? Mathematically, the idea is that you can join up any two points on the surface by a straight line drawn on the surface. A spherical surface is not plane, for example, because two points can be joined only by drawing circular arcs.

To describe a polyhedron we need to refer to the plane surfaces, which are called **faces** (not sides, note), the lines where two faces meet, called **edges**, and the points where edges meet, called *vertices* (plural of *vertex*). The term 'face' should only be used for plane surfaces, like the faces of polyhedra. It is not correct, for example, to refer to a sphere 'as a shape with one face'. A sphere has one continuous, smooth surface – but it is not 'a face'.

As with polygons, the word *regular* is used to identify those polyhedra in which all the faces are the same shape, all the edges are the same length, the same number of edges meet at each vertex in identical configurations, and all the angles between edges are equal. Whereas there is an infinite number of different kinds of regular polygons, there are, in fact, only five kinds of **regular polyhedra**. These are shown in Figure 25.6: (a) the regular **tetrahedron** (four faces, each of which is an equilateral triangle); (b) the regular **hexahedron** (usually called a *cube*; six faces, each of which is a square); (c) the regular **octahedron** (eight faces, each of which is an equilateral triangle); (d) the regular **dodecahedron** (twelve faces, each of which is a regular pentagon); and (e) the regular **icosahedron** (twenty faces, each of which is an equilateral triangle).

(a) (b) (c) (d) (e)

Figure 25.6   *The regular polyhedra*

These and other solid shapes can be constructed by drawing a two-dimensional **net**, such as those shown for the regular tetrahedron and cube in Figure 25.7, cutting these out, folding and sticking. It is advisable to incorporate some flaps for gluing in appropriate positions before cutting out.

A **prism** is a shape made up of two identical polygons at opposite ends, joined up by parallel lines. Figure 25.8 illustrates (a) a triangular prism, (b) a rectangular prism and (c) a hexagonal prism. I like to think of prisms as being made from cheese: a polyhedron is a prism if you can slice the cheese along its length in a way in which each slice is identical. Note that they are all called prisms, although colloquially the word is often used to refer just to the triangular prism.

Note also that another name for a rectangular prism (Figure 25.8(b)) is a **cuboid**: this is a three-dimensional shape in which all the faces are rectangles. A cube is, of course, a

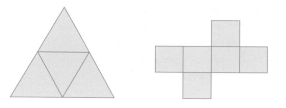

Figure 25.7   *Nets for a regular tetrahedron and a cube*

special kind of cuboid in which all the faces are squares. Note further that some 'sugar cubes' are cuboids but not cubes!

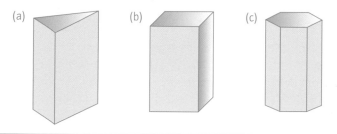

Figure 25.8   *Some prisms*

   Another category of three-dimensional shapes to be mentioned here is the set called pyramids, illustrated in Figure 25.9. A **pyramid** is made up of a polygon forming the *base,* and then lines drawn from each of the vertices of this polygon to some point above, called the *apex.* The result of this is to form a series of triangular faces rising up from the edges of the base, meeting at the apex. Note that (a) a triangular-based pyramid is actually a tetrahedron by another name, and that (b) a square-based pyramid is the kind we associate with ancient Egypt.

How does reflective symmetry
work in three dimensions?

To conclude this chapter I will make a brief mention of *reflective symmetry* as it is applied to three-dimensional shapes. In Chapter 24 we saw how some two-dimensional shapes have reflective symmetry, with a line of symmetry dividing the shape into two matching halves, one a mirror image of the other. The same applies to three-dimensional shapes, except that it is now a **plane of symmetry** that divides the shape into the two halves.

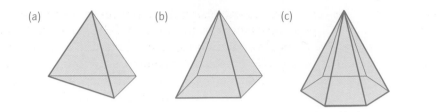

(a)   (b)   (c)

Figure 25.9   *Pyramids*

Figure 25.10   *A plane of symmetry*

This is like taking a broad, flat knife and slicing right through the shape, producing two bits that are mirror images of each other, as illustrated with a cone in Figure 25.10. This cone, of course, has an infinite number of planes of symmetry, since any vertical slice through the apex of the cone can be used. All the three-dimensional shapes illustrated in the figures in this chapter have reflective symmetry. For example, the regular tetrahedron in Figure 25.6(a) has six planes of symmetry. Children can experience this idea by slicing various fruits in half, or by using solid shapes made out of some moulding material.

Research focus

In the field of research into children's geometric learning, an influential framework has been that developed by the Dutch husband and wife team of Pierre van Hiele and Dina van Hiele-Geldof: the van Hiele levels of geometric reasoning (see, for example, Burger and Shaughnessy, 1986). There are five levels, of which only the first three are relevant to the primary school age range: (1) *visualization*, in which children can name and recognize shapes, by their appearance, but cannot specifically identify properties of shapes or use characteristics of shapes for recognition and sorting; (2) *analysis*, in which children begin to identify properties of shapes and learn to use appropriate vocabulary related to properties; (3) *informal deduction*, in which children are able to recognize relationships between and among properties of shapes or classes of shapes and are able to follow logical arguments using these properties. The implication of this framework is that geometry taught in the primary school should be informal and exploratory, aimed at moving children through visualization to analysis. Only the more able children will move into level 3. Children's experience should begin with play (van Hiele, 1999), investigating plane and solid shapes, building and taking apart, drawing and talking about shapes in the world around them. This early informal experience is seen to be essential as the basis for more formal activities in secondary school geometry.

Suggestions for further reading

1. In chapter 9 ('Thinking about shape') of Cockburn (1998) the author discusses the intrinsic mathematical and psychological problems involved for children in learning about shape and proposes some ways of overcoming these.
2. Section 4.2 ('Properties of shape') of Hopkins, Pope and Pepperell (2004) contains helpful material to reinforce your understanding of different kinds of polygons and three-dimensional shapes. The chapter in which this section comes also contains an interesting account of the historical and social context of the mathematical ideas of shape and space.
3. In a chapter entitled 'Making space for geometry in primary mathematics', in Thompson (2003), Jones and Mooney emphasize the importance of providing sufficient time and experiences for children to develop geometrical understanding, crucial for later study of mathematics in secondary school.

Self-assessment questions

25.1: Why is it not possible to have an equilateral, right-angled triangle or an equilateral, obtuse-angled triangle? (See Figure 25.2.)

25.2: What are the sizes of the three angles in a right-angled, isosceles triangle?

25.3: What is another name for: (a) a rectangular rhombus; (b) a regular quadrilateral; (c) a triangle with rotational symmetry; (d) a rectangular prism; and (e) a triangular-based pyramid?

25.4: Which of the following shapes tessellate? (a) a parallelogram; (b) a regular pentagon; and (c) a regular octagon.

25.5: How many planes of symmetry can you identify for a cube?

25.6: True or false?

   (a) All parallelograms are rhombuses;
   (b) all squares are rectangles;
   (c) all cubes are cuboids;
   (d) all squares are rhombuses;
   (e) all pentagons have five equal sides;
   (f) all isosceles triangles are acute-angled triangles.

Further practice

Glossary of key terms introduced in Chapter 25

Polygon: a two-dimensional closed shape, consisting of straight sides.

Pentagon, hexagon, heptagon, octagon, nonagon, decagon: polygons with, respectively, five, six, seven, eight, nine and ten sides (and angles).

Regular polygon: a polygon in which all the sides are equal in length and all the angles are equal in size.

Equilateral triangle: a triangle with all three sides equal in length; the three angles are also equal, and each one is therefore 60°.

Isosceles triangle: a triangle with two equal sides; the two angles opposite these two equal sides are also equal.

Scalene triangle: a triangle with all the three sides different in length.

Parallelogram: a quadrilateral with opposite sides parallel and equal in length.

Parallel lines: two lines drawn in the same plane, which, if continued indefinitely, would never meet.

Rectangle: a parallelogram in which all four of the angles are right angles. A square is a rectangle with all sides equal in length.

Rhombus: a parallelogram in which all four sides are equal in length; a diamond. A square is a rhombus with all four angles equal.

Oblong rectangle: a rectangle that is not a square.

Tessellation: a pattern made by repeatedly fitting together without gaps a collection of identical tiles; it must be possible to continue the pattern in all directions as far as you wish.

Sphere: a completely round ball; a solid shape with one continuous surface, in which every point on the surface is the same distance from a point inside the shape called the centre.

Cylinder: a three-dimensional shape, like a baked-bean tin, consisting of two identical circular ends joined by one continuous curved surface.

Cone: a solid shape consisting of a circular base and one continuous curved surface tapering to a point (the apex) directly above the centre of the circular base.

Plane surface: a completely flat surface; any two points on the surface can be joined by a straight line drawn on the surface.

Polyhedron (plural, polyhedra): a three-dimensional shape with only straight edges and plane surfaces.

Face: one of the plane surfaces of a polyhedron.

Edge: the intersection of two surfaces; in particular, the straight line where two faces of a polyhedron meet.

Regular polyhedron: a polyhedron in which all the faces are identical shapes, the same number of edges meet at each vertex in an identical configuration, and all the edges are equal in length.

Tetrahedron, hexahedron, octahedron, dodecahedron, icosahedron: polyhedra with, respectively, four, six, eight, twelve and twenty faces. The regular forms of these five shapes are the only possible regular polyhedra. A cube is a regular hexahedron.

Net: a two-dimensional arrangement of shapes that can be cut out and folded up to make a polyhedron.

Prism: a polyhedron consisting of two opposite identical faces with their vertices joined by parallel lines.

Cuboid: a rectangular prism; a six-faced polyhedron in which any two opposite faces are identical rectangles. A cube is a cuboid in which all the faces are square.

Pyramid: a polyhedron consisting of a polygon as a base, with straight lines drawn from each of the vertices of the base to meet at one point, called the apex.

Plane of symmetry: a plane that cuts a solid shape into two halves that are mirror images of each other.

26
Perimeter, Area and Volume

In this chapter there are explanations of

- the concepts of area and perimeter;

- the ideas of varying the area for a fixed perimeter, and varying the perimeter for a fixed area;

- a similar idea with volume and surface area;

- ways of investigating areas of parallelograms, triangles and trapeziums;

- the units used for measuring area and the relationships between them;

- the units used for measuring volume and the relationships between them; and

- the number π and its relationship to the circumference and diameter of a circle.

How do you explain the ideas of perimeter and area so that children do not get them confused?

Area is a measure of the amount of two-dimensional space inside a boundary. The **perimeter** is the length of the boundary. I always use *fields* and *fences* to explain these ideas. The area is the size of the field and the perimeter is the amount of fencing around the edge. Children can draw pictures of various fields on squared paper, such as the one shown in Figure 26.1. They can then count up the number of units of fencing around the edge, to determine the perimeter, which in this case is 18 units. Make sure that they count the units of fencing and not the squares around the edge, being especially careful going round corners not to miss out any units of fencing. To determine the area they can fill the field with 'sheep', using unit-cubes to represent sheep; the number of sheep they can get into the field is a measure of the area. This is, of course, the same as the number of square units inside the boundary, in this case 16 square units.

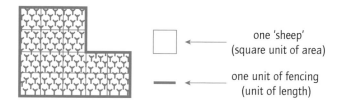

one 'sheep'
(square unit of area)

one unit of fencing
(unit of length)

Figure 26.1 *Fields and fences*

What is the relationship between perimeter and area?

In general, there is no direct relationship between perimeter and area. This is something of a surprise for many people. It provides us with an interesting counter-example of the principle of conservation in measurement (see Chapter 22). When, for example, you rearrange the fencing around a field into a different shape, the perimeter is conserved, but the area is *not* conserved. For any given perimeter there is a range of possible areas. This makes an interesting investigation for children. Again it is usefully couched in terms of fields and fences.

The first challenge is to find as many different fields as possible that can be enclosed within a given amount of fencing. Figure 26.2 shows a collection of shapes,

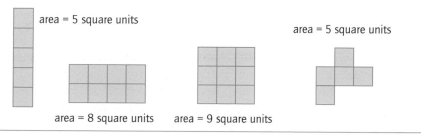

area = 5 square units

area = 5 square units

area = 8 square units   area = 9 square units

Figure 26.2 *All these shapes have perimeters of 12 units*

drawn on squared paper, all of which represent fields made up from rearranging 12 units of fencing. They all have different areas! An important discovery is that the largest area is obtained with a square field. This is the best use of the farmer's fencing material. (If we were not restricted to the grid lines on squared paper the largest area would actually be provided by a circle: imagine the fencing to be totally flexible and push it out as far as you can in all directions in order to enclose the maximum area.)

The second challenge is the reverse problem: keep the area fixed and find the different perimeters. In other words, what amounts of fencing would be required to enclose differently shaped fields all with the same area? Figure 26.3 shows a collection of fields

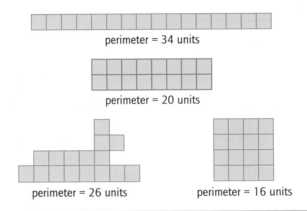

perimeter = 34 units

perimeter = 20 units

perimeter = 26 units   perimeter = 16 units

Figure 26.3   *All these shapes have an area of 16 square units*

all with the same area, 16 square units. As the 16 square units are rearranged here to make the different shapes, the area is conserved, but the perimeter is not conserved. Once again, we find the square to be the superior solution, requiring the minimum amount of fencing for the given area.

If it is not possible actually to make a square, using only the grid lines drawn on the squared paper (for example, with a fixed perimeter of 14 units, or a fixed area of 48 square units), we still find that the shape that is 'nearest' to a square gives the best solution. (The more general result, getting away from squared paper, is that the minimum perimeter for a given area is provided by a circle.) It is interesting to note that in some ancient civilizations land was priced by counting the number of paces around the boundary, that is, by the perimeter. A shrewd operator in such an arrangement could make a good profit by buying square pieces of land and selling them off in long thin strips!

What about volume and surface area?

There are parallels here with volume and surface area in solid shapes. In Chapter 22 we saw that the volume of an object is a measure of the amount of three-dimensional space it occupies, measured in cubic units. In Figure 26.4(a), for example, the cuboid illustrated has a volume of 12 cubic units, made up of 2 layers, each of which is made up of 2 rows of 3 cubic units. This illustrates how the volume of a cuboid is the product of the height, the length and the width: in this case, $2 \times 3 \times 2$ cubic units. The **surface area** of a solid object is the sum of the areas of all its surfaces, measured in square units. The cuboid in Figure 26.4(a) has four surfaces with areas of 6 square units and two with areas of 4 square units, giving as total surface area of 32 square units.

Figure 26.4(b) illustrates another cuboid with the same volume, 12 cubic units. The two cuboids in Figure 26.4 can be made by arranging 12 unit cubes in different ways. But notice that although the volume is conserved when you do this, surprisingly, the surface area is not! In cuboid (a) we saw that the total surface area is 32 square units, but in cuboid (b) it is 40 square units. This means that to cover (b) with paper you would need 40 square units of paper, but to cover (a) you would need only 32 square units. The fact that rearranging the volume changes the surface area actually explains why you sometimes need less wrapping paper if you arrange the contents of your parcel in a different way. The closer you get to a cube (or more generally to a sphere) the smaller the surface area.

(a)   (b)

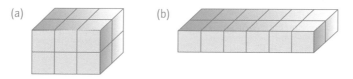

Figure 26.4   *Two cuboids with the same volume, 12 cubic units*

How can you find areas of shapes other than rectangles?

The rectangular fields in Figures 26.2 and 26.3 remind us of the simple rule for finding the area of a rectangle: that is, you just multiply together the lengths of the two sides. The reader is reminded that the visual image of a rectangular array is an important component of our understanding of the operation of multiplication, as has been discussed fully in Chapter 10 and exploited in developing a written method for multiplication calculations in Chapter 12.

The units for measuring area are always *square units*. So, for example, a rectangle 3 cm by 4 cm has an area of 12 **square centimetres**. This is abbreviated to 12 cm², but should still be read as 12 *square centimetres*. If it is read as '12 centimetres squared' it could be confused with the area of a 12-cm square, which has an area of 144 square centimetres!

The area of a right-angled triangle is easily found, because it can be thought of as half of a rectangle, as shown in Figure 26.5. In this example, the area of the rectangle is 24 square units, so the area of the triangle is 12 square units.

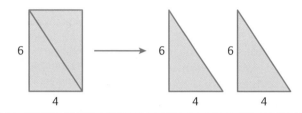

Figure 26.5   *A right-angled triangle is half of a rectangle*

More able children in primary schools might explore the areas of some other geometric shapes, so their teachers should be confident with the following material. For example, the area of a parallelogram is found by multiplying its height by the length of its base (any one of the sides can be called the base). Figure 26.6 shows how this can be demonstrated rather nicely, by transforming the parallelogram into a rectangle with the same height and the same base. For example, if the parallelogram has height 4 cm and base 3 cm, it has an area of 12 cm².

This then gives us a way of finding the area of any triangle. Just as any right-angled triangle can be thought of as half of a rectangle (Figure 26.5), so can any triangle be

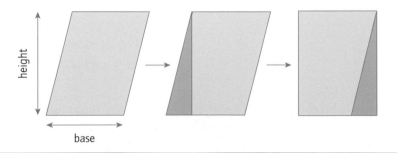

Figure 26.6   *A parallelogram transformed into a rectangle with the same height and base*

thought of as half of a parallelogram, as shown in Figure 26.7. If you make a copy of the triangle, and rotate it through 180°, the two triangles can be fitted together to form a parallelogram, with the same base and the same height as the original triangle. Since the area of the parallelogram is the base multiplied by the height, the area of the triangle is half the product of its base and height. For example, if the triangle has a height of 4 cm and a base of 3 cm, it has an area of 6 cm². Again, note that any one of the sides of the triangle can be taken as the base.

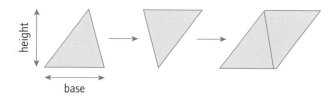

Figure 26.7 *A triangle seen as half a parallelogram*

Figure 26.8 shows a quadrilateral with just one pair of sides that are parallel. In Britain this is called a **trapezium**. This particular trapezium has a height of 3 cm and the parallel sides have lengths of 4 cm and 6 cm respectively. The area of a trapezium can be found by cutting it up into a parallelogram and a triangle, as shown in Figure 26.8. In this case we produce a parallelogram with height 3 cm and base 4 cm (area 12 cm²), and a triangle of height 3 cm and base 2 cm (area 3 cm²). So the area of the trapezium is 12 cm² + 3 cm² = 15 cm². Self-assessment question 26.6 at the end of this chapter provides the reader with an opportunity to generalize this approach and to formulate a rule for the area of a trapezium.

What should I know about the relationships between units of area?

Students often get confused when changing between areas measured in square centimetres and **square metres**. This is because they fail to recognize that there are actually 10 000 cm² in 1 m². That does seem an awful lot, doesn't it? But there are 100 centimetres in 1 metre, and remember that a square metre can be made from 100 rows of 100 centimetre squares, each with an area of 1 cm². Imagine using four metre rulers to make a square metre on the floor. You really would need 10 thousand (100 × 100) centimetre-square tiles to fill this area. So an area of 1 square metre (1 m²) is 10 000

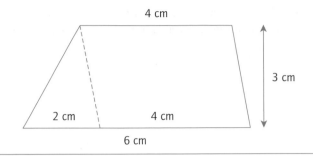

Figure 26.8   *A trapezium transformed into a triangle and a parallelogram*

cm². And an area of 1 square centimetre (1 cm²) is 0.0001 m². So converting areas between cm² and m² involves shifting the digits four places in relation to the decimal point. For example, 12 cm² = 0.0012 m², and 0.5 m² = 5000 cm².

So, for example, what would be the area of a square of side 50 cm, expressed in square centimetres and in square metres? Using centimetres, the area is 50 × 50 = 2500 cm². Using metres, the area is 0.5 × 0.5 = 0.25 m². The reader should not be surprised at this result, because they should now recognize that 2500 cm² and 0.25 m² are the same area. We might also note that a square of side 50 cm would be only a quarter of a metre square, and ¹⁄₄ expressed as a decimal is 0.25.

The potential for bewilderment is even greater in converting between **square millimetres** and square metres, since there are a million square millimetres (1000 × 1000) in a square metre.

What should I know about the relationships between units of volume?

In considering the cuboids in Figure 26.4 we noted that the volume of a cuboid, measured in cubic units, is found by multiplying together the length, width and height. Now, a metre cube is 100 layers of 100 rows of 100 centimetre cubes. So 1 m³ (a cubic metre) must be equal to 100 × 100 × 100 = 1 000 000 cm³ (a million **cubic centimetres**). So converting volumes between cm³ and m³ involves shifting the digits six places in relation to the decimal point. For example, 12 cm³ = 0.000012 m³, and 0.5 m³ = 500 000 cm³. If all this leads the reader to feel the need to brush up on their calculations with decimals, then they should now return to Chapter 18.

What is π?

A **circle** is the shape consisting of all the points at a fixed distance from a given point. The given point is called the *centre*. A line from the centre to any point on the circle is called a **radius**. A line from one point through the centre to the opposite point on the circle is called a **diameter**. The perimeter of a circle is also called the **circumference** (see Figure 26.9).

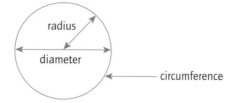

Figure 26.9 *Terms used with circles*

A point about terminology should be made here. Strictly, the word 'circle' refers to just the continuous line made up of the set of points lying on the circumference. But in practice we use the word loosely to refer to both this continuous line and the space it encloses. This enables us to talk about 'the area of a circle', meaning strictly 'the area enclosed by a circle'. Also note that we often use the words *radius, diameter* and *circumference* to mean not the actual lines but the lengths of these lines. So, for example, we could say, 'the radius is half the diameter', meaning, 'the length of the radius is half the length of the diameter'.

One of the most amazing facts in all mathematics relates to circles. If you measure the circumference of a circle and divide it by the length of the diameter you always get the same answer! This can be done in the classroom practically, using lots of differently sized circular objects, such as tin lids and crockery. To measure the diameter, place the circular object on a piece of paper between two blocks of wood, remove the object, mark the edges of the blocks on the paper and measure the distance between the marks. To measure the circumference, wrap some tape carefully around the object, mark where a complete circuit begins and ends, unwind the tape and measure the distance between the marks. Allowing for experimental error (which can be considerable with such crude approaches to measuring the diameter and the circumference) you should still find that in most cases the circumference divided by the diameter gives an answer of between about 3 and 3.3. Any results that are way out should be checked and measured again, if necessary.

This result, that the circumference is always about three times the diameter, was clearly known in ancient civilizations and used in construction. It occurs in a number of places in the Bible; for example, in I Kings 7.23, we read of a construction, 'circular in shape, measuring ten cubits from rim to rim … taking a line of thirty cubits to measure around it.'

If we were able to measure more accurately, we might be able to determine that the ratio of the circumference to the diameter of a circle is about 3.14. This ratio is so important it is given a special symbol, the Greek letter π **(pi)**. The value of π can be found theoretically to any number of decimal places. It begins like this:

3.14159265358979323846264363 … and actually goes on for ever, without ever recurring (see Chapters 13 and 18). For practical purposes, rounding this to two decimal places, as 3.14, is sufficient! Because it cannot be written down as an exact decimal, π is an example of an irrational number (see Chapter 6).

Once we have this value we can find the circumference of a circle, given the diameter, by multiplying the diameter by π, using a calculator if necessary. For example, a circle with radius 5 cm has a diameter of 10 cm and therefore a circumference of approximately $10 \times 3.14 = 31.4$ cm. And we can find the diameter of a circle, given the circumference, by dividing the circumference by π. For example, a metre trundle-wheel is a circle with circumference of 100 cm, so the diameter will have to be approximately $100 \div 3.14 = 31.8$ cm. So the radius will have to be half this, namely 15.9 cm.

There is a common misunderstanding, perpetrated I fear by some mathematics teachers who should know better, that π is *equal* to $^{22}/_7$ or $3^1/_7$. This is not true. Three-and-one-seventh is an *approximation* for the value of π in the form of a rational number. As a decimal, $3^1/_7$ is equal to 3.142857142857 …, with the 142857 recurring for ever. Comparing this with the value of π given above, we can see that it is only correct to two decimal places anyway, and therefore no better an approximation than 3.14. In the days of calculators 3.14 is bound to be a more useful approximation for π than $^{22}/_7$, which is probably best forgotten.

Research focus

To measure space and shape in two dimensions children have to co-ordinate their numerical and spatial knowledge. Children often confuse area and perimeter, because they are still wedded to a model of measuring length based on the idea of counting discrete items, like squares. This is the basis of the error that occurs when, given a rectangle drawn on squared paper, children count the squares along the inside edges of the perimeter. To grasp the concept of perimeter, children need an understanding of length as a one-dimensional continuous quantity and then to be able to extend this from one dimension (the length of a line) to two dimensions (the length of a path). Barrett and Clements (1998) reported how one 9-year-old child in a teaching experiment restructured his strategic knowledge of length to incorporate measures of perimeter. The breakthrough occurred through his response to a problem about putting a fringe on a carpet placed on a floor covered in square tiles (compare putting a fence round a field).

Suggestions for further reading

1. In chapter 9 on area, Blinko and Slater (1996) provide a range of interesting suggestions for practical classroom activities to promote children's awareness of surface and understanding of area as a measure.

2. Have a look at chapter 12 ('Area') and chapter 13 ('Capacity and volume') in Suggate, Davis and Goulding (2010). These chapters explore thoroughly the ideas of area and volume, with some interesting problems to deepen the reader's grasp of these concepts and their applications.
3. In chapter 26 ('Measuring area') of Williams and Shuard (1994) the topic of area is developed from early experiences of surfaces, through non-standard and standard units of area, to finding areas of plane shapes and surface areas of solid shapes.

Self-assessment questions

26.1: Using just rectangular fields drawn on the grid lines on squared paper, what are the dimensions of the field that gives the maximum area for 20 units of fencing?
26.2: Using just rectangular fields drawn on the grid lines on squared paper, what are the dimensions of the field that gives the minimum length of fencing for an area of 48 square units?
26.3: How can (a) 27 and (b) 48 unit-cubes be arranged in the shape of a cuboid to produce the minimum surface area?
26.4: How much ribbon will I need to go once round a circular cake with diameter 25 cm?
26.5: Roughly what is the diameter of a circular running-track which is 400 metres in circumference?
26.6: On squared paper draw a trapezium with height 10 cm and with the two parallel sides of lengths 12 cm and 8 cm. Cut this up into a triangle and a parallelogram, each with height 10 cm (see Figure 26.8) and hence find the area of the trapezium. Repeat this keeping the height and the 12 cm side fixed, but varying the length of the other side, for example, 6 cm, 9 cm, 10 cm, 11 cm, 14 cm. Think of each area as a multiple of 5. Can you now formulate a general rule for finding the area of a trapezium?
26.7: What is the area of a square of side 5 mm, expressed in square millimetres, in square centimetres and in square metres?
26.8: What would be the volume of a cube of side 5 cm? Give your answer in both cm^3 and m^3.
26.9: How many cuboids 5 cm by 4 cm by 10 cm would be needed to build a metre cube?

Further practice

From the Student Workbook
> Tasks 187–190: Checking understanding of perimeter, area and volume
> Tasks 191–194: Using and applying perimeter, area and volume
> Tasks 195–197: Learning and teaching of perimeter, area and volume

On the website (www.sagepub.co.uk/haylock)
> Check-Up 29: Knowledge of metric units of area and solid volume

Glossary of key terms introduced in Chapter 26

Area: the amount of two-dimensional space enclosed by a boundary; like the size of a field enclosed by a fence.

Perimeter: the total length all the way round a boundary enclosing an area; like the length of fencing enclosing a field.

Surface area: the sum of the areas of all the surfaces of a solid object.

Square centimetre (cm²):   the area of a square of side one centimetre; written 1 cm² but read as 'one square centimetre'. There are ten thousand square centimetres in a square metre.

Trapezium: a quadrilateral with two sides parallel.

Square metre (m²):   the SI unit of area; the area of a square of side one metre; written 1 m² but read as 'one square metre'.

Square millimetre (mm²):   the area of a square of side one millimetre; written 1 mm² but read as 'one square millimetre'. There are a million square millimetres in a square metre.

Cubic centimetre (cm³):   the volume of a cube of side one centimetre; written 1 cm³ but read as 'one cubic centimetre'.

Circle: a two-dimensional shape consisting of all the points that are a given distance from a fixed point, called the centre of the circle.

Radius: a line from the centre of a circle to any point on the circle; also the length of such a line; half the diameter.

Diameter: a line from any point on a circle, passing through the centre to the point opposite; also the length of such a line; twice the radius.

Circumference: the perimeter of a circle.

Pi (π):   a number equal to the ratio of the circumference of any circle to its diameter; about 3.14.

SECTION E
STATISTICS

27
Handling Data

What are Venn diagrams?

Sorting according to given criteria is one of the most fundamental processes in mathematics. For example, when a child in a reception class counts how many children have brought packed lunches they have first to sort the children into two subsets: those who have packed lunches and those who do not.

Technically, sorting involves the concepts of a **population** (sometimes called the **universal set**), the values of a **variable**, and **subset**. For example, the 25 children in a Year 5 class in a rural school were sorted according to how they came to school that day: walking, by bicycle, by car or by bus. In this case the children in the class constitute the *universal set*. This is the set containing all the things under consideration. In statistical language, this is called the *population*. The *variable* that distinguishes between the members of the population in this example is the way they came to school. There are four *values* of this variable: walk, bicycle, car and bus. The four different values of the variable sort the set of children into four *subsets*. The use of the word 'value' may seem a little strange here, but the concept is essentially the same as when we use a *numerical* variable to sort children, such as how many children in their family – it seems more natural now to talk about the various numbers of children in a family (1, 2, 3, 4, …) as being the values of the variable.

Set diagrams are visual structures that aid children's understanding of the process of sorting and the relationships between various sets and subsets. Figure 27.1 is an elementary example of a **Venn diagram**, where circles (or other closed shapes) are used to represent the various subsets of the 25 children. John Venn (1834–1923) was a Cambridge logician and philosopher who developed the use of such diagrams for representing various logical relationships between sets and subsets.

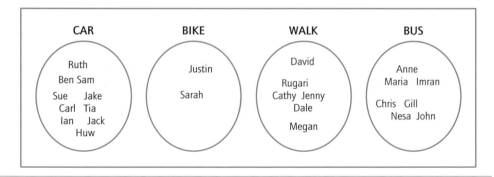

Figure 27.1   *An elementary Venn diagram: how we travel to school*

Figure 27.2 shows another kind of simple Venn diagram used for sorting. Here the questions asked is 'Did you travel to school by car?' The universal set comprises the 25 children in the class, the names of all of which are to be placed somewhere within the rectangular box. The variable is again how they travel to school. But now the sorting uses only two values of the variable, namely 'by car' and 'not by car'. All those who travel by car are placed inside the circle and all the others go outside it. The set of children who do not

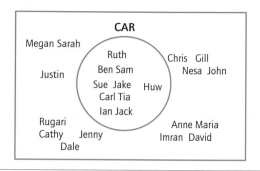

Figure 27.2 *A Venn diagram showing the complement of a set*

travel by car – those lying outside of the circle – is called the **complement of the set** of those who travel by car. This diagram is an important illustration of the partitioning structure of subtraction, linked with the question 'how many do not?' (see Chapter 7).

An interesting example of sorting using a Venn diagram occurs when two variables are used simultaneously. An example is shown in Figure 27.3, which arises from simultaneously sorting the children into those who travel by car and those who do not, and those who are girls and those who are not. This sorting generates four subsets: girls who travel by car, girls who do not travel by car, those who are not girls who travel by car, and those who are not girls who do not travel by car. If you think of each child answering the questions, 'are you a girl? and 'did you travel to school by car?' the four subsets represent 'yes, yes', 'yes, no', 'no, yes' and 'no, no'. The 'yes, yes' subset – those whose names are placed in the section of the diagram where the two sets overlap – is called the **intersection of the two sets**.

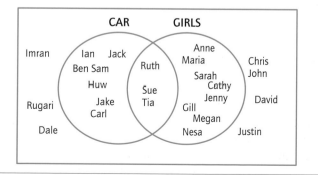

Figure 27.3 *A Venn diagram showing the intersection of two sets*

What are Carroll diagrams?

LEARNING and TEACHING POINT

A Carroll diagram is an example of a two-way reference chart, which children must learnt to use and interpret.

Lewis Carroll (1832–98) was not just the author of the *Alice* books but also a mathematician with a keen interest in logic. He devised what has become known as the **Carroll diagram**, another way of representing the subsets that occur when a set is sorted according to two variables. Figure 27.4 shows the data about girls and travel by car sorted in the same way as in Figure 27.3 but presented in a Carroll diagram. The four subsets generated by the sorting process are clearly identified by this simple diagrammatic device: girl, car; girl, not car; not girl, car; not girl, not car.

	CAR	NOT CAR
GIRL	Ruth, Sue, Tia	Anne, Cathy, Maria, Jenny, Gill, Sarah, Megan, Nesa
NOT GIRL	Ian, Jack, Huw, Jake, Ben, Sam, Carl	Imran, Rugari, Chris, John, David, Dale, Justin

Figure 27.4 *A Carroll diagram for sorting using two variables*

What do children have to learn about handling statistical data?

LEARNING and TEACHING POINT

Children should experience all four stages in handling data: collecting it, organizing it, representing it, and interpreting it.

Essentially there are four stages involved in handling statistical data: collecting it, organizing it, representing it and interpreting it. (*Note*: I adopt the current usage of *data* as a singular noun, meaning 'a collection of information'.)

Children should learn how to collect data as part of a purposeful enquiry, setting out to answer specific questions that they might raise. This might involve the skills associated with designing simple questionnaires. For example, the data used above about how children travel to school might arise as part of a geography-focused project on transport, and be used to make comparisons between, say, the children in this rural school and those in a city school. A useful technique here is that of **tallying**, based on counting in fives. Data should then be organized in a **frequency table**. Figure 27.5 shows both these processes for the information collected from our Year 5 class of 25 children.

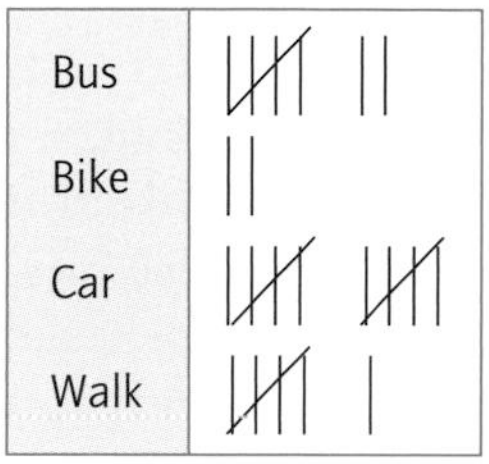

Bus	卌 ||
Bike	||
Car	卌 卌
Walk	卌	

How we travel	Number of pupils
Bus	7
Bike	2
Car	10
Walk	6
Total	25

tallying   *frequency table*

Figure 27.5   *Using tallying and a frequency table*

In undertaking a survey, primary children can be introduced informally to the concept of *sampling*. With a large population (such as the population of the city of Norwich, where I live), it is clearly not possible to gather data from all 400 000 residents. So those who do surveys will collect data from a carefully-selected **sample**. Primary children can appreciate the principle that the sample must be as far as possible a fair representation of the population. This principle resonates with their understanding of a fair test in science. Three factors can contribute to achieving a fair sample: (i) selecting members of the population at random; (ii) ensuring that the proportions of significant categories of individuals (such as male/female, employed/unemployed, age bands, social class) in the sample are similar to the proportions in the population; and (iii) making the sample as large as possible – in general, the larger the sample, the more reliable the findings. The use of sampling to estimate probabilities is discussed in Chapter 29.

Various kinds of graphs and diagrams – including Venn and Carroll diagrams, block graphs, bar charts, pictograms and pie charts – can then be used to represent the data, before the final step of interpreting it.

What is discrete data?

The word *discrete* means 'separate'. Discrete data is information about a particular population that automatically sorts the members of the population into quite distinct, separate subsets. The information about travelling to school, shown in Figures 27.1 and 27.5, is a good example of discrete data, since it sorts the children automatically into four separate, distinct subsets: those who come by bus, by car, by bicycle or on foot. Other examples of this kind of discrete data that children might collect, organize, display and interpret would include: their favourite television programme, chosen from a list of six possible programmes; the daily newspaper taken at home, including 'none'; and the month in which they were born. We can also refer to the variable that gives rises to a set of discrete data as 'a **discrete variable**'. Separate subsets are formed for each individual value taken by the variable. The number in each subset is called the **frequency**.

We have seen that sometimes a discrete variable is numerical, rather than just descriptive. For example, children might be asked what size shoes they wear, or how many pets they have. The values of a discrete numerical variable will usually be a regular sequence of numbers across a particular range. For a particular class of children, shoe sizes, for example, might be 3, 3.5, 4, 4.5, 5, 5.5, or 6. The number of pets a child has might be 0, 1, 2, 3, 4, 5 or 6. Initially, we should use variables that have no more than a dozen values, otherwise we finish up with too many subsets to allow any meaningful interpretation. Frequency data collected and organized as in Figure 27.5 can then be displayed in a conventional block graph or bar chart.

What's the difference between block graphs and bar charts?

Block graphs and bar charts are two important stages in the development of graphical representation of frequencies. In the **block graph** shown in Figure 27.6(a) each square is shaded individually, as though each square represents one child. In interpreting the graph the child can count the number of squares, as though counting the number of children in each subset, so there is no need for a vertical axis. Block

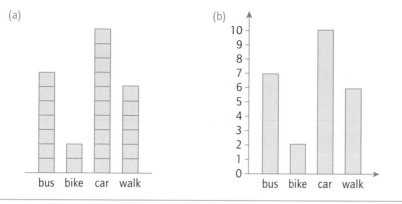

Figure 27.6   *Two stages in the use of graphs: (a) block graph; (b) bar chart*

graphs are introduced first by sticking on or shading individual squares, the number of which represents the frequency.

Figure 27.6(b) is based on a more sophisticated idea. Now, the individual contributions are lost and it is the height of the column that indicates the frequency, rather than the number of squares in the column. In this **bar chart** we read off the frequencies by relating the tops of the columns to the scale on the vertical axis. It should be noted that the numbers label the points on the vertical axis, not the spaces between them. So in moving from the block graph to the bar chart we have progressed from counting to measurement. This is an important step because, even though we may still use squared paper to draw these graphs, we now have the option of using different scales on the vertical axis, appropriate to the data: for example, with larger populations we might take one unit on the vertical scale to represent 10 people.

Notice that, in Figure 27.6, I have used the convention, sometimes used for discrete data, of leaving gaps between the columns; this is an appropriate procedure because it conveys pictorially the way in which the variable sorts the population into discrete subsets. In order to present an appropriate picture of the distribution of the data, it is essential that the columns in a block graph or bar chart be drawn with equal widths.

> **LEARNING and TEACHING POINT**
>
> When introducing block graphs to younger children, get them to write their names on squares of gummed paper, which can then be arranged in columns, so that the individual contribution of each child can be identified.

> **LEARNING and TEACHING POINT**
>
> If children are collecting (ungrouped) discrete data, use variables that have no more than a dozen values. If you want to use data about their favourite something (meal, television programme, pop star, book, and so on) then first agree with the class a menu of about six possibilities to choose from, rather than having a free choice.

What is suppression of zero?

There is a further important point to make about using bar charts to represent frequencies, illustrated by the graphs shown in Figure 27.7. This was produced prior to a general election to show the numbers of votes gained by three political parties (which I have called A, B and C) in the previous general election. The graph in Figure 27.7(a) was the version put out by our local party A candidate to persuade us that we would be wasting our vote by voting for party C. By not starting the frequency axis at zero a totally false picture is presented of the relative standing of party C compared with A and B. Because the purpose of drawing a graph is to give us an instant overview of the relationships within the data, this procedure (called **suppression of zero**) is nearly always inappropriate or misleading and should be avoided. The graph in Figure 27.7(b), properly starting the vertical axis at zero, presents a much more honest picture of the relative share of the vote.

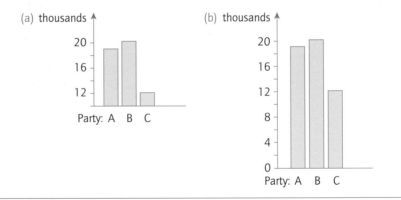

Figure 27.7   *Suppression of zero*

So what is meant by 'grouped discrete data'?

Discrete data, like that in the examples above, is the simplest kind of data to handle. Sometimes, however, there are just too many values of the variable concerned for us to sort the population into an appropriate number of subsets. So the data must first be organized into groups.

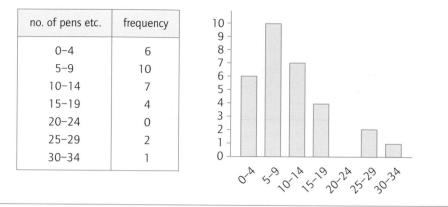

no. of pens etc.	frequency
0–4	6
5–9	10
10–14	7
15–19	4
20–24	0
25–29	2
30–34	1

Figure 27.8   *Handling grouped discrete data*

For example, a group of Year 5 children was asked how many writing implements (pencils, pens, felt-tips, and so on) they had with them one day at school. The responses were as follows: 1, 2, 2, 3, 4, 4, 5, 5, 5, 6, 6, 8, 8, 8, 9, 9, 10, 10, 11, 13, 14, 14, 14, 15, 15, 18, 19, 25, 26, 32. Clearly, there are just too many possibilities here to represent this data in a bar chart as it stands. The best procedure, therefore, is to group the data, for example, as shown in Figure 27.8.

Of course, the data could have been grouped in other ways, producing either more subsets (for example, 0–1, 2–3, 4–5, and so on: 17 groups), or fewer (for example, 0–9, 10–19, 20–29, 30–39). When working with **grouped discrete data** like this a rule of thumb is that we should aim to produce from five to twelve groups: more than twelve, we have too much information to take in; fewer than five, we have lost too much information. Note the following principles for grouping data like this:

- The range of values in the subsets (0–4, 5–9, 10–14, 15–19, and so on) should be the same in each case.
- The groups should not overlap.
- They must between them cover all the values of the variable.
- Groups with zero frequency (like 20–24 in Figure 27.8) should not be omitted from the table or from the graph.
- If possible, aim for the number of groups to be from five to twelve.

What other kind of data is there apart from discrete?

Discrete data contrasts with what is called *continuous data*. This is the kind of data produced by a variable that can theoretically take any value on a continuum. For example, if we were collecting data about the waist sizes of a group of adults, the measurements could come anywhere on a tape measure from, say, 50 cm to 120 cm. They are not just restricted to particular, distinct points on the scale. For example, the waist measurement for one individual might be about 62.5 cm. If he or she puts on some weight and the measurement increases to about 64.5 cm, then we know that the waist size would increase continuously from one measurement to the next, on the way taking every possible value in between; it would not suddenly jump from one value to the other! This is a characteristic of a **continuous variable**. The contrast with a discrete variable like, for example, the number of pets you own, is clear. If you have three pets and then get a fourth, you suddenly jump from three to four, without having to pass through 3.1 pets, 3.2 pets, and so on. Measurements of length, mass, volume and time intervals are all examples of continuous data.

Having said that, we always have to record measurements 'to the nearest something' (see the discussion on rounding in Chapters 13 and 22). The effect of this is immediately to change the values of the continuous variable into a set of discrete data! For example, we might measure waist size to the nearest centimetre. This now means that our data is restricted to the following, separate, distinct values: 50 cm, 51 cm, 52 cm, and so on. This means that, in practice, the procedure for handling this kind of data – produced by recording a series of measurements to the nearest something – is no different from that for handling discrete data with a large number of potential values, by grouping it as explained above.

It is therefore an appropriate activity for primary school children. For example, children can collect data about: their heights (to the nearest centimetre); their masses (to the nearest tenth of a kilogram); the circumferences of their heads (to the nearest millimetre); the volume of water they can drink in one go (to the nearest tenth of a litre); the time taken to run 100 metres (to the nearest second); and so on. Each of these is technically a continuous variable, but by being measured to the nearest something it generates a set of discrete data, which can then be grouped appropriately and represented in a graph. I would then suggest that we might reflect the fact that the data originated from a continuous variable by drawing the columns in the graph with no gaps between them, as shown in Figure 27.9. Any further development of handling of continuous data than this would be beyond the scope of primary school mathematics.

What about pictograms?

Figure 27.10 shows how a **pictogram** can be used to represent the data given in Figure 27.5. Here the names of the children in various sets have been replaced by

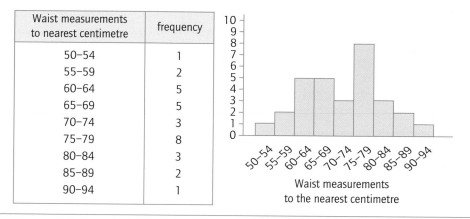

Figure 27.9 *A graph derived from a continuous variable*

icons (pictures), organized in neat rows and columns. It is essential for a pictogram to work that the icons are lined up both horizontally and vertically. The pictogram is clearly only a small step from a block graph, with the icons replaced by individual shaded squares. So, in terms of developing children's statistical understanding it should be seen as an early stage of pictorial representation of data, coming between the representations used in Figures 27.1 and 27.6.

BUS	👤👤👤👤👤👤👤
BIKE	👤👤
CAR	👤👤👤👤👤👤👤👤👤👤👤
WALK	👤👤👤👤👤👤

Figure 27.10 *A pictogram*

It is also possible with larger populations to use pictograms where each icon represents a number of individuals rather than just one. One problem with this approach is that sometimes an icon like the one used in Figure 27.10 is used to represent, say, 10 people. It seems to me rather bizarre to use a picture of one person to represent ten people! And then you have to represent numbers less than 10 with fractions of the icon. This is a popular format in newspapers and advertising, because it is more eye-catching than just a plain bar chart, so children will have to learn how to interpret them. But, mathematically, the bar chart with an appropriate scale on the vertical axis is clearer and more accurate for representing the frequencies of various subsets within a larger population.

What are pie charts used for?

The **pie chart**, shown in Figure 27.11, is a much more sophisticated idea. Here it is the angle of each slice of pie that represents the proportion of the population in each subset. It is common practice to write these proportions as percentages (see Chapter 19) within the slice itself, if possible. A really important principle of the pie chart is that the whole pie must represent the whole population. Pie charts are really only appropriate for discrete data with a small number of subsets, say, six or fewer. In fact, the effectiveness of a pie chart as a way of displaying discrete data increases as the number of subsets decreases! They are often used to show what proportions of a budget are spent in various categories.

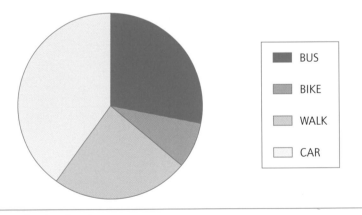

Figure 27.11   *A pie chart*

The mathematics for producing a pie chart can be difficult for primary school children, unless the data is chosen very carefully. For example, to determine the angle for the slice representing travel by bus, in Figure 27.11, we would have to divide 360 degrees by 25 to determine how many degrees per person in the population, and then multiply by 7. Using a calculator, the key sequence is: 360, ÷, 25, ×, 7, = (answer 100.8, which is about 101 degrees). This angle then has to be drawn using a protractor.

Fortunately, this can all be done nowadays by a computer. If the data in question is entered on a database or on a spreadsheet, then usually there is available a choice of a bar chart, a pie chart or a line graph (see below). Many simple versions of such data-handling software are available for use in primary schools.

When might a line graph be used to represent statistical data?

The other type of graph used sometimes for representing statistical data is the **line graph**. An appropriate example of the use of a line graph is shown in Figure 27.12. Like pie charts, line graphs are easily produced by entering the data onto a computer spreadsheet or database. Figure 27.12, showing the number of children on a primary-school roll at the beginning of each school year for a number of years, was produced in this way. For statistical data, a line graph is really only appropriate where the variable along the horizontal axis is 'time'. In this example, the movement of the line, up and down, gives a picture of how the number on roll is changing over time. A line graph would therefore be totally inappropriate as a means of presenting discrete data such as that relating to travelling to school in Figure 27.5, and similarly inappropriate for all the other examples of statistical data used in this chapter.

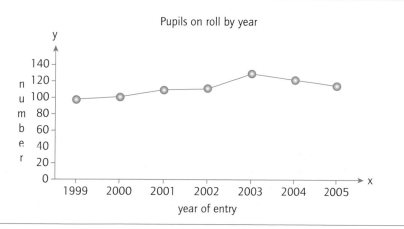

Figure 27.12 *A line graph*

What are scatter diagrams?

Various kinds of **scatter diagrams** (also called **scatter plots**, **scattergams** and **scattergraphs**) are used to show the relationship between two variables for the same members of a population. The Carroll diagram in Figure 27.4 enabled us to sort a set into four subsets according to two variables. But in a Carroll diagram each of the variables can take only two values: essentially, yes or no. This idea of using a grid to represent data from two variables can be extended to examples where the variables take more values. Figure 27.13, for example, shows an elementary form of scatter diagram. A sample of children in a school is sorted according to two variables: how they travelled to school that day and their year group. Each of these variables takes four values. The data is presented in a 4 by 4 grid, with each child represented by a small cross, placed inside one of the cells of the grid.

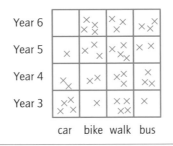

Figure 27.13   *A simple scatter diagram*

In this simple kind of scatter diagram the individuals in the set are represented by crosses or dots placed inside a cell. Because the variables have just a few values, as in Figure 27.13, it is very likely that there will be a number of crosses plotted within the same cell. When the variables are numerical and take a greater range of values it becomes more appropriate to plot the data as individual points on a graph. An example is the *scattergraph* shown in Figure 27.14. The data for Figure 27.14 has been collected by a teacher for 20 children, labelled as A–T below. The two variables are their scores in a spelling test (marked out of 10) and their performance in a reading test (marked out of 20):

Child	A	B	C	D	E	F	G	H	I	J	K	L	M	N	O	P	Q	R	S	T
Spelling	2	5	7	8	7	6	9	2	10	7	6	8	7	4	5	8	4	6	9	3
Reading	6	9	12	16	13	7	15	12	17	19	13	15	14	8	12	14	7	10	17	6

The data is entered into appropriate data handling software, such as an Excel spreadsheet. The scattergraph generated enables us to see at a glance the relationship between these two variables. The points are plotted as though they are coordinates, one point for each child. So, for example, the scores for Child G are plotted as the point (9, 15).

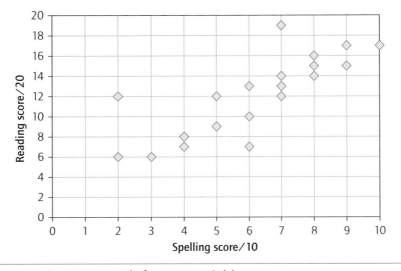

Figure 27.14   *A scattergraph for two variables*

A scattergram gives us a picture of the **correlation** between the two variables; in other words, the extent to which the two variables are related to each other. Here's a fairly basic explanation of how to interpret a scattergraph like this. A point lying somewhere in the top right-hand corner (such as the (9, 17) for Child S) represents a good performance in both tests. Likewise, a point plotted somewhere in the bottom left-hand corner (such as (2, 6) for Child A) would be a poor performance in both tests. A

point in the top left-hand corner represents a high score for reading and a low score for spelling, while one in the bottom right-hand corner is a low reading score and a high spelling score. In this example, it looks as though the points are generally clustered around a line sloping upwards. This indicates what is called a **positive correlation** between the two variables. This means that there is a statistical tendency for the two variables to be positively related to each other: when one is high the other tends to be high; when one is low the other tends to be low. A point lying approximately along this upward-sloping line indicates that the child has done about as well in one test as the other. A common error in interpreting correlation is to assume that one variable is the cause and the other the effect. In Figure 27.14, for example, it would be wrong to deduce that if we get children to be better at spelling then they will be better at reading (or vice versa). The statistics show only that the two variables appear to be related.

Sometimes the points in a scattergram seem to be clustered around a line sloping downwards. For example, I would expect this to be the case for a sample of boys across the primary school range if the two variables were (a) their age in years, and (b) the time to the nearest minute that it takes them to run 400 metres. In this case, we would probably find a tendency for the older boys to take less time and the younger boys to take longer. Of course there will be exceptions: 8-year-old Jack may run faster than 11-year-old Alex, but the scattergraph will show a general trend. It will probably have most of the points clustered around a line sloping downwards from the top left-hand corner. If this is the case, then it indicates what is called a **negative correlation**. If the points are just generally dispersed more or less randomly over the page, then this is an indication that there is no particular correlation between the two variables.

Research focus

Drawing on a bank of research and their experience with primary school children over the course of a whole year, Jones et al. (2000) have developed a useful framework for describing children's statistical thinking. This framework describes four key statistical processes. These are: (1) *describing data*, which involves extracting information from a set of data or graph and making connections between the data and the context from which it came; (2) *organizing and reducing data*, which includes ordering, grouping and summarizing data; (3) *representing data*, which refers to constructing various kinds of visual representation of the data; and (4) *analysing and interpreting data*, which involves recognizing patterns and trends and making inferences and predictions. For each of these four aspects the researchers were able to identify four levels of thinking: *Level 1*, where the reasoning is idiosyncratic, often unrelated to the given data and tending to draw more on the individual's own experience and opinions; *Level 2*, where the child begins to use quantitative reasoning to comment on the data; *Level 3*, where quantitative reasoning is used consistently to formulate judgements; and *Level 4*, which uses a more analytical approach in exploring data and in making connections between the data and the context. The framework is a helpful tool both for assessment of children's understanding and for informing teaching plans.

Suggestions for further reading

1. Chapter 9 ('Understanding data-handling') of Haylock and Cockburn (2008) uses data from a class of 7–8-year-olds to explain different kinds of data and various ways of representing it pictorially. In common with all the chapters in this book, the chapter contains some suggestions for classroom activities for younger children.
2. Read the entry on 'Cross-curricular mathematics' in Haylock with Thangata (2007). Handling data is one of the most obvious topics in the mathematics curriculum to be taught through a cross-curricular approach. The entry on this subject in this book clarifies the relationship between mathematics and other curriculum areas and provides some classroom examples.
3. The title of chapter 3 of Way and Beardon (2003), written by Perks and Prestage, is 'Spreadsheets with everything'. This helpful chapter in a book all about using ICT in primary mathematics teaching includes material on scattergraphs.

Self-assessment questions

27.1: Children in a class answer 'yes' or 'no' to these two questions: (i) are you a boy? (ii) did you walk to school today? How do their answers to these questions put the children into four subsets? How could these four subsets be represented in (a) a Venn diagram, and (b) a Carroll diagram?

27.2: Make up two questions that can be answered from the graphs shown in each of: (a) Figure 27.6; (b) Figure 27.8; and (c) Figure 27.9.

27.3: Which of these variables are discrete? Which would generate discrete data that should be grouped? Which are continuous? (a) The time it takes a person to count to a thousand; (b) your height; (c) the number of living grandparents; (d) the amount of money in coins in a person's possession; (e) a person's favourite kind of music chosen from a list of ten possibilities; (f) the number of A levels a person has passed; and (g) the mass of the classroom guinea pig recorded each Monday morning for a term.

27.4: Which of the examples in question 27.3 would be best represented in a pie chart? Which would be best represented in a line graph?

27.5: For example (d) in question 27.3, the data collected from a group of students ranged from zero to £4.59. How would you choose to group this data in order to represent it in a bar chart?

27.6: (a) In a class of 36 children, 14 come to school by car. What angle would be needed in the slice of a pie chart to represent this information? (b) What would it be for 14 children out of a class of 33?

27.7: A survey is to be conducted of the opinions of the children in a large junior school (Years 3–6) about what time the school day should start. There is a total of 500 children in the school, so it is decided to get responses from a sample of 50. One suggestion is to interview the first 50 children arriving at school one morning.

What's wrong with this method of sampling? How would you suggest the sample might be obtained?

27.8 Suggest some questions that could be asked to children aged 9–10 years to help them to interpret the scatter diagram in Figure 27.13.

27.9: In Figure 27.14, lightly draw with a pencil and a ruler a line sloping upwards from (0, 2). Do this so that about half the points lie above the line and about half below it. Which child's results are furthest away from this line? What does this indicate about this child's performance?

Further practice

From the Student Workbook

Tasks 198–200: Checking understanding of handling data

Tasks 201–203: Using and applying handling data

Tasks 204–208: Learning and teaching of handling data

On the website (www.sagepub.co.uk/haylock)

Check-Up 4: Bar charts and frequency tables for discrete data

Check-Up 5: Bar charts for grouped discrete data

Check-Up 6: Bar charts for continuous data

Check-Up 43: Interpreting pie charts

Check-Up 45: Bar charts for comparing two sets of data

Glossary of key terms introduced in Chapter 27

Population: the term used in statistics for the complete set of all the people or other things for which some statistical data is being collected; synonymous with 'universal set' in set theory.

Universal set: the term used in set theory for the complete set of all things under consideration; synonymous with 'population' in statistics. In a Venn diagram the universal set is usually represented by a rectangular box.

Variable (in statistics): an attribute that can vary from one member of a population to another, the different values of which can be used to sort the population into subsets; variables may be non-numerical (such as choice of favourite fruit) or numerical (such as the mark achieved in a mathematics test).

Subset: a set of members within a given set that have some defined attribute, or that take a particular value of a variable.

Venn diagram: a way of representing the relationships between various sets and subsets using enclosed regions (such as circles); children can use these for sorting experiences by placing the members of various sets or subsets within the appropriate regions. (See Figures 27.1–27.3.)

Complement of a set: all the things in the universal set that are not within a given set. For example, the complement of the set of 7-year-olds in a class is the set of all those who are not 7 years old.

Intersection of two sets: the set of all those things that are common to the two sets. In a Venn diagram the intersection is represented by the overlap between two enclosed regions. The intersection of the set of girls and the set of 7-year-olds is the set of 7-year-old girls.

Carroll diagram: a 2 by 2 grid used for sorting the members of a set according to whether or not they possess each of two attributes. The four cells of the grid correspond to 'yes, yes', 'yes, no', 'no, yes' and 'no, no'. (See Figure 27.4.)

Tallying: a simple way of counting, making a mark for each item counted, with every fifth mark used to make a group of five. (See Figure 27.5.)

Frequency table: a table recording the frequencies of each value of a variable. (See Figure 27.5.)

Sample: in a statistical survey a representative selection of a large population for which data is collected; in general, the larger the sample, the more reliable are the results as a representation of the whole population.

Discrete variable: a variable that can take only specific, separate (discrete) values. For example, 'number of children in a family' is a discrete variable, because it can take only the values 0, 1, 2, 3, 4, and so on. When the value of this variable changes it goes up in jumps.

Frequency: the number of times something occurs within a population.

Block graph: an introductory way of representing discrete data, in which each member of the population is represented by an individual square (stuck on or coloured in) arranged in columns. The frequency of a particular value of the variable is simply the number of squares in that column. (See Figure 27.6a.)

Bar chart: a graphical representation of data, where frequencies are represented by the heights of bars or columns. (See Figure 27.6b.)

Suppression of zero: the misleading practice of starting the vertical axis in a frequency graph at a number other than zero; this gives a false impression of the relative frequencies of various values of the variable.

Grouped discrete data: data arising from a discrete (usually numerical) variable where the different values of the variable have been grouped into intervals, in order to reduce the number of subsets. For example, marks out of 100 in a mathematics test might be grouped into intervals 1–10, 11–20, 21–30, 31–40, and so on.

Continuous variable: a variable that can take any value on a continuum. For example, 'the height of the children in my class' is a continuous variable. When the value of this variable for a particular child has changed it will have done so continuously, passing through every real number value on the way.

Pictogram: a way of representing discrete data, in which each member of the population is represented by an individual picture or icon arranged in rows or columns. (See Figure 27.10.) With larger populations, each picture or icon may represent a number of individuals rather than just one.

Pie chart: a way of representing statistical data where the population is represented by a circle (the pie) and each subset is represented by a sector of a circle (a slice of the circular pie), with the size of each sector indicating the frequency. (See Figure 27.11.)

Line graph: mainly used for statistical data collected over time; the frequencies (or other measurements) are plotted as points and each point is joined to its neighbours by straight lines. (See Figure 27.12.) A line graph is therefore useful for showing trends over time.

Scatter diagram (scatter plot, scattergram, scattergraph):   a graphical representation of data for two variables for a given set, with horizontal and vertical axes representing the two variables, and the values of the two variables for each individual in the set plotted as points.

Correlation: a measure in statistics of the extent to which two variables are related or dependent upon each other.

Positive correlation: a correlation such that when one variable is high the other tends to be high, and when one is low the other tends to be low; indicated by points tending to be clustered around an upward-sloping line in a scattergram.

Negative correlation: a correlation such that when one variable is low the other tends to be high, and vice versa; indicated by points tending to be clustered around a downward-sloping line in a scattergram.

28
Comparing Sets of Data

In this chapter there are explanations of

- how two data sets using the same variable can be presented for comparison;
- the idea of an average as a representative figure for a set of data;
- three measures of average: the mean, the median and the mode;
- how to calculate mode, median and mean from a frequency table;
- quartiles and the five-number summary of a distribution;
- range and inter-quartile range as measures of spread;
- box-and-whisker diagrams;
- percentiles and deciles; and
- the concept of average speed.

How can two data sets be presented pictorially for comparison?

Often we will want to represent two sets of data side by side for comparison. This will usually be where the same variable is used for two different populations. For example, a school may wish to compare data for 25 boys and 30 girls in a mathematics assessment. The variable here is the level achieved by each child. This variable takes values of 3, 4, 5 or 6, as shown in this frequency table:

	boys	girls
level 3	5	3
level 4	10	18
level 5	6	6
level 6	4	3

What is the best way of representing this data in one diagram so that we can visually compare the achievements of the boys with that of the girls? The first thing to note is that because the sample sizes are different (25 boys, 30 girls) we cannot really use the raw data for comparison. For example, the 6 boys achieving level 5 is a greater proportion of the set of boys than the 6 girls achieving level 5. This would not be a problem if we had two sets of the same size. But with different sized sets we need to compare the proportions of boys and girls achieving various levels. The obvious way to do this is to express the proportions as percentages:

	boys	girls
level 3	20%	10%
level 4	40%	60%
level 5	24%	20%
level 6	16%	10%

There are a number of ways of representing this data in a way that make it possible to compare them at a glance. Figure 28.1 shows two of them. Figure 28.1(a) puts the columns side by side, making it easy to compare performances for each level. Figure 28.1(b) is a better representation if you want to focus on comparing how the boys and girls were spread across the different levels. Note that the representation for each set in Figure 28.1(b) is essentially the same idea as a pie chart, but using a rectangular strip rather than a circle to represent the whole set.

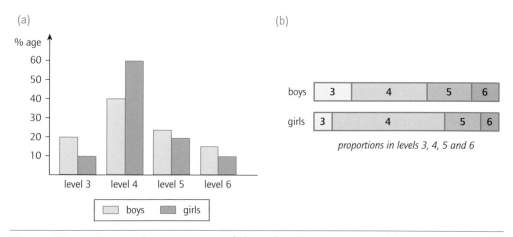

Figure 28.1 *Comparing two sets of data for the same variable*

What are averages for?

The purpose of finding an **average** is to produce a *representative figure* for a set of numerical data. There are three kinds of average to be considered: the **mean** (also called the **arithmetic mean**), the **median** and the **mode**. Although they are calculated in different ways, the important purpose shared by all three of these measures of average is to provide one number that can represent the whole set of numbers. This 'average' figure will then enable us:

> **LEARNING and TEACHING POINT**
>
> Useful sources of comparative data for using with children are: the children themselves (their ages, their heights, shoe sizes, distance of home from school, time they leave home, boys and girls in their family), the weather, sport, science experiments and most geography-focused topics (particularly for making comparisons between different areas).

1. to make comparisons between different sets of data, by comparing their means, medians or modes; and
2. to make sense of individual numbers in a set by relating them to these averages.

   In the discussion below we use these different kinds of average to consider the marks out of 100 gained by two groups of children (Group A, 14 children; Group B, 11 children) in the same mathematics and English tests, as follows:

Group A: Mathematics	23, 25, 46, 48, 48, 49, 53, 60, 61, 61, 61, 62, 69, 85
Group B: Mathematics	36, 38, 43, 43, 45, 47, 60, 63, 69, 86, 95
Group A: English	45, 48, 49, 52, 53, 53, 53, 53, 54, 56, 57, 58, 59, 62
Group B: English	45, 52, 56, 57, 64, 71, 72, 76, 79, 81, 90

How do you find the mean?

T o find the mean value of a set of numbers three steps are involved:

1. Find the sum of all the numbers in the set.
2. Divide by the number of numbers in the set.
3. Round the answer appropriately, if necessary (see Chapter 13).

For example, to find the mean score of group A above in mathematics:

1. The sum of the scores is 751.
2. Divide 751 by 14, using a calculator to get 53.642857.
3. Rounding this to, say, one decimal place, the mean score is about 53.6.

The logic behind using this as a representative figure is that the total marks obtained by the group would have been the same if all the children had scored the mean score (allowing for the possibility of a small error introduced by rounding). I imagine the process to be one of pooling. All the children put all their marks into a pool, which is then shared out equally between all 14 of them. This is an application of the concept involved in division structures associated with the word 'per' (see Chapter 10): we are finding the 'marks per student', assuming an equal sharing of all the marks awarded between them. An example that illustrates this well would be to find the mean amount of money that a group of people have in their possession. This could be done by putting all their money on the table and then sharing it out again equally between the members of the group. This is precisely the process that is modelled by the mathematical procedure for finding the mean.

We can now use this procedure to make comparisons. For example, to compare group A with group B in mathematics, we could compare their mean scores. Group B's mean score is about 56.8 (625 ÷ 11). This would lend some support to an assertion that, on the whole, group B (mean score 56.8) has done better in the test than group A (mean score 53.6).

We can also use average scores to help make sense of individual scores. For example, let us say that Luke, a child in group B, scored 60 in mathematics and 64 in English. Reacting naively to the raw scores, we might conclude that he did better in English than in mathematics. But comparing the marks with the mean scores for his group leads to a different interpretation: Luke's mark for mathematics (60) is above the mean (56.8), whilst the higher mark he obtained for English (64) is actually below the mean for his group (which works out to be 67.5). This would lend some support to the view that Luke has actually done better in mathematics than in English.

What is the median?

The *median* is simply the number that comes in the middle of the set when the numbers are arranged in numerical order. Finding this average figure is much easier therefore than calculating the mean, especially when you are dealing with a very large population with a large number of possible values for the variable being considered. It is very common, for example, for government education statistics to use medians as representative, average figures. The only small complication arises when there is an even number of elements in the set, because then there is not a middle one. So the process of finding the median is as follows:

1. Arrange all the numbers in the set in order from smallest to largest.

2. If the number of numbers in the set is odd, the median is the number in the middle.

3. If the number of numbers in the set is even, the median is the mean of the two numbers in the middle, in other words, halfway between them.

If you are not sure how to decide where the middle of a list is situated, here's a simple rule for finding it: if there are n items in the list, the position of the middle one (the median) is 'half of $(n + 1)$'. For example, with 11 items in the list the position of the median is half of 12, which is the sixth item. With 83 items in the list, the position of the median would be half of 84, which is the forty-second item. If n is even, this formula still tells you where to find the median. For example, with 50 items, the formula gives the position of the median as half of 51, which is $25\frac{1}{2}$: we interpret this to mean 'halfway between the twenty-fifth and twenty-sixth items'.

So, for example, for group B mathematics, with a set of 11 children, the median is the sixth mark when the marks are arranged in order; hence the median is 47. For group A mathematics, with a set of 14, the median comes halfway between the seventh and eighth marks, which is halfway between 53 and 60; hence the median is 56.5.

Interestingly, if we use the median rather than the mean as our measure of average we would draw a different conclusion altogether when comparing the two groups: that on the whole group A (median mark of 56.5) has done rather better than group B (median mark of 47)!

Although the median is often used for large sets of statistics, it sometimes has advantages over the mean when working with a small set of numbers, as in these examples. The reason for this is that the median is not affected by one or two extreme values, such as the 95 in group B. For a small set of data, a score much larger than the rest, like this one, can increase the value of the mean quite significantly and produce an average figure that does not represent the group in the most appropriate way. To take an extreme case, imagine that in a test 9 children in a group of 10 score 1 and the other child scores 100: this data produces a mean score of 10.9 and a median of 1! There is surely no argument here with the view that the median 'represents' the performance of the group as a whole more appropriately. All this simply serves to illustrate the fact that most sets of statistics are open to different interpretations – which is why I have used the phrase 'lends some support to … ' when drawing conclusions from the data in these examples.

Returning to Luke, who scored 60 for mathematics and 64 for English, we can compare his performance with the median scores for his group, which were 47 and 71 respectively. These statistics again lend support to the assertion that he has done better in mathematics (well above the median) than in English (well below the median).

What is the mode and when would you use it?

The mode is simply the value of the variable that occurs most frequently. For example, for group A mathematics, the mode (or the modal mark) is 61, because this occurs three times, which is more than any other number in the set. For group B mathematics, the mode is 43. This is actually a daft way of determining representative marks for these sets of data. The mode is really only of any use as a measure of average when you are dealing with a large set of data and when the number of different values in the set of data is quite small. A good example of the use of a mode would be when discussing an 'average' family. In the UK, the modal number of children in a family is two, because more families have two children than any other number. So if I were to write a play featuring an 'average' family, there would be two children in it. Clearly the mode is more use here than the mean, since 2.4 children would be difficult to cast.

Like the mean and the median, the mode enables us to make useful comparisons between different sets, when it is an appropriate and meaningful measure of average; for example, when comparing social factors in, say, parts of China, some countries in Africa and European states, the modal numbers of children per family would be very significant statistics to consider.

The mode can also be used with non-numerical variables and with grouped numerical data. For example, if we collected data about the colour of hair for the children in a class we might conclude that the modal colour is brown. If we collected the heights of children in a class, measured to the nearest centimetre, and then grouped these into intervals of 5 cm, we might conclude that the modal interval of heights is, say, 145–149 cm; meaning more children were in this interval of heights than any other.

LEARNING and TEACHING POINT

Some textbooks and some mathematics tests ask children to find the mode of a small set of items. This is bad mathematics. Explain to the children that the mode is an average to be used with fairly large samples.

How do you calculate the mode, median and mean from a frequency table?

For the median and the mean we can only do this with a numerical variable and where the data has not been grouped into intervals. So, these are procedures likely to be used for a numerical variable that takes a fairly small number of values. For example, a primary school recorded the following information regarding absences one term:

No of days absent	No of children
0	36
1	29
2	12
3	10
4	6
5	2
Total number of children	95

Of the three different averages that we could use, the mode is the easiest to read off from a frequency table like this. It is simply the value with the largest frequency, in this case the mode is 0 days. More children were absent for 0 days than for any other number of days.

It would also be quite appropriate to use the median number of days as our representative figure for this data. To find this we need the number of days absent for the child who would come in the middle if we lined them all up in order of the number of days they were absent (assuming that none of them were absent when we did this!) From the left we would have first the 36 children who were absent for 0 days, then the 29 who were absent for 1 day, and so on. With a total of 95 children the child in the middle would be the 48th child in the line. This would be one of the children in the group who were absent for 1 day. So the median number of days absent is 1 day.

The mean would also be an appropriate representative figure for this set of data. To calculate this needs a bit more work. We must first add up all the numbers of days absent for all 95 children. That is 36 lots of 0 days, plus 29 lots of 1 day, plus 12 lots of 2 days, and so on. The most convenient way of doing this is to add another column to the frequency table, showing the product of the number of days and the number of children:

No of days absent	No of children	days × children
0	36	0
1	29	29
2	12	24
3	10	30
4	6	24
5	2	10
Total	95	117

Summing the numbers in the third column gives us a total of 117 days absent, which is shared between 95 children. So, the mean number of days absent is $117 \div 95 = 1.23$ days approximately.

What is a five-number summary?

To describe a set of numerical data and to get a feel for how the numbers in the set are distributed, a **five-number summary** is often used. First, we list all the numbers in the set in order from smallest to largest. This enables us to find five significant numbers that help us to describe the distribution and to compare it with another set of data. Two of these significant numbers are simply the minimum and maximum values, the first and last numbers in the list. The third one is the median, which has been explained above.

The other two are the **lower quartile** (LQ) and the **upper quartile** (UQ). The lower quartile, the median and the upper quartile are three numbers that divide the list into four quarters. Just as the median is the midpoint of the set, the lower and upper quartiles are one quarter and three quarters of the way along the list respectively.

Here are the mathematics scores again for groups A and B considered above:

Group A: Mathematics	23, 25, 46, 48, 48, 49, 53, 60, 61, 61, 61, 62, 69, 85
Group B: Mathematics	36, 38, 43, 43, 45, 47, 60, 63, 69, 86, 95

For group B the median is the sixth score (47), the lower quartile is the third score (43) and the upper quartile is the ninth score (69). Group B is a convenient size for discussing quartiles because it is fairly easy to decide where the quarter points of the list are situated. Group A is not so straightforward. There is a similar rule to that for the median for deciding where the lower and upper quartiles come. For completeness I will explain it, but you really do not have to be able to do this! The position of the lower quartile is one quarter of $(n + 1)$ and that of the upper quartile is three quarters of $(n + 1)$. So, for group B, with 11 items, the positions of the LQ and UQ are one quarter and three quarters of 12, namely positions 3 and 9 in the list. However, for group A, with 14 scores in the list, the position of the lower quartile would be one quarter of 15, which is $3^3/_4$. This means that it comes three quarters of the way between the third and fourth scores, (46 and 48) which is 47.5. The position of the upper quartile is three quarters of 15, which is $11^1/_4$. This means that it comes one quarter of the way between the eleventh and twelfth scores (61 and 62), which is 61.25.

I should say that this kind of fiddling around deciding precisely where the **quartiles** are located between particular items in a list is definitely not necessary in practice when you are dealing with large sets of data. Anyway, the reader's requirements will be only to understand the idea of a quartile when it is met in government statistics, not to be able to calculate quartiles for awkward sets of data.

The five-number summaries for groups A and B for their scores for mathematics are therefore as follows:

	Group A	Group B
Min	23	36
LQ	47.5	43
Median	56.5	47

UQ	61.25	69
Max	85	95

This is a fairly standard way of presenting data from two populations for comparison. Teachers may well encounter government data about educational performance presented in this form. For example, the performance of primary schools in mathematics in two local authorities (LAs), X and Y, might be compared by the following five-number summaries based on data from the mathematics national assessments for 11-year-olds:

	X	Y
Min	26	23
LQ	47	48
Median	65	73
UQ	84	93
Max	96	100

The variable used here is the percentage of children in each school in the LA gaining level 4 in the mathematics assessment. For example, the upper quartile of 84 for LA X means this: if the schools in LA X are listed in order from the school with the lowest percentage of children achieving level 4 to the school with the highest percentage, then the school that is three quarters of the way along the list had 84% of children achieving level 4. Glancing at these summaries we can see that there is very little difference between the results of the bottom quarter (from the minimum to the lower quartile) of the schools in the two LAs. But the other results for LA Y are markedly better than LA X, with a higher median and a higher upper quartile. The comparison shows that the 'average' and higher-performing schools in LA Y are doing better than those in LA X.

What is the range?

We return to the test scores for group A for mathematics and English given earlier in this chapter:

Group A: Mathematics   23, 25, 46, 48, 48, 49, 53, 60, 61, 61, 61, 62, 69, 85
Group A: English   45, 48, 49, 52, 53, 53, 53, 53, 54, 56, 57, 58, 59, 62

We will compare group A's marks for mathematics with their marks for English. By looking just at the means (53.6 for mathematics and 53.7 for English) we might conclude that the sets of marks for the two subjects were very similar. Looking at the actual data it is clear that they are not. The most striking feature is that the mathematics marks are more widely spread and the English marks are relatively closely clustered together.

Statisticians have various ways of measuring the degree of 'spread' (sometimes called 'dispersion') in a set of data. The reader may have heard, for example, of the 'standard deviation'. These measures of spread have a similar purpose to the measures of average: they enable us to compare sets of data and to make sense of individual items of data.

For primary school work we would only introduce the simplest measure of spread, the **range**. This is as simple as it sounds: the range is just the difference between the largest and the smallest values in the set. So, for example, when comparing Group A's mathematics and English scores we would note that, although they have about the same mean scores, the range for mathematics is 62 marks (85 − 23), whereas the range for English is only 17 marks (62 − 45). Clearly the mathematics marks are more spread out.

What is the inter-quartile range and why is it used?

One or two exceptionally high or low scores in a set will result in the range not being a good indication of how spread out is *most* of the data in the set – it might therefore give a false impression when comparing two sets of data. So it is better to use what is called the **inter-quartile range**. This is simply the difference between the quartiles. Since this measure excludes the top quarter and the bottom quarter of the data, the set is not affected by what happens at the extremes and a better indication is given of the spread of most of the data.

In the data given above for comparing LA X and LA Y, the inter-quartile range for the data for LA X is 37 (that is, 84 − 47), whereas the inter-quartile range for LA Y is 45 (that is, 93 − 48). This indicates that there is a greater spread of percentages of children achieving level 4 in mathematics in the schools in LA Y than in LA X.

What is a box-and-whisker diagram?

A **box-and-whisker diagram** (also called a box plot or a box-and-whisker plot) is a simple way of putting the numerical information given in a five-number summary into a pictorial form. The basic ingredients of a box-and-whisker diagram for a set of data are shown in Figure 28.2.

The 'box' part contains the middle 50% of the population, and therefore stretches from the lower quartile to the upper quartile. A line is usually drawn within the box to show the position of the median. The two 'whiskers' emerging

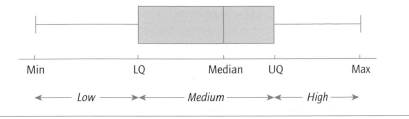

Figure 28.2   *A box-and-whisker diagram*

from the ends of the box show the range of scores achieved by the bottom and top quarters, so they stretch from the lower quartile to the minimum, and from the upper quartile to the maximum. In this way, the diagram shows very clearly the range of values of three important subsets within the data set. We can think of these loosely as 'low' (the left-hand whisker), 'medium' (the box) and 'high' (the right-hand whisker). For example, if we collected data about the heights of male schoolteachers, those represented by the left-hand whisker would be 'short teachers', those in the box would be 'teachers of medium height' and those in the right-hand whisker would be 'tall teachers'. Note that the distance between the two ends of the whiskers represents the range of values in the set, and the length of the box represents the inter-quartile range.

Figure 28.3 shows box-and-whisker plots for the data for LEAs X and Y given earlier in this chapter. The diagrams enable the reader at a glance to compare the performances of the two LEAs. The comparisons made verbally above can now be seen visually. The left-hand whiskers represent the schools with relatively low percentages of children achieving level 4 in mathematics; the right-hand whiskers represent the schools with relatively high percentages of children achieving level 4 in mathematics; and the boxes represent the schools in the middle 50%.

Note that in Figures 28.2, 28.3 and 28.5 (see self-assessment question 28.6) the box plots have been drawn horizontally. They could just as well have been drawn vertically.

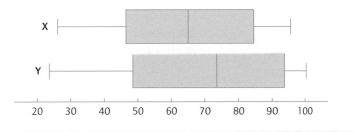

Figure 28.3   *Comparing two data sets with box-and-whisker diagrams*

What are percentiles and deciles?

The process of identifying quartiles and the median involves listing all the data in the set in numerical order and then dividing the set into four parts (quarters), with equal numbers of items in each part. With larger populations it is common practice often to divide the list into a hundred equal parts. The values used to separate these hundred parts are called **percentiles**. Note that the word 'percentile' is sometimes abbreviated to '%ile'.

If you read that the 90th percentile score in a test administered to a large number of children is 58, this means that the bottom 90% of children scored 58 or less and the top 10% of children scored 58 or more. Similarly, if you read that the 20th percentile score was 26, this means that the bottom 20% of the children scored 26 or less and that the top 80% of children scored 26 or more. It follows therefore that the lower quartile can also be referred to as the 25th percentile, the median as the 50th percentile and the upper quartile as the 75th percentile.

Often, children's performances in standardized tests will be given in terms of percentiles. For example, a report on an able 9-year-old stated that 'Tom's standardized score for reading accuracy is 125, which is at the 95th percentile.' This puts Tom in the top 5% for reading accuracy for his age range. The raw percentage scores in a numeracy test administered to a sample of 450 trainee-teachers are presented in terms of percentiles as follows:

10th %ile	58%
20th %ile	60%
30th %ile	63%
40th %ile	65%
50th %ile	70%
60th %ile	78%
70th %ile	84%
80th %ile	88%
90th %ile	92%

This example is included deliberately because it can be confusing when the numbers in the set of data are themselves percentages, as in this case. Readers should not get confused between the *percentiles*, which refer to percentages of the number of items in the set, and the *percentage scores*, which are the actual items of data in the set. The following are examples of observations that could be made from this data:

- A trainee scoring 94% on the numeracy test is in the top 10% in this sample.
- A trainee scoring 64% on the test is well below average, with more than 60% of others doing better than this.
- The median score on the test was 70%.
- The top half of the sample scored 70% or more on the test.
- The bottom 30% of the sample scored 63% or less on the test.
- The top 20% of trainees scored 88% or more on the test.
- The lower quartile was somewhere between 60% and 63%.

Sometimes reports will divide the set into ten equal parts, using what are called the **deciles**. The 90th percentile, for example, can also be called the 9th decile, and so on.

How does the idea of 'average speed' fit in with the concept of an average?

In the UK, children's first experience of speed is usually the speed of a vehicle, measured in 'miles per hour'. Note that average speed gives us another example of that important little word, 'per'.

The idea of **average speed** derives from the concept of a mean. Over the course of a journey in my car, my speed will be constantly changing; sometimes it will even be zero. When we talk about the average speed for a journey, it is as though we add up all the miles covered during various stages of the journey and then share them out equally 'per hour'. This uses the same idea of 'pooling' which was the basis for calculating the mean of a set of numbers. So if my journey covers 400 miles in total and takes 8 hours, the average speed is 50 miles per hour (400 ÷ 8).

The logic here is that if I had been able to travel at a constant speed of 50 miles in each hour, then the journey would have taken the same time (8 hours). So the average speed (in miles per hour) is the total distance travelled (in miles) divided by the total time taken (in hours). We can then extend this definition of average speed to apply to journeys where the time is not a whole number of hours; for example, for a journey of 22 miles in 24 minutes (0.4 hours) the average speed is 22 ÷ 0.4, which is 55 miles per hour. And, of course, the same principle applies whatever units are used for distance and time; for example, if the toy car takes 5 seconds to run down a ramp of 150 centimetres, the average speed is 30 centimetres per second (150 ÷ 5).

Research focus

What do you need to know to be a good mathematics teacher? Ball, Thames and Phelps (2008) have developed a useful model for analysing teacher content knowledge in mathematics. They distinguish between *common subject knowledge*, which includes recognizing wrong answers and being able to do the mathematical tasks that the children are given, and the *special subject knowledge* that is required to be an effective teacher. This includes being able to analyse errors, evaluate alternative ideas, give mathematical explanations and choose appropriate mathematical representations. Alongside this teachers need pedagogical subject knowledge. This has two strands. *Knowledge of content and learners* includes the ability to anticipate errors and misconceptions, to interpret learners' incomplete thinking and to predict their responses to mathematical tasks. *Knowledge of content and teaching* includes the ability to sequence content for teaching, to recognize the pros and cons of different representations and to handle novel approaches. Burgess (2009) showed how this model could be used to evaluate the teaching of statistics, through observing four teachers working with children aged 9–13 years on data-handling tasks involving more than one variable. The study revealed, for example, numerous instances where – because of inadequate special subject knowledge of statistics or pedagogical subject knowledge related to the learning and teaching of statistics – teachers missed opportunities to respond to and exploit the children's suggestions for processing the given data. Burgess concluded that these missed opportunities impacted negatively on the children's learning and understanding of statistical concepts and processes.

Suggestions for further reading

1 Section 4 (Statistics) of Cooke (2007) will provide useful reinforcement of the mathematical ideas that have been outlined in Chapters 27 and 28 on data handling and comparing sets of data.
2 Hansen (ed.) (2005) is an interesting book dealing with children's errors and misconceptions. In chapter 6 Surtees discusses the errors and misconceptions that arise in the context of handling data.
3 For further material to reinforce the ideas of this chapter and the preceding chapter see Hopkins, Pope and Pepperell (2004), section 3.2 'Processing, representing and making sense of data'. This includes some further examples of box-and-whisker plots, for those who enjoy that kind of thing.

Self-assessment questions

28.1: In a survey, a sample of teenagers was asked to name up to three daily newspapers. Figure 28.4 compares the proportions of boys and girls who could correctly name

0, 1, 2 or 3 daily newspapers. From the diagram, what comparisons might be drawn between the boys and girls?

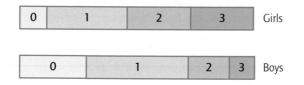

Figure 28.4 *How many daily newspapers can teenagers name?*

28.2: For this question you will need to refer again to this data:

Group A: Mathematics   23, 25, 46, 48, 48, 49, 53, 60, 61, 61, 61, 62, 69, 85
Group B: Mathematics   36, 38, 43, 43, 45, 47, 60, 63, 69, 86, 95

Group A: English   45, 48, 49, 52, 53, 53, 53, 53, 54, 56, 57, 58, 59, 62
Group B: English   45, 52, 56, 57, 64, 71, 72, 76, 79, 81, 90

(a) Compare the mean and median scores for English for groups A and B. Which group on the whole did better?
(b) Find the mean score for English for the two groups combined. Is the mean score of the two groups combined equal to the mean of the two separate mean scores?
(c) Find the median scores and the ranges for English and mathematics for the two groups combined.
(d) John, in group A, scored 49 for mathematics. How does this score compare with the performance of group A as a whole?

28.3: The table below shows the frequency of various numbers of letters in the last one hundred words in this chapter (ignoring numerals):

No of letters	1	2	3	4	5	6	7	8	9	10	11	12
Frequency	4	21	19	14	17	7	6	9	1	1	0	1

(a) What is the modal number of letters per word in this sample?
(b) Calculate the median and range for this sample.
(c) What is the mean number of letters per words in this sample?

28.4: Toy car P travels 410 centimetres in 6 seconds; toy car Q travels 325 centimetres in 5 seconds. Which has the greater average speed?

28.5: The following table shows percentages of children reaching level 2 or above in a national assessment for reading, in schools with more than 20% and up to 35% of children eligible for free school meals:

95th %ile	UQ	60th %ile	median	40th %ile	LQ	5th %ile
94	83	78	76	72	67	52

St Anne's primary school has 24% of children eligible for free school meals, so it comes into this group. In the reading assessment, 69% of their children achieved level 2 or above. How well did they do compared with schools in this group?

28.6: Primary schools with 8% or less children eligible for free school meals (group A) are compared with primary schools with more than 50% eligible for free school meals (group E) in relation to the performances of children in the national reading assessment. Figure 28.5 is a box-and-whisker diagram showing the comparison.

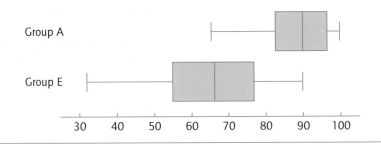

Figure 28.5   *Percentages of pupils achieving level 2 or above in reading*

(a) Just by glancing at the diagram, what is your impression of the comparative performances of the two groups of schools in the reading assessment?

(b) What is the median percentage of children for schools in group A achieving level 2 or above for reading?

(c) What is the highest percentage of children achieving level 2 or above for schools in group E?

(d) What is the median percentage of children for schools in group E achieving level 2 or above for reading?

(e) What is the lowest percentage of children achieving level 2 or above for schools in group A?

(f) Based on this evidence, which of group A or group E has the greater range of achievement in reading?

(g) Compare the inter-quartile ranges for the two groups.

Further practice

From the Student Workbook

Tasks 209–212: Checking understanding of comparing sets of data
Tasks 213–215: Using and applying comparing sets of data
Tasks 216–218: Learning and teaching of comparing sets of data

On the website (www.sagepub.co.uk/haylock)
    Check-Up 36: Calculating means
    Check-Up 37: Modes
    Check-Up 38: Medians
    Check-Up 39: Upper and lower quartiles
    Check-Up 40: Measures of spread, range and inter-quartile range
    Check-Up 41: Box-and-whisker diagrams

Glossary of key terms introduced in Chapter 28

Average: a representative value for a set of numerical data, enabling comparisons to be made between sets; three types of average are the mean, the median and the mode.

Mean (arithmetic mean):   for a set of numerical data the result of adding up all the numbers in the set and dividing by the number in the set.

Median: the value of the one in the middle when all the items in a set of numerical data are arranged in order of size. If the set has an even number of items, the median comes halfway between the two in the middle. In a set of n items arranged in order, the position of the median is $\frac{1}{2}$ of (n + 1).

Mode: the value in a set of numerical data that occurs most often; a type of average only appropriate for large sets with a relatively small number of possible values.

Five-number summary: a way of summarizing a set of numerical data by giving the minimum, the lower quartile, the median, the upper quartile and the maximum.

Lower quartile (LQ):   if the items in a set of numerical data are arranged in order of size from smallest to largest, the position of the lower quartile is $\frac{1}{4}$ of (n + 1).

Upper quartile (UQ):   if the items in a set of numerical data are arranged in order of size from smallest to largest, the position of the upper quartile is $\frac{3}{4}$ of (n + 1).

Quartiles: the three items in a set of numerical data arranged in order of size, from smallest to largest, that come one quarter of the way along (the lower quartile), in the middle (the median), and three quarters of the way along (the upper quartile).

Range: in a set of numerical data, the difference between the largest and smallest value; a simple measure of spread that can be used to compare two sets of data.

Inter-quartile range: the difference between the upper and lower quartiles; a measure of spread, not affected by what happens at the extremes.

Box-and-whisker diagram: a pictorial representation of the five-number summary for a set of data; the inter-quartile range is represented by the width of a box, with two whiskers extending to the minimum and maximum values (see Figures 28.2 and 28.3).

Percentile: the values that separate into 100 parts a large set of data arranged in order of size. To say that a child's score in a standardized test is at the 95th percentile, for example, means that the top 5% of children obtained this score or better.

Decile: the values that separate into ten parts a large set of data arranged in order of size. To say that a child's score in a standardized test is at the 7th decile, for example, means that the top three tenths of children obtained this score or better.

Average speed: the total distance travelled on a journey divided by the time taken; if the distance is measured in miles and the time in hours, the average speed is given in miles per hour.

29
Probability

What is probability?

First, we should recognize that in mathematics **probability** is a measurement, just like any other measurement such as length or mass. Second, it is a measurement that is applied to *events*. But what it is about an event that is being measured is surprisingly elusive. My view is that what we are measuring is how strongly we believe that the event will happen. We describe this level of belief with words ranging from 'impossible' to 'certain' and compare our assessment of different events by talking about one being 'more likely' or 'less likely' than another. This strength of belief is determined by different kinds of *evidence* that we may assemble.

Sometimes this evidence is simply the accumulation of our experience, in which case our judgement about how likely one event may be compared with others is fairly subjective. For example, one group of students wrote down some events that might occur during the following 12 months and ranked them in order from the least likely to the most likely as follows:

1. It will snow in Norwich during July.
2. Norwich City will win the FA Cup.
3. Steve will get a teaching post.
4. There will be a general election in the UK.
5. Someone will reach the summit of Mount Everest.

When they were then told that Steve had an interview at a school the following week for a post for which he was ideally suited, this extra piece of evidence had an immediate effect on their strength of belief in event (3) and they changed its position in the ranking.

By using 'more likely than' and 'less likely than', this activity is based on the ideas of comparison and ordering, always the first stages of the development of any aspect of measurement. The next stage would be to introduce some kind of measuring scale. A **probability scale** can initially use everyday language, such as:

impossible;
almost impossible;
fairly unlikely;
evens;
fairly likely;
almost certain;
certain.

For example, we might judge that event (1) is 'almost impossible', event (2) is 'fairly unlikely' and event (5) is 'almost certain'. When we feel that an event is as likely to happen as not to happen, we say that 'the chances are **evens**'.

To introduce a numerical scale, we can think of awarding marks out of 100 for each event, with 0 marks for an event we believe to be impossible, 100 marks for an event we judge to be certain, and 50 marks for 'evens'. For example, purely subjectively, the students in the group awarded 1 mark for event (1), 5 marks for event (2), 50 marks for event (4) and 99 marks for event (5). Event (3) started out at 40, but moved to 75 when the new evidence was obtained.

If these marks out of 100 are now thought of as percentages and converted to decimals (see Chapter 19 for how to do this), we have the standard scale used for measuring probability, ranging from 0 (impossible), through 0.5 (evens), to 1 (certain). For example, the **subjective probabilities** that we assigned to events (2) and (5) were 0.05 and 0.99 respectively.

How can you measure probability more objectively?

There are essentially three ways of collecting evidence that can be used for a more objective estimate of probability:

1. We can collect statistical data and use the idea of relative frequency.
2. We can perform an experiment a large number of times and use the relative frequency of different outcomes.
3. We can use theoretical arguments based on symmetry and equally likely outcomes.

How does relative frequency relate to probability?

The first of these three approaches, based on **relative frequency**, is used extensively in the world of business, such as insurance or marketing, where probabilities are often assessed by gathering statistical data.

For example, to determine an appropriate premium for a life insurance policy for a person such as myself, an insurance company would use the probabilities that I might live to 70, to 80, to 90, and so on. To determine these probabilities they could collect statistical data about academics of my age living in East Anglia and find what proportion of these survive to various ages. If it is found that out of 250 cases, 216 live to 70, then this evidence would suggest that a reasonable estimate for the probability of my living to this age is 86.4% (216 ÷ 250) or, as a decimal, 0.864.

Since it is normally impractical to obtain data from the entire population, this application of probability is usually based on evidence collected from a sample (see Chapter 27). For example, what is the probability that a word chosen at random from a page of text in this book will have four letters in it? To answer this we could use the last hundred words of Chapter 28 as a sample (see self-assessment question 28.3). Since 14 of these words have four letters, the relative frequency of four-letter words in the sample is 14%.

So an estimate for the probability, based on this evidence, would be 0.14. If we wanted to be more confident of this estimate then we would choose a larger sample than 100 words and make it more representative of the whole book by selecting the words from a number of different chapters.

How is probability measured by experiment?

LEARNING and TEACHING POINT

The material discussed here on experimental and theoretical probability would be excellent as extension material for children at the top end of a primary school.

The second procedure for obtaining objective estimates for probabilities applies the same idea, but to an experiment, often the kind of thing that can be experienced in a classroom. Now the 'event' in question is an *outcome* of the experiment.

For example, the experiment might be to throw three identical dice simultaneously. The outcome we are interested in is that the score on one of them should be greater than the sum of the scores on the other two. What is the probability of this outcome? A useful experience for children is to make a subjective estimate of the probability, based purely on intuition, and then to perform the experiment a large number of times, recording the numbers of successes and failures. For example, they might make a subjective estimate that the chances of this happening would be a bit less than evens, so the probability is, say, about 0.40. Then the dice are thrown, say, 200 times and it is found that the number of successes is 58. Hence the relative frequency of successes is 29% (58 ÷ 200) and so the best estimate for the probability, based on this evidence, would be 0.29. This is called **experimental probability.**

How is probability determined theoretically?

For some experiments we can consider all the possible outcomes and make estimates of **theoretical probability** using an argument based on *symmetry*. Experiments with coins and dice lend themselves to this kind of argument.

LEARNING and TEACHING POINT

'One die; two or more dice.' You might as well get it right!

The simplest argument would be about tossing one coin. There are only two possible outcomes, heads and tails. Given the symmetry of the coin, there is no reason to assume that one outcome is more or less likely than the other. So we would conclude that the probability of a head is 0.5 and the probability of a tail is 0.5. Notice that the sum of the probabilities of all the possible outcomes must be 1. This represents 'certainty': we are certain that the coin will come down either heads or tails.

Similarly, if we throw a conventional, six-faced die, there are six possible outcomes, all of which, on the basis of symmetry, are equally likely. We therefore determine the probability of each number turning up to be one-sixth, or about 0.17 (1 ÷ 6 = 0.1666666 on a calculator). We can also determine the probability of events that are made up of various outcomes. For example, there are two scores on the die that are multiples of three, so the probability of throwing a multiple of three would be two-sixths, or about 0.33 ($^2/_6 = {}^1/_3 = 0.3333333$ on a calculator).

So the procedure for determining the probability of a particular event by this theoretical approach is:

1. List all the possible equally likely outcomes from the experiment, being guided by symmetry, but thinking carefully to ensure that the outcomes listed really are equally likely.
2. Count in how many of these outcomes the event in question occurs.
3. Divide the second number by the first.

For example, to find the probability that a card drawn from a conventional pack of playing cards will be less than 7:

1. There are 52 equally likely outcomes from the experiment, that is, 52 possible cards that can be drawn.
2. The event in question (the card is less than 7) occurs in 24 of these.
3. So the probability is 24 ÷ 52, or about 0.46.

What about the 'law of averages'?

There is no such law in mathematics! A popular misconception about probability is that the more times an event does not occur then the greater the probability of it occurring next time. If the events are independent (see below) then this is not how probability works! The outcome of throwing a die has no effect on the outcome of throwing it again.

It is important to remember what I said at the beginning of this chapter about the meaning of probability. It is a measure of how strongly you believe an event will happen. So when I say the probability of a coin turning up heads is 0.5, I am making a statement about how strongly I believe that it will come up heads, based on the symmetry of the coin. To a logical person this kind of theoretical probability, provided the argument based on symmetry is valid, does not change from one outcome to the next. So the result of one trial does not affect the probabilities of what will happen in the next. If I have just thrown a head, the probability of the next toss being a head is still 0.5. If I have just thrown 20 tails in succession (which is unlikely but not impossible), the probability of the next one being a head is still only 0.5. (Of course, there might be something peculiar about the coin, but I am assuming that it is not bent or weighted in any way that might distort the results.)

What the probability does tell me, however, is that *in the long run*, if you go on tossing the coin long enough, you will see the relative frequency of heads (and tails) gradually getting closer and closer to 50%. This does not mean that with a thousand tosses I would *expect* 500 of each; in fact, that would be very surprising! But I would expect the proportion of heads to be about 50% and getting closer to 50% the more experiments I perform. It is therefore important for children studying probability actually to do such experiments a large number of times, obtain the relative frequencies of various outcomes for which they have determined the theoretical probability and observe and discuss the fact that the two are not usually exactly the same.

LEARNING and TEACHING POINT

Emphasize the idea that probability does not tell you anything about what will happen next, but predicts what will happen in the long run.

There is a wonderfully mystical idea here: that in an experiment with a number of equally likely possible outcomes we cannot know what will be the outcome of any given experiment, but we can predict with confidence what will happen in the long run!

How do you deal theoretically with tossing two coins or throwing two dice?

We do have to be careful when arguing theoretically about possible outcomes to ensure that they are really all equally likely. For example, one group of children decided there were three possible outcomes when you toss two coins – two heads, two tails, one of each – and determined the probabilities to be $\frac{1}{3}$ for each. Then performing the experiment 1000 times between them (40 times each for 25 children) they found that two heads turned up 256 times, two tails turned up 234 times and one of each turned up 510 times. So the relative frequencies were 25.6%, 23.4% and 51%, obviously not getting close to the 'theoretical' 33.3%. The problem is that these three outcomes are *not equally likely.* Calling the two coins A and B, we can identify *four* possible outcomes: A and B both heads, A head and B tail, A tail and B head, A and B both tails. So the theoretical probabilities of two heads, two tails and one of each are 0.25, 0.25 and 0.50 respectively.

In this example, the outcome of tossing coin A and the outcome of tossing coin B are technically called **independent events**. This means simply that what happens to coin B is not affected in any way by what happens to coin A, and vice versa. With experiments involving two independent events, such as two coins being tossed or two dice being thrown, a useful device for listing all the possible outcomes is a **two-way table**. Figure 29.1(a) is such a table, showing the four possible outcomes from tossing two coins.

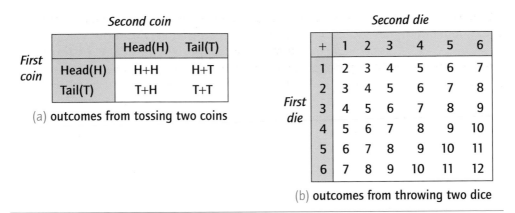

Figure 29.1 *Two-way tables for an experiment with two independent events*

Figure 29.1 (b) similarly gives all 36 possible outcomes, shown as total scores in the table, when two dice are thrown. From this table we can discover, for example, that the probability of scoring seven (seven occurs 6 times out of 36: $^{6}/_{36}$ = 0.17 approximately) is much higher than, say, scoring eleven (11 occurs 2 times out of 36: $^{2}/_{36}$ = 0.06 approximately).

An important principle in probability theory is that the probability of both of two independent events occurring is obtained by multiplying the probabilities of each one occurring. For example, if I toss a coin the probability of obtaining a head is 0.5. If I throw a die the probability of scoring an even number is 0.5. So, if I toss the coin and throw the die simultaneously, the probability of getting a head *and* an even number is 0.5 × 0.5 = 0.25. This principle can be expressed as a generalization as follows:

> If the probabilities of two independent events A and B are p and q then the probability of both A and B occurring is $p \times q$.

What are mutually exclusive events?

Events that cannot possibly occur at the same time are said to be **mutually exclusive**. For example, if I throw two dice, getting a total score of 7 and getting a total score of 11 are two mutually exclusive outcomes – since you cannot score both 7 and 11 simultaneously. However, getting a total score of 7 and getting a total score that is odd are not mutually exclusive events, since clearly you can do both at the same time. The reader should note that mutually exclusive events are definitely not independent, because if one occurs then the other one cannot.

A second important principle of probability theory is that the probability that one or other of two mutually exclusive events occurring is the sum of their probabilities. So, for example, the probability of scoring 7 or 11 when I throw two dice is the sum of $^6/_{36}$ (the probability of scoring 7) and $^2/_{36}$ (the probability of scoring 11), that is, $^8/_{36}$, or 0.22, approximately. This principle can be expressed as a generalization as follows:

LEARNING and TEACHING POINT

One obvious application of probability is to betting and lotteries. Be aware that some parents will hold strong moral views about gambling, so handle discussion of probability in a way that is sensitive to different perspectives on this subject.

If the probabilities of two mutually exclusive events A and B are p and q then the probability of either A or B occurring is $p + q$.

If you list a set of mutually exclusive events that might occur in a particular experiment that cover all possible outcomes, then the sum of all their probabilities must equal 1. For example, in throwing two coins we could identify these three mutually exclusive events: two heads (probability 0.25), two tails (probability 0.25), one head and one tail (probability 0.5). The sum of these probabilities is $0.25 + 0.25 + 0.5 = 1$.

How do you assess risk?

Taking a risk is when you invest some money or time or other resources into some action or option in the hope that the outcome will produce some reward. A simple mathematical model for assessing risk is as follows. For any individual event, the '**expected value**' in taking a risk is obtained by multiplying the probability of the desired outcome occurring by the value of the reward associated with it. For example, imagine you bought a lottery ticket for £1 in the hope of winning a prize of £100, and there were 1000 lottery tickets sold. The probability of having the winning ticket is 0.001, so the expected value of the ticket you purchased is £100 × 0.001 = £0.10. Given that you spent £1 on the ticket this represents an expected loss of 90p. What this means is that on average, over time, if you continue repeating this action you will lose 90p in every £1 invested.

LEARNING and TEACHING POINT

Children in primary school can discuss the risk associated with various actions and can begin to understand how an assessment of the probability of a particular outcome and the value of the reward associated with it might modify their behaviour and choices.

Schlottman (2001) investigated younger children's intuitive understanding of risk and whether they could simultaneously take into account both the likelihood of an outcome and the reward associated with it. Some 6-year-olds were asked to judge how happy a puppet would be to play a game in which the puppet would win a large or a small prize (numbers of crayons) depending on where a marble finished up in a tube. She discovered that these young children seemed intuitively to have a sense of the probability of winning the prizes and how the probability of winning and the value of the prize were integrated multiplicatively into a sense of how good a game it was for the puppet to play. The evidence here is that young children demonstrate a functional understanding of probability and expected value.

Suggestions for further reading

1. For more on the ideas of theoretical probability, experimental probability, mutually exclusive events, independent and dependent events see Hopkins, Pope and Pepperell (2004), section 3.3 'Probability'.
2. For an insightful chapter on probability, read chapter 7 of Cooke (2007).
3. If you really want to get to grips with probability theory applied to everyday life problems, try working through the early chapters of Tijms (2007).

Self-assessment questions

29.1: What would be the most appropriate way to determine the probability that:

   (a) a drawing-pin will land point-up when tossed in the air;
   (b) a person aged 50–59 years in England will have two living parents; and
   (c) the total score when two dice are thrown is an even number?

29.2: What is the probability that a word chosen at random in this book will have fewer than six letters in it? Use the sample of data given in self-assessment question 28.3 to make an estimate for this.

29.3: If I throw a regular dodecahedron die (with 12 faces, numbered 1 to 12):

   (a) what is the probability that I will score a number with two digits?
   (b) what is the probability that I will score a number with one digit?

29.4: See Figure 29.1(b). When two conventional dice (with six faces, numbered one to six) are thrown, what is the probability of:

   (a) Scoring a multiple of 3?
   (b) Scoring a multiple of 4?
   (c) Scoring a number that is a multiple of 3 or 4 or both?

29.5: I throw two conventional dice. Write down an outcome that has a probability of 0 and another outcome that has a probability of 1.

29.6: If you draw a card at random from a pack of playing cards, the probability that the card will be an ace is $\frac{1}{13}$. The probability that it will be a black card is $\frac{1}{2}$. Are these two outcomes independent? Are they mutually exclusive? What is the probability of getting a black ace?

29.7: If a shoe is tossed in the air, the probability of it landing the right way up is found by experiment to be 0.35. The probability that it will land upside down is found to be 0.20. Are these two events independent? Are they mutually exclusive outcomes? What is the probability of the shoe landing either the right way up or upside down? The only other possible outcome is that it lands on one of its sides; what is the probability of this?

Further practice

From the Student Workbook

Tasks 219–221: Checking understanding of probability
Tasks 222–225: Using and applying probability
Tasks 226–227: Learning and teaching of probability

Glossary of key terms introduced in Chapter 29

Probability: a mathematical measure of the strength of our belief that some event will occur, based on whatever evidence we can assemble; a measure of how likely an event is to happen.

Probability scale: a scale for measuring probability, ranging from 0 (impossible) to 1 (certain).

Evens: where we judge an event to be as likely to happen as not to happen; probability = 0.5.

Subjective probability: an estimate of the probability of some event occurring based on subjective judgements of the available evidence.

Relative frequency: an estimate of the probability of an event occurring in the members of a population, obtained from the ratio of the number of times an event is recorded in a sample to the total number in the sample.

Experimental probability: an estimate of the probability of an event occurring, obtained from repeating an experiment a large number of times and finding the ratio of the number of times an event occurs to the total number of trials.

Theoretical probability: an estimate of probability based on theoretical arguments of symmetry and equally likely outcomes; if there are n equally likely outcomes from an experiment then the probability of each one occurring is $1/n$.

Independent events: two (or more) events where whether or not one occurs is completely independent of the other; for example, throw 6 on the red die, throw 6 on the blue die. The probability of both of two independent events occurring is the product of their individual probabilities.

Two-way table: a systematic way of identifying in a rectangular array all the possible combinations of the values of two variables; used in probability to identify all the possible combinations of two independent events. (See Figure 29.1.)

Mutually exclusive events: two (or more) events such that if one occurs then the other cannot occur; for example, throw 6 on the blue die, throw 5 on the blue die. The probability that one or other of a number of mutually exclusive events will occur is the sum of their individual probabilities.

Expected value: a measure used in assessing risk. A simple model for expected value of an action is the product of the probability of success and the value of the reward associated with it.

Answers to Self-assessment Questions

Particularly where the question asks for the invention of a sentence, a question, a method or a problem, the answers provided are only examples of possible valid responses.

Chapter 3: Learning how to learn mathematics

3.1:   (a) The formal mathematical language would be 'five add three equals eight'. (b) Putting 5 fingers up on one hand and 3 on the other, children might count all the fingers and say, 'five and three make eight all together'. (c) Children might start at 5 and count on 3 to get to 8.

3.2:   Same: AB and DC are parallel to each other in both shapes; the areas are the same. Different: the diagonal line goes up from left to right in one and down from left to right in the other; AD is on the left of one shape and on the right of the other.

Chapter 4: Key processes in mathematical reasoning

4.1:   (a) Incorrect because, for example, there are four multiples of 3 in the decade 21–30 (21, 24, 27 and 30). (b) True. In each third decade the numbers ending in 1, 4, 7 and 0 are multiples of 3.

4.2:   (a) False: a counter-example is 8; (b) true; (c) false: a counter-example is any non-square rhombus (see Chapter 25).

4.3:   The square has a perimeter of 8 units. I can draw four other shapes. Checking these in turn, they each have a perimeter of 10 units, greater than that of the square.

4.4:   If there are, for example, 10 tiles along the edge, then you multiply this by 4 because there are 4 edges. But when you do this the tiles in the corners get counted twice. So you have to subtract 4. It would be the same whatever number of tiles along the edge.

4.5: The number of matches is double the number of triangles, plus 1. Explanation: put down 1 match, then 2 further matches are needed to make a triangle and each subsequent triangle. To make zero triangles does not require any matches, so this is a special case that does not fit the generalization.

4.6: This is because $7 \times 11 \times 13 = 1001$ and any six-digit number *abcabc* is the three-digit number *abc* multiplied by 1001.

4.7: Jo gets more toys. Using the principle from the problem on average speeds, the average cost of her toys will be less than the average of 50p and £1 (that is, less than 75p). If they each get £3 pocket money per week, for example, Jo gets 9 toys and Jack gets 8.

4.8: I have tried to lead you here into giving the answers: (a) 80°, (b) 100°, (c) 120°. The last of these is impossible because water boils at 100°. A little bit of flexibility in your thinking is required to obtain the correct answers: (a) 80° or 20°, (b) 100° or 0°, (c) −20° (the water is now ice, of course).

Chapter 5: Modelling and problem solving

5.1: Mathematical model is $4.95 + 5.90 + 9.95$; mathematical solution, using a calculator, is 20.8; interpretation is that the total cost is £20.80.

5.2: Mathematical model is $27.90 \div 3$; mathematical solution (calculator answer) is 9.3; this is an exact but slightly inappropriate answer, because of the convention of 2 figures after the point for money; interpretation is that each person pays £9.30.

5.3: Mathematical model is $39.70 \div 3$; mathematical solution (calculator answer) is 13.233333; this is an answer that has been truncated; interpretation is that each person owes £13.23 and a little bit; two people pay £13.23, but one has to pay £13.24.

5.4: Mathematical model is $500 \div 35$; mathematical solution (calculator answer) is 14.285714; this is an answer that has been truncated; interpretation is that it will take me 15 months to reach my target.

5.5: Problem 1. The numbers are 7, 13 and 30. Hint: if you add the given numbers, 20, 43 and 37 (= 100), each of the boxes is counted twice, so the three numbers total 50.
Problem 2. See Figure A.

5.6: Problem 5. Assuming you do buy some of each, you could get: 5 snakes and 8 alligators; 10 snakes and 6 alligators; 15 snakes and 4 alligators; 20 snakes and 2 alligators.
Problem 6: Take 60 children, because this is the largest number (less than 80) that can be divided by 3, 4, 5 and 6.

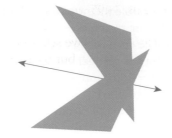

Figure A   *Solution to SAQ 5.5, Problem 2*

Chapter 6: Number and place value

6.1:   If you understand 'number' to mean integer or natural number, then the answer is 200. Otherwise there is no next number.
6.2:   32 uses the cardinal aspect; class 6 and level 4 use the ordinal aspect.
6.3:   (a) Impossible to say, or, if you like, an infinite number. (b) 19.
6.4:   It is rational and real. It is not an integer.
6.5:   It is not rational (it is irrational) but it is a real number.
6.6:   CLXXXVIII, CCLXVII, CCC, DCXIII, DCC (188, 267, 300, 613, 700).
6.7:   Four thousand one hundred (4099 + 1 = 4100).
6.8:   (a) $516 = (5 \times 10^2) + (1 \times 10^1) + 6$; (b) $3060 = (3 \times 10^3) + (6 \times 10^1)$; (c) 2 305 004 $= (2 \times 10^6) + (3 \times 10^5) + (5 \times 10^3) + 4$.
6.9:   6 one-pound coins, 2 ten-penny coins, 4 one-penny coins.
6.10: 3.2 is 3 flats and 2 longs; 3.05 is 3 flats and 5 small cubes; 3.15 is 3 flats, 1 long and 5 small cubes; 3.10 is 3 flats and 1 long. In order: 3.05, 3.10, 3.15, 3.2.
6.11: 3.405 m, and 2.500 m (or 2.5 m or 2.50 m).
6.12: (a) £0.25; (b) 0.25 m; (c) £0.07; (d) 0.045 kg; (e) 0.050 litres; (f) 0.005 m.
6.13: 3.608 lies between 3 and 4; between 3.6 and 3.7; between 3.60 and 3.61; between 3.607 and 3.609.

Chapter 7: Addition and subtraction structures

7.1:   I buy two articles costing £5.95 and £6.99. What is the total cost?
7.2:   My monthly salary was £1750 and then I had a rise of £145. What was my new monthly salary?
7.3:   The class's morning consists of 15 minutes registration, 25 minutes assembly, 55 minutes mathematics, 20 minutes break, 65 minutes English. What is the total time?
7.4:   78 pages; 256 – 178; this is an example of the inverse-of-addition structure.
7.5:   27 years; 62 – 35; this is an example of the comparison structure.

7.6:   The Australian Chardonnay is £4.95 and the Hungarian is £3.99. How much cheaper is the Hungarian?

7.7:   There are 250 pupils in a school. 159 have school lunches. How many do not?

7.8:   I want to buy a computer costing £989, but have only £650. How much more do I need?

Chapter 8: Mental strategies for addition and subtraction

8.1:   (a) $67 - (20 - 8) = (67 - 20) + 8$; general rule: $a - (b - c) = (a - b) + c$.
(b) $67 - (20 + 8) = (67 - 20) - 8$; general rule: $a - (b + c) = (a - b) - c$.

8.2:   (a) Pupil may have added, or done $2 - 0$ rather than $0 - 2$ in the tens column; (b) any subtraction involving zero gives the answer zero! (c) remembered decomposition recipe wrongly and written a little 9 instead of a little 1; (d) $7 - 1$ instead of $1 - 7$ in units, and again mystified by zero in tens column; (e) consistently taking the smaller from the larger; (f) remembered decomposition recipe wrongly and written a little 9 instead of a little 1.

8.3: $500 + 200$ makes 700; $30 + 90$ makes 120, that's 820 in total so far; $8 + 4$ makes 12, add this to the 820, to get 832.

8.4: $423 + 98 = 423 + 100 - 2 = 523 - 2 = 521$.

8.5: $297 + 304 = $ double $300 - 3 + 4 = 601$.

8.6: $494 + 307 = 494 + 6 + 301 = 500 + 301 = 801$.

8.7: $26 + 77 = 25 + 75 + 1 + 2 = 100 + 3 = 103$.

8.8: $1000 - 458 = 1000 - 500 + 42 = 500 + 42 = 542$.

8.9: $819 - 519 = 300$, so $819 - 523 = 300 - 4 = 296$.

8.10: $389 + 11 = 400$; add 300 to get to 700; then add 32 to get to 732. Then, $11 + 300 + 32 = 343$.

8.11: (a) $974 - 539 = 974 - 540 + 1 = 434 + 1 = 435$; (b) $400 - 237 = 399 - 237 + 1 = 162 + 1 = 163$; (c) $597 + 209 = 600 + 200 + 9 - 3 = 806$; (d) counting back, $7000 - 6 = 6994$; (e) counting on from 6998, $7000 - 6998 = 2$.

Chapter 9: Written methods for addition and subtraction

9.1:   Put out 2 pound coins, 8 pennies; then 1 pound coin, 5 ten-pences and 6 pennies; then 9 ten-pences and 7 pennies; there are 21 pennies; exchange 20 of these for 2 tens, leaving 1 penny; there are now 16 tens; exchange 10 of these for 1 pound, leaving 6 tens; there are then 4 pounds; the total is 4 pounds, 6 tens and 1 penny, that is, 461.

9.2: $800 + 130 + 14 = 944$.

9.3:   Put out 6 one-pound coins, 2 tens and 3 pence; take away 1 penny, leaving 2 pence; not enough ten-pences, so exchange 1 pound for 10 tens, giving 12 tens; take away

7 of these, leaving 5 tens; now take away 4 pounds; the result is 1 pound, 5 tens and 2 pence, that is, 152.

9.4: $100 + 80 + 8 = 188$.

9.5:   Put out 2 thousands and 6 units; not enough units to take away 8, no tens to exchange and no hundreds, so exchange 1 thousand for 10 hundreds, leaving 1 thousand; now exchange 1 hundred for 10 tens, leaving 9 hundreds; then exchange 1 ten for 10 units, leaving 9 tens and giving 16 units; can now take away 8 units, 3 tens and 4 hundreds; the result is 1 thousand, 5 hundreds, 6 tens and 8 units, that is, 1568.

9.6:   Add 2 to both numbers, to give $2008 - 440$; add 60 to both, to give $2068 - 500$; add 500 to both, to give $2568 - 1000$; answer, 1568.

Chapter 10: Multiplication and division structures

10.1:   I bought 29 boxes of eggs with 12 eggs in each box … (29 lots of 12). There are 12 classes in the school with 29 children in each class … (12 lots of 29).

10.2:   I bought 12 kg of potatoes at 25p per kilogram. What was the total cost?

10.3:   The box can be seen as 4 rows of 6 yoghurts or 6 rows of 4 yoghurts.

10.4:   If the length of the wing in the model is 16 cm, how long is the length of the wing on the actual aeroplane? ($16 \times 25 = 400$ cm).

10.5: $2827 \times 1.12 = 3166.24$; new monthly salary is £3166.24.

10.6:   Scale factor is 20 ($300 \div 15$); an example of the ratio structure.

10.7:   Price is 48p per kilogram-weight ($12 \div 25 = 0.48$); an example of the equal-sharing structure.

10.8:   I can afford 8 CDs ($100 \div 12.50$); an example of the inverse-of-multiplication structure, using the idea of repeated subtraction.

10.9:   I need 25 months ($300 \div 12$); this is an example of the inverse-of-multiplication structure, using the idea of repeated addition.

10.10: A packet of four chocolate bars costs 60p; how much per bar?

10.11: How many toys costing £4 each can 1 afford if I have £60 to spend?

10.12: A teacher earns £1950 a month, a bank manager earns £6240. How many times greater is the bank manager's salary? ($6240 \div 1950 = 3.2$); the bank manager's salary is 3.2 times that of the teacher.

Chapter 11: Mental strategies for multiplication and division

11.1: $1 \times 2 \times 3 \times 4 \times 5 = 10 \times 12 = 120$.

11.2:   In $288 \div 6 = 48$, 288 is the dividend, 6 is the divisor, 48 is the quotient.

11.3:   16 lots of 25 is easier to calculate than 25 lots of 16; $4 \times 25 = 100$, so $16 \times 25 = 400$.

11.4: $25 \times 24 = 25 \times (4 \times 6) = (25 \times 4) \times 6 = 100 \times 6 = 600$.

11.5: $25 \times (20 + 4) = (25 \times 20) + (25 \times 4) = 500 + 100 = 600$.

11.6: $22 \times (40 - 2) = (22 \times 40) - (22 \times 2) = 880 - 44 = 836$.

11.7: $4 \times 90 = 360$, $40 \times 9 = 360$, $40 \times 90 = 3600$, $4 \times 900 = 3600$, $400 \times 9 = 3600$, $40 \times 900 = 36\ 000$, $400 \times 90 = 36\ 000$, $400 \times 900 = 360\ 000$.

11.8: $48 \times 25 = 12 \times 4 \times 25 = 12 \times 100 = 1200$.

11.9: $2 \times 103 = 206$; $4 \times 103 = 412$; $8 \times 103 = 824$; $16 \times 103 = 1648$; $206 + 824 + 1648 = 2678$.

11.10: $10 \times 103 = 1030$; $2 \times 103 = 206$; $1030 + 1030 + 206 + 206 + 206 = 2678$.

11.11: $154 \div 22$ is the same as $(88 + 66) \div 22$ which equals $(88 \div 22) + (66 \div 22)$; hence the answer is $4 + 3 = 7$; $154 \div 22$ is the same as $(220 - 66) \div 22$ which equals $(220 \div 22) - (66 \div 22)$; hence the answer is $10 - 3 = 7$.

11.12: $10 \times 21 = 210$; another 10×21 makes this up to 420; $2 \times 21 = 42$, which brings us to 462; 1 more 21 makes 483; answer is $10 + 10 + 2 + 1 = 23$.

11.13: $385 \div 55 = 770 \div 110$ (doubling both numbers) $= 7$.

Chapter 12: Written methods for multiplication and division

12.1: The four areas are 40×30, 40×7, 2×30 and 2×7, giving a total of $1200 + 280 + 60 + 14 = 1554$.

12.2: The six areas are 300×10, 300×7, 40×10, 40×7, 5×10 and 5×7, giving a total of $3000 + 2100 + 400 + 280 + 50 + 35 = 5865$.

12.3: From 126 take away 10 sevens (70), leaving 56, then 5 sevens (35), leaving 21, which is 3 sevens; answer is therefore $10 + 5 + 3$, that is, 18.

12.4: From 851 take away 20 lots of 23 (460), leaving 391, then 10 more (230), leaving 161, then 5 more (115), leaving 46, which is 2×23; answer is therefore $20 + 10 + 5 + 2$, that is, 37.

12.5: From 529 take away 50 lots of 8 (400), then 10 more (80), then 5 more (40), then 1 more (8), leaving a remainder of 1; answer is $50 + 10 + 5 + 1 = 66$, remainder 1.

Chapter 13: Remainders and rounding

13.1: The mathematical model is: 124×5.95 (or 5.95×124); the mathematical solution is 737.8; interpretation: the total cost of the order will be £737.80; to the nearest ten pounds, the total cost of the order will be about £740; to three significant figures, the total cost of the order will be about £738.

13.2:(a) $327 \div 40 = 8.175$ (calculator), or 8 remainder 7. So 9 coaches are needed. We round *up* (otherwise we would have to leave 7 children behind); (b) $500 \div 65 = 7.6923076$ (calculator), or 7 remainder 45. So we can buy 7 cakes. We round *down* (and have 45p change for something else).

13.3: How many buses holding 50 children do we need to transport 320 children? We need 7 buses. How many tables costing £50 each can we afford with a budget of £320? We can afford 6 tables.

13.4: Calculator result is 131.88888; the average height is 132 cm to the nearest cm.
13.5: (a) 3; (b) 3.2; (c) 3.16.
13.6: 205 books per shop; that's 205 × 17 = 3485 books altogether, so the remainder is 3500 − 3485 = 15 books.

Chapter 14: Multiples, factors and primes

14.1: 3 × 37 = 111, 6 × 37 = 222, 9 × 37 = 333, 12 × 37 = 444, 15 × 37 = 555, 18 × 37 = 666, 21 × 37 = 777, 24 × 37 = 888, 27 × 37 = 999; the pattern breaks down when 4-digit answers are achieved.

14.2: (a) 47 × 9 = 423; sum of digits = 9; (b) 172 × 9 = 1548; sum of digits = 18; sum of these digits = 9; (c) 9 876 543 × 9 = 88 888 887; sum of digits = 63; sum of these digits = 9.

14:3: (a) 2652 is a multiple of 2 (ends in even digit), 3 (sum of digits is multiple of 3), 4 (last two digits multiple of 4), 6 (multiple of 2 and 3); (b) 6570 is a multiple of 2 (ends in even digit), 3 (sum of digits is multiple of 3), 5 (ends in 0), 6 (multiple of 2 and 3), 9 (digital root is 9); (c) 2401 is a multiple of none of these (it is 7 × 7 × 7 × 7).

14.4: A three-digit number is a multiple of 11 if the sum of the two outside digits subtract the middle digit is either 0 (for example, 561, 594, 330) or 11 (418, 979).

14.5: 24 (the lowest common multiple of 8 and 12).

14.6: (a) Factors of 95 are 1, 5, 19, 95; (b) factors of 96 are 1, 2, 3, 4, 6, 8, 12, 16, 24, 32, 48 and 96; (c) factors of 97 are 1 and 97 (it is prime); clearly 96 is the most flexible.

14.7: Factors of 48 are 1, 2, 3, 4, 6, 8, 12, 16, 24, 48; factors of 80 are 1, 2, 4, 5, 8, 10, 16, 20, 40, 80; common factors are 1, 2, 4, 8, 16; could have 16 rows of 3 blue and 5 red, or 8 rows of 6 blue and 10 red, or 4 rows of 12 blue and 20 red, or 2 rows of 24 blue and 40 red, or 1 row of 48 blue and 80 red!

14.8: 71, 73, 79, 83, 89, 97 (*Note:* not 91, because this is 9 × 13).

14.9: 4403 = 7 × 17 × 37.

14.10: 5, 7, 11, 13, 17, 19, 23, 25, 29, 31, 35, 37, 41, 43, 47, 49, 53, 55, 59, 61; they are all prime except 25, 35, 49 and 55.

Chapter 15: Squares, cubes and number shapes

15.1: 20 is a factor of 100; 21 is a triangle number; 22 is a multiple of 2 and 11; 23 is a prime number; 24 has eight factors; 25 is a square number; 26 is a multiple of 2 and 13; 27 is a cube number; 28 is a triangle number; 29 is a prime number.

15.2: 36 is both a triangle number and a square number.

15.3: The differences between successive square numbers are 3, 5, 7, 9, 11 … , the odd numbers; these are the numbers of dots added to each square in Figure 15.1(a) to make the next one in the sequence.

15.4: (a) The answers should be the same. (b) Whole numbers less than 100 that are both cubes and squares are 1 and 64.

15.5: (a) 57; (b) 17; (c) 42.

15.6: 14.14 m.

15.7: The cube root of 500 is between 7.93 and 7.94; so the length of the side of the cube should be about 7.9 cm (79 mm).

15.8: The answers are the square numbers: 4, 9, 16, 25, 36, and so on; two successive triangles of dots in Figure 15.5 can be fitted together to make a square number.

15.9: 20, 21 and 29 ($20^2 + 21^2 = 29^2$).

15.10: Approximately 14.14 cm.

15.11: (a) $10 > \sqrt{50}$; (b) $\sqrt[3]{100} < 5$; (c) $8 < \sqrt{70} < 9$.

Chapter 16: Integers: positive and negative

16.1: The order is B (+3), A (−4), C (−5).

16.2: (a) The temperature one winter's day is 4 °C; that night it falls by 12 degrees; what is the night-time temperature? (Answer −8); (b) the temperature one winter's night is −6 °C; when it rises by 10 degrees what is the temperature? (Answer: 4.)

16.3: (a) If I am overdrawn by £5, how much must be paid into my account to make the balance £20? (Answer: 25); (b) if I am overdrawn by £15, how much must be paid into my account so that I am only overdrawn by £10? (Answer: 5); (c) if I am overdrawn by £10 and withdraw a further £20, what is my new balance? (Answer: −30.)

16.4: My basic calculator displays −42 with the negative sign at one end of the display and the 42 at the other; this is rather unsatisfactory.

16.5: The mathematical model is 458.64 − (−187.85); the cheque paid in was £646.49.

Chapter 17: Fractions and ratios

17.1: (a) A bar of chocolate is cut into 5 equal pieces and I have 4 of them; (b) $^4/_5$ of a class of 30 children is 24 children; (c) share 4 pizzas equally between 5 people; (d) if I earn £400 a week and you earn £500 a week, my earnings are $^4/_5$ of yours.

17.2: (a) $^1/_4 = {}^2/_8 = {}^3/_{12}$; (b) $^1/_2 = {}^2/_4 = {}^3/_6 = {}^4/_8 = {}^6/_{12}$; (c) $^3/_4 = {}^6/_8 = {}^9/_{12}$; (d) $^4/_4 = {}^8/_8 = {}^{12}/_{12} = {}^6/_6$ $= {}^3/_3 = {}^2/_2 = 1$; (e) $^2/_{12} = {}^1/_6$; (f) $^4/_{12} = {}^2/_6 = {}^1/_3$; (g) $^8/_{12} = {}^4/_6 = {}^2/_3$; (h) $^{10}/_{12} = {}^5/_6$.

17.3: $^3/_5$ is $^{24}/_{40}$; $^5/_8$ is $^{25}/_{40}$; the latter is the larger.

17.4: $^1/_6$ $(^2/_{12})$, $^1/_3$ $(^4/_{12})$, $^5/_{12}$, $^2/_3$ $(^8/_{12})$, $^3/_4$ $(^9/_{12})$.

17.5: Compare by ratio the prices of two coffee-pots, pot A costing £15, pot B costing £25.

17.6: $^9/_{24}$ or $^3/_8$.

17.7: (a) $^1/_5$ of £100 is £20, so $^3/_5$ is £60; (b) £1562.50 ($2500 \div 8 \times 5$).

Chapter 18: Calculations with decimals

18.1: (a) Mathematical solution is 6.90, total cost is £6.90; (b) mathematical solution is 3.25, total length is 3.25 m; (c) mathematical solution is 0.22, difference in height is 0.22 m or 22 cm; (d) mathematical solution is 5.75, change is £5.75.

18.2: How much for 4 box files costing £3.99 each? Answer: £15.96. Method: $399 \times 4 = (400 \times 4) - 4 = 1596$, so $3.99 \times 4 = 15.96$.

18.3: Divide a 4.40-m length of wood into 8 equal parts; each part is 0.55 m (55 cm) long. (Change the calculation to 440 cm divided by 8.)

18.4: (a) 18.4; (b) 18.4; (c) 0.00184.

18.5: (a) 18 (or 18.0); (b) 18 (or 18.0); (c) 0.0018 (or 0.00180).

18.6: 0.0001; find the area in square metres of a square of side 0.01 m (1 cm).

18.7: (a) $2 \div 0.5 = 20 \div 5 = 4$; (b) $5.5 \div 0.11 = 550 \div 11 = 50$.

18.8: (a) 50; (b) 0.0005; (c) 0.005.

18.9: (a) 0.17; (b) 0.6; (c) 0.35; (d) 0.6666667 (approximately); (e) 0.1428571 (approximately).

18.10: (a) $^9/_{100}$; (b) $^{79}/_{100}$; (c) $^{15}/_{100} = {}^3/_{20}$.

18.11: $^7/_{24}$ and $^7/_{27}$ are equivalent to recurring decimals.

18.12: Largest is 1.2×10^6; smallest is 2.4×10^5.

18.13: (a) Answer should be about $3 \times 1 = 3$, so 2.66; (b) answer should be about $10 \times 0.1 = 1$, so 0.964; (c) answer should be about $28 \div 1 = 28$, so 31.

Chapter 19: Proportion and percentages

19.1: 9 euros.

19.2: 25°C.

19.3: Since one-third is about 33%, this is the greater reduction.

19.4: (a) 13 out of 50 is the same proportion as 26 out of 100. So 26% achieve level 5 and 74% do not.

(b) 57 out of 300 is the same proportion as 19 out of 100. So 19% achieve level 5 and 81% do not.

(c) 24 out of 80 is the same proportion as 3 out of 10, or 30 out of 100. So 30% achieve level 5 and 70% do not.

(d) 26 out of 130 is the same proportion as 2 out of 10, or 20 out of 100. So 20% achieve level 5 and 80% do not.

19.5: English, about 42% ; Italian, about 49% .

19.6: (a) $\frac{3}{20} = \frac{15}{100} = 15\%$; (b) $65\% = \frac{65}{100} = \frac{13}{20}$.

19.7: (a) 10% of £120 is £12, so 30% is three times this, that is, £36; (b) 10% of £450 is £45; so 5% is £22.50; 1% is £4.50, so 2% is £9; so 17% is £45 + £22.50 + £9 = £76.50.

19.8: £271.04 (275 × 1.12 × 0.88).

19.9: £150 (114% is £171 and we have to find 100%).

Chapter 20: Algebra

20.1: The relationship is $f = 3y$. Criticism: using f and y is misleading, since they look like abbreviations for a foot and a yard, instead of variables (for example, the number of feet).

20.2: (a) The total number of pieces of fruit bought; (b) the cost of the apples in pence; (c) the cost of the bananas; (d) the total cost of the fruit. Criticism: using a and b is misleading, since they look like abbreviations for an apple and a banana; so $10a + 12b$ looks as though it means 10 apples and 12 bananas.

20.3: Jenny has 11 rides. Arithmetic steps: 12 divided by 2, add 5. Algebraic representation: $2(n - 5) = 12$.

20.4: (a) 60; (b) 10.

20.5: For Figure 20.4(c): (a) add 5; (b) 498; (c) multiply by 5, subtract 2; (d) $y = 5x - 2$. For Figure 20.4(d): (a) subtract 1; (b) 0; (c) subtract from 100; (d) $y = 100 - x$.

20.6: Side by side: (a) add 2; (b) 204; (c) multiply by 2, add 4; (d) $y = 2x + 4$. End to end: (a) add 4; (b) 402; (c) multiply by 4, add 2; (d) $y = 4x + 2$.

20.7: My number is 42; the equation is $x(2x + 3) = 3654$.

20.8: The first 10 triangle numbers are 1, 3, 6, 10, 15, 21, 28, 36, 45, 55. Their doubles are $2 = 1 \times 2$, $6 = 2 \times 3$, $12 = 3 \times 4$, $20 = 4 \times 5$, $30 = 5 \times 6$, $42 = 6 \times 7$, $56 = 7 \times 8$, $72 = 8 \times 9$, $90 = 9 \times 10$, $110 = 10 \times 11$. So the nth triangle number doubled is $n \times (n + 1)$. Hence the nth triangle number is $\frac{1}{2}n \times (n + 1)$. So the one-hundredth triangle number (which equals $1 + 2 + 3 + \dots + 100$) is $50 \times 101 = 5050$.

Chapter 21: Coordinates and linear relationships

21.1: The points are (1, 2), (1, 4), (2, 5), (4, 5), (5, 4), (5, 2), (4, 1) and (2, 1). Joined up in this order they form an octagon.

21.2: They are all linear relationships, producing straight-line graphs.

21.3: (a) The total number of eggs; (b) the total number of beats; (c) the top number in the fractions in the set.

21.4: The fourth vertex is (4, 5). The sum of the x-coordinates of two opposite vertices is the same as the sum of the x-coordinates for the other two opposite vertices. The same is true of the y-coordinates. The fourth vertex to go with (4, 4), (5, 8) and (13, 6) is therefore (12, 2), because $4 + 13 = 5 + 12$, and $4 + 6 = 8 + 2$.

21.5: $2x + 1 = 6$ when $x = 2.5$.

21.6: Using the x-axis for weights in stones, the straight line graph should pass through (0, 0) and (11, 70). Then, for example, the point (10, 64) on this line (approximately) converts 10 stone to about 64 kg, and the point (9.4, 60) gives 9.4 stone as the approximate equivalent of 60 kg.

Chapter 22: Measurement

22.1: It works as far as 55 miles, which is 89 km to the nearest km (88.5115). The next value, 89 miles, is 143 km to the nearest km (143.2277), rather than the Fibonacci number, 144.

22.2: It will still be 1 kg. It will weigh less, but the mass does not change.

22.3: (a) Yes; if A is earlier than B and B is earlier than C, then A must be earlier than C. (b) No; for example, 20 cm is half of 40 cm and 40 cm is half of 80 cm, but 20 cm is not half of 80 cm.

22.4: (a) 297 mm; (b) 29.7 cm; (c) 2.97 dm; (d) 0.297 m.

22.5: (a) 250 g; (b) 2 pints; (c) 2 metres; (d) 100 kilometres; (e) 4 ounces; (f) 10 stone; (g) 9 miles to the litre.

22.6: (a) Possible – 7 tonnes is about average for an adult male African elephant; (b) impossible – it would be much more than that, probably more than 400 litres; (c) impossible to make this claim – all measurements are approximate; (d) possible; (e) impossible – I might manage it in a month; (f) possible – you should get away with one first-class stamp.

Chapter 23: Angle

23.1: $\frac{1}{8}$ of a turn (acute), 89° (acute), 90° (right), 95° (obtuse), 150° (obtuse), 2 right angles (straight), 200° (reflex), $\frac{3}{4}$ of a turn (reflex).

23.2: (a) 6 right angles; (b) 8 right angles; (c) 10 right angles. The sequential rule is add two right angles. For a figure with N sides the global rule for the sum of the angles is $2N - 4$. When $N = 100$, the sum of the angles is 196 right angles.

23.3: (a) Impossible, because two obtuse angles add up to more than 180°; (b) possible, with angles of 90°, 45° and 45°; (c) possible, for example, with angles of 100°, 100°, 80° and 80°; (d) possible, for example, with angles of 210°, 50°, 50° and 50°; (e) impossible, because the four angles would add up to less than 360°.

Chapter 24: Transformations and symmetry

24.1: (a) Translation, −6 units in x-direction, 0 units in y-direction; (b) reflection in vertical line passing through (8, 0); (c) rotation through half-turn about (5, 2), clockwise or anticlockwise.

24.2: (a) Shape Q is constructed from 45 square units, which is 9 times greater. The scale factor for area (9) is the square of the scale factor for length (3).
(b) R is transformed into Q by a scaling with factor 6. Q to R requires a scaling with factor $^1/_6$. These transformations are inverses of each other.
(c) The lines should all meet at one point. This is called the *centre of enlargement.*

24.3: A diagonal line passing through (11, 3) and (13, 1); a vertical line passing through (12, 2); a horizontal line passing through (12, 2). The order of rotational symmetry is four.

24.4: No.

24.5: No.

24.6: E has two lines of symmetry and rotational symmetry of order two. F has one line of symmetry. G has five lines of symmetry and rotational symmetry of order five.

Chapter 25: Classifying shapes

25.1: Because all the angles in an equilateral triangle must be 60°.

25.2: 90°, 45° and 45°.

25.3: (a) Square; (b) square; (c) equilateral triangle; (d) cuboid; (e) tetrahedron.

25.4: The parallelogram tessellates, as do all quadrilaterals.

25.5: Nine.

25.6: (a) False; (b) true; (c) true; (d) true; (e) false; (f) false.

Chapter 26: Perimeter, area and volume

26.1: The maximum area is that of the square field, 5 units by 5 units, that is, 25 square units.

26.2: The minimum length of fencing is 28 units, for a field that is 6 units by 8 units.

26.3: (a) As a cube with side 3 units; total surface area = 54 square units.
(b) As a cuboid, 4 units by 4 units by 3 units; total surface area = 80 square units (16 + 16 + 12 + 12 + 12 + 12).

26.4: About 78.5 cm (25 × 3.14); 80 cm to be on the safe side.

26.5: About 127 m (400 ÷ 3.14).

26.6: The area of the trapezium is 100 cm². The general rule is that the area is half the height multiplied by the sum of the parallel sides. for example, for height 10 cm, parallel sides 12 cm and 6 cm, the area is 5 × 18 = 90 cm²; for height 10 cm, parallel sides 12 cm and 9 cm, the area is 5 × 21 = 105 cm².

26.7: The area is 25 mm², or 0.25 cm², or 0.000025 m².

26.8: Volume is 125 cm³ or 0.000125 m³.

26.9: 20 × 25 × 10 = 5000 cuboids needed.

Chapter 27: Handling data

27.1: The four subsets are: boys who walked; not boys (girls) who walked; boys who did not walk; and not boys who did not walk. (a) Two overlapping circles, one representing boys, the other those who walked. (b) A 2 by 2 grid, with columns labelled boys and not boys (girls), and rows labelled walked, did not walk.

27.2: (a) Which way of travelling to school is used by most children? How many fewer children walk than come by car? (b) How many children have fewer than five writing implements? Which group has no children in it? (c) How many have waist measurements in the range 60 to 64 cm, to the nearest centimetre? How many have waist measurements to the nearest centimetre that are greater than 89 cm?

27.3: (a) Continuous; (b) continuous; (c) discrete; (d) discrete, but should be grouped; (e) discrete; (f) discrete; (g) continuous.

27.4: Examples (c) and (f), having a small number of possibilities, are best displayed in a pie chart. Example (g) is best displayed in a line graph, with the horizontal axis representing time.

27.5: Fifty-pence intervals will produce 10 groups: £0.00–£0.49, £0.50–£0.99, £1.00–£1.49, and so on.

27.6: (a) 140 degrees; (b) about 153 degrees (calculator answer: 152.72727).

27.7 Particularly for opinions about what time school should start the first 50 pupils arriving in the morning are unlikely to be a representative sample! A systematic way of getting a representative sample (of 48) would be to select 6 boys and 6 girls at random from each of the four year groups.

27.8: How many Year 5 children came by bike? How many children in each year group were in the sample? What is the total number of children who walked? For Year 5 what was the least common way of coming to school? What does the square in the top left hand corner tell you? How did most children in the sample come to school? And so on ...

27.9: The line goes approximately from (0, 2) to (10, 18). The point representing the results of Child H is furthest away from this line. This child's results show the greatest discrepancy between reading and spelling performance.

Chapter 28: Comparing sets of data

28.1: The girls in the sample were generally better than the boys at recalling names of daily newspapers. A greater proportion of boys could name none. A greater proportion of girls could name three. More than half the girls could name two or three, compared with about a quarter of the boys.

28.2: (a) Group A English, mean = 53.7, median = 53; group B English, mean = 67.5, median = 71. Both averages support the view that group B did better.
(b) The mean for English for the two groups combined is 59.8 (1494 ÷ 25). This is less than the mean of the two separate means (the mean of 53.7 and 67.5 is 60.6). Because there are more pupils in group A this mean has a greater weighting in the combined mean.
(c) With a total of 25 in the set the median is the 13th value when arranged in order; so for English, median = 56; for mathematics, median = 53. The range for English is 45 (90 − 45) and the range for mathematics is 72 (95 − 23).
(d) For mathematics, John's mark (49) is less than the mean (53.6) and less than the median (56.5), but well above the bottom of the range.

28.3: (a) The modal number of letters per word is 2.
(b) The median is 4 letters and the range is 11.
(c) The mean number of letters per word is 4.31.

28.4: P (about 68 cm per second) has a greater average speed than Q (65 cm per second).

28.5: Since the figure of 69% achieving level 2 or above falls between the 40th percentile (72%) and the lower quartile (67%) it is fair to conclude that St Anne's is performing below average compared with other schools in this group. Because their percentage is less than the 40th percentile, it means that more than 60% of schools in the group did better than St Anne's.

28.6: (a) The diagram shows a marked difference in performance between the two groups, with group A showing considerably higher levels of achievement in reading. The boxes do not even overlap. This means that all the schools in the middle 50% of group A have a higher percentage of pupils gaining level 2 or above for reading than all the schools in the middle 50% of group E.
(b) About 90%. (c) About 90%. (d) About 67%. (e) About 66%.
(f) Group E has a much greater range of achievement in reading: some schools have only 32% achieving level 2 or above for reading, whereas others get as many

as 90% of their pupils achieving this level. For group A the range is from about 66% to 100%.

(g) The interquartile ranges are markedly different, showing that group E's performance is much more diverse: group A has an IQR of 13% (from 83% to 96%); group E has an IQR of 21% (from 56% to 77%).

Chapter 29: Probability

29.1: (a) By experiment: finding the relative frequency of successful outcomes in a large number of trials.

(b) By collecting data from a large sample of people aged 50–59 years in England.

(c) Using an argument based on symmetry, considering all the possible, equally likely outcomes.

29.2: 75% in the sample have fewer than 6 letters; so estimate of probability is 0.75.

29.3: (a) $^3/_{12} = 0.25$; (b) $^9/_{12} = 0.75$.

29.4: (a) $^{12}/_{36} = 0.33$ approximately; (b) $^9/_{36} = 0.25$; (c) $^{20}/_{36} = 0.56$ approximately.

29.5: Probability of scoring 1 is 0. Probability of scoring less than 13 is 1.

29.6: They are independent but not mutually exclusive. Probability of black ace is $^2/_{52} = ^1/_{26} (= ^1/_{13} \times ^1/_2)$.

29.7: The events are mutually exclusive but not independent. Probability of right way up or upside down is $0.35 + 0.20 = 0.55$. Probability of landing on a side is $1 - 0.55 = 0.45$.

References

Ainley, J. (2001) 'Doing algebra type stuff: emergent algebra in the primary school', *Proceedings of the 23rd Conference of the International Group for the Psychology of Mathematics Education*, vol. 2, pp. 9–16, Institute of Technology, Haifa, Israel.

Anghileri, J. (2001a) 'What are we trying to achieve in teaching standard calculating procedures?', *Proceedings of the 25th Conference of the International Group for the Psychology of Mathematics Education*, vol. 2, pp. 41–8. Freudenthal Institute, Utrecht University, Netherlands.

Anghileri, J. (ed.) (2001b) *Principles and Practices in Arithmetic Teaching: Innovative Approaches for the Primary Classroom*. Buckingham: Open University Press.

Anghileri, J. (2007) *Developing Number Sense: Progression in the Middle Years*. London: Continuum.

Ashcraft, M. and Moore, A. (2009) 'Mathematics anxiety and the affective drop in performance', *Journal of Psychoeducational Assessment*, 27(3): 197–205.

Ball, D., Thames, M. and Phelps, G. (2008) 'Content knowledge for teaching: what makes it special?', *Journal of Teacher Education*, 59(5): 389–407.

Barrett, J. and Clements, D. (1998) 'Analyzing children's length strategies with two-dimensional tasks: what counts for length?', *Proceedings of the 12th Annual Meeting of the North American Chapter of the International Group for the Psychology of Mathematics Education*, Columbus, Ohio.

Beiler, A. (2000) *Recreations in the Theory of Numbers: The Queen of Mathematics Entertains*. 2nd edn. Mineola, NY: Dover Publications.

Blinko, J. and Slater, A. (1996) *Teaching Measures: Activities, Organisation and Management*. London: Hodder and Stoughton.

Boulet, G. (1998) 'Didactical implications of children's difficulties in learning the fraction concept', *Focus on Learning Problems in Mathematics*, 20(4): 19–34.

Briggs, M. (1993) 'Bags and baggage revisited', *Mathematics Education Review*, 2: 16–20.

Briggs, M. and Crook, J. (1991) 'Bags and baggage', in E. Love and D. Pimm (eds), *Teaching and Learning Mathematics*. London: Hodder and Stoughton.

Brown, J. and Burton, R. (1978) 'Diagnostic models for procedural "bugs" in basic mathematical skills', *Cognitive Science*, 2: 155–92.

Brown, T. (2003) *Meeting the Standards in Primary Mathematics: A Guide to the ITT NC*. London: RoutledgeFalmer.

Burger, W. and Shaughnessy, J. (1986) 'Characterizing the van Hiele levels of development in geometry', *Journal for Research in Mathematics Education*, 17(1): 31–48.

Burgess, T. (2009) 'Statistical knowledge for teaching: exploring it in the classroom', *For the Learning of Mathematics*, 29(3): 18–21.

Burnett, S. and Wichman, A. (1997) *Mathematics and Literature: An Approach to Success.* Chicago, IL: Saint Xavier University and IRI/Skylight.

Burton, R. (1981) 'DEBUGGY: diagnosis of errors in basic mathematical skills', in D. Sleeman and J. Brown (eds), *Intelligent Tutoring Systems*. New York: Academic Press.

Carraher, D., Schliemann, A., Briznela, B. and Earnest, D. (2006) 'Arithmetic and algebra in early mathematics education', *Journal for Research in Mathematics Education*, 37(2): 87–115.

Carraher, T., Carraher, D. and Schliemann, A. (1985) 'Mathematics in the streets and schools', *British Journal of Developmental Psychology*, 3: 21–9.

Coben, D., with Colwell, D., Macrae, S., Boaler, J., Brown, M. and Rhodes, V. (2003) *Adult Numeracy: Review of Research and Related Literature*. London: National Research Centre for Adult Literacy and Numeracy, London Institute of Education.

Cockburn, A. (1998) *Teaching Mathematics with Insight: The Identification, Diagnosis and Remediation of Young Children's Mathematical Errors*. London: Falmer Press.

Cockburn, A. (ed.) (2007) *Mathematical Understanding 5–11*. London: Sage Publications.

Cockburn, A. and Littler, G. (eds) (2008) *Mathematical Misconceptions: Opening the Doors to Understanding*. London: Sage Publications.

Cockcroft, W.H. (1982) *Mathematics Counts: Report of the Committee of Inquiry into the Teaching of Mathematics under the Chairmanship of Dr W.H. Cockcroft*. London: HMSO.

Cooke, H. (2007) *Primary Mathematics: Developing Subject Knowledge*, 2nd edn. London: Sage Publications.

DCSF/QCDA (Department for Children, Schools and Families/Qualifications and Curriculum Development Agency) (2010) The National Curriculum Primary Handbook. London: DCSF/ QCDA.

De Corte, E., Verschaffel, L. and Van Coillie, V. (1988) 'Influence of number size, structure and response mode on children's solutions of multiplication word problems', *Journal of Mathematical Behavior*, 7: 197–216.

DES/APU (Department of Education and Science/Assessment of Performance Unit) (1980) *Mathematical Development, Primary Survey Report No. 1*. London: HMSO.

DES/APU (Department of Education and Science/Assessment of Performance Unit) (1981) *Mathematical Development, Primary Survey Report No. 2*. London: HMSO.

DfEE (Department for Education and Employment) (1999) *The National Numeracy Strategy: Framework for Teaching Mathematics from Reception to Year 6*. Sudbury: DfEE Publications.

Dickson, L., Brown, M. and Gibson, O. (1984) *Children Learning Mathematics: A Teacher's Guide to Recent Research*. London: Cassell Educational.

Doxiadis, A. (2000) *Uncle Petros and Goldbach's Conjecture*. London: Faber and Faber.

English, L. (2004) 'Mathematical modelling in the primary school', in I. Putt, R. Faragher and M. McLean (eds), *Proceedings of the 27th Annual Conference of the Mathematics Education Research Group of Australasia. Mathematics Education for the Third Millennium: Towards 2010*. Townsville,Queensland: James Cook University.

English, L. and Watters, J. (2005) 'Mathematical modelling in the early school years', *Mathematics Education Research Journal*, 16(3): 58–79.

Fenna, D. (2002) *A Dictionary of Weights, Measures and Units*. Oxford: Oxford University Press.

Fluellen, J. (2008) 'Algebra for babies: exploring natural numbers in simple arrays', paper presented at the 29th Ethnography and Education Research Forum at the University of Pennsylvania. (Downloadable from www.eric.ed.gov)

Fraser, H. and Honeyford, G. (2000) *Children, Parents and Teachers Enjoying Numeracy.* London: David Fulton.

Graham, A. (2008) *Teach Yourself Basic Mathematics*, 4th revd edn. London: Hodder and Stoughton.

Groves, S. (1993) 'The effect of calculator use on third graders' solutions of real world division and multiplication problems', *Proceedings of the 17th International Conference for the Psychology of Mathematics Education*, 2: 9–16.

Groves, S. (1994) 'The effect of calculator use on third and fourth graders' computation and choice of calculating device', *Proceedings of the 18th International Conference for the Psychology of Mathematics Education*, 3: 9–16.

Haighton, J., Holder, D., Phillips, B. and Thomas, V. (2004) *Maths, the Basic Skills: Curriculum Edition*. Cheltenham: Nelson Thornes.

Hansen, A. (ed.) (2005) *Children's Errors in Maths: Understanding Common Misconceptions.* Exeter: Learning Matters.

Harries, T. and Spooner, M. (2006) *Mental Mathematics for the Numeracy Hour*. London: David Fulton.

Hart, K. (1984) *Ratio and Children's Strategies and Errors*. Windsor: NFER-Nelson.

Haylock, D. (1991) *Teaching Mathematics to Low Attainers, 8–12*. London: Sage Publications.

Haylock, D. (1997) 'Recognising mathematical creativity in schoolchildren', *International Reviews on Mathematical Education*, 3: 68–74.

Haylock, D. (2001) *Numeracy for Teaching*. London: Sage Publications.

Haylock, D. and Cockburn, A. (2008) *Understanding Mathematics for Young Children: A Guide for Foundation Stage and Lower Primary Teachers*, revd and expd edn. London: Sage Publications.

Haylock, D. with Manning, R. (2010) *Student Workbook for Mathematics Explained for Primary Teachers*. London: Sage Publications.

Haylock, D. with Thangata, F. (2007) *Key Concepts in Teaching Primary Mathematics*. London: Sage Publications.

Heirdsfield, A. and Cooper, T. (1997) 'The architecture of mental addition and subtraction', paper presented at the Annual Conference of the Australian Association of Research in Education, Brisbane, January.

Hopkins, C., Pope, S. and Pepperell, S. (2004) *Understanding Primary Mathematics*. London: David Fulton.

Hughes, M. (1986) *Children and Number: Difficulties in Learning Mathematics*. Oxford: Blackwell.

Irwin, K. (2001) 'Using everyday knowledge of decimals to enhance understanding', *Journal for Research in Mathematics Education*, 32(4): 399–420.

Jones, G., Thornton, C., Langrall, C., Mooney, E., Perry, B. and Putt, I. (2000) 'A framework for characterizing students' statistical thinking', *Mathematical Thinking and Learning*, 2: 269–308.

Koshy, V. and Murray, J. (eds) (2002), *Unlocking Numeracy*. London: David Fulton.

Liebeck, P. (1990) 'Scores and forfeits: an intuitive model for integer arithmetic', *Educational Studies in Mathematics*, 21: 221–39.

Lim, C. (2002) 'Public images of mathematics', *Philosophy of Mathematics Education Journal*, 15 (March). (Downloadable from: www.people.ex.ac.uk/PErnest/pome15/public_images.htm)

Long, K. and Kamii, C. (2001) 'The measurement of time: children's construction of transitivity, unit iteration and conservation of speed', *School Science and Mathematics*, 101: 1–8.

National Council of Teachers of Mathematics (NCTM) (1998) *The Teaching and Learning of Algorithms in School Mathematics: The 1998 Yearbook*. Reston, VA: NCTM.

Nesher, P. and Teubal, E. (1975) 'Verbal clues as an interfering factor in verbal problem-solving', *Educational Studies in Mathematics*, 6: 41–51.

Nunes, T. and Bryant, P. (1996) *Children Doing Mathematics*. Oxford: Blackwell.

Ofsted (Office for Standards in Education) (1993a) *The Teaching and Learning of Number in Primary Schools*. London: HMSO.

Ofsted (Office for Standards in Education) (1993b) *Curriculum Organisation and Classroom Practice in Primary Schools: A Follow-up Report*. London: HMSO.

Orton, A. (ed.) (2004) *Pattern in the Teaching and Learning of Mathematics*. London: Continuum.

Piaget, J. (1952) *The Child's Conception of Number*. London: Routledge and Kegan Paul.

Piaget, J. (1953) *The Origin of Intelligence in the Child*. London: Routledge and Kegan Paul.

Pimm, D. and Love, E. (eds) (1991) *Teaching and Learning School Mathematics*. London: Hodder and Stoughton, in association with the Open University.

Pound, L. (2006) *Supporting Mathematical Development in the Early Years*, 2nd edn. Maidenhead: Open University Press.

QCA (Qualifications and Curriculum Authority) (1999a) *Teaching Mental Calculation Strategies: Guidance for Teachers at Key Stages 1 and 2*. London: QCA, for the National Numeracy Strategy.

QCA (Qualifications and Curriculum Authority) (1999b) *Teaching Written Calculations: Guidance for Teachers at Key Stages 1 and 2*. London: QCA, for the National Numeracy Strategy.

QCDA (Qualifications and Curriculum Development Agency) (2010) *The National Curriculum Level Descriptions for Subjects*. London: QCDA.

Resnick, L. (1982) 'Syntax and semantics in learning to subtract', in T. Carpenter, J. Moser and T. Romberg (eds), *Addition and Subtraction: A Cognitive Perspective*. Englewood Cliffs, NJ: Laurence Erlbaum Associates.

Rose, J. (2009) *Independent Review of the Primary Curriculum: Final Report*. London: DCSF.

Rowland, T., Martyn, S., Barber, P. and Heal, C. (2000) 'Primary teacher trainees' mathematics subject knowledge and classroom performance', in T. Rowland and C. Morgan (eds), *Research in Mathematics Education*. Vol. 2, *Papers of the British Society for Research into Learning Mathematics*. London: BSRLM.

Rowland, T., Turner, F., Thwaites, A. and Huckstep, P. (2009) *Developing Primary Mathematics Teaching*. London: Sage Publications.

Ryan, J. and Williams, J. (2007) *Children's Mathematics 4–15*. Maidenhead: Open University Press.

Schlottman, A. (2001) 'Children's probability intuitions: understanding the expected value of complex gambles', *Child Development*, 72(1): 103–22.

Silver, A. and Burkett, M. (1994) 'The posing of division problems by preservice elementary school teachers: conceptual knowledge and contextual connections', paper presented to the American Educational Research Association, New Orleans, LA. (Downloadable from www.eric.ed.gov)

Squire, S., Davies, C. and Bryant, P. (2004) 'Does the cue help? Children's understanding of multiplicative concepts in different problem contexts', *British Journal of Educational Psychology*, 74: 515–32.

Suggate, J., Davis, A. and Goulding, M. (2010) *Mathematical Knowledge for Primary Teachers*, 4th edn. London: David Fulton.

Swain, J. (2004) 'Money isn't everything', *Education Guardian Weekly*, 8 June.

Tall, D. and Thomas, M. (1991) 'Encouraging versatile thinking in algebra using the computer', *Educational Studies in Mathematics*, 22(2): 125–48.

Thompson, I. (2000) 'Teaching place value in the UK: time for a reappraisal?', *Educational Review*, 52(3): 291–8.

Thompson, I. (ed.) (2003) *Enhancing Primary Mathematics Teaching*. Maidenhead: Open University Press.

Thompson, I. and Bramald, R. (2002) *An Investigation of the Relationship between Young Children's Understanding of the Concept of Place Value and their Competence at Mental Addition*. Newcastle: University of Newcastle Department of Education.

Tijms, H. (2007) *Understanding Probability: Chance Rules in Everyday Life*, 2nd edn. Cambridge: Cambridge University Press.

Turner, S. and McCullough, J. (2004) *Making Connections in Primary Mathematics*. London: David Fulton.

Van Hiele, P. (1999) 'Developing geometric thinking through activities that begin with play', *Teaching Children Mathematics*, 5(6): 310–16.

Way, J. and Beardon, T. (eds) (2003) *ICT and Primary Mathematics*. Maidenhead: Open University Press.

White, J. and Bramall, S. (eds) (2000) *Why Learn Maths?* London: London University Institute of Education.

Williams, E. and Shuard, H. (1994) *Primary Mathematics Today*, 4th edn. Harlow: Longman.

Williams, P. (2008) *Independent Review of Mathematics Teaching in Early Years Settings and Primary Schools, Final Report*. London: DCSF.

Wright, R., Martland, J. and Stafford, A. (2006) *Early Numeracy*, 2nd edn. London: Sage Publications.

Zazkis, R. and Liljedahl, P. (2004) 'Understanding primes: the role of representation', *Journal for Research in Mathematics Education*, 35(3): 164–86.

References

Index

A page number in bold refers to an entry in an end-of-chapter Glossary